Forget Me Not

Journey's End

Forget Me Not - Journey's End

Previous works by Valmai R. Harris:
1. Forget Me Not
2. Forget Me Not - The Journey Continues

Forget Me Not - Journey's End is the third book in the Forget Me Not Trilogy. Here we find the characters moving on from the war and the Spanish Flu epidemic, and adapting to life in post-war Australia.
This is a work of fiction, and any similarity between my characters and persons, living in that period, is purely coincidental.
Certain names and place names have also been changed.

Valmai R. Harris

Copyright © 2022 Valmai R. Harris
ISBN: -13: 9780645072730

valmairuthharris@gmail.com

Cover design created by Joanne Livingstone   joliving@westnet.com.au

Author Photography: imaginepictures.com.au

All rights reserved. No part of this book may be reproduced or transmitted, in any form or by any means, electronic or mechanical, including photocopying, recording or by any information storage and retrieval system, without prior permission in writing from the author.

Produced and printed in Australia by IngramSpark

'To Every Thing There is a Season: A Time For Every Purpose Under Heaven.'

Ecclesiastes 3

Verses 1 - 8

Forget Me Not

Journey's End

Introduction

The Homecoming

A keen wind blew along the Bendigo railway station, moving leaves and sneaking around the legs of those who stood waiting for the Melbourne train.

Margaret, Charles and the three children huddled together, their coats gathered around them, and hats pulled down on their heads.

"When's the train coming?" Grace was jumping up and down in anticipation.

"It won't be long," said Margaret smoothly, her hand firmly clasping that of her granddaughter.

"Hush, Gracie!" Charles laid a hand on her shoulder. "Stand still, for goodness sake! You'll see your mother soon."

"Will she be with Beau?" Ben looked up at his grandmother.

"Yes, Ben, she will."

"And are they married now?"

"Yes, they got married yesterday."

"Does that mean Beau will be living in our house?" Edward's brow was furrowed.

"Yes, Edward, he will."

"Oh!"

"You'll have to do as he says now, Edward," said Charles dryly, "with no arguing."

"Yes, Edward!" Ben gave his brother a shove, knocking him into Margaret.

"Enough, Ben!" Charles growled. "Apologise to your grandmother."

Ben looked sullen. "Sorry, grandma."

Margaret smiled thinly. Three weeks with the children had tested them all, and she was looking forward to a quiet house and no confrontations.

"Beau's always been our friend." Edward was pensive. "Does this mean that he'll be the boss of us now?"

Charles and Margaret looked at each other.

"It means," said Charles, "that he'll still be your friend, but you will need to show him some respect. It may be difficult for a time, but for your mother's sake, both of you must try to fit in."

"Hm." Edward's brow was furrowed.

"Here comes the train! Here comes the train!" Gracie resumed her jumping, golden curls bouncing beneath her blue beret.

*

Inside their carriage, Jess and Beau sat gazing out the window at the familiar landscape. They were nearly home. It had been a long twenty-four hours, and they were both tired. Jess bit on her lip as the train slowed, bringing the hills into focus. She clutched Beau's hand.

"Are you alright, Jess?" He noticed her consternation.

"I'm nervous."

"What are you nervous about?"

Jess turned to look at him. "I'm nervous about the reactions we might get."

Beau's brow furrowed. "They're your children, Jess. Of course they'll be excited to see you!"

"I know you're right, Beau, but I've been away from them for three weeks, and so much has happened to me in those three weeks."

Beau brought her hand up to his mouth, and kissed her fingers. "Trust them, Jess."

The whistle sounded as the railway workshops came into view. In a few moments they would stop, and they would step out on to the platform.

Jess released her hand from Beau's, and stood as the train thundered into the station. With a loud hiss, steam covered the crowd gathered there, and the train ground to a halt.

Beau opened the compartment door, and together they made their way to the platform. Beau was the first to step down, before reaching for Jess's hand. She took it, and he squeezed it for reassurance.

"It will be alright, Jess," he whispered. Jess nodded, as her eyes searched the crowd. There they were; she could see Charles and Margaret. She moved forward.

"Ma! Ma!" She heard Gracie's squeal, and with a quick intake of breath, opened her arms to receive her daughter. They clung together for several moments, and Jess let the tears fall as she buried her face in Gracie's golden hair.

When she lifted her tear-stained face, five pairs of eyes were watching her. Without letting go of Gracie, who hung on like a limpet, she spread one arm, and the two boys walked into the family embrace.

"Oh, my darlings, it's so good to see you."

They clung together, while Margaret, Charles and Beau looked on in silence.

Finally, shoulders aching from holding Gracie, Jess let her slide to the ground, and stood erect. Margaret walked towards her, and encompassed her in a warm hug.

"Welcome home, Jess. We've all been anxious to see how you look."

Margaret held Jess at arms length, and ran a critical eye over her. "You look better than I thought you might."

"I had the best of care." Jess looked at Beau as she spoke.

"Thank-you for bringing her back to us again, Beau."

"I had no intention of losing her, Margaret."

Charles cleared his throat. "You do have luggage, I presume?"

"Oh, yes, in the luggage van."

"I brought the motorcar, so perhaps you and I can get the luggage, Beau?"

"Certainly, Charles."

"Good to have you here," Jess heard Charles say to Beau, as the two men walked away. "Welcome to the family."

Jess turned to Margaret. "It's going to be alright, isn't it, Margaret?"

"Of course it is, dear."

"You're not angry that we married in Sydney?"

"No, dear." Margaret smiled. "It was the best thing to do under the circumstances. Besides, we can have a celebration when everything settles down."

Jess looked down at her children, who were regarding her seriously.

"Did you nearly die, ma?" Edward's blue eyes were questioning.

"I was very sick, Edward, but Beau wasn't going to let me die." Jess took her two boys by the hand, while Margaret took a firm hold of Gracie. "Now, what's been happening here while I've been away?"

"Oh, Jess," said Margaret, "we have so much to tell you, don't we, children?"

The boys nodded enthusiastically.

"Really? Well, how about you tell me while we head for the motorcar. I need to get home" Jess looked up to see Beau coming down the steps of the pedestrian bridge. She smiled softly. "We need to get home. We have so much to tell you, too."

Margaret watched, as the distance decreased between them. Gracie let go her hand, and ran to meet Beau. He swung her up in his arms, and she smiled down at him. Margaret breathed a soft sigh of relief. There was plenty of time to tell Jess what had really been happening.

"Come on, grandma!"

Margaret smiled softly as she walked slowly up the steps.

Part One

A Time For Change

Coming Home

Charles pulled the car up to the kerb, and silenced the motor. Everyone sat still; not a word was spoken. Jess looked up at her house, and then turned her eyes to Beau. He was quietly watching her, and as their eyes locked, he smiled softly.

"You're home, Jess."

"We're home, Beau." Jess reached for his hand and squeezed gently.

"Well," said Charles brusquely, "we'd better get all this luggage out." He slid out of the driver's seat, and moved to the back of the car.

Margaret, who had been nursing Gracie, gave her a hug, and set her on the running board.

"Out we get, children. Let your mother have some breathing space."

Ben and Edward, who had been sitting on their mother's knees, scrambled out on to the footpath, followed by Margaret. Jess and Beau remained seated for a couple of moments, as they took in their surroundings, and felt the overwhelming emotion of coming home. Tears sprang to Jess's eyes as she contemplated the future for all of them. There would certainly be changes and quite possibly obstacles, but she was prepared for that, and smiled through her tears.

Beau stepped out from the vehicle, and reached out a hand to Jess.

"Come on, Mrs. DuBois. You can't sit there all day."

Jess took his hand and stepped on to the footpath. The children had all reached the verandah, and stood looking down at their mother, as she made her way slowly up the steps. Beau went to assist Charles with the luggage, and soon they were all standing silently on the verandah, while Margaret unlocked the front door.

"Welcome home, Jess and Beau," she said quietly.

Beau turned to Jess. "There's one thing I must do, if you will all excuse me. I need to carry my wife over the threshold."

Jess stared at him, her eyes wide. "Beau, don't be ..." she began, but immediately found herself scooped up in his arms.

Ben and Edward slapped their thighs and laughed uproariously, while Margaret smiled softly and Charles grunted his disapproval. Grace was unsure of what was happening, and clutched at Margaret's hand, as they all watched Jess being carried through the front door, and along the passage.

"Beau, put me down!" she protested, to no avail.

It wasn't until they reached the kitchen that Beau let her slide to the floor. He kept his arms around her, as the rest of the family entered behind them. Jess shook her head as she smiled at their bemused expressions.

"It's a tradition," she explained to her children, "that a new wife be carried over the threshold." She shrugged. "It's probably a sign of good luck."

"But you're not a new wife, ma." Ben looked puzzled.

Jess glanced swiftly at Beau, before ruffling her son's hair. "I'm Beau's new wife, Ben."

"Oh."

"Well, anyway," muttered Charles, breaking the uncomfortable silence. "It's good to have you home. Margaret and I will leave you now to settle in."

Margaret moved towards the stove. "I've got a stew cooking for you, Jess, so you won't have to bother about this evening's meal."

"Thank-you, Margaret. It smells wonderful." Jess turned to Charles. "Thank-you, Charles, for all you've done. We are deeply grateful."

Charles cleared his throat, and taking Margaret by the arm, headed for the door. "We hope everything goes well." At the door, he turned. "Oh, by the way, Beau, I've had a word with the Hospital Board, and they want to interview you. I've told them that you would be an asset to the hospital. They'll be contacting you shortly."

Beau's eyes registered surprise. "I'm much obliged, Charles. Thank-you."

Charles nodded brusquely, and then he and Margaret left the kitchen. Their footsteps echoed along the passage, before the family heard the front door close firmly.

Jess looked down at the three children silently watching her, and smiled brightly.

"Let's bring the luggage in, shall we?"

"I'll bring the luggage in, Jess." Beau touched her arm. "You talk to the children. I think they might need a little reassuring." He smiled and then was gone.

Jess sat heavily on one of the kitchen chairs. Suddenly she felt very tired, and three pairs of eyes were watching her solemnly. She opened her arms.

"Come here." They moved into her embrace. "I have missed you, my darlings."

"It's going to be different now, ma, isn't it?" Ben's brown eyes regarded her seriously.

"In what way, Ben?"

"It won't be just us anymore."

"No, it won't, Ben, and I think that's a good thing, don't you?"

"Yes." He paused. "I think so."

"Beau wants to make us all happy, and what we have to do in return, is make him happy. Do you think we can do that?" Jess ruffled the boys' hair, and smiled at them as they slowly nodded their heads. "You'll still be able to do all the things you used to do together, when he was just your friend. That won't change."

"Will he take us rabbiting?" Edward asked enthusiastically.

Beau, who had been standing quietly at the kitchen door, moved forward. "Yes, Edward," he said, "I'll certainly take you rabbiting."

Jess looked up as Beau stood behind her, and she reached for his hand. "You'll be able to do all sorts of exciting things together." She smiled into his eyes.

"Me, too?" piped up Gracie, as she scrambled on to her mother's knee.

"Yes, you too!" Jess laughed. "Now, I need to get out of these clothes that I've been in for at least twenty-four hours, and you boys can go and collect the eggs." She lifted Grace from her knees, and was met with a loud protest. "Go and help the boys, Gracie."

As the screen door slammed behind the children, Jess stood up and slid her arms around Beau.

"It will be alright," she whispered. "We'll make sure of that."

Beau gave her a gentle squeeze. "Yes, we will."

*

Later that evening, Jess was standing at the sink, washing the last of the dishes, when she paused to listen to the laughter that was issuing from the bathroom. She smiled. Beau was in charge of bath-time, and it sounded as though he was doing a good job of it. Jess wiped her hands on the towel, and tiptoed to the bathroom door. Beau was on his haunches beside the big enamel bath, and three wet children were splashing water on him, while they squealed with laughter.

Jess stood by the door, and as she watched, she remembered the last night that Jack had bathed the children before he went away. Her heart gave a sudden spasm, and she blinked away the tears that threatened. Beau turned and saw her standing at the door.

"I think they're all washed," he said, as he brushed water from his face.

"I think you're all washed!" Jess laughed shakily, and grabbed for the towels that hung behind the door. "Come on, Gracie! You're first."

As Jess made a grab for Grace's naked body, she darted past her mother, and was out the door, heading along the passage to the lounge.

Jess threw two towels at Beau, said, "The boys are all yours," and headed out after Grace.

She found her standing on the mat before the fire, and Jess suddenly realised how much her children had grown in the few weeks that she had been away.

Grace pressed her face against her mother, and Jess breathed in the clean smell of her youngest child as she towelled her dry.

"I missed you, ma," Grace murmured. "Don't go 'way again."

"I won't, Gracie. I promise."

The lump in Jess's throat threatened to choke her, but she was saved by the arrival of the two boys, followed by Beau, carrying their pyjamas.

"They can get themselves dressed." Jess laughed at Beau's expression. "They'll have you doing everything for them if you let them."

"Your mother has spoken!" Beau threw the pyjamas at the boys, and promptly sank into the old brown couch. "I'm done!"

"We haven't finished yet, Beau. We still have story-time before they go to bed."

Beau sighed. "I have a lot to learn, don't I?"

"Yes, you do." Jess smiled at him as she finished dressing Gracie.

The boys, now in their pyjamas, sat on the couch beside Beau, and when Jess set Gracie on her feet, she immediately scrambled onto his knees.

Jess picked up the towels and looked down on the foursome. "I'll get a book, shall I?"

"Yes!" chorused the children.

"Gulliver's Travels!" called Ben as she left the room.

Jess returned some moments later, 'Gulliver's Travels' in her hand. She handed it to Beau. "Your turn," she said sweetly.

Beau grimaced, but opened the book, while Jess sat on the rug at his feet.

"Where do I start?" asked Beau, looking sideways at the two boys.

"Where the bookmark is!" laughed Edward.

Beau cleared his throat. Jess leaned her head against his knees, closed her eyes, and let his voice transport her to Lilliput.

It wasn't until she felt a tap on her shoulder that she came back to reality, and looked up at Beau. He gestured to Grace, now asleep against his chest.

"I think it's time to stop," he whispered.

Jess got to her feet. Taking Grace from Beau's arms, she indicated to the boys that it was time to go to bed. Edward was about to protest, but Jess shook her head at him.

"Time for bed," she whispered. "Make sure you clean your teeth." As they both scrambled from the couch, she added, "Say goodnight to Beau."

"Goodnight, Beau," they said in unison.

"Goodnight, boys."

"Can we go rabbiting tomorrow?" Edward fixed his gaze on his mother.

"We can talk about that in the morning," she whispered. "Now, go!"

Jess turned at the door. "Stay there, Beau," she said over her shoulder. "I'll get the children to bed, and then I'll make us a cup of tea."

"That sounds wonderful." He sighed, as he stretched his legs towards the open fire.

When Jess returned, some minutes later, Beau had his eyes closed and his arms stretched across the back of the couch.

"Cup of tea, Beau," she whispered, as she smiled down on him.

Beau opened one eye, and stretched out his hands for the cup. "Wonderful."

Jess sat beside him, and curled her knees up, so that she was resting against him. Together they sipped their tea in silence, while the fire crackled before them.

"You did very well with the children tonight, Beau," Jess said finally.

Beau turned to look at her. "Do you think I'll make a good father, Jess?"

"Oh, without a doubt!" Jess leaned forward and kissed his cheek. "I do have a word of advice, though."

"And what is that?"

"Don't let the boys manipulate you, especially Edward. He will try, you know."

Beau laughed. "I've already learnt that. So, do I take them rabbiting tomorrow or not?"

"Don't be in too much of a hurry to agree. Let them wait." Jess took his empty cup. "I don't know about you, but I'm very tired, so I'll wash these cups, and then I'm going to bed. We've had a couple of very long days."

"We have." Beau smiled. "The sleeper on the train was not altogether successful, either."

"It certainly wasn't." Jess laughed as she recalled their struggle to remain on the narrow bunk. "It was never meant to be a honeymoon suite." She uncurled her legs and stood up.

"I'll be along in a few minutes, my love," said Beau softly, answering the question in her eyes. "I can't waste the last of this fire."

"Alright, but don't be too long." Jess moved towards the door.

As she headed for the kitchen, Jess pondered Beau's reluctance to leave the fire. Was he feeling apprehensive, knowing that he was no longer in his own familiar surroundings? She could understand that, as she had felt the same way in Sydney. He was going to feel like an interloper for a time, and she had to give him space until he felt comfortable.

With the cups washed, the stove banked for the night, and the porridge oats soaking, Jess grabbed a shawl from behind the kitchen door, and stepped out into the night. She shivered. For the past few weeks she had experienced the luxury of not having to venture outside to the lavatory.

Once her ablutions were completed, Jess returned to her bedroom, noticing that the light was still on in the lounge. She undressed hurriedly, and slipped between the cold sheets. Hopefully, Beau would not be long.

Jess woke with a start. What was the time? How long had she been asleep? She swivelled around to peer at the bedside clock. It was 1am, and she was still alone in the bed. Sighing, she slid her feet out on to the cold floor, and padded to the door. After turning up the light, she pulled her dressing gown from its hook behind the door, and hurriedly slipped it on, shivering convulsively as she stepped out into the passage.

There was no light beneath the lounge door. Jess pushed it open. The moon shining through the front windows, gave her enough light to see her way to the couch. Beau was still there, and the fire was out.

"Beau!" she whispered. "Why are you still here?"

He moved, and rubbed a hand across his eyes. "I must have gone to sleep." He yawned.

Jess sat beside him, wrapping an arm around his chest.

"It's freezing in here," she murmured, "and you're as cold as ice. Come to bed, please?"

Beau was silent, but he slipped an arm around her, and gave her a gentle squeeze.

"I think I know what this is about, Beau." Jess touched his scarred cheek. "There are no ghosts, I can assure you. They've been put to rest, so please come to bed. I need you with me."

Beau turned to look at her in the moonlight. Her eyes were searching his face, and he knew that she was right.

"I'm sorry, my love, and it probably sounds foolish, but…"

Jess placed her fingers across his mouth. "Hush! I don't want to hear it." She smiled suddenly, as she stood and took his hands. "We're wasting precious time while we're freezing to death in here."

A New Day

Jess awoke to the sound of laughter coming from the direction of the kitchen. She rubbed her eyes and sat up. The other side of the bed was empty. The sheet was cold to her touch, so she concluded that Beau had been gone a while.

Reluctantly she threw back the covers and reached for her slippers and dressing gown. Padding quietly along the passage, she stopped at the kitchen door. Beau was at the stove with the two boys, his shirtsleeves rolled up as he stirred vigorously at the porridge pot. They didn't hear Jess tiptoe silently across the room to stand behind them.

"It's very thick, boys," Beau was saying. "What would your mother do with it?"

"I'd put some more milk with it," answered Jess, causing them all to turn.

"Good morning, my love." Beau smiled at her, and then grimaced as he looked at the gluggy mass in the saucepan. "I've never made porridge before, and I wanted to surprise you, but now I need some help."

"Ben, fetch the milk from the ice-chest, please? We'll try to resurrect this…"

"Mess?" offered Beau.

"Hm." Jess smiled, and taking the saucepan from Beau, placed it back on the stove. "Something else to learn, Beau?"

He grinned. "It seems like it."

Ben returned from the verandah with a jug of milk, and handed it to his mother.

"Watch carefully, Beau, and then you'll know next time." Jess smiled up at him, before pouring milk into the saucepan.

Using the wooden spoon, she whisked the porridge until the lumps were gone, and then she added hot water from the kettle to smooth the mixture further.

"There! That's how it should look."

"I see." Beau looked impressed.

"Bowls please, boys!"

While the boys were getting bowls from the kitchen dresser, Beau kissed Jess on the cheek, as she continued to stir the porridge.

"I hope you slept well, my love," he whispered.

"Like a top," she whispered back, smiling into his eyes.

Their moment of intimacy was broken by the arrival of Grace at the kitchen door. She carried her rag doll, and she made straight for her mother.

As Jess ruffled her hair, Grace turned her attention to Beau, now holding the saucepan.

"I don't want porridge." Her green eyes regarded him solemnly.

"Yes you do, Grace," said Jess sharply. "We're all having porridge, so sit down, please, and we can all eat together."

"But I don't want it!" insisted Grace.

The two boys sniggered as they sat waiting for their porridge.

Beau looked at Jess as her face creased into a frown, and to stop from smiling, he began to ladle steaming porridge into the bowls.

Jess lifted Grace and sat her firmly at the table. Then she spooned honey on to the porridge, and poured a little extra milk on the top.

"There you are! I've made it nice and sweet for you."

Grace pouted and pushed the plate away. Jess sat and reached for a bowl, while Beau sat opposite and did likewise.

"Let's eat, shall we?" said Jess brightly. "If Grace doesn't want her porridge, she can sit there until we've all finished, and then she'll have to go hungry until lunchtime."

Grace began to cry. "I want grandma!" she hiccoughed.

Jess closed her eyes momentarily, to hide the feeling of hurt that suddenly overwhelmed her. "Grandma's not here, Grace," she said huskily.

Beau, looking on, sensed Jess's dilemma. "What if I help you, Gracie?" he said softly, as he picked up her spoon.

Grace turned tear-filled green eyes in his direction, and she studied him for a moment before opening her mouth. Beau looked quickly at Jess, who returned his look as she shrugged.

The situation had been saved, and Grace silently ate her porridge.

"Are we going rabbiting today?" Edward broke the silence.

"We can, if your mother agrees," said Beau slowly, looking in Jess's direction.

"There are chores that have to be done first, Edward." He nodded vigorously. "When the chooks have been attended to, and wood stacked on the verandah, then you can go."

"We can take Mack!" Ben hurriedly finished his porridge and pushed back his chair.

Edward followed suit, and after placing their bowls in the sink, they rushed outside.

Jess sighed and looked across at Beau. He was smiling.

"They need a heavy hand," she said slowly, "but right now I'm not in the mood to give it to them."

"We'll all be feeling our way for a while, Jess." Beau reached for her hands across the table. "We need to cut each other some slack, and that includes the children."

"I know." Jess sighed, and looked at Grace who was regarding her solemnly. "I know."

*

Some time later, when Beau and the boys had gone, and the house was quiet, Jess contemplated her movements for the day. It was time to remove Jack's belongings from the bedroom. This was a task that she had been dreading, and now it was deemed necessary. She would put his clothes in the sleep-out, to await distribution to the local thrift shop. It was important now, that Beau be made to feel as comfortable as possible, and she had told him that there were no ghosts, so that was the way it had to be.

Gracie was playing quietly with her dolls, so Jess marched resolutely to her bedroom, and opened the wardrobe doors. For a moment her nerve seemed to leave her, and her hands faltered on the door handles. No, she told herself, **this has to be done, and done now!**

Trying hard not to become emotional, Jess began to gather the few clothes that Jack possessed, and clutching them against her breast, carried them out to the sleep-out, where she laid them on the bed. She made three trips before the wardrobe was empty.

Beau's case lay on the floor beside the bed. Jess opened it, and began to hang the neatly folded shirts in the wardrobe. He had two suits, sundry items of underwear, and two pair of shoes, socks, and two woollen jumpers. At the bottom of the case, Jess found her crayon portrait. Slowly she took it out, and saw Celia's scribble. She shook her head, and pondered on the state of mind of someone who would do that.

Jess sat the picture carefully on the dressing table. As she went to close the case, she spied a grey tobacco tin on the bottom. Without thought, she picked it up, and was about to set it on the dressing table, when she heard something rattle inside it. She shook it. There was something other than tobacco in the tin. Jess tried to prise the lid open, but it wouldn't budge. What was in there?

Suddenly Jess felt like an intruder, and she put the tin hastily on the dressing table. Whatever it was, it belonged to Beau, and she had no right to be prying.

She closed the case, and slid it into the bottom of the wardrobe. Shutting the doors, she walked quickly from the bedroom, just as the telephone rang shrilly in the passage. It was Izzy.

"Jessie!" Her voice came through the line, loud and clear. "You're home!"

"Hello, Izzy! Yes, we arrived home yesterday."

"What's this I hear about you being secretly married?" Izzy followed this statement with a laugh.

"It wasn't secret, Izzy. It seemed like the proper thing to do."

"Hm! Well, you're not going to do me out of a celebration, sister dear."

"No, we intend having a family celebration at some point."

"Good!" Izzy paused. "Now tell me, what is it like living with Beau?"

Jess knew what her sister was implying. "Izzy, we've only been married for three days!"

"Yes, I know, but how is it?"

"It's good, Izzy. I don't know what else you want me to say."

"Is he the lover you imagined he would be?" Izzy giggled mischievously.

Jess was silent for a moment. "Now you are being vulgar, Izzy!"

"Not at all, Jess. Beau is a very passionate man, and I thought…"

"Keep those thoughts to yourself, Izzy. We are…working things out."

"Good!" There was a pause. "How are you after the influenza?"

"I'm feeling quite well now. It was a harrowing time… for everybody."

"It certainly was. We…"

"Are you extending?"

"Yes. We have a quarantine camp here at the reserve, where I believe travellers must remain for a week before going over the border."

"It's the same at Albury," said Jess, "although we had an exemption because I had recovered from the influenza, and Beau was my doctor."

"Your doctor, eh? Lucky you!"

"I hope he can get a position here in Bendigo, Izzy. Charles has put in a recommendation to the Hospital Board."

"That would be wonderful, Jessie!"

"Yes, it would."

"Listen, sister dear, we are going to be cut off shortly, so I'll say good-bye, and it's wonderful hearing your voice again."

"You, too, Izzy. Take care of yourselves, and we'll talk soon.'"

The line went dead. Jess replaced the receiver and stood for a moment before realising that Grace was standing silently beside her. Jess smiled down at her.

"That was Auntie Izzy, Grace."

"Are we going to see Auntie Izzy?"

"No, not yet. We will soon, I promise."

*

A short time later, Jess and Gracie stood at the side entrance to the Grey Goose Hotel. Jess rapped loudly on the knocker. They waited until they heard the sound of footsteps within. Jean opened the door, and her face broke into a smile as she saw Jess standing on the footpath.

"Jessie! How wonderful! Come in, come in!" The door opened wide, and Jess and Grace were ushered into the passageway. "Come to my sitting-room; it's warm in there."

Soon they were standing in front of the open fire, and while Jean threw another log on to the embers, Jess removed her coat and beret.

The fire crackled and sizzled as flames licked around the dry log. Jean stood for a moment, poker in hand, to make sure it didn't tumble out on to the floor. Then after placing the poker carefully in its wrought-iron stand, she turned to face Jess.

"Give me a hug, Jessie girl," she said, as she opened her arms. "What a worrying time you have given us all."

Jess fell into her arms, and Grace watched silently as the two women cried on each other's shoulders.

"I know," stammered Jess, as she moved out of Jean's grasp. "I'm sorry you all had to suffer."

"Sit down, dear, and tell me all about it." Jean looked at Grace. "Would you like me to find you some toys, Gracie?"

Grace shook her head, and clambered on to her mother's knee as she sat beside the fire. Jess managed a tearful smile, as she hugged Grace to her.

"She wants to be with me, Jean. We have missed each other."

"Of course you have, dear." Jean settled into the armchair opposite Jess. "Margaret has done a sterling job looking after the three of them. I was very concerned about her, and asked if I could help, but she said she could manage. I don't think she's..." Jean stopped and shook her head.

Jess frowned. "Is she not well?"

"Oh, I don't know. Tired, more like it."

"Yes, I suppose she is."

There was silence for a moment, before Jean cleared her throat.

"So, you're Mrs. DuBois now?" Her eyes twinkled. "I must say we were all surprised, but happy, nonetheless. The boys came by this morning with Beau, and collected Mack to go rabbiting." Jean's eyes squinted. "The boys seem to have accepted Beau."

"Oh, yes, while ever he gives in to them, they'll be very happy."

Jean laughed. "I see. And you, Jess, are you happy?"

Jess smiled softly. "Of course I am, Jean."

*

The front door slammed. Jess looked up from stirring the stew on the stove, to see Ben heading towards her. He buried his head in her skirts, as Edward and Beau entered the kitchen.

"What's wrong, Ben?" Jess could hear him snuffling into her skirt.

Beau placed three dead rabbits on the kitchen table, before turning to answer Jess's query.

"I don't think rabbiting is Ben's idea of a good time," he said quietly.

"Oh?"

"Ben's a sook, ma!" Edward's eyes were shining. "He didn't like the rabbits being killed."

Jess felt a sudden wave of guilt. Of course he wouldn't! Ben hated his chooks being killed, even when necessity demanded it. She placed an arm around his heaving shoulders.

"It's alright, Ben. You don't have to do that again." She looked up at Beau. "I'm sorry, Beau, I should have known that he would be upset."

"I wasn't, ma!" said Edward gleefully. "I'm going to help Beau skin them."

"Are you? Well, into the wash-house, both of you, and don't leave anything in my trough."

Edward grabbed the rabbits eagerly, and headed for the back door.

"Come on, Beau!" he exclaimed. "I want to keep the skins."

Jess shook her head at Beau. "They are so different," she said with a sigh.

"Maybe next time it won't seem so bad." Beau had his hand on the wire door, and he turned towards Jess. "It is a fact of life, Jess, and Ben may have to get used to it."

Jess stared incredulously at him. "Oh? He can't help his nature, Beau."

Beau merely smiled and followed Edward to the washhouse.

Jess stood for a moment, her hand on Ben's head and her thoughts in disarray. Suddenly she knew that life was not going to be idyllic all the time; there would be rough patches to negotiate. Beau's childhood was surely going to dictate how he handled discipline. Hadn't he spent most of his young life under the guidance of a tutor? Somewhere in the back of her mind she remembered him telling her this. His father had mostly been absent.

"I don't want to go rabbiting, ma," Ben was saying, as he turned tear-filled eyes towards his mother.

"Don't worry about it, Ben."

"But Beau might make me." He hiccoughed loudly.

"No, he won't." Jess ruffled his hair. "I'll talk to Beau."

*

The children were in bed, the Lounge fire crackled up the chimney, and Jess sank gratefully on to the couch, stretching her feet towards the flames.

"That feels good," she sighed.

Beau turned from shifting the burning logs with the poker, and smiled at her.

"Stay there, Jess." He sat the poker back in its stand. "I'll make you a cup of tea."

"That would be nice." She bent to unbutton her boots.

"There are a couple of things we need to talk about."

Jess looked up sharply. "A couple?"

"Yes." He smiled, and Jess watched as he moved out of the Lounge, closing the door quietly behind him.

She sat back against the cushions, feeling the warmth of the fire on her bare feet. Was she in for a lecture? Charles had been hard on the boys in the early days of Jack's absence, but since his heart attack, his discipline had waned, and she knew that in some respects, Beau was right. Life did have to be faced, and she was prepared to listen to what he had to say.

Her thoughts were interrupted as Beau appeared, carrying two steaming mugs of tea. He handed one to Jess, and then sat beside her. Jess tucked her knees up, so that she could lean against him, as she liked doing.

"Well, what do we need to talk about?" Jess smiled into his eyes.

"I shocked you this afternoon, when I said that Ben may have to get used to facing up to life."

"I was a little dismayed, I have to admit, but I know you're right."

"Ben is very compassionate, just like his mother, and life is not going to be easy for him, whereas Edward, now he's a very different proposition."

Jess smiled. "Yes, he is."

Beau touched her face. "I won't force Ben to go rabbiting if he doesn't want to."

"Thank-you." She leaned across and kissed his cheek. "Now what else did we have to discuss? You said there were a couple of things."

"Oh, yes. You emptied my case today?"

"I did."

"And you found a tobacco tin?"

"Yes." Jess's brow crinkled. "What's in it, Beau? I know it's not tobacco."

Beau put down his mug. "No, it's not tobacco. You didn't open it?"

"I must admit I tried, but it wouldn't open. Then, as it was really none of my business, I put it on the dressing table."

"It's not for your eyes yet, Jess." Beau was looking intently at her. "One day I'll show you."

"But not yet?"

"No." It was said with a tone of finality.

Jess sighed and rested her head against his shoulder. "I can wait."

They were silent for a long minute, as the fire crackled and spat in front of them. Finally Jess stirred, placed her empty mug on the floor, and stretched her legs out towards the warmth.

"Beau?"

"Yes, my love."

"Did you notice anything unusual about Margaret yesterday?"

"What do you mean?"

"Does she look well, to you?"

Beau's brow furrowed. "I wasn't paying particular attention. Why? Do you think she is unwell?"

"I don't know. Jean said something today that made me think that maybe she isn't well."

"What do you want me to do?"

Jess turned and grinned at him. "Cast your experienced eye over her, when she's not looking."

He smiled suddenly, and reached out to pull her into his arms. "I'll cast my experienced eye over you, if you're not careful, my girl."

"Is that a threat or a promise?" Jess settled into his embrace, and tilted her face for a kiss.

"A promise," he murmured.

Sid O'Connor

The next day, after the boys had left for school, and the house was quiet, Jess turned her attention to the pile of Jack's clothes lying on the spare bed in the sleep-out. Should she offer them to Beau, or would that be too awkward? She lifted a pair of boots and turned them over in her hands. There was practically no wear and tear, and it seemed a shame to send them to the thrift shop if Beau could wear them. He had worn Jack's clothes before, but that was a long time ago, when Jack was away and…

There was a sudden loud hammering on the front door. Jess put down the boots and headed across the verandah to the kitchen. As she opened the door to the passage, she heard Beau's voice.

"Ah! Mr. O'Connor!"

Jess stopped. It was Sid at the front door.

There was silence for a moment before she heard Sid clear his throat.

"What are you doin' here?"

"I live here now, Sid."

"Do ya?"

"Yes. Now what can I do for you?"

"Where's Mrs. Stanley? I wanna speak with her."

"Mrs. Stanley and I are married, Sid, so she is now Mrs. DuBois."

"I see."

Jess heard him cough loudly as she made her way to the door.

"Good morning, Sid," she said pleasantly. "Are you delivering wood?"

"Yeah." Sid snatched the dirty cap from his head, and looked at his feet. "Is it true then, what 'e tells me? You're married?"

"Yes, Sid."

"Will ya still want me wood?"

"Of course." He nodded his head slowly, but didn't look up. "I'll open the gate for you."

"No, I'll do that, Jess." Beau moved past her, and headed for the kitchen.

Sid looked up then, and stared balefully at Jess through the wire door.

"That was a shock," he muttered, his eyebrows drawing together. "I didn't expect that."

"I don't suppose you did." Jess smiled a little awkwardly. "Well, anyway, you'd best get the wood unloaded while I find you some money."

He looked as though he wanted to say more, but shrugged instead, and replaced his greasy cap.

"Good day to ya, Mrs. Dubois."

Jess detected a note of scorn in his voice as he stepped off the verandah and headed out the gate.

Before closing the front door, she stood and watched him disappear along the street. Hoping that there wouldn't be an altercation between Sid and Beau, Jess made her way to the kitchen, where she stood by the window, hidden from their view by the lace curtains.

She saw Beau opening the back gate, and as she watched, Sid brought his horse and cart into the back yard. He jumped from the cart and tied the black horse to a stake beside the vegetable patch. Jess watched as he clambered back on to the cart, and began throwing the logs to the ground. Beau was stacking them alongside the shed, as fast as Sid threw them. She could see that they were speaking to one another, but she couldn't hear the conversation. Their body language didn't indicate that it was a heated discussion, so Jess turned from the window and reached for the tin that stood on the mantel. Opening it, she counted out nine shillings and slipped the coins into her apron pocket.

When she could see that the cart was almost empty, Jess stepped outside on to the verandah. The two men looked in her direction as she made her way towards them.

"I have your money, Sid," she said, smiling as she held out her hand.

Sid removed his cap and scratched his head, before taking the proffered silver.

"Thanks, Mrs…DuBois." The name obviously felt strange to his tongue.

Beau was watching keenly as Sid pocketed the money before unhitching the grazing black horse. Clicking his tongue, he carefully turned the beast and the cart, and headed towards the gate.

"I'll see ya in about four weeks then?" The question hung in the air.

"Yes," said Beau. "We should have enough wood to last that long."

"Right." Sid clambered up on to the cart, flicked the reins, and they lumbered out of sight.

Beau secured the gates before turning to Jess.

"I don't want you here on your own when he comes, Jess."

"He's hardly going to do anything, knowing that you are likely to be somewhere around."

Beau rolled down his sleeves. "Don't bet on it. He only has to decide that he'll have a couple of pints before he comes, and anything could happen."

"He's off the drink."

Beau laughed. "He told you that?"

"Yes."

"Darling girl, I've told you before that you are too trusting." Beau gave her a gentle squeeze. "Believe me, he was not too pleased to hear our news."

"What did he say?"

Beau glanced sideways at Jess, and his expression was serious. "It wasn't what he said, but rather what he didn't say that concerns me."

"You worry about me too much, Beau." Jess slipped an arm around his middle. "Come on, let's have a cup of tea, and I'll show you a pair of boots that I think might fit you, if you want them. Then," she tickled his ribs, "I want to go and see Margaret, so that I can cast my experienced eyes over her."

"Do you just?" Beau made a grab for her, but Jess was too quick, and scurried up the steps, across the verandah and into the kitchen.

Beau followed, and as she busied herself at the stove, he came up behind her and slipped his arms around her.

"You are being very cheeky this morning, young lady," he whispered in her ear. "I might have to chastise you for that."

Jess squirmed around to face him. "And just what do you propose to do?" she laughed coyly, cocking her head to one side.

"Well, to start with…"

"Ma!" Grace's voice interrupted the banter.

Beau rested his head on Jess's shoulder and groaned deeply.

"What is it, Grace?" Jess covered an involuntary laugh, and moved out of Beau's embrace.

"Can I go to grandma's?"

"Yes, we're going after we've had a cup of tea."

"A cup of tea wasn't what I had in mind," whispered Beau, and Jess stifled another laugh.

"No, I don't suppose it was, but you'll have to settle for second best."

Beau sighed as he retrieved two cups from the sink.

"I hope I don't always have to settle for second best," Jess heard him mutter, as he went out on to the verandah to fetch milk from the ice chest.

"I'll have to make sure you don't," Jess whispered, but he didn't hear her.

Margaret

An hour later, Jess, Beau and Grace stood waiting outside Margaret's door.

"Grandma!" Grace jumped up and down, her golden curls bouncing beneath a blue beret.

They heard footsteps on the linoleum inside, and Margaret appeared. She smiled as she opened the door, and ushered them all inside.

"Come in, come in! I was wondering when we'd see you."

"I thought you might be glad of the rest, Margaret," chided Jess.

"Oh, I've had enough rest. You know I love to see my babies."

Jess laughed. "They're not babies now, Margaret."

She led the way to the lounge, where Charles was seated before the fire, a newspaper in his hands. He looked up as they all entered, and smiled over the top of his spectacles.

"Well, this is a nice surprise." He folded the newspaper, and beckoned them to sit.

Jess and Beau sat on the plush green sofa. Grace waited for Margaret to sit opposite Charles, and then she clambered on to her knee. Jess hid a smile.

"To what do we owe this visit?" Charles looked from Jess to Beau and back again.

"We only saw you for a few minutes when you dropped us home on Saturday," said Jess. "So I thought it was time to check on you both, and see how you survived after having the children for so long." She stole a look in Beau's direction. He was watching Margaret closely.

"It wasn't so bad," said Margaret lightly. "When the boys were at school, it was just Gracie, so we managed to amuse ourselves quite well, didn't we, Gracie?"

"We made lots of biscuits." Grace moved her hands in an exaggerated sweep.

"Which were soon eaten, when the boys came home from school," muttered Charles. "Speaking of biscuits, are we having a cuppa, Margaret?"

"Not for us, thank-you," said Jess hurriedly. "We had one before we left." "Oh!" Charles raised his bushy eyebrows. "I'd like one, please Margaret."

As Margaret set Grace on the floor and stood, Jess rose from the sofa. "I'll help you, Margaret."

"It's alright, dear, I can manage."

Nevertheless, Jess followed Margaret to the kitchen, and as she pushed the kettle over to boil, Jess broached the subject of Margaret's health.

"Is everything alright with you, Margaret?"

"What do you mean, Jess?"

"Are you well?"

There was a slight hesitation before Margaret spoke. "Yes. Why do you ask?"

Jess couldn't say that Jean had implied that there was something wrong, so she moved to the kitchen dresser as she searched for a suitable answer.

"I thought you looked a little pale when you met us at the station." She took down two cups and saucers, and set them on the table. "I hope the children weren't too much for you."

Margaret turned brown eyes in Jess's direction. "Maybe I am a little tired," she confessed, "but the children are not to blame for that."

"Then what is?"

Margaret sighed. "I don't want to discuss this right now."

Jess moved to her side, and placed an arm around her. "If there is something wrong, I want to know about it."

"I appreciate your concern, Jess," she hesitated, "but I'm alright, really."

Jess was not convinced. "I have just come through a life and death experience, Margaret," she whispered, "and I know how much I needed the love of those around me."

Margaret nodded, and Jess saw her eyes fill with tears. "I understand, Jess."

"You will tell me if there's something troubling you?" Margaret nodded. "Promise?"

"Yes." She took a deep breath. "Now I must get Charles his cup of tea."

In the lounge, Grace had made herself comfortable on Beau's knee, while Charles surveyed them over the rim of his spectacles. He cleared his throat.

"We have a Hospital Board meeting on Thursday night, Beau. I think it might be a good time to introduce you to the committee. What do you think?" His thick eyebrows drew together.

"I'm happy to do that, Charles."

"Good! Good!" Charles settled back in his chair. "I'll put you on the agenda. I look forward to hearing about what you have been doing in Sydney, and how you deal with the influenza up there."

"It wasn't our primary concern, Charles, but it became necessary to stay on top of the cases that came our way. Hospitals are still being inundated, I believe."

"It's of great concern. Even here now we have numerous cases."

"It is sporadic, but we need to remain vigilant, and the public needs to be aware that this is not going to go away overnight."

"No, I see. Public awareness is crucial?"

"Most definitely."

Margaret and Jess took that moment to enter the lounge, and Beau slanted a glance over them. They both looked subdued, and Jess's eyes told him that something had transpired.

Margaret placed a cup on the small table beside Charles, before seating herself beside him.

"Please excuse us," she said quietly, "if we drink our tea."

"Don't mind us," said Jess quickly, as she sat beside Beau.

"Charles has just asked me to attend the Hospital Board meeting on Thursday night, Jess." Beau turned to look at her.

"That's wonderful, Beau!" Jess smiled at him, before turning her gaze on Charles. "Make sure they know what a wonderful doctor he is, Charles." Her eyes returned to Beau. "He rescued me from the clutches of the influenza."

Margaret saw the undisguised look of love that passed between them, and she blinked away the tears that threatened to spill. It was something else that she must get used to.

*

An icy wind had picked up, by the time Jess, Beau and Grace headed for home. Jess tucked her arm in Beau's, as they hurried along the deserted street. Grace skipped ahead.

"Well, there is definitely something wrong with Margaret," panted Jess, as she tried to slow the pace, "but she wouldn't tell me what it is. Beau, can you slow down, please! You are not in Sydney now, and I'm struggling to keep up with you."

Beau slackened his pace. "I'm sorry, my love. Old habits die hard."

"Yes, well as I was saying…"

"You quizzed Margaret, and got no result, right?"

"Right. Could you tell by looking at her that there was something wrong?"

Beau smiled. "I'm not a magician, Jess. Without examining her, I would just be guessing."

"Guessing what?" Jess jerked on his arm and he stopped walking.

"Who's her doctor?"

"Doctor Simmons. Guessing what? Beau?"

"She might just be low on iron, but she needs to see Doctor Simmons. I can't prescribe anything for her."

"The only thing she said was that she is a little tired, and she didn't want to discuss it."

Beau sighed. "Try to convince her to see Doctor Simmons, and suggest some blood tests."

"Doctor Simmons will know where that came from."

"From me?"

"Yes."

"Well, in my humble opinion, he should have already suggested it. She is deathly pale."

"Maybe she hasn't even been to see him."

Beau pulled Jess into motion again. "Maybe she hasn't. Come on. Grace is getting too far ahead of us, and we need to get home before it decides to rain."

Jess smiled up at him. "It's lovely to hear you say 'home', Beau."

The Hospital Board

It was Thursday evening, and Beau was dressed in his best grey suit; the suit he'd been married in. Jess walked into the bathroom as he was combing his hair, and sliding her arms around him, she sighed and murmured against his back.

"Was it only a week ago that you wore that suit, and promised to love me for the rest of your life?"

Beau turned slowly. "Yes, it was, and yes, I did."

"You look so handsome when you're dressed up, Beau."

He frowned. "'Handsome' is not a word I'd use to describe myself, Jess."

"Oh, I would." She ran her fingers down his scar, as she smiled up at him.

Beau pulled her close, and buried his face in her hair. "I don't deserve you, Jess," he murmured.

"Don't say such things!" Jess shook him gently. "Now, it's time to prepare yourself to meet the intimidating Doctor Simmons."

"Intimidating?" Beau raised his head.

"Oh, he can be very intimidating."

Beau frowned suddenly. "He will remember my history, and that could go against me."

"Nonsense! Circumstances were very different then. Besides, you'll have Charles in there batting for you, so don't worry." Jess smiled as she smoothed the front of his white shirt.

Beau looked quickly at his watch. "Charles is calling for me at seven. It's nearly that now."

The blast from a horn, followed by running footsteps along the passage, made them both look up. They heard Ben shout, "Granddad's here!"

Beau took a deep breath, and Jess reached up to kiss him briefly.

"Wish me luck, Jess."

"You'll be fine, Beau." She smiled. "Go on! Don't keep Charles waiting."

Beau gave his tie a nervous tug, before heading into the passage. At the bedroom door, he picked up his briefcase, looked once more in Jess's direction, and hurried out the front door.

Ben shut it behind him, and turned to his mother.

"Is Beau going to work with Granddad?"

"Not exactly, Ben. Granddad is on the Board of Management at the

Hospital, and he would like to see Beau get work there, so he's taking him to a meeting to introduce him to the committee."

"That would be good, wouldn't it, ma?"

"It certainly would, Ben."

"Do you think they'll want him?"

"I don't see why not, Ben. Hospitals can't run without doctors, and I know that there is a shortage of qualified men at present."

"Why's that, ma?"

"Because of the war, Ben. So many went overseas, and of course, a lot didn't come back."

Ben's brow furrowed. "Like dad," he muttered softly.

"Yes, like your dad."

*

The linoleum squeaked beneath their feet, as Charles and Beau walked the length of the wide hospital corridor.

"The meeting-room's just along here," Charles was saying, and his voice echoed in the empty space. "We meet once a month under normal circumstances, but tonight we need to discuss a new strategy that will meet the current demands of this influenza pandemic."

"Do you have many cases here in Bendigo?" asked Beau.

They had reached a door, which Charles pushed open. "Yes, indeed we have." He ushered Beau into the room, and closed the door quietly behind them.

Beau inhaled quickly, as the smell of tobacco assailed his nostrils, making him cough. The air was hazy with smoke from cigars and cigarettes, as men stood talking in groups. At Charles's appearance, many sought the ashtrays on the long table dominating the room, and conversations hushed. Men moved to the straight-backed chairs that lined the table, and sat in their appropriate places.

All eyes turned to Charles and Beau as the clatter ceased, and an uncomfortable silence filled the void. Charles placed his briefcase on the table, and turned to Beau.

"Gentlemen," he began, "I want to introduce you to Doctor DuBois, who has come here from Sydney to live, and who is well-versed with what the medical profession is doing, regarding the influenza. He is here at your request, to tell us about himself and his work." There was a general murmur amongst the men, and Charles made his way to the empty chair at the centre of the table. "Doctor DuBois, if you wouldn't mind sitting at the end there, we will get started."

Beau was ushered to an empty chair, by an elderly gentleman with a large grey beard, and bushy eyebrows.

"Welcome, Doctor," he murmured. "Please don't be intimidated by what you see here. We are friendlier than we look." He smiled reassuringly at Beau, and resumed his seat.

Beau sat, a little self-consciously, and looked along the row of mainly bearded faces. He wondered briefly which one was Doctor Simmons. He was soon to find out.

A tall man with flecks of grey in his dark hair, and a short, clipped beard, stood and fixed his gaze on Beau. Clearing his throat, he introduced himself.

"Doctor DuBois, you may not remember me. I am Doctor Raymond Simmons." His gaze stretched along the table as he addressed the committee. "I had occasion to attend to Doctor DuBois two years ago, after an unfortunate mishap." His eyes returned to Beau. "I am pleased to see you are now in good health, Doctor."

Beau felt the weight of his words and sucked in his breath, as he met the cool gaze with a confidence that he didn't quite feel.

"I had the best of treatment," he said carefully.

"I'm pleased to hear that." Doctor Simmons sat, as Charles banged a gavel on the table.

"Can we get down to business, gentlemen?" A murmur went along the table. "We'll dispense with the formalities." He shuffled some papers. "The first item I have on the agenda is the present situation, with the increase in influenza patients. We have urgent need of more rooms and more staff to attend to them."

"We may have to set up tents like we've done before," voiced one committee member.

"We need somewhere to isolate them," called another.

"We are putting our general patients at risk."

"Maybe we need to commandeer the Town Hall."

"What's wrong with the YMCA building?"

"Gentlemen! Gentlemen!" Charles called them to order. "I have a suggestion which is much closer to home. If we could secure the use of a floor in the Benevolent Asylum next door, then I think our problems would be solved."

There was silence for several moments as the idea took hold.

"And how do you propose to do that, Charles?" Doctor Simmons' voice rang out. "We would still have the problem of putting other patients at risk, and these are very vulnerable people we're talking about here."

Beau, who had been listening intently, felt the need to interject, so he stood.

"Mr. Chairman," he began, and the silence trickled around him.

Charles looked in his direction. "Doctor DuBois, do you have something to say?"

"I do."

"Very well. You have the floor. Please indulge us with your experience."

Beau took a moment to compose his scattered thoughts as all eyes turned in his direction. He licked his dry lips.

"Gentlemen, I have been working in an Institution in Sydney, where the welfare of returning soldiers has been our priority. As you now know, many have returned with afflictions that cannot be healed with traditional medicine." A murmur went around the group. "I myself suffered from the dreaded condition known simply as shellshock, and as a result, had no control over my emotional wellbeing. This condition has been largely ignored, and termed in some quarters, cowardice. Let me tell you it is not cowardice to be faced with enemy gunfire, and know that at any moment you could die."

"And you have recovered from this?" Doctor Simmons turned steely eyes in Beau's direction.

"I believe I have." Beau returned his stare.

"And your work with these men has brought results?"

"Yes, it has."

"And the influenza? How did you deal with that?"

Beau took a deep breath. "As the numbers in the hospitals grew, we were asked to open our doors to patients with the influenza. We were reluctant to do so, as those men and women we were dealing with, were vulnerable, and we didn't want to expose them to anything else. However, we had to comply, and we opened four rooms, which was all we had."

"How did you keep them separated?"

"We were fortunate I suppose. Our building had a back entrance, and the rooms we made available were far enough away from our regular patients, that we could quarantine the back section of the second floor, and hospital staff would use the back entrance. So there was virtually no contact between our patients and the patients with influenza."

"So the hospital provided staff?"

"Some, but at times not enough, so my colleague and I had to step in and assist."

"That would make you susceptible to this infection, would it not?"

"Yes, it did. My colleague actually contracted the influenza."

There was a low murmur.

"Did he recover?"

"Yes." Beau paused, his palms sweating with this bombardment of questions. "Unfortunately he developed tuberculosis, and is now at a sanatorium in the mountains."

Another murmur followed this blunt statement.

"So how did you stop the spread of this dreadful disease?"

"Diligent disinfecting of public spaces, masks, gowns, and inoculations, of course." Beau smiled briefly as he recalled Nurse Flanagan and Edwina Evans. "We were very lucky to have staff who recognised the severity of this virus, and carried out their duties to the letter."

"So what is happening up there now, Doctor?" Raymond Simmons was looking at him intently. "You are here, and your colleague is in a sanatorium, so who's running the institution?"

Beau glanced at Charles, who nodded his head.

"Tell us all, Beau," he said finally.

All eyes turned towards Beau. "As you may or may not know, I married your Chairman's daughter-in-law, Jess, a week ago, in Sydney." Beau noticed some smiles, and heard the odd chuckle. "I had already planned on leaving Sydney to marry Jess, well before this, but with Doctor Morley falling victim to the influenza, plans were up in the air. However, steps were already in place to replace me at the Clinic, and the Institution. Then of course, Doctor Morley contracted tuberculosis, which meant he would be gone for possibly twelve months, and a replacement Psychiatrist needed to be employed straight away."

"So you weren't prepared to wait that long?" Doctor Simmons persisted.

"No. There were other factors at play here, which I won't go into. We had a very supportive committee, and I have no doubt that Serendipity Lodge (which is the name of the Institution) and its associated Clinic, will be well serviced."

"So your hope is to get work here, Doctor DuBois?" Steely blue eyes were still regarding him.

"Yes."

"Can I ask how you were received by the Medical Board on your return from the warzone?"

Beau was silent for a moment. "Not favourably, but I can assure you my registration is current, and I can practise medicine." He paused. "I was trained in orthopaedics, but the war left me with tremors in my hands, so I am no longer able to perform surgery."

"That's unfortunate." Doctor Simmons dropped his gaze, but Beau saw his lips twitch.

"I have all my papers here, if you care to look at them, along with a letter of reference from my former committee."

"We will need to see those of course," said Charles, his eyes on Doctor Simmons. "Is there something else you'd like to say, Raymond, before we continue our discussion on alternative measures for influenza patients?"

Doctor Simmons toyed with a pencil on the table before him, before switching his gaze to Beau. "No, I don't think so," was all he said.

"Good." Charles was relieved. "Then if someone will move a motion, we'll go from there."

The elderly man who had seen Beau to his seat, stood slowly.

"I propose that we meet with the Board of the Benevolent Asylum, with the view to discussing the likelihood of our obtaining rooms at their facility for the use of influenza patients."

There was a murmur of agreement from most members of the committee.

"Can we discuss this proposal, gentlemen before we move a motion to the effect?" Charles glanced along the table.

"I wish to amend the wording to be that we send representatives to meet with the Board."

"I think Doctor DuBois needs to be present at this meeting," offered one gentleman, and was met with a disapproving stare from Doctor Simmons.

"Doctor DuBois is not a member of this committee," he said icily.

Charles glanced swiftly at Beau, to gauge his reaction. His jaw was set, but his expression remained passive as he waited to see where this led. Charles could see that there was going to be no love lost between these two. It was up to him to smooth the way.

"That is true, gentlemen, and I can see only one way to rectify this. Doctor DuBois, would you mind stepping out of the room for a few minutes, please?"

Beau complied, and made his way out into the cold corridor. The door was shut firmly behind him, and he waited in the silence. Eventually the muffled sound of raised voices reached him, but he could not distinguish words. He walked to the end of the corridor, his footsteps echoing in the empty space. This was not going to be a fait accompli. Doctor Simmons had ammunition that could well put him out of the picture altogether. How many other committee members were aware of the circumstances of two years ago? Possibly none.

Beau turned and retraced his steps slowly. If he was not accepted here, then he would have to look elsewhere for work, and that would take him away from his beloved Jess.

As he neared the meeting-room, the door opened suddenly and Doctor Simmons strode out. He passed Beau, and without a backward glance headed along the corridor. Beau watched as he disappeared around a corner, and then he turned to see Charles standing in the doorway. His expression was tight.

"Come in, Beau," he said shortly.

Beau followed Charles into the room, and his glance along the row of faces told him that an upset had taken place. He resumed his seat at the end of the table.

Charles moved to his seat, and sighing loudly, rested his hands on the table and looked at Beau.

"We have had a vote, and the majority ruled in favour of you being instated as a member of this Board, and as a general Medical Practitioner here at the Hospital."

Polite applause followed, and Beau saw many heads nodding. He wanted to ask why Doctor Simmons had left so abruptly, but decided against it. No doubt Charles would enlighten him later.

"Thank-you," he said quietly. "I hope I can live up to your trust."

"You will, Beau," said Charles. "I am certain of that." He leafed through some papers. "Now, back to the business at hand. We need a motion on the books so that we can move forward with plans for our influenza patients. Andrew, refresh our memories on your proposal…"

*

The children were in bed, and Jess was anxiously waiting for Beau to return. She put another log on the lounge fire and settled herself on the couch, but she couldn't relax. Her mind kept leaping to all the things that could go wrong, and her apprehension increased as the minutes ticked by. Doctor Simmons could quite easily put a spanner in the works, as he knew what Beau had attempted two years ago. Would Beau be able to escape his past?

A car door banged, and Jess rose quickly to her feet. She heard footsteps on the verandah, and then the front door opening. A moment later, Beau appeared in the lounge doorway.

"Well?" Jess felt rooted to the spot. "How did you get on?" Her heart was thumping loudly.

Beau placed his briefcase on the floor, and walked towards Jess. His expression was unreadable.

"I've been accepted," he began, and Jess flung herself into his arms, not waiting to hear any more.

"Oh! That's wonderful news, Beau!" Her cheeks were wet as she pressed her face against his.

"It is and it isn't," he said, as he extricated himself from her arms.

"What do you mean?" Jess was confused. "What happened?"

Beau took her arm and led her to the couch. "Sit down, and I'll tell you all about it."

Jess sat abruptly, and Beau sat beside her.

"It's either wonderful news or it's not, Beau! It can't be both."

"Yes it can. There was only one vote against me, Jess."

"And that was Doctor Simmons?" Jess slumped. "What did he say?"

"I don't know. I wasn't in the room at the time, and Charles didn't say much on the way home, but I gather he just walked out of the meeting."

"So he didn't say anything about…"

"No, he didn't."

"That's good then, isn't it?"

"I suppose it is, but I will have to work with the man, which from what I have seen of him, could be a little difficult."

Jess slid her arms around him. "You'll work it out, Beau, I'm sure. Your life in Sydney wasn't exactly a bed of roses, you know?"

Beau kissed the top of her head. "No, you're right there."

"So when do you start?"

"As soon as a room is made available for consultation."

"I'm so happy for you, Beau." Jess reached for a kiss. "I know it will all turn out for the best."

"I hope so." Jess didn't see his troubled expression.

A Meeting with Doctor Simmons

Beau waited for several days to hear from Charles, so in the meantime he put his energy into cleaning up the back yard, which had been neglected for some weeks. Jess would stand and watch him through the kitchen window, as he toiled in the vegetable garden.

On one occasion, when the weather was reasonably dry, she pulled on her gardening boots and went out to join him. Beau stood up as Jess approached, and stretched his back. The hard physical work was beginning to play havoc with his injuries, but he couldn't tell Jess this. He smiled as she picked up the hoe.

"Need some help?" she queried.

"I won't say 'no'," answered Beau, as he leaned on the shovel for a brief moment.

Jess began to hoe around the cauliflowers that had suddenly appeared from behind the weeds.

"I'm glad to see that we still have produce growing amongst the sour grass," she said. "I thought all would be lost after my absence."

"You still have a few cabbages, and some carrots now that I have thinned them out. There's also plenty of rhubarb, and I have dug up some potatoes." Beau wiped his forehead on a handkerchief.

"So we won't go hungry?" Jess looked up at him and smiled.

"No, definitely not." Beau pushed his foot on to the shovel.

"When do you think you'll hear about your job?"

"Soon, I hope. I need to talk with Doctor Simmons, and the sooner we can do that, the better."

"Is Charles going to organise that?"

"I presume so. The last thing he said to me was, and I quote, 'I will have a chat with Raymond, and see if I can talk him around.'"

"Well, if anyone can talk him around, it will be Charles. He does get things done."

"I'm pleased to hear you say that, Jess." The voice came from behind them.

They both turned to see Charles coming across the yard. He stopped at the edge of the garden bed, drew a paper from his coat pocket, and held it out towards Beau.

"Hello, Charles." Beau pushed the shovel into the earth, wiped his hands down his trousers, and took the paper from Charles. "What's this?"

"Your contract."

Jess put down the hoe, and stepped across the garden to the two men. Beau opened the paper, and they both scanned its contents. There at the bottom they saw two signatures. Charles Stanley was the first, and the second was Raymond Simmons. Beau looked up at Charles.

"Doctor Simmons has signed this?"

"That's right."

"So, you've spoken to him then?"

"I have."

Jess gave Beau a squeeze. "That's wonderful! You talked him around?"

Charles frowned. "Not exactly."

Jess sighed with exasperation. "What does 'not exactly' mean?"

"It means," said Charles, "that I have opened the conversation, and Beau can do the rest."

"So does this call for a cup of tea and a freshly-baked scone?"

"I'll be in that!" said Charles enthusiastically.

Beau folded the paper, and tucked it into his shirt pocket. "I won't say no, either."

"Good!" Jess beamed at both of them, before heading for the verandah.

*

Two days passed before Beau heard from Doctor Simmons. Jess was washing the breakfast dishes when the telephone rang in the passageway. Her hands stopped as she heard Beau answer it. Straining her ears, she tried to hear what he was saying, but his voice was low and all she heard was, "Thank-you. Yes, I'll be there."

She waited.

"I'm meeting with Doctor Simmons at two this afternoon."

Jess turned. Beau stood in the doorway.

"That's wonderful news, Beau!" Jess wiped her hands on her apron as he crossed the kitchen.

"I have to go to his rooms." Beau sighed as Jess slid her arms around his neck. "He sounded pleasant enough on the telephone."

"It will be alright, Beau! I've told you that before. He can be rather brittle, but I think, underneath, Doctor Simmons is a reasonable man."

"I hope so. I must confess that I've been troubled by this all along. It wasn't only Celia's veiled threats that concerned me."

"Well, be positive, my dearest, knowing that you have all the right credentials." Jess gave him a quick kiss. "Now, I must iron your white shirt. My reputation is at stake here, too." She laughed.

*

Beau rapped on the door with the gold plaque, which read: Dr. Raymond Simmons. His heart was beating rapidly, and in spite of Jess's words of encouragement, he felt less than confident. He twitched at his tie as he waited to hear footsteps on the other side of the door.

Finally it opened, and Doctor Simmons stood there, unsmiling.

"Doctor DuBois," he said tightly. "Come in."

Beau stepped into the passage, with its gleaming grey-flecked linoleum, and a strong smell of disinfectant. He followed as Doctor Simmons entered the second doorway, which was the consulting-room. Beau stood uncomfortably while Doctor Simmons moved to his deep leather chair behind the large polished desk. He sat, and beckoned Beau to do the same.

Beau sat stiffly, feeling like an errant schoolboy, awaiting the judgement of the Headmaster.

"So, Doctor DuBois, it seems that we will be working together." Blue eyes regarded him coolly.

"Yes, I believe so."

"I have to be honest with you; I was not in favour of this, given the circumstances that occurred two years ago."

"I can understand that." Beau clenched his hands. "I can assure you that those circumstances no longer exist, and my life has moved on since then."

"No longer exist? Surely, Doctor, from what I have read about the affliction known as shellshock, it is always there, ready to flare up at any time."

"Unfortunately that is true in many cases. I believe I have conquered my fear, as I have been free of the tremors for over twelve months now. I am happy with my life."

"Hm." Doctor Simmons picked up a paper, which Beau recognised as his reference from Clarence Bonner-Smyth. "Dealing with sufferers is not a problem to you?"

"Not now, no."

"So it was at first?"

"Yes, it was."

"This is a glowing report of your work in Sydney. You obviously had to deal with many issues."

"As I said at the meeting, we were dealing with very vulnerable people, and sometimes the situations became quite volatile."

"You are not a Psychiatrist though?"

"No. My colleague was the Psychiatrist. I was generally under his instruction, but I relied on my own experiences to work with certain patients."

"Your colleague didn't see this as a problem?"

Beau frowned. "No, not at all. He let me handle cases as I saw fit, and he was there to offer his advice if necessary."

"And the influenza patients? You dealt with them, too?"

"Yes. We only had a few at Serendipity, so the problem was not overwhelming."

Doctor Simmons sat back in his chair, and regarded Beau over the rim of his spectacles.

"We need to work out a roster, if this arrangement is going to work."

"A roster?"

"We will have to share the surgery for the time being."

"Oh, I see."

"You're not happy with that idea?"

"Oh –um- yes, I think so. What about the patients?"

Doctor Simmons adjusted his glasses. "You will have some of my patients, and that will free up my time to be at the hospital." He stared at Beau. "This will be a temporary arrangement, of course, until we see how things work out."

Beau nodded. "Of course."

There was silence then as the two men pondered their changed circumstances.

Beau broke the silence when he extended a hand across the table.

"Can we shake hands on the beginning of a good working relationship?"

There was a slight pause, before Doctor Simmons took Beau's extended hand.

"I'm prepared to shake hands on the beginning of a trial period for this working relationship."

"Very well. To a trial period." Beau paused. "Can we start with you calling me Beau?"

"I would prefer to keep things formal," was the stiff reply.

Beau was somewhat taken aback. "As you wish."

"Now let's talk about a roster."

Beau had to concede that it was going to take some time to convince Doctor Simmons of his ability to perform in the workplace.

*

Later, sitting opposite Jess at the kitchen table, a cup of tea between his hands, Beau related the details of his meeting with Doctor Simmons. Jess listened closely.

"He's not going to let me off the hook easily, Jess. I'm going to have to prove my worth."

"You will, Beau." Jess reached across the table and placed her hands around his. "He'll soon find out what an asset you are, and maybe then he'll allow you to call him Raymond." She chuckled. "So that's the way he wants to play, is it?"

"Yes."

The back wire door slammed, and Ben and Edward entered the kitchen. Ben threw down his bag and headed for the table. He had a letter in his hand.

"This is for you, ma, from Mr. Granger."

"Thank-you, Ben. I should have been in touch with Mr. Granger about my job at the school." Jess opened the envelope and slid out a folded piece of paper.

Opening it out, her eyes skimmed down the page, widening as she reached the scrawled signature at the bottom. She looked up at Beau.

"Mr. Granger is unable to employ me," she said, "because I am once again a married woman, with a husband who will support me." She raised her eyebrows. "Well, we may be able to vote, but we're still a long way off being able to have a say in our own future."

"So you won't be working at the school, ma?" Edward was frowning at her.

"No, Edward, I won't be working at the school."

"Aw! I told all my friends that you would be."

"Well then, you'll have to 'untell' them, won't you?" Jess looked across at Beau. "I was looking forward to being able to contribute to the reading program."

"Not all jobs are closed to married women, Jess. You'll find something if you really want to."

Jess nodded vaguely. "I suppose so."

"In the meantime," said Beau, rising to his feet, "you have all of us to look after, and that will be challenging enough." He smiled at her dejected expression. "Now I'd better get out of my best suit, and look as though I've got work to do."

The Dinner Party

"Anybody home?" The voice came from the back door.

Jess appeared from the washhouse, wiping perspiration from her brow. "I'm here!" she said.

Charles turned at the sound of her voice. "Ah, Jess!"

She wiped her wet hands on her apron. "What brings you here, Charles?"

"An invitation." He was smiling broadly.

"An invitation to what?"

"Dinner at our house."

"Oh? What's the occasion?"

"I've invited Louise and Raymond Simmons to dinner tomorrow night, and I'd like you and Beau to be there. Neutral territory, so to speak."

Jess frowned. "Are you sure that's a good idea, Charles?"

His bushy eyebrows lifted in surprise. "Of course."

"It's just that Beau's meeting with Doctor Simmons was not altogether friendly."

"Well they've agreed to come to dinner."

Jess had another thought that concerned her. "Is Margaret happy to do this?"

"Yes. Why wouldn't she be?"

That was so like Charles; he probably hadn't consulted Margaret at all.

"Well, I shall insist on helping with the food."

"You'll have to talk with Margaret about that." He looked at his watch. "I must go. I have a meeting with my employees." He sighed. "They are wanting to down tools, and I have to put a stop to it before it starts." He turned to leave.

"What about the children, Charles? Are they invited?"

"Er – perhaps not, on this occasion. Find someone to sit with them." Charles waved his hands in the air, and strode off without a backward glance.

Jess watched him disappear around the corner of the house. She didn't know whether to be indignant or amused. The one thing she was sure of was that she had to speak with Margaret, and offer to provide food. Shaking her head, she returned to the washhouse. There was also the problem of who would sit with the children? Jean was the only candidate of course. Maybe she wouldn't mind. She couldn't ask either of her neighbours. Mrs. Palmer was as deaf as a post, and she really hadn't had much to do with the new couple who had moved in on the other side.

Jess continued with her washing, in a slight state of anxiety. Meeting socially with Raymond and Louise Simmons was not something she particularly wanted to do, but if Beau was to work amicably with the good doctor, then she knew it was inevitable. She sighed as she pushed the sheets through the wringer.

"That was a big sigh, my love." Beau's voice sounded close to her ear.

Jess half turned, startled. "Beau! Where did you spring from?"

"From the bedroom. I saw Charles leaving a few moments ago. What did he want?"

"He came to invite us for tea tomorrow night."

"That was nice of him."

"Doctor Simmons and his wife will be there."

"Oh!" Beau frowned.

"Yes, 'oh' indeed! No children are invited; just us."

"And are we going?"

"We are expected to be there, yes. It's a chance for you two to meet on 'neutral' territory."

"Then we mustn't disappoint them."

"I'm just a bit concerned about Margaret. I don't think Charles has given a thought as to how she might feel about it."

"I'm sure Margaret can speak for herself."

"Not where Charles is concerned."

Beau shrugged. "Well, I'll let you take care of that, my dear." He kissed her nose. "I'm off to the hardware shop to buy some nails."

"What for?"

Beau was already out the door. "There are one or two jobs that require nails." He was gone.

Jess sighed. Men certainly had a different way of thinking about so many things.

*

Jean was very apologetic when asked if she could sit with the children.

"I'm sorry, love," she said, "it's my Bingo night, and I'm the organiser." She paused. "Why don't you ask Audrey Maitland? I'm sure she'll jump at the chance."

Audrey did jump at the chance when Jess knocked on her door later that day.

"I'd love to, Jess," she beamed. "I don't get out much these days."

Jess left Audrey and headed towards Margaret's house, knowing that she was probably on a fruitless mission. Margaret would no doubt have it all under control.

She was right. Margaret was adamant that she needed no help with the catering, and Jess left there feeling guilty that she hadn't insisted. Maybe she would make a batch of scones. Margaret would hardly knock them back. It was all making for a very interesting evening.

*

The following evening, Audrey Maitland arrived at precisely six o'clock, and after listening to Jess's seemingly endless list of instructions, shooed them out of the door.

"I've raised children, Jess," she said, "so I know what has to be done. You go and enjoy yourselves while you can. We'll be fine, won't we, children?"

This was received with enthusiastic nods all around.

"Behave yourselves, and do as Mrs Maitland asks." Jess bent to kiss each cheek.

"We will, ma!" was the combined chorus.

Beau took Jess's arm and steered her down the front steps.

"Come on, Jess, before you remember something else to tell Audrey."

The front door closed as they stepped on to the footpath. Jess clutched a paper bag full of scones in one hand, while she tucked her other arm in Beau's.

"Do I look presentable enough to meet with the good doctor and his wife?" she asked as their footsteps echoed on the asphalt.

"My darling, you would look presentable in cheesecloth." Beau was smiling indulgently.

"Be serious, Beau!" Jess gave him a nudge. "Do I look alright?"

"Of course you do, Jess. I'm sure you could stand up against Louise Simmons any day."

"You haven't met her, Beau. She is very stylish."

"Hm, well she'll have to look good to beat you and the red dress."

Jess sighed. "If we're going to be socializing with medical royalty, I need to have more than just this red dress. I'll have to talk with Izzy."

"By all means, Jess, if you think that's necessary."

Jess rolled her eyes. "Men!"

They reached Charles and Margaret's front gate just as Doctor Simmons' black Wolesley pulled up in the driveway. Jess tightened her grip on Beau's arm, and he patted her hand as reassurance.

Doctor Simmons stepped out of the driver's seat, and walked around to open the passenger door for his wife. Louise stepped out on to the footpath and Jess swung a quick glance in Beau's direction. Her gown of shimmering green taffeta rustled as she moved. Over her shoulders was draped a fur cape, and her blonde hair was caught up with matching green combs.

"Good evening, Jess," she said warmly, as her eyes travelled quickly over Beau.

"Good evening, Louise." Jess smiled nervously.

Charles appeared in the doorway at that precise moment, saving them from any embarrassment.

"Welcome!" he boomed. "Come in! Come in!" He held the door wide as the four visitors filed past him. "Into the lounge, if you please! We'll have a drink before dinner."

Jess clutched Beau's arm as they entered the familiar lounge with its deep armchairs and polished wood sideboard.

"What's wrong?" he whispered.

"Don't let me have any alcohol, Beau," she whispered back, recalling the evening at Mario's Restaurant in Sydney.

Beau chuckled, as he also remembered. "Lemonade for you, my dear."

Charles turned to his guests. "Do we all know each other?"

"I haven't met Doctor DuBois," said Louise coolly, smiling in Beau's direction.

"Forgive me," muttered Charles. "Beau, meet Louise Simmons, President of the local Red Cross Society, and wife of Doctor Raymond Simmons."

Beau extended a hand. "I'm very pleased to meet you, Louise."

"Likewise, Beau." They shook hands.

Doctor Simmons stood silently watching the introduction, his brow furrowed.

"Good!" Charles clapped his hands. "Now what will you all have to drink?"

Jess was anxious to slip away to the kitchen, to give Margaret the bag of scones still clutched in her hand, so while Charles moved to the sideboard to pour drinks, she made her escape.

In the kitchen she found Margaret bending over a pot of soup. She turned as Jess walked in, and smiled a little hesitantly.

"Jess dear, could you please taste this, and tell me if it's alright?"

"Of course." Jess put the bag of scones on the kitchen table. "I made some scones for supper, if you want them."

"Thank-you, dear." Margaret's face was flushed, and Jess noticed beads of perspiration on her top lip. "I haven't thought of supper."

Jess picked up a spoon and dipped it in the bubbling soup. "Very nice," she said after tasting it. "Do you need any help in here, Margaret?"

She shook her head. "No, but you can tell Charles that I am ready to serve the soup, so he can move everyone to the dining-room."

The dining room was only used on special occasions, and Jess couldn't remember ever eating a meal in there. The door was always closed.

Jess headed along the passage to the lounge. At the doorway she stopped as her eyes took in the scene. Charles was deep in conversation with Doctor Simmons, and Louise was standing close to Beau, her hand on his arm. They were both laughing. Jess felt a twinge of annoyance, and took a deep breath to control the feeling. Louise looked in her direction and smiled.

"Beau has been telling me about your wedding, Jess," she said smoothly, removing her hand from his arm. "It sounds so romantic."

Beau moved slightly to include Jess in the conversation.

"I wouldn't call it romantic exactly," he said, looking keenly at Jess. "It did follow rather a harrowing time, what with Jess being so ill with the influenza."

"Yes, indeed." Louise's radiant smile vanished and was replaced with an expression of sympathy. "How awful it must have been for you."

Jess squeezed Beau's hand. "I had the best medical care."

"Quite." Louise dropped her gaze.

"I need to speak to Charles. Margaret is ready to serve the soup." Jess smiled quickly before moving across the room to Charles.

He saw her hovering beside him, and interrupted his conversation with Doctor Simmons.

"What is it, Jess?"

"Margaret said to tell you that soup is ready, so if you wouldn't mind moving to the dining-room, she'll begin serving."

"Oh! Goodo! Did you hear that, everyone? Soup is about to be served. Follow me."

Jess hung back to walk with Beau.

"I wondered where you had disappeared to," he whispered.

"You were doing alright without me," she whispered back, and followed it with a smile.

A fire crackled in the dining-room fireplace, giving off a warm glow. The table was covered with a white damask cloth, on which stood two silver candelabras with flickering candles. Margaret had set out her best cream crockery with the tiny rosebuds, and Jess noted that the silverware had been meticulously polished.

"The table looks wonderful!" exclaimed Louise, as she slipped off her fur cape.

A glittering diamond pendant sat at her throat, and the green gown revealed a generous amount of smooth bare shoulders. Jess turned away as she slipped off her shawl. She felt like the poor relation, and she pressed her hands down her red dress, wishing that she could feel comfortable. Looking up, she caught Beau watching her. He smiled reassuringly, and pulled out a chair for her.

"You look beautiful," he whispered, as he draped her shawl across the back of the chair.

"You would say that," she murmured, unconvinced.

Jess found herself seated beside Doctor Simmons. She stared across at Beau, who was seated beside Louise. Charles was at the head of the table. Margaret came in with a large tureen, which she placed on the table. Jess watched her closely, noticing how her hand trembled when she dished soup into each bowl. She shouldn't be doing this on her own. Jess decided then that she would help with the serving of the main course, whether she was wanted or not.

When Margaret was seated, Charles said a brief blessing, and the meal began.

"This is absolutely delicious, Margaret!" enthused Louise, smiling in Margaret's direction. "You never let us down."

Margaret acknowledged the compliment with a simple "Thank-you, Louise."

When the bowls were empty, she collected them and retreated to the kitchen as the conversation began. Charles wiped his mouth on the linen napkin, folded it and looked up at his guests.

"I am pleased to be able to announce to you, doctors, that the committee for the Benevolent Asylum, has agreed to let us have the top two floors for influenza patients. That means we can cater for at least twenty patients on each floor, more if necessary. And," he added imperiously, "Council has agreed to assist with the cost to ensure that the asylum inmates are not put at risk."

"How many beds are there?" asked Beau.

"We will have to provide our own beds."

"And staff?" It was a pertinent question from Doctor Simmons.

"Ah!" Charles paused. "We will provide our own staff, doctors included, plus cleaning staff."

Doctor Simmons expelled an impatient breath. "Is all this really necessary, Charles? How many extra patients do we have?"

"Raymond, the hospital is seriously over-crowded."

"I've been there with the Red Cross," interrupted Louise, "and I've seen how crowded it is." She was staring at her husband. "Are you telling us, Raymond, that you hadn't noticed?"

He frowned, his face flushing. "I'm not on the premises all the time,

Louise."

"Well, they've obviously run out of space!" Louise was matching her husband's mood.

"Louise, this is really none of your concern."

"It is very much my concern, as a constant visitor. What do you think, Jess?" Louise's eyes turned to Jess, who had been listening, wide-eyed, to the discussion.

She cringed, suddenly realising that four pairs of eyes were focused on her.

"Louise, I'm afraid I haven't seen the conditions at the hospital, but I do know that patients with the influenza need to be isolated as much as possible." Jess stared helplessly at Beau.

"There you are, you see!" Louise exclaimed gleefully. "Jess agrees with me."

"Louise, I think it would be wise for you to leave the decision-making to the committee."

"Oh! You mean the men, Raymond?"

"Louise!" There was a note of warning in his tone.

Margaret hovered in the doorway, uncertain whether to interrupt or not. She was saved from making a decision, by the shrill sound of the telephone in the passageway. Charles rose quickly.

"I'll get it, Margaret." He moved from the room, and an uneasy silence fell over the group.

"I'll serve the main course, if everyone is ready," said Margaret quietly, moving into the room.

"I'll help you, Margaret." Jess laid her napkin on the table and rose hurriedly.

"There's no need, Jess. I can manage."

Jess took Margaret by the arm. "I'm helping, and that's all…"

"Over my dead body!" Charles' raised voice could be heard coming from the passageway.

Margaret's hands flew to her mouth.

The receiver was slammed down, and Charles appeared in the doorway, his face beet red.

Margaret rushed to his side. "What was that all about, Charles?"

"Nothing for you to worry about, Margaret." Charles brushed her aside and resumed his seat at the table. "I think it's time for the main course, don't you?" His eyes scanned the group silently looking in his direction. "If you're ready, Margaret?"

"Yes, Charles."

Jess followed Margaret from the room. In the kitchen they stared at one another in consternation.

"Something is going on, Jess," gulped Margaret, "and Charles won't talk to me about it."

"You mean with his work?"

"Yes. He has one or two trouble-makers who are making things difficult for all of them."

Jess bit her lip. Charles had already inferred to her that his workers wanted to 'down tools', as he put it. Was Margaret aware of this, she wondered?

"I'm sure Charles will sort it out, whatever it is," she said lamely. "Now come on, we need to feed them all, and soften the atmosphere in there. It was getting a bit tense. What are we having for the main course, Margaret?"

"Beef Wellington."

"It sounds wonderful!" Jess was already removing the dinner plates from the hob, where they had been warming.

*

The meal continued amid the hum of general conversation, and after a dessert of delicate orange flummery, the ladies retired to the lounge, and left the men to consume the mandatory glass of port, and talk about those things that did not include the women.

"It really is time that men listened to what we have to say!" expounded Louise, as she sank into one of the lounge chairs. "Raymond seems to think that I don't have any brains at all!" She sighed.

"I'm sure that isn't true, Louise," said Margaret, lowering herself into the opposite chair. "It's hard for men to get used to the idea that we do have a voice, and some of us want to use it."

Louise laughed. "I would just like to win an argument occasionally." She turned to Jess, who was seated on the couch. "How about you, Jess? Do you win arguments with Beau?"

Jess frowned. "We don't really argue, Louise."

"What! Never?"

"We have differences of opinion, and can usually settle them amicably."

Louise laughed. "Wait until you've been married as long as we have." Her eyes narrowed. "And did you argue with Jack?"

Margaret sucked in her breath, as she waited for Jess's reply.

"No, Louise. There was never any need to argue with Jack."

"Are you telling me that your men usually get their own way?"

Jess bit her lip as she looked in Margaret's direction. "No, I'm not saying that. I like to think that lively discussion is the best way to handle a situation."

"Hm." Louise sipped from the wineglass she held in her hand. "I must admit that I do get angry very quickly, particularly over issues that affect people's wellbeing. Raymond can be so devoid of feeling sometimes."

"He does see the ugly side to life, Louise," said Jess carefully. "I suppose that can make a person more cynical."

"You're probably right, Jess." Louise sighed. "Your Beau would have seen enough during the war, to make him cynical."

"He tries not to think about it."

"Hm." Louise took another sip of the wine. "Well, I wish him good luck working with Raymond. It won't be easy for him." She stared at Jess. "It probably won't be easy for either of them."

*

It was time to leave the warmth of the Stanley home, and head out into the chilly night air. Beau wrapped Jess's shawl about her shoulders, while Louise attended to her own fur cape. Her husband was deep in conversation with Charles.

"Can we give you a ride home?" Louise looked casually in Beau's direction.

"No," he said hastily. "It's not far, and we like to walk."

"Oh." Louise smiled at Jess. "Settled amicably?" The question hung in the air.

Jess looked momentarily startled.

"Sometimes there's no need for discussion," she said, smiling at Louise's amused expression.

"I see."

"Are you ready, Louise?" Raymond had appeared at her shoulder.

She paused before answering. "I believe I'm ready, Raymond." Smiling sweetly at Jess and Beau, she said, "It was lovely meeting you, Beau, and I wish you well in your new job."

Beau inclined his head. "Thank-you, Louise."

Raymond cleared his throat. "I'll see you tomorrow, Doctor DuBois," he said stiffly, "and we'll have a look at the space in the Benevolent Asylum. Shall we say four o'clock?"

"That suits me," answered Beau, careful not to use his name.

Charles and Margaret appeared beside them, and Jess placed her arm through Margaret's.

"Thank-you for a wonderful meal, Margaret," she said softly. "I'll see you tomorrow."

"Certainly, Jess."

"Goodnight, everyone." Charles shook both men by the hand, and inclined his head at the two women. "We'll see how things go tomorrow. Beau, do you want to borrow the car?"

"Thank-you, Charles. I would appreciate that. You won't be needing it?"

"No, not tomorrow."

Raymond had taken Louise by the arm. She stumbled as they headed towards the car, and Jess heard him say, "You're drunk, Louise!"

She didn't wait to hear Louise's answer. Instead, she clutched Beau by the arm.

"Come on, it's cold standing here."

They stepped it out along the footpath, walking close together to keep warm. Jess shivered.

"You need a wrap like the one Louise was wearing," said Beau lightly.

Jess turned to look at him in the moonlight. "I don't think so, Beau."

"Why not? She looked very warm."

"Did she now?"

"What was the meaning of her last comment, Jess?"

She laughed. "Oh! We had a discussion on whether we argue with our spouse, or not."

"And you said?"

"I said that we don't argue, we discuss."

"I'd say they have lots of arguments," said Beau, pulling Jess closer to his side.

"Yes, I'm sure they do." She paused. "I had the impression tonight, Beau, that Louise was flirting with you."

Beau stopped walking, pulling Jess to a halt beside him. "What did you say?"

"Louise was flirting with you, Beau."

He laughed. "No woman consciously flirts with me, Jess."

"She was, and you obviously didn't notice." They started walking again. "Louise is a very attractive woman, Beau."

"Do I detect a note of jealousy, Jess?"

"No. It was just an observation, that's all."

Beau stopped walking again, and drew her into his arms. "Listen to me, Jess. Louise Simmons could never hold a candle to you, my dearest. My eyes only see you. Never forget that." He kissed her then, igniting the familiar flame inside her. "Come on, let's go and relieve Audrey, so that we can finish what we have now started."

A Package From Angela

The following morning, after the boys had gone to school, and Beau had taken Grace for a walk to the grocer, Jess decided that it was time to flick a duster around the bedrooms, and polish the floorboards along the passageway. She was on her knees with a tin of beeswax and a polishing cloth, when there was a loud knock on the front door.

Jess scrambled from her knees, pulled off her headscarf, and opened the front door. George the postman stood there, holding a large package.

"Good mornin' Mrs. Stanley," he said pleasantly. "I have a package addressed to here, but the name says Mrs. DuBois." He looked at Jess, puzzled.

"Thank-you, George." She smiled. "I have recently married, and I'm now Mrs. DuBois."

His bland face registered surprise. "Blimey! I didn't know that."

Jess knew that the whole street would soon know, but she had to accept the fact that George loved to gossip. She took the package from his outstretched hands.

"Well, good day to you, Mrs. DuBois, and congratulations." George smiled, and nodded towards the package. "It's from Sydney."

"Yes, I see. Thank-you, George." Jess managed to close the front door, and she listened as his footsteps crossed the verandah. The gate squeaked as he closed it.

Jess turned the package over, and there on the back was scrawled the name Angela Rickard. So that was Angela's name? Rickard. Jess had not heard it mentioned in all the time she was in Sydney. What could Angela be sending her?

Jess laid the package on the bed and began to carefully open it, gasping as the final layer of paper fell off. It was the wedding gown she had borrowed. Angela had insisted that she keep it, but Jess had been reluctant, and so had left it behind. Now it seemed that Angela definitely wanted her to have it. Jess sighed as she fingered the soft fabric. It was a beautiful gown.

She picked up a note that lay on top, and sat on the bed to read it.

> *Dear Jess and Beau,*
> *It is so quiet here since you left, and the city is like a ghost town. People are only getting about to do what is absolutely necessary, which means that businesses like mine are starting to suffer. Not much laughter happening.*
> *I am sending you the wedding dress, Jess, because I really did want you to have it. There are no memories attached to it, if that's what you were thinking when you left it behind. Show it to your family, and tell them what a marvellous day it was for all of us. I will never forget it.*
> *By the way, I have been out to dinner with Clarence. He took me to Mario's as a thank-you for my part in your recovery from the influenza. He is a very nice man, underneath that pompous exterior. He told me that his son-in-law, Matthew, is doing reasonably well, and his daughter will stay indefinitely at the sanatorium. That is heartening news, Beau, and I thought you would like to know.*
> *Take care of yourselves, and I hope you are enjoying married life. I miss you both terribly, and I will make it my business to come down and see you as soon as we are allowed to travel without restrictions.*
> *Write to me, please.*
> *Love to you both,*
> *Angela*

Jess wiped the tears from her eyes, and folded the note. Yes, she would certainly write to Angela. She had been a tower of strength during those dramatic days in Sydney.

The front door slammed, and she heard Beau's voice.

"We're home, Jess! Where are you?"

"I'm in the bedroom," she answered.

Beau and Grace appeared in the doorway. Beau was carrying a large canvas bag, which he dumped on the bed. "I hope I've got everything you wanted." He spotted the open package. "What have you got there?"

"The wedding dress." Jess slipped the handkerchief into her apron pocket. "Angela sent it to me. Here's the note that came with it."

Beau took the note, and sat beside Jess, while Grace touched the silken fabric spilling from the open package.

"That's pretty, ma," she said, her eyes widening.

"That was ma's wedding dress, Gracie." Jess ran her fingers over the fabric.

"You wore it, ma?"

"Yes, I did."

Beau looked up from reading the note. His eyes were moist.

"Angela really wanted you to have it, Jess. She's such a kind-hearted soul." He handed the note back to Jess. "Fancy Clarence taking her out to dinner at Mario's? I told you they were getting on well together, but I didn't anticipate that." He paused. "I must write to Matthew. I feel dreadful about the way things happened, but there wasn't much I could do about it."

"Beau, it wasn't your fault, so don't start blaming yourself." Jess patted his hand. "It's probably for the best. It will give Matthew and Celia a chance to renew their feelings for one another, and it will give Clarence a chance to…"

Beau smiled. "A chance to make new acquaintances?"

"Possibly."

"Come on, Jess, admit it! Angela will be good for Clarence."

"But he has a wife, Beau."

He sighed. "He has a wife who doesn't know him, Jess."

*

Later that day, as Beau was preparing for his meeting with Raymond, Jess decided that she would walk with him to see Margaret. Their previous conversations had been unfinished, and she wanted to get to the bottom of what was going on with her mother-in-law's health. Besides, she wanted to show Margaret the wedding gown.

She was bothered also by the telephone call that Charles had received the night before, and if it spelt trouble among his workers, Jess feared for his health.

It was about half past three when Jess, Beau and Grace set off for the Stanley residence. Jess had left a note for the boys, saying where they were, and for them to walk around to grandma's place.

The day was blustery, and they held their coats around them as they walked.

"What do you hope to learn by going to see Margaret, Jess?" asked Beau.

"Something more than I know already."

"Which is?"

"That she's worried about something."

"Don't press her too hard, Jess. She might not want to burden you with whatever it is."

"I might not get a chance to say anything if Charles is there. I think he's oblivious to any problem Margaret might have."

"Yes, well he has a few of his own."

"He told me the other day that some of his workers are threatening to 'down tools'."

Beau stopped walking. "Charles told you that?"

"Yes, and I would say that was what the telephone call was about. They are threatening to strike."

Beau pursed his lips. "You're right, Jess," he said soberly. "Charles admitted it to Doctor Simmons and myself last night. He's very worried about the whole thing."

"I'm sure he is. Margaret is unaware of the actual problem."

"He needs to tell her."

"You know Charles, Beau. Women don't feature very prominently in his estimation."

"He might need to change his attitude."

Jess laughed. "Pigs might fly, Beau! It's too ingrained. Mind you, he's not the Charles he used to be. He has mellowed somewhat."

As they rounded the corner, they could see Charles pacing on his front verandah. He saw them approaching, and hurried down the steps to meet them.

"Hello Charles," said Beau. "Is anything the matter?"

"I'm coming with you." His face was flushed, and sweat was visible on his top lip.

Beau looked quickly at Jess, who was frowning. "Certainly, Charles."

"You can drive." Charles was already clambering into the passenger seat of the grey Chevrolet.

"I'll see you later, Jess." Beau gave her a quick kiss. "I'll see if I can get to the bottom of this."

"Please do, Beau."

Jess grabbed Grace by the hand, and together they watched as Beau backed the vehicle out of the driveway. He waved, and they set off along the bumpy dirt road.

Jess watched as the car disappeared, and then smiling at Grace, she opened the front gate.

The door was ajar, so Jess pushed it open, calling out as she entered.

"Are you there, Margaret?"

There was silence for a moment before Margaret appeared from the kitchen. She was smiling, but Jess could see that her eyes were puffy.

"Oh, hello Jess! Hello Gracie! I wasn't expecting you."

"I did say last night that I would see you today, Margaret."

"Yes, of course you did, dear. I had forgotten." She took a deep breath. "Come into the kitchen. It's warm in there, and I'll pop the kettle on." Margaret spotted the parcel that Jess was carrying. "What have you got there, Jess?"

Jess opened the parcel on the table. "This came today, Margaret. It's the borrowed wedding gown I wore. My dear friend, Angela, has sent it to me. She wants me to keep it."

"Oh, my goodness! Was it her wedding gown?" Margaret fingered the delicate fabric.

"It was, but she didn't get to wear it. Her fiancé was killed at Gallipoli."

"Oh, how very sad." Tears were brimming, and Margaret groped for a handkerchief in her apron pocket. "It's a beautiful gown, Jess. I wish we had all seen you in it."

Jess put her arms around Margaret and held her as tears washed down her cheeks.

"You'll get to see me in it, one day, when we have a family celebration. Now sit down. I'll make the tea, and I want you to tell me what is going on, with both you and Charles."

Margaret sniffed, and sat heavily at the table. Grace was watching her, with eyes like saucers.

"What's the matter, grandma?" she asked plaintively. "You're crying."

"I know, dear." Margaret brushed her fingers across her wet cheeks. "Come here to grandma. She needs a cuddle."

Grace obliged, and sat on her grandmother's knee, wrapping her chubby arms around her.

"Gracie make it all better," she said softly.

"Yes, dear." Margaret rested her head on Grace's golden curls.

Jess pushed the kettle over to boil, and then sat beside Margaret.

"Now," she said matter-of-factly. "Tell all."

*

Meanwhile Beau had pulled up at the front of the impressive cream brick Benevolent Asylum. He turned to Charles, who was sweating profusely, despite the cold weather.

"Do you want to tell me about it?" he asked.

Charles wiped a handkerchief across his face. "I think I have been very foolish," he muttered.

"What have you done?"

"The man I was telling you about last night; the one who's joined the Trade Union movement, well, I've just paid him out, and told him to leave."

Beau whistled softly. "He could make trouble for you, Charles."

"I know, and he probably will."

"What about your other workers?"

"They haven't joined the Union, although they did listen to him when he said that they should all down tools and demand an increase in wages." Charles pounded his forehead. "I pay them a fair wage, and this is the thanks I get!"

"Have you talked to them?"

"No. Come Monday when Russell doesn't appear, they'll want to know why."

Beau drummed his fingers on the steering wheel. "I'm afraid I don't have any answers for you, Charles. Have you told Margaret?"

"Good heavens, no! It's not her concern."

"I think you'll find that she'll want to know."

Charles turned his piercing stare on to Beau. "She is not to know! Is that understood?"

Beau shrugged. "It's your business, Charles, but Margaret is no fool. She's aware that something is going on." He paused. "If you keep this pressure on yourself, it will only elevate your blood pressure, and knowing your history, could bring on another heart attack."

Charles groaned. "I know," he muttered.

"Then you must tell Margaret."

Raymond Simmons appeared beside them.

"Good afternoon, gentlemen," he said politely. "Glad you could join us, Charles."

They both stepped out of the car, their conversation interrupted. Charles pulled his hat firmly on his head, and walked around to join the two doctors.

"I-er-I managed to free up some time," he said quickly.

"Then let's get this over with." Raymond was already striding towards the stairs that led up to the main entrance.

The building reminded Beau of Serendipity, with its cream masonry gleaming in the watery sunlight. He took Charles by the arm.

"Come on, or we'll be left behind," he muttered wryly.

Margaret's News

The children were in bed, and Jess was waiting in the lounge for Beau to return from the back verandah with more firewood. She kicked off her boots, as was the custom, and settled into the couch. This was their special time together, when they could concentrate on each other without interruption from the children. However, tonight would be different because they both had information to share about Charles and Margaret. Jess frowned as she pondered on Margaret's shock announcement, and its ramifications for all of them.

Beau soon returned and dropped an armload of wood into the box on the hearth. He placed a log on the fire, making flames crackle and sizzle up the chimney. After brushing the bark from his sleeves, he turned to Jess. They stared, unblinking, at on another for a long moment.

"What a strange day," said Beau finally. "I have so much to tell you."

Jess patted the couch beside her. "Come and sit with me, Beau," she said quietly. "I have a lot to tell you, too."

Beau removed his shoes and sat beside Jess. She flung her arms around him and pressed her face against his chest. He placed an arm around her shoulders.

"I think you should go first, Jess." He kissed the top of her head.

Jess lifted her tear-stained face. "You told me not to press her, Beau, but I had to know."

"So what did she tell you?"

Jess gulped and sat up, wiping her cheeks with the back of her hand. "Doctor Simmons thinks that Margaret may have a chronic blood disorder."

"Like Leukaemia?"

"She didn't actually say."

"And I'm guessing that Charles doesn't know?"

Jess shook her head. "No. She had blood tests just before we came home."

"Oh, Jess, that's not good news. Are you sure it's not anaemia?" Beau took a deep breath.

"I'm just telling you what Margaret said." Jess blew her nose.

Beau wrapped his arms around her and held her tight. "I wish there was something I could do, but leukaemia is one of those diseases that we know very little about."

"What will happen if it is leukaemia?"

"I'm afraid she will become more and more fatigued as her red blood cells are gobbled up."

"And there's nothing that can be done?"

"Not a lot. Perhaps I need to talk with Doctor Simmons."

"Yes, please do that. Maybe Margaret got it wrong."

"Possibly." Beau shrugged.

They sat in silence for a few moments, while the fire crackled warmly in front of them.

"Margaret is more worried about Charles than she is about herself. He won't talk to her about his problems at work, and she's afraid that he will have another heart attack."

"He will have a heart attack if he's not very careful."

"He'll never cope if anything happens to Margaret." Fresh tears began to fall.

"Don't lose heart yet, my love."

"No, I mustn't get all teary in front of the children." Jess smiled suddenly. "Gracie cuddled Margaret this afternoon, and told her that she would make it all better."

Beau sighed. "If it could all be that easy."

A flaming log rolled out of the fire, landing on the brick hearth. Beau leapt to his feet, and grabbing the poker, moved it back into the fire, where it crackled and hissed, as though in defiance.

"How did you get on with Charles and Doctor Simmons this afternoon?" Jess asked as Beau settled back on to the couch. He grunted.

"Well, Charles has sacked his trouble-maker, and is now awaiting the repercussions."

"Oh! And Doctor Simmons?"

"He was very cool towards me, but we managed to come to an amicable arrangement with the two floors of the Asylum." He turned to Jess. "It is so much more spacious than Serendipity. We have enough room for at least twenty beds on each floor, plus areas where we can completely isolate a patient if necessary. It should work well. Mind you, I haven't seen conditions at the hospital, so I'm just guessing, after hearing Louise's outburst last night, that it is extremely over-crowded."

"That's a positive step then?"

"Indeed. It cheered Charles up no end, and made him forget his own troubles for a short time."

"Charles and Margaret need to tell each other their problems!" Jess sounded exasperated. "They're not going to go away just because they can't talk to each other."

Beau took Jess's hand and squeezed it gently. "They've lived in separate worlds for so long, Jess, that it won't be easy for either of them."

"Then we have to intervene!"

"Charles told me that on no account was I to tell Margaret."

Jess slumped. "But they need each other now, more than ever."

"Jess, not all couples relate to each other easily."

"You mean they're not like us?" Jess looked into his grey eyes.

Beau shook his head. "No, they're not like us." He stared absently into the fire. "Not all men treat their wives with the respect they deserve, Jess."

"What do you mean, Beau?" He didn't answer for a long moment, so Jess gave him a gentle nudge. "Beau?"

He tore his eyes away from the fire, and looked at Jess. For a brief moment she saw a look of utter despair in his expression, but it was soon gone, replaced by a soft smile.

"Where were you then, Beau?" she asked quietly.

"I was thinking of my own parents."

"Your father was a hard man?"

"He was."

"I remember you telling me that your mother was sickly."

Beau nodded. "I was too young to question why that was, and it's probably wrong of me to blame my father. Hindsight is a very fine thing, Jess." He squeezed her hand.

"You're not saying that your father mistreated your mother?" Jess was shocked.

"No." Beau took a deep breath. "I think it was more that he ignored her, and didn't include her in any of his decisions. Taking to her bed was the only way she could handle it."

Jess removed her hand from his, and stroked his cheek. "I'm so sorry, Beau."

"I don't want to be like that, Jess."

"You're not." Jess smiled serenely. "Although I do remember being left out of certain wedding arrangements."

Beau groaned. "Oh! Don't remind me of that! I was under a great deal of stress at the time."

"I know." Jess leaned forward and kissed him. "I was only joking. Now can we please forget about everyone else's problems for a few minutes?"

"With pleasure, my love, but we might need more than a few minutes."

"Take all the time you need."

Beau Begins Work

The telephone rang shrilly as Jess was seeing the boys off to school. She stood on the front verandah, her dressing gown wrapped tightly around her, and listened as she heard Beau answer it.

He was silent for a long moment, and Jess immediately thought of Matthew. Maybe something had happened and Beau needed to be notified? She waited with bated breath.

Finally she heard him answer whoever was on the other end of the line.

"Yes, I'm happy to do that. I presume you have a receptionist who will fill me in on patient information."

Jess expelled her held breath. It wasn't Matthew.

"Yes, I can be there by eleven. Thank-you, Raymond."

Jess heard the click of the receiver, and she turned as Beau appeared at the front door.

"That was Doctor Simmons," he said.

"I know, and you called him Raymond."

Jess saw him shrug. "It slipped out, I'm afraid. Never mind. I have to be at the surgery by eleven. He's off to Melbourne for two days, and I've been left to hold the fort."

"That's good, isn't it?"

"Yes; yes it is."

"Well!" Jess opened the screen door. "I'd better press your suit. You must look your best on your first day." She kissed him hurriedly, and headed along the passageway. Beau walked into the bedroom, grabbed his suit from the wardrobe, and followed her.

In the kitchen, Jess quickly cleared the table of breakfast dishes. She pushed the flat iron to the middle of the stove, and retrieved a large folded cloth from the dresser. Spreading it on the table, Jess smoothed it out with her hands.

Beau placed his suit over the back of a chair and turned towards the door.

"I'll go and have a shave," he said as he ran his fingers over the dark stubble on his chin.

Jess looked up and smiled. "You could grow a beard again, and save yourself all that extra time."

He turned back, looking at Jess quizzically. "Do you mean that?"

"No, silly! You'd look like every other man then."

Beau grinned. "Are you saying I'm unique?"

"Hm! Possibly."

Beau crossed to where Jess was standing at the table, and grabbing her around the waist, rubbed his whiskered chin against her cheek.

"Ouch!" Jess brushed a hand across her cheek. "Go and shave, Beau!"

"I'm going! I just wanted you to know what you'll be missing."

"Go!"

Jess was smiling as she grabbed the iron, licked her fingers and tested the base for heat. She wrung out a wet cloth and placed it over the suit coat, testing it gingerly with the hot iron.

This was what Beau needed; the opportunity to prove to Doctor Simmons that he was worthy.

*

At ten minutes to eleven, Beau stood at the gate of the narrow red brick terrace building. There on a shiny brass plaque was written: Dr. Raymond Simmons, G.P.

Beau took a deep breath, opened the wrought-iron gate and stepped along the narrow path that led to the front door. As he pushed it open, a brass bell rang loudly, heralding his arrival. He walked into a passageway that smelled strongly of antiseptic. The grey linoleum squeaked beneath his shoes as he headed for the window where a large sign read: Please see receptionist upon arrival.

Beau heard footsteps, and a young woman in grey nurse's uniform, appeared at the window. She smiled at him from behind thick glasses, reminding Beau of Nurse Flanagan at Serendipity.

"Can I help you, sir?" she asked pleasantly.

"I'm Doctor DuBois," said Beau, hoping that it would be self-explanatory.

"Yes, Doctor DuBois!" the nurse breezed. "I was told that you would be coming."

"Is Doctor Simmons here?"

"No, he caught the ten-fifteen train to Melbourne. I'm to fill you in on patient details. I'm Norma Allen, by the way."

"I'm pleased to meet you, Miss Allen."

She blushed. "I'm Mrs. Allen, actually. My husband died overseas. Please call me Norma."

"Oh, I am sorry. I was over there myself."

Norma nodded towards his scar. "I take it you got that over there?"

"Yes, unfortunately."

"But you're alive to tell the tale." Her brown eyes misted.

"Indeed." Beau felt somewhat embarrassed.

"Alright, Doctor," said Norma, rousing herself. "I'll show you the consulting-room."

"I have been there before."

"You have?"

"Yes. Doctor Simmons interviewed me some days ago."

"A grilling, more like it," Beau heard her mutter as she came out into the passage to meet him.

Beau smiled to himself. It seemed he wasn't the only one with an opinion of Doctor Simmons.

"You have three patients this morning, and then ten this afternoon, including several children." Norma Allen turned her bright smile on Beau. "Do you think you can handle it?"

"We'll see, shall we?"

They passed a waiting room, where Beau could see a mother pacing with a baby in her arms, and two older men, both suppressing coughs.

"That's Mrs Leonard with the babe, and the other two are miners, both suffering the lung condition that comes with working underground."

Norma unlocked the consulting-room door, and they stepped inside. It was as Beau remembered it, the highly polished desk dominating the space, and the leather seat behind it. Norma placed a manila folder on the desk, arranged the medical instruments on a large tray, and checked the inkwell.

"I think you have everything you need, Doctor. Let me know if there's anything else you require." She turned at the door. "I'll bring you some sandwiches and a cup of tea at noon." She smiled. "I'll give you five minutes before I send Mrs. Leonard in." The door swished shut and she was gone.

Beau moved the leather chair back, and stood for a moment, taking in his surroundings. Along one wall was a patient's examination bed, covered with a white sheet, and half obscured by a folded hospital screen. Beside the bed was an enamel washstand. On the wall in front of him were two large coloured prints; one of the circulatory system, and the other outlined the muscles. On one side of the door stood a skeleton, its head at rather a bizarre angle, and on the other side of the door stood a wooden coat stand. Beau wondered fleetingly whether the skeleton was inadvertently used as a coat stand from time to time.

The door opened at that moment, and the young woman he had seen in the waiting room, walked in. Beau beckoned her to sit on the chair opposite, and when she was seated, he sat also. Norma appeared in the doorway.

"This is Mrs. Leonard, Doctor," she said quickly. "All her information is in the file."

As she left the room, Beau smiled at the young woman, an infant in her arms.

"I'm Doctor DuBois," he said, as he opened her file.

"Where's Doctor Simmons?" she asked abruptly.

"He's not here today." Beau looked at her notes. "What can I do for you?"

"It's the baby." She began to unwrap the infant from the grubby blanket that swaddled it. "She's not doin' very well. I can't get 'er to feed."

Beau stood. "Pop her on the bed over there, and I'll have a look at her. What's her name?" He picked up the stethoscope.

"Charlotte."

Beau felt a sickening shockwave for a moment, and breathed quickly.

"Are you alright?" The young woman stared at him.

"Yes." Beau shook away the thoughts that accompanied the sound of his sister's name.

The young woman laid the infant carefully on the bed, and opened the blanket. The child responded to the handling by crying weakly. Beau could see immediately that she was under weight.

"What do you feed her?" he asked, as he warmed the stethoscope with his hand.

"I feed 'er meself, but she won't drink. I've tried cow's milk, but that gives her diarrhoea. I don't know what else to do!" The young woman was obviously distressed.

"How old is she?" Beau put the stethoscope on the tiny chest.

"Four months."

Beau listened to the heartbeat. It sounded strong enough. Large brown eyes stared up at him.

"Have you introduced solid foods?"

The young woman shook her head. "Should I'ave?"

"It would be a good idea," said Beau quietly, so as not to distress the woman further. "Do you have regular visits to the infant welfare nurse?" He already knew the answer to this.

The young woman shook her head, and her brown eyes filled with tears.

"Fred says we can do this on our own. We don't need anybody's help." She gulped.

"You do if your child is not drinking."

"So it's my fault?"

"No, Mrs Leonard, but I do think that your baby needs to be supplemented with formula."

"I can't afford formula!"

Beau took a deep breath. "I'll give you a note to take to the local dispensary, and they will give you a tin of formula." Beau moved to the desk, and began to write on a slip of paper. "I want you to give Charlotte two scoops in six ounces of boiled water, twice a day. Hopefully this will give your body a chance to replenish your own milk supply."

The young woman was clutching the child to her bosom. "She won't die, will she?" Her voice quivered with anguish.

"No, she won't die."

"But I can't pay for the formula."

"There's no need to." Beau smiled sympathetically. "I would like to see you both in a week's time, and in the meantime, if you have any concerns, I want you to get in touch with the surgery, and we'll fit you in."

"Thank-you, doctor."

"She's a beautiful baby, and we want to give her every chance." He paused. "Maybe you could start introducing her to a few teaspoons of mashed potato."

"I can do that." The woman smiled tremulously at Beau. "You're very kind," she murmured.

Beau handed the woman the note for the chemist. "Your child is very precious."

The woman nodded her thanks and left the room.

Beau sat, and the harshness of reality suddenly hit him. Here was a woman who loved her child, but who without help, could possibly lose her. If she had a husband who would not accept help, then the situation was doomed. Beau prayed that he would be receptive to the child having formula. He had done as much for her as he could safely do. The rest was up to her.

Beau looked up to see Norma Allen regarding him seriously from the doorway.

"What did you do for Mrs. Leonard, Doctor DuBois?" she asked.

"I tried to give her a helping hand."

"There are many young women out there, just like Mrs. Leonard, Doctor DuBois. Unfortunately you can't help all of them."

"I know, but I can help her. I told her to get a tin of baby formula."

"She won't, you know. It's too expensive."

"I'll pay for it."

Norma rolled her eyes. "Her husband might not thank you."

Beau's eyes narrowed. "The child is his, too."

Norma Allen nodded, but didn't answer. "I'll send in your next patient."

Beau's Dilemma

The rest of the morning progressed without drama. Mr. Longmire simply wanted a repeat for the prescription that Dr. Simmons had given him to suppress his 'miner's' cough. It was the same with Mr. Bartlett, except that his cough was more persistent. Beau asked him how long he had been working underground, and he confessed that he had been just a nipper when he had first gone underground back in Yorkshire.

"Started off leadin' the ponies, and bein' responsible for the canaries," he wheezed.

"How old are you?" Beau asked, as he looked at the man's grimy skin and rheumy blue eyes.

"I'll be forty-eight next birthday."

Beau thought he would have been older. "How long do you intend working in the mines?"

The man shrugged. "Dunno. Gotta feed the family. Got a wife and two lads dependin' on me."

"Does the cough syrup help?" Beau was writing on the prescription pad.

"Doctor Simmons says it's the best we can do."

"Have you thought about wearing a mask to prevent the dust from getting into your lungs?"

He shrugged his lean shoulders. "No. Too late for that."

"Not necessarily."

Mr. Bartlett picked up the prescription, tucked it in his jacket pocket, and stood up.

"Thanks, Doctor DuBois," he wheezed. "I'll think about it."

Beau sat back as Mr. Bartlett shuffled out of the room, and pondered on this town and its problems. Gold mining was an important industry here, and no doubt a lot of the miners were suffering from the condition known as Miners' Thysis. Beau needed to read more about the disease, in order to help these men.

At precisely twelve o'clock, Norma Allen swept into the consulting-room, a plate of sandwiches in one hand and a cup of tea in the other.

"Lunchtime!" she said cheerfully. "You have an hour before the next patient."

"What can you tell me about this miners' complaint? I have a feeling it's pretty prevalent here?"

"Oh, yes! Most of the miners have it, and there's not much can be done about it. It's all part of working underground."

"They should be wearing masks."

Norma shrugged. "Some wear a scarf wrapped around their face, but find it hard to wield a pick."

"How do they cope with it?" Beau drummed his fingers on the desk.

"They learn to live with it." Norma leaned on the desk. "That is, until it beats them."

"Not much of a life, is it?"

"The point is, Doctor DuBois, most of them don't know anything else." She straightened her back. "You'd better drink your tea before it gets cold." Smiling, she left the room.

*

It was as Beau had feared; six more miners entered his consulting-room that afternoon, and all of them required the same treatment. Surely there was something that could be done for these hard-working men? The suffering showed on their lined faces, as they struggled to breathe.

As well as the stoic miners, Beau ministered to four young children; two who were suffering with croup, one small boy who had trodden on a nail, and a little girl whose hand had been slammed in a door. All had been intrigued by the new doctor's scarred face, and as fortune would have it, was ultimately a distraction from their immediate problems.

As the last patient walked out the door, Beau gave a sigh of relief. He had not dealt with children since before the war, and so now had to arm himself with all the tactics required to mend tiny limbs, and cope with the tears. He would have to pick Jess's brains for this one.

Beau reached for his coat, and as he did so, he heard voices in the passage. He opened the door in time to hear Norma say, "I'm sorry, Mr. Leonard, you can't come in here. The doctor has finished for the day. I'll make you an appointment for tomorrow."

"I wanna see 'im now!" The voice was raised in anger.

Beau strode down the passage to the front door. "What seems to be the trouble, nurse?"

"Mr. Leonard wants to see you, but he'll have to come back tomorrow."

Beau looked at the young man standing on the doorstep. He could have been no more than twenty years of age, well built with curly brown hair and an olive complexion. He scowled at Beau, as he twisted a cap in his hands.

"You the doctor?" he asked angrily.

"Yes, I am." Beau was mentally putting two and two together, as he realised that this was baby Charlotte's father. "It's alright, nurse," he said to the agitated Norma Allen. "I'll see Mr. Leonard now. You go home, and I'll lock up."

"I can't do that, doctor." Her voice was rigid. "I'll wait."

"As you wish." Beau turned to the young man. "Come this way."

As he strode back to the consulting-room, he heard the clump of Mr. Leonard's boots on the linoleum behind him. Once in the room, Beau shut the door and turned to the angry young man.

"Sit down, Mr. Leonard. What seems to be the problem?"

"I'll stand," said the young man belligerently.

"Suit yourself." Beau seated himself behind the desk.

"My Gertie was in 'ere today," the young man began, "an' you told 'er to give Charlotte formula!"

"Yes," said Beau quietly, "I did."

"We can't afford bloody formula!" A clenched fist was brought down on the desk. "Gertie can do it 'erself. Doctor Simmons said so!"

"When was the last time your wife saw Doctor Simmons?"

The young man shrugged. "I dunno! Why?"

"The situation has obviously changed since then, Mr. Leonard. Your wife is not producing enough milk to feed her baby."

"What d'you mean?" His face was etched with a frown.

"I mean that Charlotte is not being nourished as she should be."

He was silent for a moment. "You mean she's hungry?"

"Yes." Beau paused. "The formula will give your wife's body a chance to produce milk again. Otherwise it will have to be a wet nurse, I'm afraid."

"What's a wet nurse?"

"A woman who has had a child, and has milk to spare."

"You mean someone else would be feeding Charlotte?"

"That's right." There was silence as the young man took in all of this information. "Blimey!"

Beau leaned forward on the desk. "Mr. Leonard, it is vitally important that your wife takes Charlotte to see the Infant Welfare Nurse. She is not expected to know all of these things, and I suspect that she is quite young."

"Gertie's eighteen an' I'm twenty."

Beau sat back. "Do you understand what I'm saying, Mr. Leonard?"

He nodded, and the belligerence was replaced with sadness. "We can't afford luxuries like formula, doctor. My wage at the Deborah barely makes ends meet as it is."

"You're a miner?"

"Yeah."

"There's no need to pay for the formula." At the young man's sudden frown, Beau added, "It is a medical requirement, and will be taken care of. Now you go home to your wife and that beautiful child of yours, and I'll see them both in a week. If you have any concerns, contact this surgery, and I'll be happy to do a house call."

The young man stared at Beau for a long moment. "Why are you doin' this?"

"I'm doing it because I want to see that baby thrive."

"I came in 'ere ready t'have a go at ya, Doctor." His bottom lip trembled.

"I know." Beau smiled.

"Looks like someone beat me to it." He pointed to Beau's scar.

"That was during the war."

"I wanted t' join up, but I was too young."

"I'm glad. It was no place for boys."

"So I heard. Well, thank you, Doctor, an' I won't take up any more o' your time."

"Good-bye Mr. Leonard."

"Name's Fred." He pushed his grubby cap on to the unruly curls. "Thanks again."

Beau listened as his footsteps echoed in the passageway. He heard the door shut, and a moment later, Norma Allen appeared, her eyes questioning.

"I think we sorted it out, nurse." Beau sighed. "There's so much ignorance out there in the community. People think they are doing the right thing, but all they need is the right advice."

"Mr. Leonard is like many men, Doctor. They think having children is in the natural order of things for a woman. They don't realise that nature doesn't always get it right."

"I hope I've convinced him of that." He looked up at the nurse. "The mother is only eighteen."

"Yes, I know."

Beau pushed the chair back, and stood up. "The next thing I have to do is talk with Doctor Simmons, and hope that he'll see things my way."

Norma laughed. "Don't count on it!"

*

Jess heard the front wire door slam, and reached for a pot mitt. Beau appeared in the doorway just as she slid a hot plate on to the table.

"How did it go?" She lifted the lid from the steaming plate of stew.

"Interesting." Beau loosened his tie as he sat heavily.

Jess pulled out the chair opposite, and sat facing him, her eyes questioning. "As you expected?"

"No." Beau picked up his fork. "There's a lot I have to learn about this town and the people who live here. They are not city folk, and their needs are quite different."

"In what way?"

"Well, the miners, for instance. Their work is killing them, and we don't have any answers."

Jess smiled. "It's how they live, Beau."

"I know, but I should be able to relieve their suffering, and I can't do that."

"You're not God, my love."

Beau took a mouthful of the steaming stew. "This is good, Jess." He looked around. "Where are the children?"

"In their rooms. I told them not to disturb us."

Beau smiled as he chewed. "I don't mind their company, Jess."

"Not when you've just come home from work, and I want your full attention."

"I'll read to them afterwards."

"Good. Now tell me more."

"I had the usual croup and accident cases." Beau put down his fork and looked straight at Jess. "I had a mother come in with her baby. The child was under-nourished, and the mother was at a loss. I suggested baby formula as a supplement, but she said she couldn't afford that."

"So what did you do?"

"I told her to get it anyway. I'll cover the cost."

"What!"

"I didn't tell her that. I said it would be covered."

Jess sat back and exhaled. "You do have a lot to learn about the people of this town. They are poor, mostly, but they are also very proud."

"So I found out. Her husband came this evening to have a go at me." Beau leaned forward. "Jess, he was just a boy." He shrugged helplessly. "They need the right advice, and they're not getting it."

"You can't help them all, Beau."

"My nurse said the same thing, but I would be failing in my duty if I sat back and did nothing. I can't do that, Jess!" His eyes glistened with unshed tears.

She stared at him. "You'll do your best, Beau, and that's all you can do."

"The child's name is Charlotte. She's four months old."

Jess reached for his hands across the table. "And it triggered memories of your sister?"

"Yes. You're right. I do need to find her, if it's not thirty-four years too late."

Jess squeezed his fingers. "I've been thinking about it, too, Beau, and I know who can help you."

"Who?"

"Angela. I'm sure she'd be only too happy to do some sleuthing for you."

"I don't know, Jess."

"I'll write to her, and if you give me the information you have, then we'll see what happens."

"She may not…"

"Let's ask her, Beau. It's a mystery that needs to be solved."

Beau looked at her quizzically. "Do you read detective stories?"

Jess laughed. "No!" Her face became pensive. "It will take my mind off all the other things that are happening around us at present."

"That's true."

Jess roused herself. "I have rice pudding for dessert."

As she pulled her hands away from Beau's, he grasped them. "Jess, do you know how good it is to come home from work to someone who cares about you and wants to hear all about your day?"

"I'll get your rice pudding," she answered softly.

Louise

Beau was ready for work, and anxious to be gone before the rainclouds that were threatening, dropped their deluge on an already sodden landscape. He had spent the previous evening penning a letter to Matthew, while Jess had been busy writing to Angela. As she wrote, she questioned him on what he remembered of his sister's removal from the family home. Beau could not remember much, except that he had heard the name 'Sisters of Mercy' mentioned. As an eight-year-old, he had not been privy to adult conversations, so apart from seeing his mother's tears and her fretfulness at that time, he was told nothing.

Jess placed the letters on the table in the passageway. She would post them later in the morning, after a visit to see Margaret.

"Take an umbrella with you." Jess now stood at the front door as Beau buttoned his coat against the wind, and pulled a hat low on his forehead.

"No, it will only catch the wind," He said, before giving Jess a quick kiss. "I'll catch the tram."

"Good luck!"

He waved as he headed off along the street, and Jess watched until he disappeared around the corner. She heard the clang of the tram in the distance, and hoped that Beau would be in time to catch it.

Shutting the door, she looked at the two letters waiting to be posted, and wondered what response they would bring. They had heard nothing of Matthew since their return, except what Angela had told them, and Beau was anxious to know how he was faring. Jess needed to thank Angela for the wedding gown. She smiled as she pictured Angela's face after reading her request to seek information about Beau's sister. *What! You want me to go digging?*

Now it was time to get ready to go and see Margaret, hopefully before the next shower came. Jess pulled off her apron as she entered the bedroom to collect her coat and beret.

Grace appeared at the door as Jess was pulling a green beret over her hair.

"Are we going somewhere, Ma?" she asked.

"Yes, Gracie. We'll go and see grandma, and then I might leave you there while I go and post some letters, if you're a good girl."

"I'll be good, ma!" Grace did a little skip, her green eyes dancing.

"Good, then get your coat and beret, and we'll go, before it rains again."

*

Meanwhile, Beau had missed the tram, and was hurrying along the Pall Mall, dodging scurrying pedestrians, all on the same mission; to get where they were going before the rain. He picked his way across the High Street, narrowly missing being run down by a black Wolesley motorcar, and then finding his trouser legs covered in mud.

As he reached the footpath, he saw the offending vehicle stop, and heard a woman's voice. "Doctor DuBois! Beau! I am so sorry!" Beau looked up to see Louise Simmons waving to him from the driver's seat. He frowned as she gestured towards the passenger seat. "Jump in!" she called out. "I'll give you a ride."

Beau hesitated, and then decided that it would be rude to refuse. He opened the passenger door and stepped up into the comfortable luxury of Doctor Simmons' Wolesley.

"Thank-you," he said somewhat stiffly. "I'm heading to the surgery."

"I thought you might be." Louise laughed gaily, as the car jerked into motion. "I wasn't trying to run you down. It's a bit like Russian roulette on the road at this time of day. Everyone's trying to get to work." She glanced down. "I hope I haven't ruined your trousers."

"They'll dry."

Beau sat stiffly while Louise ploughed through the traffic, narrowly missing a horse and cart, and managing to hit every pothole in the road.

"Raymond doesn't like me driving," she said, laughing self-consciously. "You're not going to tell on me, are you, Beau?" She slanted a glance in his direction.

I can see why, thought Beau wryly. "No, of course not."

"Good."

They had reached the surgery without any more mishaps, and Louise pulled to an abrupt halt.

"Here you are, Doctor; safe and sound."

"Thank-you, Louise." Beau stepped down on to the footpath, and watched as with a wave of her gloved hand, she put the vehicle in motion and jerked away from the kerb.

Shaking his head, he opened the gate, and walked up the path to the front door, just as heavy raindrops spattered on the ground. The bell clanged as he stepped into the passage, and Norma was there to greet him with a wide smile.

"I see you had a ride, Doctor?"

"Yes," said Beau, looking down at his mud-splashed trousers. "She tried to run me down first."

Norma laughed. "I'll fetch you a cloth to wipe off the worst of the mud."

"Thank-you." Beau paused at the door of the consulting-room. "How's today's schedule?"

"Much the same as yesterday, but there are several with flu symptoms, so I've left you a mask to wear," and at Beau's quizzical look, "to be on the safe side."

"Yes, of course."

Beau entered his consulting-room, pondering over the erratic behaviour of Louise Simmons. He could have sworn he smelt liquor on her breath, and at ten in the morning, that was concerning, particularly as she was driving her husband's luxury motorcar. The possible consequences of that were horrendous.

Beau shook away the worrying thoughts, and picking up the surgical mask that lay on the desk, tied it around his face. It was time to push Louise's problems from his mind, and concentrate on those who were going to walk through his door.

*

Jess grabbed Grace by the hand as large raindrops began to fall, and hurried her the last few yards to Margaret's house. As they climbed the steps, Jess noticed that the car was gone, which meant that Charles was not at home. She rapped on the brass knocker.

Margaret appeared a few moments later, and ushered them into the lounge-room.

"Come in! Come in! It looks as though you have just beaten the rain." The drops were heavier now. Jess pulled off her beret and shook out her hair.

"It might be setting in for the day, too."

"Oh dear!" Margaret was peering through the lace curtains. "It's our Red Cross meeting today, and Charles is not here to take me."

"Never mind." Jess sat on the chair that Charles usually occupied. "Maybe you can ask Louise to pick you up in the motorcar?"

Margaret frowned. "I don't think so. I'll walk if it's not raining."

"I should go with you. I've missed quite a few meetings." Jess unbuttoned her coat. "Are there any new projects that I should know about?"

Margaret sighed as she sat opposite Jess. "There are the usual knitting projects for the needy."

"Why don't we ask Louise if we can turn out attention to young mothers with babies. Beau was telling me of a case he had at the surgery yesterday, of a young mother whose baby is not feeding properly. Maybe we could visit these young women, and offer our experience?"

"Isn't that what those new Infant Welfare nurses are supposed to do?"

Jess shrugged. "I don't know. They weren't around when I had my children."

"No." Margaret stared off into the distance.

"What's the matter, Margaret?"

"I'm worried about Charles. He had a meeting with his labourers this morning. There's some sort of trouble brewing, but he won't talk to me about it."

Jess leaned forward. "Have you talked to Charles about what is troubling you?"

"No, dear."

"Why not?" Jess sat back against the cushions.

"Doctor Simmons has gone to Melbourne to the laboratory place where they analyse blood and tissue samples. I won't know what the outcome is until he returns." Margaret's brown eyes were large and fearful. "There's no need to worry Charles just yet. It could be that I'm anaemic."

"Anaemia is still a worrying condition, Margaret."

"I know, but let's wait and see, shall we?" Margaret turned to Grace who had been standing quietly, listening to the conversation. "How's my little Gracie today?"

"I'm alright, grandma. Are you feeling better?'

"Yes, of course, dear." Margaret opened her arms and Grace clambered on to her knee. "I'm feeling much better." She looked at Jess across the top of Grace's head. "Much better."

*

Beau's day was almost at an end. He had seen to wounds, recommended gargle for several sore throats, talked with two more miners about their dusted lungs, and listened to another mother whose infant was irritable and refused to feed. Beau ascertained that the boy was teething, and prescribed a soothing rub for his gums. Once again he asked the mother if she had visited the Infant Welfare Nurse. The answer was an emphatic 'no!'

"Why not?" asked Beau, puzzled by the mother's obvious reluctance to use the service provided.

"She's not got no children!" the woman answered scornfully. "What does she know?"

"I don't have any children, and yet you come to me," said Beau cautiously.

"Because you're a doctor."

Beau wasn't about to argue with her logic. "I still think you should be checking with her at least once a month."

When he quizzed Norma about the reluctance of mothers to take their children to the Infant Welfare Nurse, he received a very blunt answer.

"It's all new to them. It will take a while for the idea to be accepted."

"In the meantime, children are suffering."

Norma raised her eyebrows. "Children have always suffered. Where have you been, Doctor DuBois? Infant mortality rate is still too high. There's no question about that."

Beau sighed. "I know, but surely it doesn't have to be."

"It's ignorance in most cases. Mothers usually want what's best for their children, but they are very cautious when it comes to anything new." She smiled. "You've been out of General Practice for too long, Doctor."

"I'm afraid so. I've spent a great deal of time…"

They were interrupted by a female voice calling out from the passage.

"Norma! Where are you?"

Norma frowned. "I do believe that is Mrs Simmons. I wonder what she wants." She hurried out into the passage and Beau heard the exchange clearly.

"Oh! Norma! There you are!"

"What can I do for you, Mrs. Simmons?"

"Is Doctor DuBois here?"

"Surgery has finished, Mrs Simmons."

"That's not what I asked you! Is Doctor DuBois here?"

"Yes, he is, but..."

"I want to see him."

Beau heard footsteps along the passage, and Louise Simmons appeared in the doorway, carrying a fur coat. She made her unsteady way across the room, and sat heavily on the chair opposite Beau. He looked beyond her to see Norma hovering at the door, her mouth set in a straight line.

Louise brushed stray blonde hairs from her flushed face, and stared at Beau.

"I need you to do me a favour," she blurted out.

"What sort of favour?"

"I need you to drive me to the station to pick up Raymond." She shrugged theatrically.

Beau's eyes narrowed. "Have you been drinking, Mrs. Simmons?"

"None of your business!" she snapped, her blue eyes glittering.

"Where is your car?"

"Down the road a bit." She waved a hand vaguely.

Beau saw Norma mouth the words, 'Fox and Lair'.

"Maybe you need to join a Temperance group, if you are having problems." Beau was now treading on very dangerous ground.

"Temperance!" Louise's voice rose with indignation. "I don't need Temperance! I have the Red Cross! They're..." She stopped suddenly, clapping a hand across her mouth. "Oh, Lord!" she groaned. "I should have been at a meeting today." She slumped in the chair.

Beau looked at Norma. "Could you make Mrs. Simmons a strong cup of coffee, please Norma?"

"Certainly, Doctor." She disappeared from the doorway.

Beau turned his attention back to Louise, who was sitting quietly sobbing now.

"What time does the train arrive?" he asked as gently as he could.

"Six o'clock!" she wailed, rubbing a hand across her wet cheeks.

Beau looked up at the clock on the wall. It was five-thirty. "Very well! We have half an hour to get you sober."

"Raymond shouldn't go away so often!" she sobbed. "He knows I hate being alone."

"Why don't you go with him?"

"No!" she hiccoughed. "The laboratories are no place for a woman, so

Raymond says."

Beau looked at her with pity. The crumpled woman sitting opposite him bore no resemblance to the glamorous Louise Simmons who had arrived at the dinner party several nights ago. Not so long ago it had been Celia who craved attention, particularly from her husband. Now it seemed that Louise was suffering the same anxiety. Celia turned to spite to get attention, and Louise was obviously turning to the bottle.

Norma took that moment to enter with a steaming cup of coffee.

"Here, drink this, Mrs. Simmons. It will make you feel better."

Louise took the cup in trembling fingers, and stared up at Norma. "Thank-you."

Beau stood up. "I'll fetch the car while you're drinking that."

"I feel so foolish," murmured Louise, while Norma merely shook her head.

*

Beau stepped out on to the street. Daylight was waning and there was a distinct chill in the air. He pulled his coat on as he walked in the direction that Louise had vaguely indicated. **Finding the vehicle won't be that difficult at this time of day,** he thought. How had she managed to walk from the hotel to the surgery in the state she was in, and in the high-heeled shoes she was wearing?

Beau walked quickly, and soon came in sight of the 'Fox and Lair'. Raymond's black Wolesley was standing outside. He cranked the motor to life, and jumped into the driver's seat. As he pulled away from the kerb, a voice shouted out from the footpath.

"Hey! What do you think you're doin'?"

Beau turned to see a man waving his arms and running beside him. He idled the motor.

"This is Doctor Simmons' car!" Beau called out. "I'm Doctor DuBois, and I'm taking it to his wife. She's at the surgery."

A burly man appeared beside him. He studied Beau through squinted eyes.

"How can I be sure o' that?" he asked, poking a blunt finger at Beau.

"You'll just have to take my word for it," answered Beau. "Louise has asked me to drive her to the station to pick up her husband."

The burly man placed his hands on the edge of the door. "And Louise is alright?"

"Apart from consuming too much alcohol, I'd say she's alright. Now if you'd be so kind as to let me go, I have a train to meet at six o'clock."

The man took his hands from the door. "I'll remember your face, mate, if this is not fair dinkum."

Beau smiled wryly. "Yes, I bet you will."

He eased the car on to the road, and headed up the hill towards the surgery. In the rear vision mirror, Beau could see the man standing with his hands on his hips, watching his departure.

At the surgery he left the motor idling, while he ran up the path and into the building. Norma was helping Louise on with her fur coat, and they both looked up as Beau entered the room.

"I think I had a run-in with the publican," he said, as he collected his briefcase from behind the desk. "He wanted to know why I was driving your vehicle."

Louise laughed. "That would have been Cyril Bainbridge. He's not the publican, but he spends a good deal of his time there."

Beau wanted to say 'as you do', but a look from Norma silenced him. Instead he glanced up at the clock. It was ten to six.

"Come on, we'd better go."

Louise seemed to have gained some control of her movements as they headed for the front door. "I'll lock up!" Norma called out, as they negotiated the path.

"Thank-you, Norma. I will possibly see you next week." Beau felt a twinge of uncertainty, as he helped Louise into the passenger seat. His job might be over, when all of this surfaced.

As darkness was now falling, he lit the gas headlights before climbing into the driver's seat. Stealing a glance at Louise, he moved the vehicle on to the road.

"I'm so sorry about this," she murmured, as they headed for the centre of the town. "I'm going to have some explaining to do."

"You asked me to drive you to the station. Raymond shouldn't have a problem with that."

Louise sighed. "No, he won't have a problem with that, but he'll know I've been drinking, and when he finds out that I missed a Red Cross meeting, he'll be furious."

Beau had no answer for that, so he remained silent.

By the time they reached the station, the train was already in, belching steam on to the platform. Beau climbed out of the car, leaving it idling.

"You stay here," he said to Louise. "I'll meet Raymond."

Beau made his way towards the platform. Raymond was striding towards him, an overnight bag in one hand and a briefcase in the other. He stopped as he saw Beau.

"Ah! Doctor DuBois! What brings you to the station?"

"I'm here to collect you," said Beau lightly.

"Where's Louise?"

"She's in the car."

Beau heard his quick intake of breath. "Is she alright?"

"Yes. She asked me to drive her here."

Beau didn't miss the frown that creased his brow. "Did she now?" Raymond brushed past Beau and hurried towards the parking area. Beau followed.

At the car, Raymond stopped and peered at his wife in the gathering gloom. "Louise?"

"Yes, Raymond."

"What is happening here? Why did you have to trouble Doctor DuBois?"

"Please can we talk about this when we get home, Raymond?"

He sucked in his breath as he turned to Beau. "Can I give you a ride home?"

"No, thank-you. It's not far; I can walk."

"Are you sure?"

"Positive."

Raymond cleared his throat. "I must apologise for the inconvenience that this has been for you."

"Not at all," answered Beau quickly. "I'll just retrieve my briefcase from the front, and I'll let you both get on your way."

Beau grabbed his briefcase from beneath the front seat, and stepped back as Raymond climbed in beside Louise.

"You've got some explaining to do, Louise," he heard Raymond say, as the car pulled away.

Beau sighed. He felt drained, and all he wanted to do now was go home to Jess. Walking quickly, he headed up the steps of the pedestrian bridge.

*

Jess was clearing away the tea dishes when she heard the front door opening. Resisting the urge to run and meet Beau, she waited until his footsteps stopped at the kitchen door.

"I'll get your tea." She smiled at him as she moved towards the stove.

"No!" Beau put down his briefcase. "Not yet. Come here, Jess."

She walked across the kitchen and into his open arms. Beau buried his face in her neck.

"Darling girl," he sighed. "You have no idea how good it is to be here with you at this moment."

"Did you have a bad day?" Jess smoothed his hair with gentle fingers.

Beau raised his head. "It was an interesting day, to say the least." He looked around the kitchen. "Where are the children?"

"They're playing in their rooms."

Beau frowned as he looked at Jess. "You don't have to hide them from me, Jess."

"I know." She touched his face. "But this is our time, and I've told them that we'll read to them after you've had your tea." She moved out of his arms. "Are you ready for it now?"

Beau shook his head. "I want to tell you about my day first. Is the fire going in the lounge?"

"Of course."

"Then let's go and sit in there. I have a lot to tell you."

As they walked into the passage, the door to the boys' room burst open, and Edward appeared.

"Is it story-time yet?"

"Wait just a little longer." Jess smiled at his crest-fallen expression.

Beau was settling himself in the old brown couch as Jess closed the door quietly behind her.

"Now tell me what happened." She sat beside him, and took his hands in hers.

Beau turned to look at her. "I had Louise Simmons in to see me today."

"Oh?" Jess raised her eyebrows. "She missed our Red Cross meeting this afternoon."

"And I know why."

"You do? Then you'd better tell me." Jess's tone had a slight edge to it.

Beau took a deep breath and began with the incident that morning, when Louise had nearly run him down. Jess listened as the events unfolded, finishing with the drive to the station to pick up Raymond. She took a deep breath as Beau finished speaking.

"I can't say I'm surprised about the drinking. Louise has seemed rather on edge of late."

"She's like Celia in many ways, Jess. They both crave attention, and will try anything to get it."

"I think Raymond ignores her." Jess looked down at her hands, still holding Beau's. "Louise is a very intelligent and beautiful woman, but Raymond doesn't see that."

"She told me that she would love to go with him to Melbourne to the laboratories."

Jess shook her head slowly. "And he won't allow it?"

"No."

"What would you do, Beau, if it were me?"

"I would be happy to share my knowledge with you, Jess."

"Would you?" Jess smiled at him. "You're not like most men, Beau. Why is that?"

Beau released his hands and cupped her face, as he looked deep into her eyes.

"Darling girl, I would walk over hot coals if necessary, to make you happy."

"I hope you never have to do anything quite so drastic, Beau." Jess laughed softly as she placed her hands over his. "Now come and have your tea. Three anxious children are waiting for our attention."

An Uneasy Truce

The following morning, Beau and Edward set off into the bush to hunt for rabbits. Ben had shaken his head vehemently when asked if he wanted to join them, and Grace had stamped her feet with anger, when told that she was too young to go. Jess was busy pacifying her when there was a loud knocking on the front door. Frowning, she hurried to see who was there. It was Doctor Simmons.

"Good morning, Mrs. DuBois." He raised his hat as Jess opened the door.

"Oh! Good morning, Doctor Simmons. What can I do for you?"

"I wish to speak with your husband."

"I'm sorry, Doctor. You've just missed him. He's taken Edward rabbiting."

"Rabbiting?" Jess saw his aristocratic nostrils quiver slightly.

"Yes. It's a week-end treat for both of them."

"I see." His tone was disdainful, making Jess hide a smile. "When do you expect them home?"

"Certainly not before lunch."

He pursed his generous mouth. "If I come back at say, two o'clock, they'll be home?"

"I would think so." Jess laughed. "Hunger will drive Edward home before then."

"Good. I shall return at two." He raised his hat once more. "Good day to you, Mrs. DuBois."

Jess watched him walk down the steps, before she closed the door. He probably wanted to talk with Beau about what had transpired the previous day. Poor Louise! Jess could only imagine what a lecture she would have got about her embarrassing behaviour.

*

Beau and Edward arrived home just a little after twelve, two rabbits slung over Edward's shoulder. He displayed them proudly on the kitchen table. "Mack and I caught these, ma!"

"Wonderful, darling, but could you put them in the washhouse, please? I'm about to set the table for lunch." Jess caught Beau's look of amusement, and wrinkled her nose at him.

"I left two rabbits with Jean," he said, "in case you're wondering why we have only two."

"Good!" Jess clapped her hands. "Now out to the washhouse, both of you!"

As Beau reached the back wire door, Jess moved swiftly after him.

"Beau!" He stopped. "I had a visit from Doctor Simmons this morning. He's coming back to see you at two this afternoon."

"What did he want?"

"He didn't say."

Beau opened the wire door. "It will be about yesterday, I imagine."

"Yes, I would say so."

*

At precisely two o'clock there was a loud knock on the front door.

"I'll get it," said Beau quickly. "We'll go into the lounge, if that's alright, Jess?"

"Yes, of course."

Beau opened the front door. Raymond Simmons stood there, his expression dour.

"Good afternoon, Doctor DuBois," he said stiffly, as he removed his hat.

"Good afternoon, Raymond." Beau made a point of using his Christian name. "Come in."

Opening the door, he ushered Raymond Simmons into the passageway.

"We'll go into the lounge where it's quiet, and we won't be interrupted."

He led the way into the lounge, where the fire crackled in the grate, and the room was warm.

"I won't beat about the bush, Doctor DuBois." The two men stood facing one another across the room. "I come with an apology from my wife. She told me everything that happened yesterday, and I am deeply sorry that you had to be drawn into such a shameful incident."

Beau looked at the man. His haughty features now expressed a degree of sorrow, and he twisted the brim of his hat between his fingers.

"Before we talk about yesterday," said Beau, with a forcefulness that he didn't really feel, "I would like to clear up one little thing, if I may?"

"And what is that?"

"I'm afraid I don't like the formality of being called by my full title. I insist that you call me Beau, and if I can call you Raymond, then we can reserve formality for professional occasions."

There was a pause before Raymond answered.

"Very well."

Beau held out his hand, and it was shaken firmly.

"Good!" said Beau, releasing his hand. "That's out of the way. Now, back to yesterday. I'm glad I was able to help, and it was a good thing that Louise had the foresight to come to me. She was in rather a bad state, if you don't mind me saying so."

Raymond nodded his head slowly. "Yes, I believe she was." He paused. "I've known she had a problem for a little while now, but we've always managed to hide the fact."

"Hiding the fact is not going to solve it, Raymond." Beau wasn't sure how far he should go in this vein. "Perhaps Louise needs some professional advice, or…"

"You mean a psychiatrist?" Raymond's tone was sharp.

"I know very little about Louise, but I have observed that she is very intelligent, and I just wonder whether involving her brain in something that interests her, might be a better option."

"Is that your professional opinion, Beau?" There was a slight sting in his tone.

"No." Beau kept his voice level. "Simply an observation, that's all."

"Thank-you, but I can deal with Louise."

Beau shrugged. "I'm trying to be helpful here, Raymond."

"Yes, I'm sure you are. After all, you did deal with similar problems in Sydney."

"Drug addiction and alcoholism were all part of dealing with life in a post-war existence. Yes, I saw it all, unfortunately."

Raymond stopped twisting the brim of his hat, and began to brush imaginary fluff from its crown. Beau, watching on, recognised the signs of a very stressed man. Going to the door, he opened it and called into the empty passage.

"Jess, love!" She appeared from the kitchen. "Could we have a cup of tea, please?" Beau turned to Raymond. "Do you have milk and sugar?" He shook his head. "Black tea, please Jess."

Back in the lounge, Raymond had moved to a position in front of the fire. As Beau returned, he placed his hat on the mantel, and stood with his hands behind his back. Beau drew one of the lounge chairs closer to the fire, and motioned his guest to sit.

"We might as well be comfortable," he said lightly, as he waited for Raymond to be seated.

"I'd like to discuss with you a roster for the surgery, if I may."

"Yes, indeed," said Beau, as he seated himself on the couch.

"If it works for you, I would like you to do Mondays, Wednesdays and Fridays. That way we can both have two days at the hospital, and the annexe at the asylum. I will have to speak with the Registrar about that, but I'm not expecting that there will be a problem. Apart from two College Graduates, plus the nursing staff, of course, you and I will have to oversee the patients there. Hopefully this will allow me one day a week to visit the Laboratories in Melbourne."

"I'm happy with that arrangement, and then we can both have continuity with our own patients."

Beau saw Raymond's eyes flicker at that suggestion, and fully expected to be contradicted, but there was silence, indicating that he wasn't averse to the idea.

"Good!" Raymond's features seemed to relax somewhat, as he settled into the comfortable horsehair lounge chair with its colourful crocheted rugs.

Jess took that moment to appear with a tray, on which were two cups of tea and a plate of scones with jam. As she looked around for somewhere to put the tray, Beau rose from the couch and carried a small polished wood table to the rug in front of the fireplace. Jess placed the tray on the table, and smiling at Beau, was about to leave the room.

"Get yourself a cup of tea, Jess, and join us."

Jess looked at Raymond for a reaction to Beau's statement. He merely inclined his head.

"Very well," she said slowly. "As long as I'm not interrupting anything."

"No." Beau also looked in Raymond's direction. "I think we've finished here."

"Certainly, Mrs. DuBois. You can help us eat these delicious scones."

For a moment Jess saw a spark of humour in Raymond's blue eyes, and at the door she stopped.

"On one condition," she said, tilting her head slightly.

"And what is that?"

"That you call me Jess."

A smile lit his face, startling both Jess and Beau. "As you wish."

When Jess returned a few minutes later, a cup of tea in her hand, the two men were devouring the last of the scones. She looked at the near empty plate, and cocked an eyebrow.

"You're obviously enjoying those scones," she said, as she sat beside Beau.

"We did leave you one, my love." Beau grinned at her, as he wiped jam from his mouth.

"Louise has never learnt to master the art of cooking scones." Raymond brushed the crumbs from his tweed jacket as he glanced in Jess's direction.

She also caught the look from Beau that said: *Here's a perfect opening for you, Jess.*

Picking up the last piece of scone, Jess looked directly at Raymond.

"We'll have to do something about that, Raymond. Maybe I can show her how it's done?"

"Would you?" There was that smile again.

"Certainly."

*

Ten minutes later, Jess and Beau were standing on the front verandah, watching as Raymond's black Wolesley pulled away from the kerb. Jess tucked her arm in Beau's.

"Well, you won him over with your scones, Jess." Beau squeezed her arm.

"He actually smiled, Beau! Can you believe that? I've never seen him smile before, in all the years I've been attending the surgery. He always looks so solemn."

"It was the scones, my darling. You know the way to a man's heart is through his stomach?"

"I don't want his heart, Beau, but I have to admit that he is almost as handsome as you, when he smiles." Jess turned to look at him, and he grinned.

"Almost?"

"That's what I said."

Margaret

Beau arrived at the surgery at nine o'clock the following Monday morning, to find Norma already there, arranging files for the day's schedule. She looked up and smiled as Beau entered the consulting-room. He hung his coat and hat on the stand beside the door, and was surprised to find the room was warm. Looking around, he saw that a kerosene heater had been placed beside the desk, and was glowing red, indicating that it had been on for a while.

Norma saw Beau glance at the heater. "It's a very cold morning, Doctor," she said, as a way of explanation.

"Yes, it is. You must have arrived early, Norma?"

"There's not much to do at home, so I might as well be here." She laid a pile of manila folders on the desk. "How did you get on with Mrs. Simmons, Doctor?"

"We arrived at the station in time to meet the train. Doctor Simmons was rather surprised to see me." Beau opened the top folder, and his eyes skimmed down the page. Another miner.

"I'm sure he was." Norma picked up a surgical mask that lay beside the folders. "Don't forget to wear your mask, Doctor. We have a few influenza patients today. How serious they are, I don't know, but we mustn't take any risks." She smiled serenely at Beau, and headed for the door. "The first patient is a Mr. Reynolds. He has an injury to his leg. I'll send him in at half-past-nine. That will give you time to check the information that's there." She nodded towards the files.

Beau sat behind the desk. "Thank-you, Norma." He looked up. "Has Doctor Simmons spoken to you about our roster?"

"No."

"Well, I'll be here on Mondays, Wednesdays and Fridays, and Doctor Simmons will do Tuesdays and Thursdays. That may have to be flexible, of course."

"Of course." Norma was about to say more, but decided against it. "I'll leave you to it, Doctor."

She closed the door quietly behind her.

Beau glanced quickly through the files, checking occupations and history of illnesses. Most were miners. There were a couple of injuries had to be checked and dressed, and several who were concerned about flu symptoms.

As he reached the middle of the files, the name Margaret Stanley jumped out at him.

Beau sat forward in his chair, and his eyes quickly scanned Margaret's file. On the first page he saw her blood test results, from the Laboratory in Melbourne. It was as he had suspected, and bad news for Margaret and the family. He sat back, trying to digest what he had read, and thinking of the repercussions when the news reached Jess.

Beau put Margaret's file back in the queue, and pondered on what he should say to her. She would be expecting to see Doctor Simmons when she arrived later in the day, and it was possible that she would prefer to speak with him. Beau had to be prepared for a negative reaction.

The door opened and Norma ushered in a young man on crutches.

"This is Harold Reynolds, Doctor DuBois." She smiled before making her exit.

"Where's Doc Simmons?" the young man asked as he sat awkwardly on the chair facing Beau.

Picking up his file, Beau scanned it before answering.

"Doctor Simmons is not here today. I'm new to the Practice, and I'll be sharing Doctor Simmons' patients." He smiled behind his mask.

The young man studied him from above a thick growth of dark beard.

"He told you about me, has 'e?"

"No. I only have what information there is on your file." Beau nodded towards the man's injured leg. "So you caught your foot in an animal trap?"

"Yeah. Stupid of me, because I set 'em meself."

"You set them to trap what, may I ask?"

"Foxes, rabbits, dogs sometimes." He shrugged.

Beau bit back a scathing comment, and walked around the desk.

"Could you sit on the bed while I have a look at what's going on with your leg?"

"Yeah, alright." Harold Reynolds limped across to the bed, and seated himself.

Beau washed his hands at the sink, dried them and began to unwrap the ankle that was encased in bandages. As he got near the end, he smelt rotten flesh, and he looked up quickly at the young man seated above him.

"When did Doctor Simmons see this?" he asked.

The young man wrinkled his nose. "Dunno! About a week ago, I think. Stinks, don't it?"

"It certainly does." Beau completed the unwrapping, and stared at the wound on the man's ankle. It was septic and the exposed bone was inflamed. Beau had not seen a wound like this since the war. "This will need to be bathed in disinfectant, and I suggest you try to keep off it for the next week or so."

"I gotta go t'work."

"You work in the mines?"

"Yeah."

"Well, Mr. Reynolds, if this wound is not bathed every day, you run the risk of losing it."

"Losin' it! Ya mean have it chopped off?"

"That's exactly what I mean."

"Bloody hell!" The man's face had blanched, and he stared at Beau. "That can't happen, Doc."

Beau stood up. "I'll get the nurse to attend to you, and I want you back again tomorrow."

"I'll lose me job." It was a whisper now.

"I'm sorry, but I've given you the alternative."

"The wife won't be pleased."

Beau moved to the door. "Excuse me for a moment."

Norma was at her desk when he walked into the waiting room. She looked up and smiled behind her mask.

"Yes, Doctor?"

"Could you attend to Mr. Reynolds' wound, please Norma?" he lowered his voice, as the waiting room was full of curious onlookers. "It's turned septic, and I've told him to come back tomorrow."

Norma raised her eyebrows. "Very good, Doctor." She kept her voice low. "I'm not surprised at that. I wasn't at all happy with it when I saw him last week."

"He should have been having it dressed daily."

Norma sighed. "You're probably right, but the men here are in constant fear of losing their jobs."

"It's that, or lose his leg. I'll leave a note for Doctor Simmons, and I'll see Mr. Reynolds on Wednesday. I'll send him into the dressings room, and then I'll see the next patient."

"Yes, Doctor."

Beau hurried back to the consulting-room, where he picked up the crutches, and handed them to Harold Reynolds, who was staring bleakly at his mangled ankle.

"Come with me," said Beau as he helped the handicapped man from the bed. "Nurse Allen will see to your wound, and remember, I want to see you on Wednesday."

Harold Reynolds grunted an expletive, and hobbled after Beau.

*

The morning continued with fretful children, miners looking for their dose of special cough elixir, and a young woman with a swollen nose. When Beau quizzed her as to how she received the bruising, she told him to 'mind y'r own bleedin' business', and if he could just give her something to take the swelling down, she would not bother him again.

After she had gone, Beau checked her case files, and found that she regularly attended the surgery with similar injuries. He felt certain that they could only be as the result of being beaten, so he made a note to discuss her case with Raymond.

At twelve o'clock Norma bustled in with a plate of sandwiches and a cup of tea.

"How are you going, Doctor?" she breezed. "Finding your way, now?"

"Yes, thank-you, Norma." Beau picked up the cup. "This is quite a treat, having lunch supplied."

Norma laughed. "You Doctors wouldn't eat, if I didn't look after you."

"Well, thank-you. It's much appreciated."

Norma paused at the door, her eyes above the mask, serious. "I don't think you'll be seeing Mr. Reynolds on Wednesday, Doctor."

Beau shook his head. "He'll lose his leg if it's not treated."

"I know, but these men are stoic, and refuse to be seen as weaklings."

"And if I do a house call?"

"I don't know. Doctor Simmons only does house calls for extreme emergencies."

"I would call this an extreme emergency."

"It's worth a try. I'll get you his address."

"Thank-you, Norma."

Beau sat back as she left the room, and pondered on the circumstances of these stoic miners and their families. He had not encountered people like them before, and he would have to change his way of thinking to match theirs.

The afternoon continued in the same vein, and at three o'clock, Beau prepared himself for the arrival of Margaret. Her file lay on the desk in front of him, as he waited for her knock on his door. It came at two minutes after three.

"Come in," said Beau, and the door opened slowly.

Margaret hesitated before entering the room. "I expected to see Doctor Simmons," she said quietly.

"I'm sorry, Margaret, but he's not here, so you'll have to talk to me." Beau smiled above his mask.

"Don't apologise, Beau. I don't suppose it matters who gives me the news." Margaret sat slowly, and looked across the desk at Beau. "So what is the news, Beau?"

He took a deep breath, as he picked up the paper with the blood test results.

"You do have blood cancer, Margaret, but I suspect that you knew that."

"Yes. I was fairly sure, although I hoped that I was wrong."

Beau leaned forward. "There are things we can do, Margaret, to help you."

Margaret shook her head. "No. I don't want my life extended, if the end result is still the same."

Beau was at a loss for words. "You will have to tell the family, Margaret."

"I know, but not yet, Beau." She sighed, and a tear escaped, sliding down her pale cheek.

"Charles needs to know, Margaret, and the sooner the better."

"I'll tell him when I'm ready. He has enough on his mind at the moment." She looked intently at Beau. "And I must ask you not to tell Jess that I've seen you today. Please, Beau!"

There was silence for a long moment before Beau shrugged. "As you wish, Margaret, but don't leave it too long. Jess already fears the worst."

Margaret brushed at the tears on her cheeks. "How long do you think I've got, Beau?"

"I really don't know, Margaret." He hesitated. "It could be weeks, or it could be months."

"So it's time to get my house in order?" It was just a whisper.

Beau could only nod his head. His throat had closed, and no words would come.

*

Beau walked home slowly that evening, his heart heavy with the knowledge that his family would soon be facing another cruel blow, and he was powerless to do anything about it. He would have to bide his time, and be ready to pick up the pieces when the moment of realization came.

He pulled his coat around him, and shivered as a chill wind swept straight through him. Whether it was from the cold, or a sense of dread, he didn't know, but as his footsteps neared home, the chill increased. Jess would know instinctively that something was wrong, but he was sworn to silence. He must not give her any reason to suspect that he was keeping something from her.

At the front gate he stopped to gather his senses, and prepare for a thorough quizzing. Jess would want to know all about his day, and under normal circumstances he would be happy to share that, but not tonight.

Taking a deep breath, Beau pushed the front gate, climbed the steps and opened the front door.

"Jess, love! I'm home!"

Confrontation

Beau arrived at the Surgery on the Wednesday morning, to find Norma waiting for him. As he stepped into the passage, she hurried to meet him, her face anxious.

"What is it, Norma?"

"Doctor Simmons is here," she whispered furtively, "and he wishes to speak to you. He doesn't look all that pleased, I must say."

Beau smiled reassuringly. "Well, I'd better see what he wants." He patted her arm. "Don't worry."

He headed for the consulting-room, and paused before opening the door. Turning, he saw Norma watching him, a frown on her normally smooth brow. Beau knew there were several issues that could be the reason for the visit, and he took a moment to mentally prepare himself for a verbal altercation.

Opening the door, he saw Raymond Simmons behind the desk, several files in front of him. He looked up as Beau entered, and slowly put down the file he had been reading.

"Good morning, Raymond," said Beau brightly, as his heart thumped erratically.

Raymond removed his spectacles and placed them on the desk, before looking up at Beau.

"Good morning," he said brusquely. "Sit down, Beau. I need to speak to you." Beau sat obediently, and placed his briefcase on the desk. "We seem to be in disagreement over a number of things, and I'd like to clear them up." Beau waited, sensing what was coming. "I had a couple of issues yesterday; one with Mrs. Leonard and one with Mr. Reynolds."

"Ah!"

"Can you explain to me why you provided Mrs. Leonard with a tin of baby formula?"

"It was simple really. The child needs sustenance, and her mother is unable to provide it for her."

Raymond scowled. "And are you going to do that for every mother who comes in here?"

"Raymond, that child was heading for certain death. I couldn't have that on my conscience, knowing that I could have helped her." Beau paused. "Mrs. Leonard came to see you yesterday?"

"Yes, she did."

"And the child?"

"She had the child with her."

"Is she responding to the formula?"

Raymond coughed. "It appears that she is."

"That's marvellous! So what is the problem? The fact that I provided the formula?"

Raymond shuffled the files in front of him, before looking across at Beau. "The problem is that Mrs. Leonard will tell other mothers, and they will expect the same treatment. We're not a benevolent society."

Beau bit back the initial retort that rose to his lips. Instead he took a deep breath.

"Well, maybe we should be encouraging them to seek advice from the Infant Welfare Nurses. After all, isn't that what they have been set up to do?"

"The mothers are reluctant to do so."

"Then we need to find a way to educate them, particularly the young ones like Mrs. Leonard."

Raymond sat back in the chair, his hands folded under his chin. "How do you propose we do that? You are forgetting, Beau, that new mothers make up only a small percentage of our patients. We have more pressing issues to deal with, like the influenza, for instance."

"There is no issue more pressing than a child's life." Beau's head was spinning as an idea occurred to him. "Leave it with me, Raymond. I have an idea that could work."

Raymond's thick eyebrows rose. "Very well," he said cautiously. "Now there's the matter of Mr. Reynolds. He came in here yesterday saying that you insisted he have his ankle dressed every day. That's asking the impossible of these men."

"Does he want to lose his leg? I saw a lot of similar injuries during the war, Raymond, and believe me, without constant treatment, they all finished up with amputation."

"He doesn't want to lose his job." Raymond drummed his fingers on the desk. "It's a no-win situation, isn't it?" He looked across at Beau, his brow furrowed.

"Indeed it is. He stands to lose both." Beau leaned forward. "We are duty-bound to take care of the leg." He shrugged as he sat back. "I'm afraid we are powerless to do anything about his job."

"He's terrified of losing his leg, or even part of his leg." Raymond looked up at the clock. "We'll attend to the dressing as long as Mr. Reynolds keeps coming through that door, but if he decides not to come, then I'm not going to press him further." Raymond stood up, pushing back the chair. "Other than that, I think everything else is in order."

"There is another patient that I'd like to discuss with you."

"Oh? And who is that?"

"Margaret Stanley."

"Ah! I see her blood test results are back. She saw you yesterday?"

"Yes." Beau stopped. "She wants no medical intervention."

Raymond took a deep breath. "That's her choice, of course. Does Jess know?"

"I've said nothing, although she does fear the worst after talking to Margaret recently."

"Keep it that way. Margaret will tell them in her own time." Raymond smiled tightly. "In the meantime, it's nearly ten o'clock, and your patients will be arriving on the doorstep. Keep me informed, Beau, if hard decisions need to be made." He moved to the door. "I'll be at the Benevolent Asylum if you need me. We have sixteen influenza patients settled there, which has eased the hospital situation greatly."

"There is one more thing, Raymond."

"And what is that?"

"The Miners. Surely we can do more for them."

Raymond stood for a moment, his hand on the door handle. "You can't change the world in a day, Beau, no matter how hard you try." His eyes bored into Beau's. "We'll discuss them another time." He opened the door. "You have patients waiting."

With that he swung the door shut behind him.

Beau heaved a sigh of relief. That could have been a lot worse. He walked around the desk, pushed in the chair, and sat heavily. It was time to start his day.

Margaret Breaks The News to Charles

Margaret was seated on the front verandah, a crocheted rug around her knees. Closing her eyes, she lifted her face towards the wintry sunlight that filtered through the cream-painted iron lacework and created patterns on the wall behind her. Weariness was beginning to overtake her, but she felt at peace with the silence that surrounded her. The garden was dormant, but it wouldn't be long before the spring buds started to appear. She heard the warble of a magpie close by, and opening her eyes she saw one sitting on the verandah railing, its head cocked to one side and its beady eyes watching her. Margaret smiled.

"You've come for some food, have you?" she said softly, and the magpie ruffled its feathers.

The screen door opened beside her, and Charles appeared, his spectacles pushed to the top of his head, and the daily newspaper in his hand.

"So this is where you are?"

The magpie immediately flew off, landing some distance away on the front lawn.

"Yes." Margaret patted the seat alongside her. "Come and join me, Charles."

He frowned, but sat nevertheless. "The fire's going in the lounge. You don't have to sit out here in the cold, you know!"

"I'm not cold." Margaret turned to look at him. "Charles, there's something I need to tell you, but before I do, I want you to tell me what's going on with your workers."

"It's nothing for you to concern yourself about, Margaret. I've told you that before."

"Whether it is or not, Charles, I want to know." Margaret laid a hand on his arm.

Charles made a grunting noise, and shifted uneasily on the seat. "It's all under control, Margaret, so there's no need to go into details."

"Charles?" Margaret's brown eyes were suddenly keen as they bore into him.

He sighed. "Very well. If you must know, I had to sack my overseer."

"Harold Mayberry? Why? What did he do?"

"He was stirring up the young apprentices to go out on strike."

"So he's a Union Member?"

Charles raised his eyebrows. "Yes he is, and what's more, he was using bully-boy tactics to get the young ones to lay down their tools and demand higher wages."

"So what did you do?"

"I told him that there are plenty of men out there, looking for work, and if he wasn't happy, then he had better find a job elsewhere, or words to that effect."

"So he's gone?"

"I heard on the grapevine that he's got work with Abe Taylor & Son." Charles chuckled. "He won't want to fall out with Abe. He's a harder taskmaster than I am."

"And have you given your workers a pay rise?"

"A pay rise? Margaret, I pay them a fair wage." Charles snorted loudly. "Anyway, now that you have wheedled that out of me, what is it you want to tell me?"

"I did not wheedle!" Margaret smiled softly, and took his hand in hers. "I have had tests, Charles."

"Tests? What kind of tests?"

"Blood tests." Margaret looked into his eyes. "I have a chronic blood disorder, for which there is no cure."

Charles stared at her for a long moment. "What are you saying, Margaret?"

"I'm sick, Charles, and I won't get better."

"Have you spoken to Beau about this? Is there something he can do?"

"Yes, I have spoken to Beau, and he said that this is something the doctors know very little about, and although there are things he can do to help me, there is no cure."

Charles squeezed her hand tightly. "Maybe they got it wrong," he said hoarsely, and Margaret noticed tears in his eyes. "Maybe you should ask for the tests to be done again?"

"Margaret shook her head. "They didn't get it wrong, Charles."

"Are you sure?"

Margaret lifted her free hand, and stroked his cheek. "We've had thirty-six good years together, Charles, and we'll see out what time I have left." Her own vision was blurred. "Besides, I could still outlive you, if you don't behave yourself." She laughed shakily.

"Does Jess know?"

"Jess suspects."

Charles shook his head sadly. "I had no idea, Margaret. I've been so wrapped up in my own problems, that I haven't noticed anything else. I'm sorry, my dear."

They sat in silence for a few minutes, while the magpie warbled cheerily on the grass below them.

"Come on," said Charles finally. "Let's go in. You must be getting cold now."

As they stood, Charles wrapped his arms around Margaret, burying his head against her shoulder.

"You've shocked me, Margaret," she heard him murmur. "I need time to let this sink in." His body shook as he held her. "I don't know what I'll do without you."

Margaret smoothed his hair. "Don't think about it yet. Come inside, and we'll have a cup of tea."

Part Two

A Time To Find and a Time To Lose

Matthew and Celia

Celia shivered as she pulled her coat around her shoulders. She was seated on a wicker chair on the wide balcony that overlooked a heavily wooded valley. Gums rose from the valley floor, to a height where she could see the top branches, and moisture dripped from the sodden leaves to the floor close to where she sat. The air was crisp and sweet, and the sound of currawongs filled the silent spaces.

Celia turned to look at Matthew as he lay on a narrow cot at her side. His features were pale and gaunt, and he was breathing with the aid of an oxygen mask. Speaking was difficult, so for most of the time he remained silent. Celia sighed and stood up. Walking across to the balcony railing, she let her eyes skim across the wet landscape to the road that led away from Willowbank Sanatorium, and on through the mountains to Sydney.

Slipping her hands into the pockets of her heavy black coat, her fingers encountered the letter from Beau, written to Matthew, and which she had read to him as he lay passively beside her. She pulled it out now, and unfolded it. It had been two weeks since Beau had moved to Victoria, and she had to admit that she missed him, and wished that he were here to help her through the lonely vigils with Matthew. Leaning on the balcony, she read Beau's words again:

> *Dear Matthew,*
> *You are in my thoughts constantly, and I feel a certain amount of guilt at the way things unfolded in Sydney. I was between the devil and the deep blue sea, so to speak.*
> *Your condition was out of my hands, and with Jess being so desperately ill at the same time, I had to be with her. I know you will understand, and when I can see my way clear, I will come and visit you up there in the mountains.*
> *I have a position here in Bendigo, as a General Practitioner, and as the hospital is opening up special wards for influenza sufferers, I will assist there, too.*
> *I miss the hustle and bustle of the city, but I am enjoying a freedom*

that I haven't had for a long time. Jess is my rock, and I love her completely. I look forward to the day when you can meet her, Matthew. I know you two will get along.

Please ask Celia to write and let us know how things are progressing. We are anxious to know.

Your lifelong friend

Beau

Celia folded the page, and slipped it back into her pocket. Matthew had not registered any emotion when she had read it to him, except that she had seen a tear slip silently down his cheek. She turned to look at him now, and the fear that she had felt over the past two weeks, suddenly overwhelmed her. That such a strong man could be reduced to a shadow in such a short time challenged her reasoning. Matthew was the last person to succumb to weakness, and yet here he was, completely reliant on those around him. He stared at her now, above the contraption that covered the lower part of his face. His eyes were bleak, and Celia blinked back the tears that threatened. She walked across the balcony and sat beside him, taking his hand in hers.

"I must write to Beau, Matthew," she whispered. "Do you recall me reading the letter from him?"

Matthew's head nodded slightly, and one hand fumbled with the oxygen mask, as he tried to remove it. Celia took the mask and laid it on the cot beside him.

"He's gone?" he gasped.

"Yes. He's now in Bendigo with Jess, and apparently has work with the hospital there."

Matthew nodded. "I hope… he's happy."

"It sounds as though he is." Celia shivered. "Matthew, it's very cold out here. I'm going to call an orderly to take you back to your room. Fresh air is beneficial, I know, but I think you've had enough for one morning. I know I have." She patted his hand. "Besides, I'm getting hungry. It must be lunchtime."

Celia opened the glass door that led into the building. She walked quickly, her footsteps echoing in the empty corridor. At the entrance to Matthew's room, she stopped, and looked inside. The bed had been made and the floors disinfected, but nobody was there. Celia continued along the corridor, until she heard the sound of someone whistling. She followed the sound, and in one of the rooms she saw an orderly, dressed in white from head to toe, a bucket and mop in his hands.

"Excuse me," said Celia loudly. The man turned. "Doctor Morley needs to come in from the balcony. Could you assist, please?"

"Certainly, ma'am." His reply was muffled behind a white surgical mask. "I'll get a wheelchair, and I'll be there shortly." He placed the bucket and mop against a wall.

"Thank-you." Celia turned back towards the balcony.

As she walked along the corridor, she heard a familiar voice filtering up from the floor below. She stopped. It was her father. Stifling a sob, she hurried towards the stairwell, and headed down the stairs. She hadn't seen Clarence in over two weeks, and she needed his brusque reassurance.

At the foot of the stairs she spied him heading towards her, so she ran the last few steps, and fell into his large embrace.

"Whoa! Steady on!" Clarence patted her shoulders as she clung to him.

"Oh, daddy!" Celia stammered. "It's so good to see you."

"Well, I must say that this is a pleasant surprise." Clarence laughed. "You're not always this pleased to see me."

Celia finally pulled away, and wiping at her eyes, looked up at her father. He was still the dominating figure that he had always been, and his piercing gaze still struck a certain amount of awe, but at that moment, he suddenly became the one sure anchor that would hold her fast in the turbulence she was enduring. She groped in her pocket for a handkerchief, found one, and blew her streaming nose. It was only then that she noticed that her father was not alone. A dark-haired young woman stood beside him, quietly watching the reunion between father and daughter. Celia had seen her before somewhere.

Blinking rapidly, she turned enquiring eyes back to her father. Clarence smiled down at the young woman beside him, and placed an arm across her shoulders.

"Celia, I'd like you to meet Angela Rickard, who kindly consented to accompanying me here today. It's a long drive on one's own."

Celia shook her head, and the security bubble that she had experienced only moments ago, suddenly crumbled into a thousand pieces.

"We've met before," she said stiffly.

"Yes," said Angela, smiling. "Doctor DuBois brought you to my patisserie some time ago."

"That's right." The memory of French pastries and Beau's news that he was going to marry Jess came flooding back. Celia stared up at her father. "How do you know each other?"

Clarence's face suddenly suffused with colour. "We met at Beau and Jess's wedding."

"I see." Celia's tone was cool.

"I think your father was struck by my cooking." Angela laughed self-consciously.

Clarence, perturbed by the friction that was evident between his daughter and his companion, took each by the arm, and steered them towards the stairs.

"Come!" he said. "Let's go and see Matthew. I want to see how he's faring."

They walked up the wide stairway, three abreast, their footsteps in sharp unison. When they reached the top, they saw Matthew being wheeled along the corridor towards them. Celia broke free of her father's restraining hand, and hurried towards the approaching wheelchair.

"Matthew!" Her voice was high-pitched. "Daddy's come to see us! Isn't that wonderful?"

Matthew opened his eyes and stared at Celia for a moment, before registering what she had said.

He nodded his head, and the ghost of a smile reached his eyes.

Clarence released Angela's arm, and moved forward to shake Matthew's hand. His throat was tight as he looked at the shadow of a man who lay in the wheelchair, his face partly covered by an oxygen mask, and the cylinder wedged between his feet.

"Matthew, my boy," he muttered hoarsely. "How are you?" Clarence already knew the answer.

Matthew shrugged, and pulled off the mask. "I've been...better," he murmured.

Celia turned to the orderly who was waiting patiently to take Matthew to his room, and gave him the signal to move. As Clarence took Angela's arm and made ready to follow the wheelchair, Celia held up her hands.

"We'll wait here, daddy, until Matthew's been put to bed. Then I'll go and order us some lunch."

"There's no need to do that," said Angela quickly, looking up at Clarence from beneath her broad-brimmed straw hat. "I have a hamper of food in the car."

"I'll get it." Clarence started to move away, but Angela placed a restraining hand on his arm.

"No," she said firmly. "You stay here with Celia, and I'll get it."

"Are you sure?" Clarence looked from Angela to Celia.

"Certainly!" Angela didn't wait for a reply, but turned and headed for the stairs.

Clarence and Celia stood silently, listening as her footsteps echoed around the corridor. When all was silent, Celia rounded on her father.

"What are you thinking, daddy?" Her eyes blazed.

"I don't know what you mean, Celia." Clarence tried to remain calm.

"Yes, you do! Angela is half your age, and anyway, what about mother? She does exist, you know, or have you forgotten?"

"No, I haven't forgotten, Celia." His voice quivered. "Angela is a very good friend, and I don't want you saying anything that will upset her."

Celia stared at her father for a moment, and then bowed her head. "I thought I had you to myself, daddy," she whispered miserably. "You don't know what it's like sitting here every day with Matthew, who rarely talks. It's soul-destroying." She hiccoughed loudly.

"I know only too well, Celia." Clarence patted her shoulder. "I sit for hours with your mother, and when I leave, she doesn't even know that I've been. So, yes, I know how soul-destroying it can be." Celia moved into his arms, and he held her tight, while she sobbed against his tweed jacket.

They moved apart as they heard footsteps on the stairs, and Celia wiped hurriedly at her tear-streaked face. Angela appeared, this time without her hat and with a large wicker basket in her hands. Clarence stepped forward and relieved her of the basket.

"What have you got in here, Angela?" he chided. "A dead body?"

She laughed as she ran her fingers through her dark hair. "Ah! You'll have to wait and see."

Her eyes had already taken in the tear-stained appearance of Celia, and she guessed as to the reason. It didn't come as a surprise that Celia resented her presence, but Clarence had insisted that she accompany him, and a day trip out of the city was too tempting to pass up.

The orderly appeared at Matthew's doorway, breaking the awkward silence that had grown between the three in the corridor.

"Doctor Morley's ready," he said. "You can come in now."

Celia was the first to move, pushing her way past the orderly, as he manoeuvred the cumbersome wheelchair into the corridor. Clarence ushered Angela ahead of him, and smiled graciously at the young orderly.

"Thank-you," he murmured, and received a nod in response.

Celia was stripping off her coat as Clarence and Angela entered the room, and the space suddenly seemed diminished as they looked around for somewhere to sit. There was one straight-backed chair beside the bed.

"I'll go and find some chairs," said Clarence as he put the picnic basket on the floor.

When he had gone, Celia looked across the bed at Angela, and then down on Matthew's pale countenance. She took his hand as she spoke.

"Matthew, this is Angela, a friend of Beau's, and…an acquaintance of daddy's."

Matthew turned his head slightly to look at Angela.

"The lady…with the…cake shop." He lifted the mask from his face. "I've heard… about you."

Angela smiled. "I know all about you, too, Doctor Morley."

Matthew managed a faint smile. "Not all…I hope."

"Maybe enough for me to say I'm pleased to meet you."

Clarence appeared in the doorway, a straight-backed chair in his hands. "I've taken a couple from the visitors' room downstairs." He placed the chair near Angela. "I'll fetch the other one," he whispered conspiratorially, and with that he disappeared.

Angela removed her camel-coloured coat and scarf, and pulling the picnic hamper towards her, sat beside the bed. Celia sat opposite, and silently studied the well-proportioned young woman with the merry dark eyes and clear skin. Angela looked up and caught Celia's eyes on her. She smiled.

"I have some custard tarts here that I thought Doctor Morley might like," she said brightly. "I know Jess enjoyed the custard when she was so ill." She felt a hand touch her arm.

"Call me…Matthew."

"Very well, Matthew it is."

"Matthew needs to have some beef broth before he attempts custard," said Celia tightly. She looked at her watch. "It should be arriving shortly."

Clarence arrived back with the chair, at the same time as a young nurse bustled in with a tray.

"Lunchtime, Doctor Morley!" she breezed, placing the tray on a table beside Celia. "Can I leave you in charge, Mrs. Morley?"

"Naturally!" snapped Celia

The young nurse smiled at the two visitors, and hurried from the room.

"Well!" boomed Clarence into the uncomfortable silence, "I'm hungry, so let's eat, shall we?"

*

When the much-depleted picnic basket had been packed away, Celia stood up. "If you don't mind, I'm going outside for a cigarette," she declared, slipping her arms into her coat.

When she had gone, the three left in the room, looked at one another. Matthew focused his gaze on Angela.

"I wish…I could send her… home with you," he gasped, "but I know… she wouldn't…go."

Angela touched his hand as it lay on the sheet. "No, she wouldn't, Matthew."

An awkward silence filled the room, broken only by the scratchy ticking of a clock on the wall above Matthew's bed. Clarence stood, and walked across to the large bay window that looked out on the dewy landscape. He stretched his large frame.

"It is quite a beautiful place, isn't it?" The remark was directed at Angela.

"Yes, it is." She rose and went to stand beside him. "It's almost as though the building has risen out from the top of the trees, and is hovering in the air."

Clarence raised his thick eyebrows as he looked down on her. "That's very poetic, Angela," he said. "But you're right. It does give that impression, doesn't it?"

"Why is it called Willowbank? I didn't see any willows."

"I don't know." He shrugged. "Maybe there were willows here at one stage."

"Hm, possibly. Anyway, it's so nice to get away from the noise and bustle of the city. Thank-you, Clarence, in case I forget to say it later."

"I've enjoyed your company, Angela. Thank-you for saying 'yes'."

They smiled at each other just as Celia returned, and a bubble of anger caught in her chest.

"What have I missed?" she said stingingly, as she flung her coat across the back of her chair.

"Nothing, my dear," said Clarence soothingly. "We were just admiring the view."

"I can see that!"

Celia rolled her eyes as she sat beside the bed. Matthew had his eyes closed, but he must have sensed the tension, because he lifted his mask and turned towards Celia.

"Please, Celia…" He coughed. "Your father…didn't come all this way… to be barked at."

Celia expelled a quick breath. "Is that what you think I'm doing, Matthew?"

"I know…you are."

"Very well, I'll keep silent." Celia folded her arms and stared out through the window.

Angela returned to her seat, and reaching into the pocket of her coat, pulled out an envelope.

"I had a letter from Jess, yesterday," she said, as she looked in Celia's direction.

"Matthew had one from Beau," said Celia without turning her head. "What did Jess have to say?" She still faced the window.

Angela looked up at Clarence before speaking. "They want me to see if I can trace Beau's sister."

Celia spun around. "What sister?" She turned startled eyes on Matthew. "I didn't know he had a sister. Matthew, did you know?"

Matthew's head nodded briefly. "There was mention… a long time ago."

Celia looked across at Angela. "This is all news to me. You'd better tell me what Jess had to say."

"Better still," said Angela, passing the envelope across the bed, "read it for yourself."

Celia leaned forward on her chair, and grasped the letter, opening it with nimble fingers. There was silence as her eyes skimmed the lines on the single sheet of paper. When she had finished, she looked across the bed at Angela and then up at her father, who was standing behind her.

"My God! What a revelation! Did you know about this, daddy?"

Clarence cleared his throat. "Not until today. Angela read it to me on the way here this morning."

Celia sat back, exhaling loudly. "You've never thought to mention it, Matthew?"

"Not my business." Matthew was beginning to tire, and he reached for the oxygen.

"So how do you propose to go about finding someone who's been out of the equation for over thirty years?" Celia's black eyes bore into Angela.

She shrugged. "I'll have to start with the Convents, and the Sisters of Mercy. There must be records kept of the girls who finished up in such places."

"I have agreed to help where I can," cut in Clarence, "even if it's only to drive Angela around to the various Convents." Celia opened her mouth to retort, but Clarence went on. "This is something I want to do, Celia, so there's no point in objecting."

Celia closed her mouth.

Matthew began to cough, and at that moment, a nurse bustled into the room, with a rustle of starched uniform. She surveyed the group over the rims of her spectacles.

"I will have to ask you all to adjourn to the visitors' lounge downstairs," she said crisply. "Doctor Morley needs attending to, and then he must rest."

Celia stood, and gathered her coat from the back of her chair. Angela did the same, before picking up the empty picnic basket. Clarence lifted the two borrowed chairs, and looked apologetically at the nurse.

"I'll return these to the visitors' lounge."

"Indeed you will!" she retorted sharply.

Quietly the three left the room, as the nurse removed Matthew's oxygen mask, and slid a thermometer into his mouth.

"Time to check your temperature, Doctor Morley," they heard her say, as they stepped into the empty corridor.

Celia reached for her packet of cigarettes. "I'll be down in a few moments," she said quickly, as she headed for the balcony. Clarence watched her retreating figure, and sighed heavily.

Jess and Louise

Jess stared at Beau incredulously. She was standing by the sink, and Beau was sitting at the kitchen table, a cup of tea in his hands.

"Have you been reading my mind, Beau?"

"Why? Have you been thinking the same thing?"

"Yes. In fact I thought I'd go and see Louise this afternoon, (while you're here to look after the children), show her how to make scones, and bring up the subject of new mothers and how the Red Cross can help them. It's a project that could be very beneficial to those young women who find that raising a child is extremely difficult without assistance."

"My thoughts exactly." He looked across at Jess, and a frown etched his brow. "What do you mean by 'while you're here to look after the children?'"

"Exactly what I said." Jess placed her hands on her hips, and gave him her sweetest smile.

Beau shook his head. "And what if I say 'no'?"

"But you're not going to, are you?" Jess moved swiftly around the table until she was behind him, and slid her arms around his neck. "Are you?" She kissed his ear.

Beau sighed with resignation. "Probably not, seeing as you asked so nicely."

"Thank-you, my dearest." Jess looked past Beau to where rain was beating a tattoo against the windowpane. "Although, we could be in for a wet afternoon."

"That means board games or jigsaw puzzles." Beau drained his teacup. "Edward won't be happy. I think he was planning on going rabbiting."

"Well he can't, even if it does stop raining." Jess straightened up. "That boy has to learn that the world does not revolve around him and what he wants to do. Besides, I still have two rabbits in the ice chest."

"Jess?"

"Hm?"

"I noticed a bicycle in the shed."

"That was Jack's bicycle." Jess stared off into the distance. "It hasn't been used for a long time."

Beau took her hand and squeezed it gently. "Do you mind if I have a look at it, and see what needs doing to make it rideable?"

"No, I don't mind." Jess smiled briefly.

"I could ride it to work."

"Yes." Jess shook away the thoughts of Jack arriving at her lodgings on his bicycle, and the bumpy rides she had, seated on the bar in front of him. "Yes, that sounds like a wonderful idea." She cleared her throat to remove the lump that had lodged there.

Beau noticed the mood change, and pulled her towards him. "Did it bring back memories?"

"Yes." Jess took a deep breath.

"If you don't want me to…"

Jess brushed a hand through his hair. "No, it's not that. You repair it, by all means, and maybe the boys can help you." She smiled down at him. "That could be a rainy day project."

"If you're sure?"

"Yes, I'm sure. It would be good to see it used again." She paused. "So that only leaves Grace."

"Grace?" Beau was puzzled. "You've lost me, Jess."

"For you to look after."

"Oh! This afternoon?"

"Yes. I could drop her off at Margaret's, but I don't want to worry her at present."

"No, of course not." Beau bit his lip. "Grace will be alright here."

Jess leaned forward and slipped her arms around his neck. "Thank-you, my darling."

"Don't make a habit of it," he whispered against her cheek.

*

The rain had eased by the time Jess stood on the front verandah of the Simmons' red brick terrace house. She pressed the shiny brass doorbell. As she waited, Jess glanced around at her surroundings. Shrubs along the edge of the verandah were neatly trimmed, the lawn edges were straight and roses lining both sides of the path had been recently pruned. The timber verandah had been freshly lacquered, and the iron lacework gleamed with new paint. Jess also noticed a ladder leaning against the wall, and she smiled as she envisaged Doctor Simmons climbing the rungs with a paintbrush in one hand.

She shook away the image as the front door opened and Louise appeared, clad in a multi-coloured silk dressing gown, and holding a wine glass in one hand. Her blonde hair hung loose, and her face was devoid of make-up. She stared at Jess for a long moment, before realising who was standing on the verandah.

"Jess! What are you doing here?"

"I've come to see you, Louise. There's something I'd like to discuss with you."

"Oh?"

"Is… your husband at home?" Jess was beginning to feel a little uncertain.

Louise shook her head. "No. Saturday is his golf day."

"In this weather?" Jess laughed.

Louise shrugged. "Golfers don't care about the weather." She opened the screen door. "Come in. I'm afraid you have caught me resting." She sighed. "It's what I do best."

"Well," said Jess, as she stepped into the hallway. "I might be about to change all that."

"What do you mean?"

"I have a suggested project for our Red Cross group."

Louise ushered Jess into the front lounge room, and walked unsteadily across to a large sideboard, where she placed her glass, before turning to Jess.

"Please sit by the fire, Jess." She indicated one of the plush red velvet armchairs placed at either side of the large open fireplace, where a substantial fire blazed. "Tell me more."

There was interest now in Louise's blue eyes, as both women sat facing each other. Jess turned her gaze to the fire before launching into the speech she had mentally prepared.

"Beau is concerned about the new mothers who are reluctant to visit with the Infant Welfare Nurses. I can see a role for us here." She turned to look at Louise. "We can act as a sort of go-between, and steer the mothers in the right direction."

"How would we do that?"

"By visiting them in their homes, and being a shoulder for them to lean on, I suppose."

Louise was frowning. "Why are you so concerned about them, Jess?"

"Babies are dying unnecessarily, Louise, because mothers are afraid to ask for help."

Louise sighed heavily. "Unfortunately I know nothing about children."

Jess leaned forward. "Maybe not, Louise, but you would know when walking into a home, whether the mother is coping or not."

"Possibly." Louise frowned. "Mothers may not take too kindly to extra interference from women they don't know."

Jess sat back. "When I had my children, I was just as ignorant about what was expected of me, but I was fortunate. I had Margaret to advise me, and my babies thrived. A lot of women are not so fortunate."

"No. Well, we can certainly discuss it at our next meeting." Louise looked down at her hands, clasped in her lap. "I must apologise to the meeting for my non-attendance last week." Her eyes sought Jess's. "I suppose Beau told you what happened?"

"Yes, he did, but don't worry about it, Louise. We all suffer memory loss from time to time."

"Mine wasn't just memory loss. I behaved very badly." A heavy silence followed this last statement, before Louise took a deep breath. "Jess, how would you like to chair our Red Cross meetings? Elections are coming up shortly."

"Me? Oh, no! I couldn't possibly do that."

"Of course you could. You would be marvellous!"

"No." Jess shrank back in the armchair.

"That way, you could certainly get your project off the ground." Louise was studying her intently. "Think about it, Jess."

"I'll think about it, but I won't promise anything."

"Discuss it with that charming husband of yours. I'm sure he would be in favour of it."

Jess felt her cheeks flushing under Louise's intense scrutiny. She needed to change the subject.

"The other thing I came around here to do, is to show you how I make my scones."

Louise sat back and laughed. "My husband put you up to that one, didn't he?"

"Not exactly."

"Of course he did!" Louise snorted. "Alright! I'll get dressed, and you can show me how you make your beautiful scones." She stood, a little unsteadily. "Maybe I can prove to Raymond that I'm not as useless as he thinks I am."

*

Jess's steps were light as she headed home some time later. Having caught Louise off-guard, she now had a different perception of her. The woman was lonely. All she needed was the company of another woman to bring out her true character. Together they had laughed over the scone making, and had enjoyed eating some of the spoils, as they downed cups of tea. Louise had been careful to keep aside the better-looking scones for Raymond, and had spontaneously hugged Jess as she prepared to leave.

"I've really enjoyed today, Jess," she had said. "Thank-you, and please come again."

Jess was still smiling as she rounded the corner into Oleander Street, and was not prepared for what greeted her there. The sound of laughter made her look up quickly, and her feet stopped as she saw a bicycle heading along the roadway towards her. Beau was riding it, and in front of him sat Grace, squealing with delight as her hands held fast to the handlebars. Ben and Edward ran alongside, and all were laughing. Jess stared at the foursome, her mouth open.

"Ma! Look at me!" Grace had spotted her mother.

Jess took a gasp of air, as the sight of her daughter kindled a rush of emotion. She was rooted to the spot as they all stopped in front of her. Beau lifted Grace from the bicycle, and she slid to the ground at Jess's feet.

"Did you see me, ma?" she squealed, as she jumped up and down. "I was riding the bicycle!"

"Yes!" gasped Jess. "I saw you." She looked up at Beau, who was grinning widely.

"We've all had a turn!" shouted Edward. "It was fun, ma!"

"It's in pretty good nick, Jess," said Beau, referring to the bicycle. "It just needed a bit of grease here and there, and some adjustment to the chain. The seat is a bit worn, but as you can see, it's quite rideable."

"I'm so glad!" Jess joined in the laughter as she quelled the memories of Jack and his bicycle.

"It's my turn next!" Ben was clutching at Beau's sleeve.

"Yes, alright Ben, but let me talk to your mother first." Beau turned the bicycle around, and Jess fell into step with him as they all headed back along the street.

"You've obviously had a very successful afternoon." Jess slipped her arm through Beau's. "I might have to leave you all to your own devices more often." She grinned at his mock scowl.

"Will you indeed?"

"Yes."

"And how was your afternoon with the glamorous Mrs. Simmons?"

"She was not so glamorous, and we had a lovely afternoon. Needless to say, Raymond was not there. He was out playing golf." Jess wafted a hand in the air.

"How were the scones?"

"Oh, the scones were a great success."

"And the discussion?"

"It will go to the next meeting." Jess paused briefly. "Louise wants me to consider the position of Chairwoman at the next election."

Beau stopped walking, bringing them all to a halt. "And you told her that you would love to?"

"I told her I'd think about it."

"Jess! Come on! You'd be very good at the job."

"You'd have to look after the children more often."

Beau grinned. "I didn't think of that! No, seriously, Jess, you need to consider it."

"Maybe I will."

"Good! Now, who said you can't change the world in a day?"

"I don't know. Who did?"

Beau leaned in to kiss her cheek. "It doesn't matter, because we know it can be done. Anything is possible."

Margaret Breaks The News to the Family

The following afternoon, Jess was seated on the front verandah, a shawl wrapped around her, watching Beau giving the boys bicycle riding lessons on the road outside their gate. Edward was mastering the art at a faster rate than Ben, and Jess had to smile as she watched him pushing Beau's hands from the back of the seat.

"I can do it!" he yelled, and the bicycle wobbled forward for several yards as Beau ran beside it.

The inevitable happened, of course, and Edward toppled to the ground before Beau could stop the fall. Jess sprang to her feet, and hurried down the steps to the gate. Edward was bellowing like a wounded bull as Beau lifted the bicycle from on top of him.

"Edward!" she cried. "Are you hurt?"

Beau was kneeling beside him. "Just a few grazes, Jess. This is what happens when you learn to ride a bicycle. Edward?"

"What," sobbed Edward, as he studied the blood on his bare knee.

"The best thing to do when you fall off is to get up and get right back on again. Do you think you can do that?"

Edward nodded slowly. "I think so."

As Beau helped him to his feet, Jess bit on her lip. She wanted to intervene, but Beau's glance in her direction told her that he was in control, so she stepped back, wrapping her shawl around her.

"Right, Edward! On you get! This time I'll hold the seat, and I'll be the one who says when you are ready to go solo. Understood?"

"Yes, Beau."

"Good." Beau saw Jess frowning, and smiled reassuringly. "Don't worry, Jess."

She walked back to the footpath, upset that Beau had left her out of the situation, but in her heart she knew that he was right. He was in charge, whether she liked it or not, and to question his authority would only confuse Edward. Beau was going to continue where Charles had left off, in toughening her boys for the real world that was out there, and which they would both have to face.

Jess climbed the steps to the verandah, and leaned on the rail. Edward was now riding fairly confidently, as Beau ran alongside, holding the seat. As they passed her, she heard Beau call out,

"Your turn next, Jess!"

She shook her head. "I don't think so, Beau."

"It's fun ma!" Edward had obviously forgotten his fall already.

"I don't think I'll have any more turns today, ma." Jess turned to see Ben standing beside her.

"Don't you, Ben? Why not?"

"I don't want to fall off."

"You heard what Beau said, Ben. It's part of learning how to ride." Jess placed an arm about his shoulders. "Can I tell you something Ben?" He nodded. "Your father and I used to ride that bicycle. I would sit on the front, and we would ride for miles. I remember we both fell off once, when we hit a pothole in the road. That was the only time. We both lay on the road, covered in mud, and laughing at how ridiculous we looked."

"Did you get hurt?"

"No, Ben, only our dignity." Jess gave him a gentle squeeze. "Oh, look Ben! I see grandma and granddad heading this way. Let's go and meet them, shall we?"

Together they stepped on to the footpath, and headed towards Margaret and Charles, who had stopped to watch Edward riding the bicycle. Margaret had her hands pressed to her mouth, but Charles was clapping his hands enthusiastically.

"Well done, Edward!" he shouted, as the bicycle wobbled to a halt in front of them.

"I fell off, granddad, and Beau made me get back on again."

"Very good, Edward." Charles grabbed his arm as he clambered from the bicycle.

Jess and Ben reached the scene, as Edward was showing off his grazed knee to his grandfather.

"Is that Jack's bicycle?" Margaret was eyeing it closely.

"Yes, it is," said Jess as she gave Margaret a hug. "Do you remember the day when we both fell off it, and had to walk home, covered in mud, and Jack carrying the bicycle?"

Margaret laughed. "I do remember that, Jess, and I remember telling you how foolish you were to be riding it in the first place."

"Yes, you did." Jess shot a covert look at Beau, who was staring at her, his eyebrows raised. She blushed. "Come on, I think it's time we all went inside. It's getting very chilly out here."

They all headed for the house, and as Beau lifted the bicycle up the step to the front yard, he turned to Jess.

"So you have ridden it?" he whispered.

"Many times, much to Margaret's horror."

"You surprise me, Jess. I was only joking when I said 'your turn'."

"You forget that I was raised on a farm, Beau. I did a lot of things when I was younger; things that would not be classed as ladylike."

"Such as?"

Jess was spared from answering, as Charles' voice boomed from the verandah.

"We'll head for the lounge, Jess. Margaret and I have something to tell you."

Jess looked quickly at Beau, and then up at Charles. "We'll be there in a minute." She looked back at Beau, her eyes wide. "What are they going to tell us, Beau?"

He caught her look of fear, and had it not been for the bicycle between them, he would have drawn her into his arms, because the moment he had feared had arrived.

"I don't know, Jess. Let's wait and see."

She gulped. "I'd better send the children off to their rooms. If the news is bad, I don't want them hearing it just yet."

"I'll put the bicycle in the shed, and I'll be with you shortly."

Jess hurried up the steps to the verandah, and into the house. Margaret was seated on the couch in front of the fire, and Grace, who had appeared from her room, was sitting close beside her. Charles stood with his back to the fire, his arms folded across his ample chest.

Jess beckoned to the boys, who were about to sit on the couch.

"Children," she said as calmly as she could, "I want you to go to your rooms for a short while."

"Why can't we stay here?" Edward asked petulantly.

"Because Beau and I want to talk to grandma and granddad alone. Now go, please?"

Beau entered the room, as three dejected children filed out into the passage.

"It's not fair!" he heard Edward grumble, as Ben tried to pacify Grace, who had burst into tears.

When they had gone, Beau shut the door and walked across the room to stand beside Charles. Jess seated herself beside Margaret, and looked up at Charles.

"What is it you want to tell us, Charles?" Her voice had a slight quiver.

"Margaret has been diagnosed with blood cancer."

The seconds ticked by, as the news penetrated Jess's brain. She reached for Margaret's hand, and held it tightly, but her eyes were still on Charles.

"What is going to be done about it?"

"Nothing." It was Margaret who spoke, and Jess turned to look at her.

"Nothing?" she whispered. "Margaret, there must be something that can be done, surely." She shifted her gaze to Beau. "There must be something."

He shook his head. "There's not a lot we can do, Jess. We don't know enough about it."

"I don't want any interference, Jess," said Margaret slowly. "I'd already told Beau that."

Jess stared accusingly at Beau. "You knew, and yet you didn't tell me? Beau?"

"I couldn't tell you, Jess. I'm sorry, but it's a part of my profession that becomes very difficult. We are not allowed to breach patient confidentiality."

"Not even to me?"

"No."

Jess turned back to Margaret, her eyes swimming. "We will find a way through this, Margaret," she said in desperation. "There has to be a solution."

Margaret wiped a hand across Jess's wet cheek. "Don't fret, Jessie dear. I'm going to be around for a while yet." She laughed softly. "I told Charles that I'll outlast him if he doesn't behave himself. Now come on, dry those tears and let me see my grandchildren. Nothing is going to happen today or tomorrow, or even the day after."

*

Later that night, cradled in Beau's arms, Jess reflected on the events of the day. It was true that no matter what plans were made, life had a habit of directing the movements. She wanted so desperately to see a solution to Margaret's problem, but it seemed there was none. Life was no longer black and white; there were many shades of grey in between, and many hurdles, seen and unseen, that would have to be negotiated.

The one good thing that had come out of this day was that Edward and Beau had found some common ground, and Jess smiled to herself. It was a relief to know that her strong-natured, stubborn little boy had finally met his match in Beau, and as long as she knew when her interference was necessary, all would be well. She sighed as she snuggled closer.

"What have you been thinking about?" Beau's voice sounded in her ear. "You've been very quiet. You're not still angry with me, are you?"

Jess lifted her head. "Angry with you?"

"Yes, for not telling you that Margaret had been to see me at the surgery."

"No, I'm not angry." She rested her head back against his chest. "I'm sad that this is happening, and that there's nothing we can do to prevent it. I don't like the thought of being without Margaret. She's always been here for us, and in her own quiet way, has seen us through some tough times. Charles will miss her. She's his anchor, although he is unaware of it."

"I think he might be aware of it now."

"How long do you think she's got, Beau?"

"I can't predict, Jess. It's in the lap of the gods, or in Margaret's case, she's in God's hands."

Jess sighed. "We must have our wedding celebration soon, while Margaret is still well enough to enjoy the company. We can invite friends and family to share a special day with us. I know Izzy will be ecstatic, and maybe we can invite Angela, if she's able to travel this far." She looked up at Beau. "I would love to invite Matthew and Celia, but I know that's out of the question."

"Matthew won't be able to travel for a long, long time, supposing that he does recover." Jess felt the tremor that ran through his body.

"Oh, Beau! I am so sorry." She held him tight. "Matthew has been a very important part of your life for a long time. We must remain positive, just the same." She stroked his cheek. "We have each other, and I count my blessings every day."

"What did I do to deserve you, darling girl?"

"You love me, and that's all that matters."

Beau reached for a kiss, kindling the flame of their desire for one another.

Surprise Discovery

The high ivy-covered brick wall of the convent stretched away in both directions. The iron gates were padlocked; there was no way in. Angela and Clarence stood staring into the courtyard, pondering their next move. This was the fourth convent they had visited in their search for records of Beau's sister, Charlotte. So far the answers had all been the same; there was no record of her being sent to any of the cloisters.

Angela turned her gaze to the man standing at her side, and gave a little sigh of frustration.

"I'm sorry, Clarence," she murmured. "We seem to be on a wild goose chase, and it looks as though we're not likely to gain entry here."

"On the contrary, my dear." Clarence smiled down at his companion, his eyes twinkling. "If I give that bell a tug, I can guarantee someone will come running."

He stepped forward and grabbing the rope hanging down from a large iron bell set against the wall, he shook it with force. The noise was ear splitting. Angela placed her hands across her ears, and winced. Clarence stepped back with a grunt of satisfaction.

"That should do it!" Within two minutes they spotted a black-clad figure hurrying across the courtyard towards the gate. "What did I tell you?" Clarence was beaming with pleasure.

The figure stopped at the gate and peered at the intruders from beneath her wimple.

"Yes? What is it?" She was out of breath.

Clarence removed his trilby, and smiled at the woman behind the gate.

"My apologies, Sister," he said in his most cultured voice. "I am Clarence Bonner-Smythe and my companion here is Angela Rickard. We wish to speak with the Reverend Mother, if you please."

The nun stared at them for a moment. "What is it about?"

"It is of a personal nature."

"You'll have to wait here. I will see if the Reverend Mother wishes to speak with you."

"Thank-you."

The nun hurried back the way she had come, leaving Angela and Clarence standing on the footpath. They looked at each other, and Clarence gave Angela's arm a gentle squeeze.

"Don't look so worried, my dear," he said, in response to her furrowed brow. "I am enjoying this little escapade. I haven't had this much fun for a long time, and I owe it all to you." His blue eyes reflected what he had said, making Angela blush.

"I have to say, and it is with a twinge of guilt, that I am enjoying all this, myself. Thank-you, Clarence, for agreeing to come along as my chauffeur."

Clarence threw back his head and laughed loudly. "Chauffeur? Angela, I would say I'm your partner in…sleuthing." He suddenly became serious. "I've spent so much time between the asylum and the Clinic, that I had forgotten that life has some lighter moments. All my energy has been focused on Celia and my wife." His blue eyes bored into Angela, making her quake. "Now I have discovered that I too have a life, and by God, I am going to live it!"

Angela looked away, afraid that he was going to say something he could regret. She focused on the gate, and prayed fervently for the nun to reappear. Spending time with Clarence had been refreshing, and since the departure of Beau and Jess, it had filled that awful void of loneliness. She was extremely grateful to him for this, but a feeling of apprehension was settling on her. Their compatibility was obvious, even to his daughter, and Angela had a sudden feeling of uncertainty. If he wanted more than friendship then…

Her thoughts were interrupted by Clarence's voice. "Here she comes. I hope she has good news."

The nun appeared at the gate, and in her hand she held an enormous bunch of keys. Selecting one, she slid it into the padlock, and it clicked open.

"The Reverend Mother will see you," she said shortly. "Follow me, please." The gate creaked as she pushed it open, and Angela and Clarence stepped into the compound.

As soon as they were in, the gate was swiftly closed and the padlock re-instated.

They followed the black-clad figure as she hurried across the grass towards the building that towered in front of them. It was three storeys of red brick, almost entirely covered with ivy, except for the windows staring sightlessly out from the foliage. Above the slate roof rose at least six chimneys, only one from which there issued smoke.

They followed their guide in through a massive oak door, and along a cold corridor, dimly lit by candles set in sconces in the walls. Angela glanced at Clarence whose eyebrows were raised. At the end of the passage, their guide rapped on a heavy door, and waited for a response from within. At the sound of a voice, she turned to the visitors.

"The Reverend Mother will see you," she murmured, as she pushed the heavy door.

As it swung open, the nun scurried away. Clarence ushered Angela into the room ahead of him, and they stood on the carpet square as their eyes became accustomed to the semi-darkness. A round face, circled in white peered at them from behind the large desk that dominated the room. Candles in sconces were the only source of light, as the heavy drapes had been drawn across the windows. Angela had a strong desire to pull them apart and let the light stream in.

A voice came from the face across the desk; a strong, resonant voice that commanded attention.

"Mr. Bonner-Smythe, I have heard of you. This visit wouldn't by any chance lead to a charitable donation for the Convent?" The question hung in the air.

Clarence looked stunned for a brief moment, before recovering his composure.

"It possibly could, Reverend Mother, but it is not the reason we are here."

Her eyes moved to Angela, standing quietly to one side. "A new novice for the Order?"

Angela stiffened visibly. "No!" she retorted sharply.

"What a pity. You look a strong young woman, capable of hard work."

Angela bristled, and was about to retort, but Clarence placed a hand on her arm.

"The reason we are here, Reverend Mother," he said calmly, "is because we are searching for someone who has been separated from her family for over thirty years."

The eyes narrowed. "And what makes you think that I can help you?"

Clarence continued. "This woman was sent to a Convent at the age of eighteen, for reasons we don't know, but her brother, who was a mere child when his sister was removed from the family home, would now like to find her."

"After thirty-odd years?" The disembodied face laughed. "She could be anywhere."

"Yes, we know that, but we are starting with the Convents around Sydney, and then if necessary, will widen our search."

There was silence for some moments. "What was this young woman's name?"

Clarence looked at Angela, and nodded, as much as to say 'you take it from here.'

Angela stepped forward. "Her name was…is Charlotte DuBois."

"I see." The Reverend Mother sat back on her chair, and stared at the two in front of her. "And she was eighteen when she was sent to a Convent?"

"Yes." Angela's mouth was dry.

Another long silence ensued, before the Reverend Mother lifted herself from her chair.

"Wait here." It was a command.

She moved quickly around the desk, across the room, and was gone, closing the door behind her. Angela and Clarence looked at one another in disbelief.

"Where do you think she's gone?" whispered Angela.

"I don't know, but I hope she's not gone long. I have a strange feeling about this place."

"So do I." Angela shivered. "And I must say it is extremely cold." She glanced at the enormous empty fireplace that occupied one wall. "You'd think there'd be a roaring fire on a day like this."

"No, m'dear. It's all about depriving oneself of creature comforts, in order to achieve salvation."

"I don't know about salvation, but a little warmth can't be all that bad."

Clarence chuckled suddenly. "You realise, Angela, that I am not going to get out of this place without a sizeable donation to the cause."

"Well," said Angela with merry laugh, "you will have to stipulate that it is for firewood."

As the minutes ticked by, and the room became colder, Angela began to feel apprehensive.

"Perhaps we should go, while we can," she whispered.

"You're forgetting, my dear, that the gate is padlocked. We wouldn't get very far," Clarence responded, as he began to prowl the room, checking the bookshelves, and the paintings that adorned the walls. "No, we'll wait."

A large portrait of the Virgin Mary hung above the empty fireplace, and alongside, he pondered over two landscapes that looked vaguely familiar in the semi-darkness.

"They have a Tom Roberts look about them," he muttered, almost to himself, "but I doubt very much whether a place like this would have originals." He shrugged. "Copies, maybe?"

At that moment the door creaked open and a black-clad figure entered the room, gliding silently across the carpet. Angela turned to speak, thinking it was the Reverend Mother, but this nun was much taller, and carried herself with poise.

"How may I help you?" she asked in a cultured voice.

Angela blinked, and suddenly her legs would not hold her. She grabbed a chair for support as she found herself looking into a familiar face.

"You're Charlotte," she whispered hoarsely, and Clarence walked swiftly to her side.

The nun with the grey eyes looked at Angela for a long moment, before sighing deeply.

"I was Charlotte." Her chin rose slightly. "I am now Sister Agnes, and have been for the past twenty-nine years. Why are you looking for Charlotte?"

Angela swallowed hard. The resemblance between Beau and his sister was uncanny. She stumbled over her words. "We're here on behalf of your brother."

"Little Beau," they heard her murmur. "He was only a child."

"Yes, but now he's a man with quite a story to tell, and he wants to find you."

"Is he well?"

"He is now. He recently married and is settled in Victoria. He's a doctor of medicine."

"Ah!" A smile touched her face. "He was a bright little boy. I hated leaving him there."

"Leaving him where?" Clarence interrupted.

"At that house."

"With your parents?"

The grey eyes regarded Clarence thoughtfully. "With father."

"Beau doesn't remember much about your departure, but he thinks that maybe you...had a child?"

Her back stiffened and her gaze became hard. "There was no child," she said dispassionately.

"So you left of your own free will?" Angela felt there was more to Sister Agnes than met the eye.

The gaze dropped. "I couldn't stay there."

Angela was not satisfied, but she decided that it would be best to leave further questions to Beau. They had located his sister, and that was all that was required of them.

"Beau will be so thrilled that we've found you. Do you want him to contact you?"

Sister Agnes looked up, and a sad smile touched her mouth. "I think it would be best if you merely tell him that I am alive and well, and have found a new life." She moved towards the door. "Tell him... that not a day has gone by when I haven't thought of him and prayed for him."

The door swished shut behind her. Angela and Clarence looked at one another.

"She's not telling us everything," whispered Angela.

"Never mind, m'dear, our job is done. Beau is resourceful enough to follow up." He patted Angela's arm. "I think that for you and me a celebration is in order. What do you think?"

Angela laughed softly. "If someone lets us out of here. I don't fancy being a permanent resident."

Clarence reached into the breast pocket of his overcoat, and produced a chequebook. "I'll leave a donation for the Reverend Mother, and then you and I had better see if we can find the nun with the large bunch of keys. The sooner we're out of here the better." He found a fountain pen on the desk, scribbled a figure on a cheque, and placed it where the Reverend Mother would find it. "There! Now let's head to Mario's. Is that alright with you, m'dear?"

"Whatever you say, Clarence." Angela smiled coyly.

Making Plans

Jess threw herself into the task of planning a belated wedding celebration with family and friends. Her original plan was to have a gathering when the weather became warmer, but now there was an urgency to have it while Margaret was well enough to enjoy it. Postponing it wasn't an option.

The most important thing she had to do was to speak with Jean about using the Hotel as a venue. Knowing that a lot of public places had been shut down to combat the spread of the influenza, she hoped that what she had planned would fall under the guidelines of the local council.

Jean was more than happy to host the celebration, and pooh-poohed the idea of it not happening.

"Of course it will be alright, Jess love!" she enthused, as she stood with Jess in front of the roaring fire in her private sitting room. "We have plenty of room, both inside and out, so don't worry your head about that. I can deal with the council."

"Are you sure, Jean?" Jess was a little apprehensive. "I don't want you getting into trouble."

"There won't be any trouble, Jess." Jean flapped her fleshy arms in a gesture of confidence. "So when are you planning for this event to be held?"

Jess held back from telling Jean the reason for the snap decision. "Maybe three weeks from now, if that suits you? I have the invitations ready to send.

All I need is a date and a venue."

"Well, let's say we make it the last Sunday in August?"

"That was about the time I had in mind. Thank-you, Jean."

"I always planned, love," said Jean sagely, "that you would get married from here."

"I know, Jean, and I went and spoilt it all."

Jean's eyes twinkled. "No, you didn't. I still get to have my day."

Jess laughed softly. "You're a good friend, Jean, and I appreciate what you are doing."

"Is it going to be a full wedding service, with the vows and everything?"

Jess didn't want to dampen Jean's enthusiasm. "No, Jean, but we will dress in our wedding finery, and maybe add a few extra touches."

"Do you want me to make the cake?"

Jess felt a sudden wave of sadness. "I'd better ask Margaret first, Jean."

Jean had seen the look that passed across Jess's face. "Of course, dear," she said slowly. "Is everything alright, Jess?"

Staring at her friend's concerned face, Jess felt the tears well in her eyes. "No," she whispered.

"What is it?"

"It's Margaret." Jess gulped. "Please don't say anything, but she has an incurable blood disorder."

Jean wrapped her arms around Jess, and held her against her ample bosom. "I am so sorry, my dear. I shouldn't have asked, but you looked so pained. When did all this come about?"

"In the last few days," sobbed Jess.

"If there's anything I can do, you just have to ask, Jess."

"Yes, I know. This is the reason for the hasty decision to have a wedding celebration." Jess moved away from Jean's warm embrace, and wiping her eyes, tried to regain her composure. "We all need to act as though nothing is wrong. I don't want the children to sense that we're hiding something from them."

"No, of course not." Jean breathed hard. "Life is uncertain, I must say. Still, wherever there's life, there's hope, I say, so let's hope for the best, shall we?"

"Yes, of course."

"Well, if you feel like it, love, we'd better get down to the nitty gritty."

*

"Jessie! That's marvellous!" Izzy nearly came through the telephone. "What do you want me to do? I can design some place cards, or…"

"Jean and I have it all under control, Izzy. I want you to simply enjoy yourself."

"Jean?" Izzy sounded put out. "I thought I was going to hold the reins on this occasion."

Jess was not in the mood for a confrontation with her sister. "Things have changed, Izzy, and as Jean is here, and we'll be using her establishment, then it seemed the practical thing to do."

There was silence on the other end, before Izzy spoke again.

"Is there something you're not telling me, Jess?"

"No, Izzy!" Jess felt herself snap. "Why does it always have to be something I'm not telling you?"

"Well, what things have changed, for instance?"

Jess softened. "It isn't going to be a full wedding service, Izzy. It will be a get-together with all our friends and family. That's what I meant. There won't be balloons or decorations."

"Oh!" Izzy sighed. "I'm sorry, Jess. Let's start again, shall we?"

"Maybe we should, Izzy." Jess swallowed hard. She didn't want to tell Izzy what was happening with Margaret. "I'm sending out the invitations today, and I wanted to speak to you before you received yours." She stopped. "If you like, you could do a painting, as a gift for Jean."

"Yes, alright. Maybe I could do a still life? Flowers perhaps?"

"That sounds lovely, Izzy."

"Are you extending?"

"Yes," said Izzy quickly, then she stopped.

"Well?" Jess spoke into the silence. "What else did you want to say, Izzy?"

"Three weeks is not long to plan an occasion like this, Jess. You're not pregnant, are you?"

"Izzy!" Jess was losing patience again. "No, I am not!"

"I just thought..."

"We both know where your thoughts lead, Izzy, so please, just this once, behave!"

Izzy laughed suddenly. "You know I can't do that, Jessie."

Jess began to laugh, too. "Yes, I know."

*

Later that evening, Jess went over all the day's planning with Beau, as they sat in the lounge, having their last cup of tea for the day. He listened quietly to the details as Jess related her conversations with both Jean and Izzy. When she got to the suggestion from Izzy that perhaps she was pregnant, Beau turned startled eyes on her.

"Do you both know something that I don't?"

"No." Jess smiled coyly. "Izzy has an obsession about these things, I'm afraid."

"It would be nice." Jess heard the longing in his voice.

"Yes, I know it would, but we have to give it time, Beau. It will happen." He was silent as he stared into the fire, and Jess saw that sad, faraway look in his eyes that she'd seen before. **Where are you, Beau? Come back where I can reach you,** her heart was saying.

She touched his arm. "How was your day?" she asked quietly.

Beau dragged his eyes away from the fire, and stared at her for some moments. "Did you say something, Jess?"

"Yes, I did, Beau. I asked about your day. How was it?"

He took a deep breath. "I'm what is termed a new broom, Jess, and it's going to take a little while for me to sweep clean the habits and superstitions that exist in this town."

"Meaning?"

"Meaning that not all things can be changed in a day, as I had hoped."

"You'll make them happen, Beau, eventually."

He smiled. "At least Mr. Reynolds has consented to having his leg dressed each day, although it means he won't be working at the mines for some time." His eyes found hers. "How will he survive in the meantime? He has a family to support."

"They rely on their families and friends. They look out for one another, Beau."

A Letter From Angela

Jess was changing the linen on the beds, and had her arms laden with sheets, when she heard the sound of the postman's whistle. Dropping the sheets on the floor of the passage, she hurried out the front door, and down the steps to the letterbox. George, the postman, was ambling along the street, and he turned as he heard her open the box.

"Good day, Mrs. DuBois!" he called cheerfully. "Letter from Sydney for you this mornin'."

"Thank-you, George!" she called back, as her hand reached into the letterbox.

There was a letter, and it was post-marked from Sydney. Jess shook her head as she looked up to see George grinning foolishly at her. There wasn't much that slipped by him, unfortunately, and she knew that the rest of the street would know 'how lucky she was to be receiving mail from as far away as Sydney.' Smiling at him, she turned the letter over. It was from Angela. Her heart gave a little leap. Did she have news already of Beau's sister?

Jess hurried up the steps, and into the house. Stepping over her pile of washing, she headed for the kitchen. There she pulled a chair towards the stove, opened the oven door, and with anxious fingers, opened the envelope. She pulled out two sheets of paper, and Angela's neat handwriting leapt out at her.

Dear Jess and Beau,
We have found Charlotte! Yes! I can't believe it myself.
When I say 'we' I mean Clarence and myself. He took it upon himself to escort me to the various Convents, and at the fourth one we

found her. As soon as I laid eyes on her, I knew she was your sister, Beau. You have the same eyes.
I need to rewind. We arrived at this bleak Convent with its gates padlocked, and Clarence had to ring a bell to gain admittance. We were nearly ready to forget the whole idea, but a nun came out and let us in. It was the gloomiest place I have ever been in, and as cold as charity itself.
Nevertheless the Reverend Mother agreed to see us, I think on the grounds that she knew of Clarence Bonner-Smythe, and expected a donation from him.
When Clarence said what we were there for, she left the room and was gone for ages. We stood in that cold room, and I was about to leave, when another nun walked in. I knew who she was immediately. Beau, your sister is now Sister Agnes, (the Order is The Sisters of Mercy) and has been for the past twenty-eight years.

Jess stopped reading, and gave a little sob of disbelief. Charlotte was a nun? What was Beau going to think about that? She read on:

She looked very sad when I said her brother wanted to find her, as I really don't think she wanted to be found. She has made another life for herself.
Beau, she said to tell you that not a day has passed when she hasn't thought about you and prayed for you. She also said, in answer to my query, that there was no child. I had a strange feeling about that, but I will leave you to pursue it further, Beau, if you wish to do so. Charlotte (Sister Agnes) is well and seems happy with the life she has chosen.
By the way, Clarence did leave a donation for the Convent. It's my hope that they buy firewood with it. I have never experienced such a cold place.
On another note, I accompanied Clarence when he went to see Matthew and Celia recently. Celia seems very unsettled and edgy, and Matthew is struggling to stay on top of his disease. The Sanatorium is a beautiful place, set high in the mountains, and he is receiving the best of care, so we can only hope that in time he will recover.
I hope you are both keeping well, and I look forward to seeing you again one day.
Your friend
Angela

Jess expelled a long, shaky breath. Angela's letter was good news and yet an element of sadness rose from its pages. Whatever had happened in Charlotte's past, had been buried with her name, and it seemed that she was at peace with her new identity.

Jess folded the letter and placed it carefully back in the envelope, which she then put on the kitchen dresser for Beau. His reaction would be mixed, she felt sure, but at least he could be content in knowing that Charlotte still lived.

Jess went about her duties for the rest of the day, in a state of anxiety, as she waited for Beau to return from work. It was almost dark when she heard him walk through the front door, and her nerves tingled as she took the letter from the dresser. The children had eaten their tea, and were settled in their rooms, waiting for story time.

Jess heard Beau speaking with the boys as he passed their door, and she stood with her back against the sink, waiting for the kitchen door to open.

Beau took off his hat as he entered the kitchen, and looked up, surprised to see Jess standing quietly by the sink. He frowned.

"Is everything alright, Jess?" He hung his coat and hat behind the door.

Jess held out the letter. "This came today," she said huskily. "It's from Angela."

Beau took the letter from her outstretched hand, and opened it. Jess watched as he silently read the contents before looking up at her. He stared at her for a moment, before folding the letter and pushing it back into the envelope. Jess waited as the seconds ticked by. Finally he spoke.

"From what I remember of my sister, she would not have voluntarily chosen to cloister herself away in a Convent. She was far too outgoing for that." He gave a ragged laugh. "But I suppose I have to be satisfied that she's happy." He sighed as he looked at Jess. "Can you understand my reluctance to find her, Jess? It has brought up too many questions that may never be answered."

Jess cleared the lump from her throat. "I can understand, Beau." She took the letter from his hand, and placed her other hand in his. "At least you know you can see her if you want to. Now come and have your tea before it gets cold. All this is a lot for you to take in." She smiled.

"There was a child, Jess. I'm almost sure of that."

"Perhaps it died. Perhaps she miscarried."

"Then why become a nun?" His voice rose. "That I don't understand."

"Like you said, Beau, you were only a child at the time."

*

Jess had banked the stove for the night, and prepared the porridge oats for the morning. Looking at the dwindling wood supply, she realised that Sid O'Connor should have been back with a load before now, and she made a mental note to speak to Beau about it. She gave a cursory glance around the kitchen, before closing the door and walking silently along the passage to the lounge. The door was ajar, allowing light to seep out into the passage. Pushing it open, she saw Beau lying full length on the couch, Angela's letter in his hands.

Jess closed the door quietly. Beau looked up, saw her and shifted to a sitting position on the couch. He patted the seat alongside him, and Jess sat, tucking her feet beneath her.

"You're reading it again?"

Beau stretched one arm behind her. "Yes. The initial shock has passed, and I wanted to see if I'd missed anything the first time."

"And had you?"

"Only the fact that Clarence is paying a lot of attention to Angela." Beau looked sideways at Jess, and a slight smile touched his mouth.

"That's good, isn't it?" Jess noticed the smile, and felt some of her own tension being released.

"Yes and no."

Jess sighed. "Beau, it's either 'yes' or 'no'. It can't be both."

"Yes it can. It's good because it gives them time away from the things that consume their lives."

"And 'no'?"

"And 'no' because I'd hate to see either of them being hurt."

"I don't really know Clarence, but I would hate to see Angela suffer. She's suffered enough."

"Hm." Beau leaned back on the couch and closed his eyes.

Jess resisted the temptation to stroke his cheek. Instead she leaned forward and kissed him. Beau's eyes fluttered open. "What was that for?"

"I felt like it." Jess leaned her head against his shoulder. "I posted the invitations today."

Beau smiled. "Did you? And who are the lucky ones getting an invitation to this event?"

Jess snuggled closer. "Well, apart from family and Jean, of course, I've invited Angela, Nancy, Sally, and Mary and George Walker. Mary is dying to meet you."

"Is she now?"

"Yes. Is there anyone you'd like to invite, Beau?"

He didn't answer immediately. "Maybe Raymond and Louise."

"So your relationship with Raymond is improving, is it?"

"Yes, it is." Beau gave a sudden chuckle. "I saw something very funny during my hospital rounds today, Jess. The Matron was entertaining the children, and she had a cockatoo on her shoulder."

Jess laughed. "Yes, I know. Absurd, isn't it? The patients love it."

"So she's been around for a while?"

"Many years. She actually retired some years back, but returned, probably because she can't stay away from the place."

"It's not something you would see in the city, I must say."

"Probably not, but this is not the city, Beau."

"I am beginning to realise that."

"By the way, Beau," said Jess as she watched the dying embers of the fire, "we're nearly out of firewood. I thought Sid would have been back by now."

"Yes, I know. We can't rely on him, Jess. I've made other arrangements."

"You have? You're not going to collect firewood yourself?"

Beau shrugged. "The thought did cross my mind, but no, Albie Blake is happy to do it."

Jess bit her bottom lip. "I did promise Sid that I'd give him a chance."

"He's had his chance, Jess. According to Albie, he's disappeared again."

"Oh? On a drinking spree, you mean?"

"Probably. Now don't you worry your pretty head about Sid O'Connor. He's a bad penny."

"Yes, and bad pennies have a habit of turning up."

Louise's Visit

Jess was rudely awakened by the sound of loud knocking at the front door. After the talk about Sid the previous evening, she had a tight feeling in her chest. She sat up quickly, glancing at the bedside clock as she threw off the covers. It was nine o'clock. Why hadn't Beau woken her before this? As she slid out of bed, she heard his voice at the front door.

"Louise! This is a surprise. Come in."

It wasn't Sid, but it certainly was a surprise. As Jess grabbed for her dressing gown, Beau appeared in the doorway.

"Why did you let me sleep in?" Jess pushed her feet into her slippers, and attempted to smooth her hair with agitated fingers.

"You needed it," whispered Beau, closing the bedroom door behind him. "It's Louise, and I've asked her to wait in the lounge. She seems very excited about something."

"She must be, for her to be here at this time of the morning." Jess groaned. "I haven't got time to get dressed, but I need to visit the lav. and the bathroom. Oh dear! I was having such a lovely dream, too."

"Beau grinned. "About me?"

"Maybe."

Jess opened the bedroom door, and fled silently along the passage, through the kitchen and out the back door. It was Saturday, and Beau had obviously fed the children, because they were all outside. Ben and Edward were tinkering with the bicycle, and Grace was digging holes in the vegetable patch. Jess had no time to chastise her. She completed her ablutions and hurried back into the house.

In the bathroom she managed to comb the knots out of her hair, sprinkle a little cologne on her neck, and take a deep breath before heading to the lounge.

Louise was standing on the rug in front of the fire, her face wreathed in a wide smile. She had dressed carefully that morning, and her pale blue coat brought out the colour of her eyes. In her blonde hair she had tied a matching blue scarf. Jess smiled apologetically as she crossed the room.

"I'm sorry, Louise. You have me at a disadvantage this morning."

"That means we're even, Jess. You caught me the other day, remember?"

"Yes, I do remember." Jess laughed self-consciously.

"You're probably wondering why I'm here so early on a Saturday morning?"

"Well, yes."

"I have managed to persuade Raymond to find out who among his new mothers would like visits from our Red Cross ladies." Louise smiled widely at Jess. "Isn't that wonderful?"

"It certainly is, Louise. I was wondering how we could diplomatically do this."

"And..."

"There's something else?"

"Yes." Louise was squirming with excitement. "He also suggested that we might visit with other patients who have nobody to check on them."

"He did?"

"I don't know what's triggered the change in Raymond, but I suspect it has something to do with his association with Beau."

"With Beau?" Jess felt a little like a parrot.

"Raymond seems so much more relaxed." Louise giggled suddenly. "So, while he's in this mood, I am going to persuade him to allow me to accompany him to Melbourne when he visits the Laboratories." Her blue eyes shone. "I might not get another chance."

"That's a marvellous idea, Louise! I do hope he agrees."

Louise gave a little sigh of satisfaction. "You can get dressed now, Jess. I'll leave you in peace."

"There is one other thing we could discuss, Louise."

"And what is that, Jess?"

"Your suggestion that I take over as President of the Red Cross at the annual meeting."

"Would you like to?"

"I am going to suggest that you have another year. You have a worthwhile project now, and I can see that you're looking forward to getting on with it."

Louise nodded enthusiastically. "I am, Jess. Thank-you."

As she moved towards the door, Jess glanced out the window.

"How did you get here? I don't see your car."

"I walked. Raymond has the car. It's his golf day." She rolled her eyes.

Jess looked down at the boots Louise was wearing. "You walked in those heels?"

"I'm used to them." Louise lifted her coat, displaying slender ankles above her button-up boots.

As she did a little pirouette, Beau appeared, taking them both by surprise. Louise quickly let go of her coat, flushing in the awkwardness of the moment.

"Oops!" she said, to cover her embarrassment, and then she laughed softly. "I'll go, Jess, before I make a fool of myself again." She flashed a smile at Beau before hurrying out the door.

They heard the click of her heels on the linoleum, before the front door opened and then shut.

Jess expelled a long breath, while Beau stood shaking his head.

"I only came in to give her an invitation," he said. "I didn't expect to see that."

"Louise is very excited, Beau. Raymond seems to have mellowed, and has even offered to suggest to his new mothers that maybe a visit from ladies of the Red Cross would be a good thing."

"Well, well! That's a turnaround for the books."

"Isn't it?" Jess smiled coyly. "Louise thinks it's your influence, my dear husband."

"Does she now?"

"Yes." As Beau moved to pull her into his arms, Jess slipped past him and reached the door. "I must get dressed before the morning has gone altogether."

They turned as they heard running footsteps along the passage, and Edward appeared at the door.

"Can we ride the bicycle today, Beau?" he asked eagerly, as he looked from one to the other.

Beau glanced at Jess before answering. "We can as long as your chores have been done."

Edward nodded enthusiastically. "Yes, everything's done."

"Properly?" Beau smiled at Jess's attempt to look severe.

"Yes, ma!" Edward groaned.

"Very well then." Edward rushed back along the passage, as Jess called after him. "Not until Beau is ready, Edward! Do you hear me?"

"Yes, ma!" came from the direction of the back door.

Jess sighed as she turned back to Beau. "Don't let him wear you out, Beau."

"He won't, I promise you."

Preparations

The next three weeks flew by, as Jess began the preparations for the wedding party. Acceptance notes had been received from Mary, who was highly delighted, Nancy, who asked what she could do to help, and Sally, who asked if she could bring a friend. Angela was waiting to see whether she could travel across the border, and would they mind if Clarence joined her? Jess sent back a note, saying 'by all means, bring Clarence.'

Louise and Raymond, when the invitation was finally delivered to them, accepted graciously, and even offered their home as accommodation for two of their guests. Jess puzzled over this, and after discussion with Jean, decided that Mary and George Walker (and baby Jack) would be the most compatible couple for the Simmons'.

Jean was happy to open up the hotel for those who needed a bed, and with Jess's help, aired the rooms and prepared the necessary beds.

Whenever she could, Jess checked in on Margaret as discreetly as possible. She seemed to be in reasonable spirits, and was anxious to make the wedding cake, in spite of Charles's opposition.

"It's too much for you, Margaret!" he chided, to which Margaret replied,

"It may very well be the last thing I do, Charles, so let me do it."

Charles had to give in, but for a man who had previously been oblivious to his wife's needs, he was now paying a great deal of attention.

"Now I know what I sound like," Margaret said to Jess on more than one occasion. "Charles is like a mother hen, and so protective that I suddenly feel smothered."

Jess had merely smiled, but underneath she felt the pain that was surely coming.

Izzy was constantly on the telephone with suggestions about food and table decoration. Jess listened vaguely and finally had to consent.

"Alright, Izzy! You win."

"Good!' declared Izzy, as permission was granted. "We'll come down on the Saturday, and I'll keep out of your hair, I promise."

"You'll be sleeping at the hotel, I'm afraid." Jess expected a negative response to this remark, but it washed over Izzy, in her excitement.

"Wonderful! I'll be on the spot. It's going to be a celebration to remember, sister dear!"

It certainly was, thought Jess, as she replaced the receiver, and in more ways than one. There was a bittersweet irony about it, for the few who were aware of the circumstances.

*

Finally the Saturday arrived, and with it the promise of fine weather for the coming days. Jess spent the morning baking fruit pies and scones, having been told categorically by Jean that everything else was taken care of, including the enlisting of help to wait on the tables. At Jess's enquiry as to who was in charge of waitressing, she was told that Louise had it all in hand, and that meant the Red Cross ladies had been shanghaied, so to speak.

Angela had telephoned to say that she and Clarence would be arriving on the Sunday morning train from Melbourne. Jean said primly that she would be giving them separate rooms, and Jess smiled at the implications of Angela sharing a room with Clarence.

She voiced this thought with Beau as they sat in their favourite place, before the dying embers of the lounge fire, on the final evening. He smiled indulgently.

"What they do in private is not our business, Jess."

"Jean obviously thinks it is."

"Yes, well she's in charge of the sleeping arrangements." He laughed suddenly. "Am I relegated to the couch tonight?"

"No. Why would you be?" Jess frowned.

"You're forgetting, my darling, that Angela forbade us to be together before the wedding, and I thought that the rules might still apply."

"No." She planted a kiss on his cheek. "We're inseparable now."

Beau studied her face for a long moment before standing and moving towards the door.

"Wait here, my love."

"Where are you going?"

"I need to show you something. I won't be a moment."

He was gone for no more than a minute, and when he returned, he sat facing her on the couch.

"Close your eyes Jess."

She stared at him for a moment, before closing her eyes. Beau took her hand and placed something cold and metallic on her palm. He folded her fingers over it.

"You can open them now," she heard him say.

Jess opened her eyes and stared down at her hand. "What is it, Beau?"

Slowly she opened her fingers, revealing a heart-shaped gold filigree brooch, set with three brilliant emeralds. Jess gulped as she stared at the extraordinary beauty and delicacy of the jewellery.

"It was my mother's," he said huskily. "It's the only thing I have of her, and I did intend waiting until the birth of our first child." Beau stared intently at Jess.

"So why didn't you?"

"I thought it would look perfect on your wedding dress."

"Oh, Beau!" Jess felt the tears behind her eyes. "Is this what you had in the tobacco tin?"

He nodded, unable to speak. Jess slid her arms around his neck, drawing him close to her, feeling the wetness of his tears on her face.

"This is all you have of your mother? I will treasure it, Beau, and I will wear it tomorrow." She lifted his face, and they stared mutely at each other.

Finally Beau brushed a hand across his eyes and drew a deep breath. "It should have been Charlotte's, as the firstborn, but was eventually left to me when father died."

"It's all so tragic, Beau." Jess stared down at the brooch. "It makes me wonder about Charlotte."

"Let's not go into that now, Jess." He cupped her face in his hands. "It's yours."

Celebrations

"Is anybody there?"

Jess stopped stacking scones into a large wicker basket, and rushed to open the front door.

Izzy stood on the other side, her arms wide to receive her sister.

"It's so good to see you, Izzy! It's been an age."

"It certainly has, Jessie." Izzy stood back to survey her sister. "You look well, Jessie, I must say."

"As do you, Izzy. Come on in. The scones and fruit pies are nearly ready to go."

"Good." Izzy followed Jess to the kitchen, where Beau was placing a tea towel across the top of the wicker basket. He looked up as Izzy entered the room.

"Hello Izzy!" he said warmly. "Come to collect the goodies, have you?"

"Hello Beau." Izzy smiled serenely. "Yes, and I've come to collect three children, too."

"Oh?" Jess looked puzzled. "But they're not ready yet."

"That's alright. I thought if I take them now, then you two can get yourselves ready in peace."

"Give me a minute, Izzy. I'll collect what they need." Jess glanced up at the kitchen clock, before dashing from the room. It was just past midday.

She quickly went through the children's rooms, finding their best clothes. As she folded them into a suitcase, she could hear laughter coming from the direction of the kitchen. Izzy turned as Jess appeared in the doorway.

"I've been telling Beau the plans for your arrival at the hotel this afternoon," she said as she took the suitcase from Jess.

"Oh?" Jess glanced quickly at Beau.

"Yes. He'll tell you, sister dear. Now, where are the children?"

"In the back yard."

"Good. I'll fetch them. They can carry some of this stuff." Izzy laughed.

At the back door she called their names, and the three children came running.

"My word, you have grown!" she exclaimed, as she hugged each one in turn. "We're going to the hotel, so that your mother and Beau can get ready without having to worry about you three."

Within a few minutes they had all gone, and the house was quiet. Jess turned to Beau.

"So what's the actual plan, Beau?" Her voice had a slight edge to it.

He slipped his arms around her, drawing her against him.

"Charles is picking us up in the car at five minutes to two."

"But we're only going as far as the hotel."

"I know, but do you really want to walk along the street in a wedding dress?"

Jess sighed. "Probably not."

"Alright then. Let's enjoy the time of solitude that we have." His arms tightened.

*

Two hours later, Jess stood surveying herself in the cheval mirror that stood in one corner of the bedroom. Angela's gown looked just as beautiful as it had done on her actual wedding day. Jess adjusted the coronet of silk magnolias on her head, and smoothed her hair. Beau stood behind her, and they gazed at each other in the mirror. He held the sapphire brooch in his hand. Jess turned and he fastened it to the bodice of her gown, as she smiled up at him.

"It's beautiful, Beau," she whispered.

"Like its wearer," responded Beau, as he kissed her cheek.

"Will we impress the crowd?" Jess smoothed her hands down the silky fabric of the gown.

"Undoubtedly."

They both looked up as they heard the sound of a car horn, and Beau picked up his black top hat from the bed. He held out his arm, and Jess linked hers through it.

"Come, Mrs. DuBois, our chariot awaits."

"Let's enjoy this day, Beau."

They made their way out the front door, and Beau locked it behind them. Charles, resplendent in light brown suit and cream silk cravat, was standing beside his gleaming Chevrolet, and as they descended the steps, he opened the door with a flourish.

Jess stepped up on the running board, and Beau handed her into the immaculate vehicle. The black leather had been polished meticulously, and smelt strongly of beeswax. Jess sat, gathering her skirts around her, and Beau sat beside her as Charles closed the door. Flashing them a beaming smile, he hurried back to the driver's seat.

"Never could get the hang of these gears," he muttered as the car jerked forward. "I hope you don't mind, but we're doing the scenic route today," he added over his shoulder.

Jess and Beau looked at one another and grimaced.

"We're in your hands, Charles," said Beau, as he took Jess's hand and squeezed it.

"Good!"

As the car crunched along the dirt road, Jess noticed that small groups of her neighbours had gathered along the footpath. She smiled and waved. Children waved back, but she couldn't help noticing the looks of disapproval on some of the women, as they stared at her.

"They don't look very impressed," whispered Beau.

"How did they know?" Jess was puzzled by the fact that the whole neighbourhood seemed to be on the footpath at that moment. "The boys must have said something at school."

"More than likely."

Charles took them around the block, and eventually they pulled up beside the Grey Goose Hotel.

He climbed out, and opened the door for them. Beau stepped out on to the road, and stretching up his arms, took Jess by the waist and lifted her to the ground. He held her for a moment, before taking her hand in his.

"Come on, we'd better face the music."

They entered the hotel by the side door. Charles stepped ahead of them, and stopped in front of the Ladies' Lounge.

"Wait here," he whispered. "I'll herald your arrival."

Jess turned to look at Beau, and her nerves were tingling. In that room were people she hadn't seen for quite a while, and their approval was paramount. She smiled nervously.

"Ladies and gentlemen!" They heard Charles's booming voice. "I give you Dr. and Mrs. DuBois!"

The applause was deafening as they stepped into the Ladies Lounge, their hands tightly clasped. Jess blinked away the tears as she looked around the faces. There was Sally Mitchell on the arm of a tall young man. Mary and George Walker were smiling broadly, and she saw Mary mouth the words 'I approve'. Standing alongside them, Louise and Raymond were silently watching the reactions. Nancy stood to one side, her smile soft and gentle. Angela and Clarence were clapping loudly, and Angela had tears streaming down her cheeks. Izzy and Harry stood in the centre of the room, surrounded by Jess's three children and Freya. Izzy managed to hide her emotions behind hands that were tightly pressed against her mouth.

As Jess's gaze swept around the room, she saw Jean quietly dabbing at her eyes with a handkerchief. There was one person missing. Jess scanned the room again, and at last her eyes rested on Margaret, seated at one of the round tables. She, too, was weeping silently, and Jess felt a sudden rush of sadness as she gazed at her.

The look did not escape the notice of Izzy, and her gaze slid from one to the other, resting finally on Jess. It could have been simply the memories of Jack that had triggered such an expression of sadness, but Izzy, knowing how well she could read her sister, had an uneasy feeling. She would have to get to the bottom of it.

"Ladies and gentlemen, I am to be your Master of Ceremonies today, probably because I have the loudest voice." All attention turned to Charles. "These are my instructions." He reached for spectacles in his breast pocket, and unfolded a sheet of paper. "Firstly, there is to be a time of mingling and reuniting with the newlyweds." He gazed around the faces. "I must ask you to please refrain from lots of hugging and kissing. We have Medical personnel here, and in the current influenza crisis, we are asked to comply." There was a brief murmur of resignation. "This will be followed by a sumptuous wedding feast. Lastly, there will be the cutting of the wedding cake, made and decorated by Margaret." His voice quivered slightly, but he quickly recovered his composure, and tucked the paper into his jacket pocket. "Are there any questions?"

There were no questions, and so the mingling began. Beau removed his top hat, and had it immediately whisked from his grasp by Jean.

"I'll take care of that," she whispered. "You go and mingle."

Jess could see Angela and Clarence bearing down on them, and had to stop herself opening her arms for an embrace. Instead she smiled broadly.

Angela gripped her hands, and her face was beaming. "You look so happy, Jess," she gushed.

"I am, Angela." Jess looked at Beau. "This man has breathed life into me again."

"I can see that. How are you, Beau?"

"Never better, Angela, and I can say the same about this woman." He smiled.

Angela glanced coyly at Clarence, who was smiling indulgently down on her.

"Could I ask you both," said Beau tentatively, "if there's anything else I need to know about my sister? Does she want me to get in touch with her or am I excluded from her life?"

It was Clarence who answered. "I did get the impression, Beau, that she wants to leave the past where it is, and that includes you. She seemed anxious that we let you know that she thinks of you, but I don't think she wants to renew the relationship. Was that your impression, Angela?"

"I'm afraid so, although I do feel that she wasn't telling us everything. The years have been too long, and the wounds too raw to be healed."

"Yes, I suppose so." Beau sighed. "Thank-you, anyway."

"We enjoyed it, Beau. It was such a refreshing change from the problems at home."

"How is Matthew?"

"He's struggling, but he refuses to give in to the wretched disease."

"And Celia?"

Clarence shook his head. "She's struggling, too, and I'm waiting for the day when she says she can't do it any longer. She has amazed me, as it is."

Angela had spied the brooch on Jess's bodice. "What a beautiful brooch, Jess!" she exclaimed. "It matches your eyes perfectly."

"It belonged to Beau's mother," said Jess quietly, as she ran her fingers over the filigree.

"Can we butt in?" It was Mary, who had been waiting to speak with them.

Angela turned. "Certainly! We didn't mean to monopolize the happy couple." She stepped back and Mary moved forward to clasp Jess by the hand.

"Jess, you look truly radiant!" she enthused, before turning her attention to Beau. "Beau, I'm Mary Walker, and this is my husband, George. We have so been looking forward to meeting you."

Beau inclined his head to Mary, and shook George by the hand. "And I you," he said briefly.

"Where's baby Jack?" asked Jess, looking around for the child.

"He's upstairs sleeping."

"Let me introduce you to Beau's colleague, Raymond Simmons, and his wife, Louise."

"Oh yes," said Mary. "We've already met."

As they stepped forward, Jess spied Sally Mitchell trying to get her attention. She turned to Beau.

"Please excuse me for a moment. Sally seems anxious to speak to me."

Jess threaded her way towards Sally and her young man. They clasped hands.

"It's so good to see you, Sally."

"You too, Jess. Can I say that you look absolutely gorgeous, and Beau looks divine."

"Divine?" Jess laughed.

"Well, I can't say that he looks gorgeous, so 'divine' is the next best thing."

"I see." Jess looked up at the young man by Sally's side. "Are you going to introduce us, Sally?"

"Yes, of course," breathed Sally. "Jess, I'd like you to meet Simon Carter." She flushed prettily as she gazed up into his brown eyes. "We're getting married at the end of the year."

"That's wonderful! Congratulations, and I'm very pleased to meet you, Simon." Jess shook his hand. "I have known this young lady for a long time." She looked from one to the other. "We expect an invitation, of course."

Sally nodded her head. "Yes, definitely, Jess."

"Ladies and gentlemen!" boomed Charles, above the hum of conversation. "If you have all finished mingling for the time being, I believe the food is ready. If you would like to make your way to the buffet, you can help yourselves, and then find a table, where you can resume conversation. The bar is of course not open, but there's plenty of fruit punch and lemonade."

As Jess headed for the buffet, she felt someone touch her arm. Turning, she saw Nancy Weatherall standing beside her.

"I think it might be my turn," she said softly.

"Nancy! How are you?" Jess grasped her hand.

"I'm very well, Jess, and I must say that you look…exquisite."

Jess laughed. "I've been described in many ways today, Nancy. 'Exquisite' is a first."

"It's true."

"Well, can I say that you look stunning? That blue suit matches your eyes perfectly."

Nancy blushed. "I bought the suit in preparation for Martin's wedding."

"Oh my! When is he coming home?"

"November, hopefully." She sighed wistfully.

"You miss him, Nancy?"

"Oh, yes. In fact," she took a deep breath, "I'm thinking of going to France with him."

"To live?"

"Yes."

"That's a big move." Jess was shaken by this news.

"There's nothing here for me, Jess. Martin is my world, and I've been without him for so long. He is in favour of my decision."

"Yes, I can imagine he is."

Beau appeared at Jess's side. "Come and eat, my love," he said, as he took her arm. "Hello, Nancy. It's always nice to see you."

"Thank-you, Beau, and congratulations to both of you."

"Beau, Nancy was telling me that she's considering moving to France, to be near Martin."

Beau smiled at Nancy. "I think that's an excellent idea. France will be a wonderful country again, now that the war is over."

"Martin loves it there."

"Izzy and Harry will miss you, Nancy."

She shrugged. "I'll miss them, too, but I need to be with my boy." Jess noticed tears in her blue eyes. "If Martin won't come back here to live, then I must go there."

"Yes, I see."

*

Jess needed to find Margaret. She had caught up with most of her guests, but she hadn't spoken to the most important guest of all, and it would soon be time to cut the wedding cake. She made her way across the room to where she had last seen her, seated at one of the round tables. Yes, she was still there. Jess sat beside her.

"How are you, Margaret?" Jess took the older woman's hand. "I haven't had a chance to get to you until now." They smiled at one another. "Are you enjoying yourself?"

"Yes, I am, Jess. Today is a good day, in more ways than one. It's wonderful to meet your friends." Margaret stretched her free hand out to touch the brooch at Jess's shoulder. "That's a fine piece of jewellery, Jess. Where did you get it?"

"It belonged to Beau's mother. He gave it to me last night."

Margaret looked up, and Jess saw tears in her eyes. "You look so happy, Jess, and I am pleased that you are, but…don't forget Jack, my dear."

Jess felt the weight of her words, and her own resolve crumbled. "I'll never forget Jack, Margaret. He will always have a place here." She placed Margaret's hand over her heart.

Across the room, Izzy was watching the exchange between Jess and Margaret, and a frown creased her brow. There was something amiss, she was sure of it.

Charles interrupted her thoughts, as he appeared at her elbow.

"Is it time for the cake, Isobel?"

"Yes, Charles. I think everyone has eaten their fill."

"Good. I'll get their attention." He clapped his hands. "Will the bride and groom make their way to the centre of the room, please? We are about to cut the wedding cake."

Jess looked around for Beau. He was deep in conversation with Clarence. At the sound of Charles's voice, he looked up, caught Jess's eye, and made his way towards her.

"Where are the children?" she asked, looking around the room.

"The last I saw of them," said Beau, "Harry was taking them outside."

"Could you track them down, please Beau? I'd like them here for the cutting of the cake."

As Beau moved away, the children and Harry appeared, flushed and dishevelled.

Jess frowned, as she began to brush grass from Grace's pretty yellow frock. "Harry!" she chided. "What have you been up to?"

Harry straightened his flamboyant green tie, before running a hand through his receding hair.

"I thought I'd take them outside for a while, and they wanted to play 'hide and seek.' Hence the state of our clothes." He brushed at the grass stains on his trousers. "Isobel won't be pleased, either," he muttered.

The rest of the guests had gathered around the central table, on which stood the two-tiered wedding cake, wrapped in white icing and decorated with handmade gardenias. The family stood to one side of the cake, as everybody admired it.

Charles had a camera pointed at them. "Smile, please!" he shouted.

Isobel appeared with a large knife, and handed it to Beau.

"Both hands on the knife!" called someone.

"Don't cut right through!" called someone else.

"Make a wish!"

Together they plunged the knife into the cake, and smiled as Charles took a photograph. As Jess looked around for Margaret, she saw Charles hand the camera to Harry, while he made his way through the crowd to where Margaret was still seated. Jess watched as he took her arm, and escorted her to where the family were gathered.

"Harry," Jess noticed the quiver in his voice, "take a picture of all of us, please?"

As they stood waiting for Harry to press the shutter, Jess heard a voice begin to sing 'For they are jolly good fellows.' It was Mary. Her tone was warm and true, and everyone joined in. Jess placed an arm around Margaret, and smiled through her tears.

*

"There you are, Jess! I've been searching everywhere for you." Izzy stepped carefully across the grass in her flimsy high-heeled shoes. Sitting beside her sister on the wooden garden bench, she breathed a heavy sigh. "What are you doing out here?" She slanted a glance at Jess.

"I needed a few moments to myself," answered Jess, avoiding her sister's glance.

"You need a shawl if you're going to stay out here, or you'll catch your death otherwise."

"I'm not cold."

"Come on, out with it! Something's bothering you, Jess. I can read you like a book."

Jess shook her head. "No," was all she said.

"No what?" Izzy grabbed her sister's hands. "Is it something to do with Margaret?" Jess turned to stare at her. How could she have guessed? "It is, isn't it?"

"There's not much I can hide from you, Izzy."

"No, there isn't, so out with it! I'm not leaving here until you tell me what's going on."

A tear slid silently down Jess's cheek. "Margaret has an incurable blood disorder."

Izzy was silent for a moment, before drawing Jess into her arms. "Oh, Jessie, that is terrible. I am so sorry. Is there nothing Beau can do for her?"

"No!" sobbed Jess, against Izzy's shoulder. "That's why we had to have this celebration now, in case anything happens."

Izzy laughed softly. "And there I was, thinking it was because you were pregnant. I can be so tactless sometimes." She sighed.

Jess raised her head, and rubbed a hand across her wet cheeks. "Yes, you certainly can."

"I deserved that," said Izzy wryly.

Footsteps made them both look up to see Beau crossing the grass towards them.

"So here you are?" Beau looked from one to the other, and frowned. "What's the problem?"

"In my usual clumsy way, Beau, I asked about Margaret."

"Oh."

Izzy sighed heavily. "I didn't expect the answer that I received."

"Jean is the only other one who knows, Izzy," said Jess quickly. "We'd like to keep it that way."

"I can be secretive if I have to be, Jess."

"Yes, I know."

Beau held out his hands to both women. "You are required inside. We're about to wind up the afternoon, and Charles has asked me to give a short speech. You won't want to miss this."

"We certainly won't!" Izzy was the first one on her feet. "Come on, Jessie."

*

The applause died down, and everyone focused their attention on Beau and Jess, as they stood together in the centre of the Ladies' Lounge. Beau took Jess's hand, and turned her to face him. She saw him mouth the words 'I love you' before he turned to face the crowd.

"Ladies and gentlemen, (and children, of course,) on behalf of my wife and myself…" This brought more spontaneous applause. Beau raised a hand and the silence resumed. "On behalf of my wife and myself, I want to thank you all for being here today. The support you have shown to Jess and me is overwhelming, and your presence here is much appreciated." He stopped for a moment before continuing. "When I met Jess, nearly three years ago, I was homeless, penniless and without a friend in the world, except for my dog. This woman you see here, wanted to give me a chance, and trusted me without knowing my circumstances." He smiled at Jess, whose eyes were brimming. "She didn't see the damaged person I was; she saw someone who needed a friend." He brushed a hand across Jess's wet cheek. "I have given her some traumatic and awkward moments over this time, and I thank her for her resilience and her courage… When I asked her if she would do me the honour of being my wife, I didn't expect that I would be marrying a whole family." A murmur went around the room. "Such warmth I had never known, but I was drawn into this family and accepted without hesitation. Family is everything, and I have finally found mine." He stopped, and taking Jess by both hands, looked into her eyes. "Jess, I promise, in front of all gathered here today, that I will love you unconditionally until the time when I take my last earthly breath."

Several women reached for their handkerchiefs, as the silence followed this statement. Beau drew Jess against him and cupped her face in his hands. As he bent to kiss her, she heard him whisper so that only she could hear, "You are my world, darling girl."

Angela

Jess was seated on the front verandah, enjoying the solitude after several hectic days. The boys had gone to school, Grace was playing in the back yard, and Beau had ridden to work on Jack's bicycle, after finding trouser clips in the shed. Izzy, Harry, Freya and Nancy had boarded the morning train to Swan Hill, unable to extend their stay because of the shop. Mary and George were staying on for an extra day with the Simmons's, and Louise was excited about showing them the sights of Bendigo. Sally and Simon were doing their own exploring, pleased to be out of the city for a short while. That left Angela and Clarence. They too had decided to extend their stay, saying that it was a long way to come for two days. Besides, the accommodation at the Grey Goose was, in Clarence's words, 'thoroughly commendable.'

Jess yawned. It had been very late when they finally got to bed. The party hadn't ended after Beau's speech. Conversations had continued until late in the evening. The children were bedded down upstairs, which left parents free to relax and enjoy the company of those they'd just met, and those they hadn't seen for a while. At Jess's request, Mary had agreed to sing a few favourite songs, which were received with well-deserved acclamation. Jean was sorry that the old piano in the Bar couldn't be used on this occasion.

"I should have thought of it, earlier," she grumbled, "and had it shifted into the Ladies Lounge."

It was ten o'clock when Jess decided that as the coming day was a school day, they should really get the children home. So they had been carried out to Charles's car, and driven the short distance home, where they were soon transferred to their own beds. Jess and Beau had finally got to bed, but talked into the early hours. Jess smiled as she recalled asking him how long it had taken him to mentally prepare his speech.

"There was no preparation, Jess. It was straight from the heart."

Yes, she knew that was the case, as did all those present, judging by their reactions.

Jess roused herself. It was time to head along to the hotel and help Jean with the washing and cleaning up after the previous day's party. Reluctantly she stood, and was about to fetch Grace, when she saw a familiar figure walking along the street towards her, from the direction of the hotel. It was Angela.

She was dressed smartly in a suit of a rich burgundy colour, and a straw hat covered her thick dark hair. Jess walked down the steps, and opened the gate for her.

"Angela! This is a surprise. Come and join me. I've been contemplating the events of yesterday."

"It was a wonderful day, Jess, and I'm so glad we could be here."

The two women seated themselves on the bench, and gazed out upon the empty street.

"It's so different to Sydney; so quiet and peaceful." Angela sighed as she visibly relaxed.

"What have you done with Clarence this morning?" asked Jess.

"Oh, Charles has taken him to have a look around the hospital. So I thought I'd come along and annoy you." Angela squeezed Jess's arm. "It's so good to see you again, Jess. I have missed you dreadfully, and Beau, of course."

"I've missed you too."

They were silent for a full minute, before Angela turned to Jess, her expression serious.

"Clarence wants me to work at the Clinic, as a receptionist."

Jess raised her eyebrows. "Does he? What about your shop?"

"The way things are going, I'll be closing the doors before long."

"No!" Jess was shocked. "You can't do that!"

"With the influenza pandemic continuing, businesses like mine are closing all over the city."

"That's terrible."

"The only way I can continue is to cut down on staff, and only open on certain days."

"And that's possible if you have a job elsewhere?"

"I've been over it with Clarence, and yes, it is possible."

Jess sat back, expelling a long breath.

"Jess?" Angela turned to look at her again. "Does my relationship with Clarence bother you?"

"What do you mean?"

"I mean, knowing that he has a wife, does that bother you?"

Jess clasped her hands. "No, of course not, Angela! You enjoy each other's company, so why shouldn't you spend time together? Besides, it's nobody else's business."

"I just thought that maybe people think we have… an intimate relationship, which we haven't." Angela flushed. "Celia is not at all in favour of any of it, and has made that very clear." She looked earnestly into Jess's eyes. "I'm very fond of him, and I'm no longer lonely. Can you understand that, Jess?"

"Yes, I can understand that, Angela."

She gave a tinkling laugh. "I'm so glad you don't disapprove, Jess. That means a lot."

The front door opened, and Grace appeared at the screen door.

"I'm hungry, ma. Is it lunchtime yet?"

"Probably," said Jess. "Come inside, Angela, and we'll have some lunch, and then I must go and help Jean with the washing." As they stood, Grace opened the screen door for them.

"My goodness, she's so like you, Jess," said Angela as she smiled down on Grace.

"In more ways than one, Angela."

*

Later that afternoon, when all the chores at the Grey Goose had been completed, Jess decided to walk around to check on Margaret. Angela declined the offer to accompany her, saying that she would have a rest before Clarence returned. He was taking her to the Shamrock Hotel for their evening meal. So Jess, after prising Grace away from Mack (the terrier), headed along the street towards Margaret's.

Grace skipped ahead of her, and when they reached the house, she was the first to stretch up on her toes to reach the shiny brass knocker. They waited. There was no answer.

"Come on, Gracie, we'll go around to the back. Grandma should be home."

Together they walked along the side of the house, and around to the back door. Jess knocked. There was no answer, but the door was unlocked. They entered the kitchen. Everything was in place and the room was warm.

"Margaret!" Jess called out. "Are you here?"

She heard a sound coming from the front bedroom, so she walked quickly through the passage to the front of the house. Opening the bedroom door, she saw Margaret in the big double bed, the blankets pulled up to her chin, and a frilly pink nightcap covering her hair. She smiled as the two faces appeared at her door.

"Come in Jessie." Her voice was weak. "I heard you at the door." Margaret patted the bed covers. "Come and sit with grandma, Gracie." She clambered up on the bed.

"Are you not so well today, Margaret?" Jess pulled Grace's boots from her feet.

"A little tired, that's all. Yesterday was a big day." She smiled as she stroked Grace's hair. "Charles has gone out with that nice man from Sydney, to show him the hospital."

"His name's Clarence Bonner-Smythe," said Jess. "Yes, I believe so."

"It was lovely yesterday, Jess, really lovely."

"Would you like me to make you a cup of tea?"

"Yes, dear, that would be nice. Charles should be home soon. I didn't expect him to be gone this long." She smiled. "Although he does tend to get carried away when he talks about the hospital. Anyone would think that he owned it."

"Have you had lunch, Margaret?" Jess realised that Charles had been gone since the morning, and it was now close to three o'clock in the afternoon.

"Yes, dear, but I wouldn't mind a biscuit." She smiled at Grace. "You'd like one too, wouldn't you, Gracie?"

"Yes please, grandma."

"Oh, and if you wouldn't mind filling this up again for me?" Margaret produced a hot water bottle in a pink knitted cover, from beneath the blankets, and handed it to Jess.

In the kitchen the kettle was singing quietly on the stove, and Jess noticed that there was a bowl and a cup in the sink. Margaret had eaten something for lunch, thankfully. The biscuit tin was almost empty, and Jess made a mental note to replenish the supply.

When the tea was made, and the last of the biscuits set on a plate, Jess looked for a tray. She could hear Grace laughing, and knew that this would be good for Margaret. With the afternoon tea ready, Jess emptied the hot water bottle, and refilled it from the kettle.

Tucking it under her arm, she picked up the tray and headed for the bedroom. As she reached the door, Jess heard the car pull up alongside the house. A car door slammed, and this was followed by the quick crunch of footsteps on the gravel. Finally the back door opened and she heard Charles moving about in the kitchen. Quickly she placed the tray on the bedside table, handed Margaret the hot water bottle, and retraced her steps to the kitchen. Charles was removing his boots, and looked up as Jess entered.

"Ah, Jess, I'm glad you're here. I didn't mean to be so long." He slid his feet into slippers that sat on the hearth in front of the stove.

"It's alright, Charles." Jess could sense that he felt guilty about being late. "I've made Margaret a cup of tea, and she's resting in bed."

A frown crossed his brow. "Is she feeling alright?"

"She's a little tired, that's all. Yesterday was a big day for her." Jess laughed softly. "It was a big day for all of us."

"Indeed it was, but it was a good day, Jess, and I think Margaret enjoyed the fellowship. You have a wonderful group of friends." Charles headed for the passage. "By the way," he added as Jess followed him to the bedroom, "Clarence was very impressed by our hospital."

Margaret looked up as he entered, and a smile lit her pale face. "I'm glad you're here, Charles."

"I'm sorry, m'dear. I didn't intend staying away for so long."

"Never mind." Margaret smiled at Grace. "Gracie has been entertaining me. Now come and have a cup of tea." She looked apologetically at Jess. "You'll have to make another one, Jessie."

The Unwelcome Encounter

The train thundered into the station in a cloud of steam. Jess and Grace stood on the platform, as Angela and Clarence prepared to board for their journey to Melbourne. Angela turned to Jess, and swiftly pulled her into an embrace.

"It has been so good, Jess. I wish you and Beau well, and maybe we'll see each other again some time." Her eyes were moist as she then bent towards Grace. "Goodbye little Gracie. You are a delightful little girl, and I have enjoyed meeting you."

Grace looked solemnly up at her with large green eyes.

"She's not always this quiet," laughed Jess.

Clarence held out his hand and Jess found hers squeezed in a vice-like grip. "Goodbye, Jess. We shall tell Matthew and Celia all the news when we see them." He turned to Angela. "Well m'dear, shall we go? This beast won't wait for us, and we have a long couple of days ahead of us."

"Yes, Clarence. Goodbye, Jess. Goodbye, Gracie."

Jess watched as they boarded the train, which started to move with a great screech of metal. Angela was at a window, waving and holding a handkerchief to her nose. Jess wondered whether she was crying, or whether the steam and smoke was affecting her. She waved back, until the train was out of sight, and then catching Grace by the hand, headed for the pedestrian bridge.

"Come on, Gracie, let's pay Mrs. O'Malley a quick visit, shall we?"

"And Mack?"

"Yes, and Mack."

As they headed along the street, Jess thought back on the celebration, and was satisfied that everybody had had a good time, and new friendships had been forged. Mary and George had been persuaded by Louise to stay an extra day, to take in more of the sights. Their company would be good for Louise, and discussion about young mothers was sure to come up. Mary, being a nurse, was a suitable ear for Louise to bend, in her quest to come up with an answer for the mothers of the town. This was just what Louise needed.

Jess's thoughts turned to Nancy, and her decision to move to France to be with her boy. For a shy person like Nancy, this was going to be a huge change and…

Her thoughts were interrupted by a loud familiar voice behind her. She turned.

"Oi! Missus whatever you call yourself now, I wanna talk to you!"

It was Sid O'Connor. Jess clutched Grace's hand and walked quickly, but he caught up with her, and loped alongside. Jess could smell the alcohol on his breath.

"What do you want, Sid?" she said quickly, as she hurried in the direction of the Grey Goose.

"What's the meanin' of givin' my job to Albie Blake, eh?"

"You weren't around, Sid, and we needed wood."

"You promised me the job."

"Only under certain conditions, and you let me down."

Sid grabbed her wrist, forcing her to a halt beside the south wall of the Grey Goose. His fingers bit into her flesh.

"Let me go, Sid! You're hurting me!" she managed to stammer. "I'll call out if you don't stop this nonsense at once!"

"It was that husband of yours, wasn't it?" His face was close to hers. "He never did like me."

"Sid, please stop right now, and I won't take this further."

"Take this further?" he parroted. "Sure you won't." With that he flung her arm away from him, and Jess felt her knuckles scrape against the rough brick wall of the hotel. A searing pain went through her hand, and she yelped as she clutched it to her breast.

Sid whirled around, suddenly aware of what he had done, and with a look of panic, jabbed a dirty finger at Jess.

"Don't you tell no-one, you hear?" With that he loped away, down the hill towards the station.

Jess stood for a moment, her legs shaking and her hand throbbing. Grace was staring up at her, with eyes like saucers and her bottom lip trembling.

"I'm alright, Gracie." Jess smiled reassuringly. "Come on, we'll go and see Mrs. O'Malley."

They were only a matter of feet away from the side entrance, and Jess made her way to the door.

Ushering Grace inside, they headed towards the bar door. Jess could hear laughter issuing from inside, and she saw Jean talking to Billy Maitland, who was seated at the bar.

"Jean!" Jess called out.

Billy turned, saw her, and said something to Jean. She wiped her hands on a cloth, before speaking to her barman, Norman, and then she shuffled across to the door.

"Jess, whatever's the matter?" Her eyes suddenly took in the hand that Jess had clutched against her breast. Blood was issuing from her knuckles. "What have you done, girl?"

Jess began to shake violently. Jean took her by the arm and led her to her sitting room. Grace followed, crying inconsolably and unsure of what was happening.

"Sit down, Jess, and I'll get some salve for that hand of yours."

Jess sat heavily in the armchair, and Grace climbed on to her knee.

"I'm sorry, Gracie," said Jess through chattering teeth. "Ma needs to let Mrs. O'Malley look at her hand." She tentatively straightened her fingers, relieved that nothing was broken.

Jean returned moments later, a bowl of warm water in one hand, and a cloth and ointment tin in the other.

"Let's have a look at the damage," she said, as she placed the bowl on a small table beside the chair, and wrung out the cloth in the warm water. "What on earth did you do?" She patted the bloodied knuckles with the damp cloth. "Did you have an encounter with the footpath?"

Jess shook her head. She was unsure whether to tell Jean what had actually happened. However, the decision was made when Grace, in all her innocence, set the story straight.

"It was Sid, wasn't it, ma?"

Jean looked from one to the other. "Sid? Sid O'Connor did this?"

Jess nodded. "Yes."

"Then you'd better tell me what happened." Jean rubbed some soothing salve into the red knuckles, before wiping her hands, and then seating herself opposite Jess. "Out with it!"

So rather reluctantly, Jess told Jean what had transpired right outside the hotel. Jean shook her head in disbelief.

"That's assault, Jess," she muttered. "You can have him charged for that."

"Yes, I know." Jess rubbed the ointment into her inflamed knuckles.

"What are you going to tell Beau?"

Jess looked up quickly. "I – I don't know."

"I do." Jean looked meaningfully at Grace, pressed up against her mother. "You have to tell him the truth. Besides, you can't hide an injury like that from him."

"No, I don't suppose I can." She paused for a moment. "I'm afraid of his reaction, Jean."

"Well, whatever he does, Sid's got it coming, and when I tell Billy…"

"No! Jean, you mustn't tell Billy."

"Why not?" Jean laughed. "He's been looking for an excuse to have a go at that little weasel for a long time. He'll enjoy a confrontation." Her eyes twinkled. "Well, I'd better get back to the bar." She stood up slowly. "You stay here for as long as you want, dear."

After Jean had left the room, Jess leaned back against the comfortable lounge chair. Her hand throbbed, and she knew that Beau was going to be extremely angry; not with her, but with the man who had inflicted pain on her. She shuddered, causing Grace to look up at her.

"You alright, ma?"

"Yes, Gracie. We'll sit here for a little while before we go home. I don't think my legs will carry me at the moment."

They sat in silence, as the clock ticked above the mantel. It was getting towards three o'clock, and the boys would be home from school soon. She sighed heavily.

There was a tap on the door, and Billy Maitland appeared in the doorway.

"Can I come in, Jess?" he rasped, his voice still affected by the gas during the war.

"Yes, Billy."

He squatted on the floor in front of her, his brown eyes troubled.

"Mrs. O'Malley told me what happened, Jess. That little bas..." He stopped. "That little rat has a lot to answer for. Just say the word, an' I'll fix 'im proper!"

"No, Billy. He's not worth going to gaol for."

Billy laughed scornfully. "I won't be the one goin' to gaol, Jess, I c'n assure you!" He took her wounded hand and studied it carefully. "He needs to be punished for what he's done." He looked up at Jess. "You leave 'im to me."

"Billy, I appreciate what you are saying, but I don't think Sid will hang around now."

Billy shrugged. "I'll find 'im. We have our own scores to settle."

"You be careful."

"I didn't come 'ome from the war for nothin', Jess."

"No, you didn't."

*

Jess made her slow way home, troubled by Billy's obvious need for revenge. She felt sure that Sid had not intended for things to happen the way they did. The look of panic on his face was proof of that, but Billy and Beau had not seen that look, so their minds would be already made up as to Sid's intentions. She chewed anxiously on her bottom lip as she thought of Beau's reaction. She had no doubt that it would be explosive.

As they neared the front gate, Jess saw Ben and Edward ambling along the street, throwing stones into the gutter and scuffing their shoes in the gravel. They spotted their mother, immediately stopped what they were doing and ran in her direction. Jess opened the front gate, and followed them as they ran up the steps to the verandah.

"What happened to your hand, ma?" asked Edward, always the curious one.

"I had an accident," said Jess, as she unlocked the front door.

"What kind of accident?" persisted Edward.

"I grazed it on a wall." Jess didn't want to explain the circumstances to the boys.

Edward's brow was furrowed. "That doesn't sound like an accident."

"Well it was, now stop asking questions and change out of your school clothes. You both have chores to do before tea."

No more was said. The boys went to their room, and Jess gave a small sigh of relief. It was time to prepare tea, and wait for Beau to come home.

*

Jess heard the squeak of the front gate, and stood in front of the stove until she heard Beau step on to the back verandah. She heard him removing his shoes, and then the door opened. His smile faded as he looked at her, and immediately he saw that something was amiss.

"What's wrong?"

Jess's throat was working, but no words would come. Beau crossed the kitchen in two strides, and placing his hands on her arms, tried to draw her to him, but she resisted.

"Jess! What is it?" Slowly she lifted her hand so that he could see it. Beau let go of her arms, and took her hand in his. "How did you do this?" He prodded her knuckles gently.

"Sid," was all she could whisper.

"Sid O'Connor?" His voice was sharp and his eyes narrowed. "Sid O'Connor did this?"

Jess nodded mutely.

"How?" he steered her towards a kitchen chair. "I think you'd better tell me what happened."

Slowly Jess related what had taken place, including what Jean and Billy had said. Beau listened intently, and Jess watched the changing expressions on his face. When she stopped, he rubbed his hands through his hair in a gesture of frustration.

"You need to have him charged, Jess. He is not going to get away with this." He thumped a hand on the table, making the cutlery rattle.

"Beau, I'm sure he didn't intend for this to happen," whispered Jess.

"I don't care! It did happen, and one way or another, he is going to pay for it!"

"He was as shocked as I was, and I doubt very much whether anyone will find him now. He'll have gone into hiding. He seems to do that."

"Jess, I did warn you about him, but this is totally unexpected." Beau drew a shaky breath. "No-one could have predicted this."

"No." Jess took his hand. "I'm alright, Beau; just a little shaken up." She tried to smile. "No bones broken, so I suppose I can say I'm lucky."

"First thing tomorrow, we'll go to the police station and put in a complaint." As Jess tried to object, Beau placed a finger over her mouth. "No 'buts', Jess. This is a serious assault. Nobody does this to my girl and gets away with it." He drew her to her feet, and gathered her into his arms.

"Oh, Jess," he murmured against her hair, "this is all my fault. If I hadn't…"

"It's not your fault, Beau. Please don't blame yourself." Jess felt his body tremble, and knew that this incident had affected him deeply; how deeply remained to be seen.

*

Beau was not the only one affected by what had happened. Grace woke during the night, and her sobbing sent Jess running to see what was wrong. She lifted her up in her arms, and in spite of the pain in her hand, carried her back to her own bed. There she laid her between herself and Beau, and held her tight, whispering words of reassurance until the nightmare subsided, and Grace was asleep. Jess didn't sleep, however, and spent the remainder of the night going over what had happened, and wondering if it could have been avoided.

By the time daylight filtered through the bedroom window, she was stiff from lying in the one position, and mentally drained. Beau had managed to sleep through most of the drama, for which Jess was extremely thankful, and now it was time to rise and face the day ahead.

Seeking Retribution

At nine-thirty, Jess, Beau and Grace stood in the Police Station, facing a burly Constable, who stood frowning at them from behind a glass partition.

"You want to file a complaint against a Sid O'Connor?" His thick eyebrows beetled.

"That's right," said Beau. "He assaulted my wife yesterday, outside the Grey Goose Hotel."

"The hotel?" He looked from one to the other. "Had he been in there?"

"No," said Jess quickly, "but he had been drinking."

"I see. And you, ma'am, had you been in the hotel?"

"No! I was making my way home from the station, and he came up behind me."

"Any provocation?"

"Absolutely not!" Beau was barely holding on to his anger.

"If you don't mind, sir," said the constable patiently, "I need to ask your wife these questions, to ascertain the background."

Jess could hear Beau grinding his teeth in agitation, so she laid a hand on his arm, and managed a smile. "It's alright, Beau. I can answer the questions."

"Were there any witnesses to this assault?"

Jess shook her head. "Only my daughter."

"The child?" The constable scowled down on Grace, who stared up at him with wide eyes.

"Yes. Grace was with me when it happened."

"We can rule her out as a witness," said the constable. "She's too young."

"You can see what he did to my wife," said Beau, taking Jess's wounded hand and showing it to the constable. "I want him charged."

The constable held up his hands. "First things first, sir, if you don't mind." He looked at Jess. "And you say you didn't provoke him?"

"No. I tried to get away from him, and he followed me."

"And what did he say, exactly?" The constable chewed on the end of a pencil, before poising it over a notebook.

Jess went through the incident, and the constable wrote in his notebook, stopping her every now and then, to question a comment.

Finally he closed the book, and looked at the trio before him.

"Right!" he said matter-of-factly. "I've got all that." He peered at Beau. "It seems he was angry with you, sir, am I right?"

"No doubt he was," said Beau stiffly, "but he had no right to take it out on my wife."

"Have you had trouble with him before?" The constable looked from one to the other.

"Yes," said Jess.

"Reported?"

"No."

The constable sighed. "Very well, we'll look into it." He looked them over once more. "You may go. We'll be in touch. In the meantime, I suggest you stay out of his way."

"Jess, I don't want you home alone while I'm at the Surgery. Please take Grace to Margaret's, and stay there until I come home." They were standing on the footpath outside the Police Station, and Beau took hold of Jess's arm, forcing her to look at him. "Did you hear me, Jess?"

"Yes, Beau, I heard you. I don't think it's a good idea for me to be at Margaret's all day."

"Where else can you go?"

Jess thought for a moment. "Mary and George are still at Louise's place, and it's not far from the surgery. We could go there, but I don't want to stay all day. I can't stay all day."

"I want you safe, Jess, and while that man is at large, you are not safe."

"I'll stay until school finishes, and then I'll walk home with the boys."

Beau nodded. "Alright, but please, Jess, don't put yourself in harm's way."

"I won't, Beau." Jess touched his cheek. "I really think that Sid is no longer in town."

"I hope you're right." Beau looked at his fob watch. "I must get to work." He leaned forward and kissed her cheek. "Promise me you'll go straight to Louise's place, and no detouring on the way?"

"I promise." Jess smiled at his concern.

Within fifteen minutes, Jess and Grace were standing at Louise's front door. Jess rang the doorbell, and it was Mary who answered.

"Jess! Come in! George and I were going to call in on you on our way to the station this afternoon." She opened the door. "We're heading back to Melbourne on the two o'clock train."

As Jess and Grace were ushered into the hallway, Louise appeared at the kitchen door, wrapped in an apron, her hands covered with flour.

"Jess! How wonderful! Can you guess what I'm doing?"

"Making scones, if I'm not mistaken," answered Jess, smiling.

"Yes, and you're in time for morning tea. I was showing off my skills to Mary." She stopped. "Goodness gracious! What have you been doing to yourself?" Louise had spotted Jess's hand.

"It's a long story," sighed Jess.

"We've got time, haven't we, Mary?" Louise bustled back into the kitchen.

"Yes, of course."

Jess followed Mary into the warmth of the large kitchen, and was immediately ushered to a chair. Grace scrambled on to her knee, and buried her face in Jess's coat.

"Hello Gracie." There was silence. "We're not talking today?" Louise looked meaningfully at Jess.

"Apparently not." Jess ruffled Grace's hair.

Louise shrugged, and pulled out a chair. "Well, Jess, you'd better tell us what happened." She looked up at the clock above the range. "The scones will be ready in ten minutes."

The women sat silently while Jess related what had transpired the previous day, and what had led up to it. Their eyes opened with horror at what had happened to their friend, so soon after the wonderful celebrations that they'd all enjoyed.

"Beau doesn't want me home on my own, until Sid is apprehended, so that's why I've come here, but I'd say Sid is no longer in town."

"How awful for you!" Louise looked at Grace, still tucked up against her mother. "And Gracie was with you? No wonder she's upset, poor little mite." She stood up, and grabbed a pot mitt from beside the range. "Maybe a scone will do the trick."

Louise opened the oven door, and the aroma of fresh baked scones filled the kitchen. She pulled out the tray and sat it on the top of the range. Pulling a couple of scones apart, she checked the bottoms to make sure they were cooked. Jess smiled to herself. That was one instruction she hadn't forgotten. Louise saw the smile.

"I've remembered everything, Jess!" she boasted, as she tipped the scones on to a tea towel and wrapped the corners over the top. "Five more minutes and we can eat these beauties."

The sound of a baby crying caused Grace to come out of hiding. She looked up at her mother.

"I can hear a baby, ma."

"Yes, Grace, it's baby Jack. Do you want to go and see him?"

Grace nodded.

"Come with me," said Mary, holding out her hand.

Jess breathed a sigh of relief as Grace took Mary's hand and went with her.

"She's been very clingy since yesterday," she said to Louise, who was splitting the scones with a knife.

"I'm not surprised." Louise reached for the butter dish. "I'm so proud of my efforts, Jess. Even Raymond is impressed." She smiled benignly.

"Is he ready to take you to Melbourne with him?"

"Let's just say it's beginning to look like a possibility." Her eyes were shining.

"That's wonderful, Louise!"

"Mary has been so helpful, Jess. She's given me lots of ideas to throw open at our next meeting. I feel as though I've been given a second chance, and I want to prove to the ladies, and Raymond, that I can do a good job."

"And you will, Louise." Mary stood in the kitchen doorway, her child on her hip, and Grace beside her. "I have no doubt about that."

Louise flushed. "Thank-you, Mary. It's wonderful knowing that I have so much support." She breathed deeply, "I think we're ready to eat."

"We'd better leave some for George and Raymond," laughed Mary.

"Where are they?" enquired Jess.

"Raymond took George to show him our hospital, and the facilities we have for influenza patients," said Louise. "They'll be home in time for lunch."

Mary looked up at the kitchen clock above the range. It was eleven o'clock. "I hope so. We'll have to get packed as soon as George returns."

"Plenty of time, Mary!" Louise fluttered her hands in the air. "Let's enjoy these first."

*

"Are you sure you don't want me to drop you off at home, Jess?" shouted Louise above the roar of the car engine.

"Yes, I'm sure!" replied Jess, who was sitting in the passenger seat, Grace on her lap. "I need to go to the school and wait for the boys."

"Right!" Louise changed gears with an ominous screech, and the Wolesley jerked away from the train station. "I'm going to miss Mary and George."

"They knew Jack during the war."

"Yes, Mary told me. They even named their baby after your Jack." Louise looked sideways at Jess's profile. "That was a great honour, Jess."

"Yes, it was." Jess tightened her grip on Grace.

Louise was silent as she drove towards the school. Mary had filled her in on many things over the past two days, including the death of her friend, Meg Harper, and the subsequent letter from Beau. It seemed that life was full of surprises, and now she, Louise, had a few surprises of her own to share, in due course. She smiled smugly.

The Wolesley pulled up in front of the school, and Jess lifted Grace from her lap.

"Thank-you, Louise. I'm grateful for your time and the ride." Jess pushed the door open, and stepped on to the running board. Grace jumped to the ground.

"My pleasure, Jess. Take care of yourself." The gears grated as Jess stepped on to the road, and with a wave, Louise accelerated away.

Jess watched her disappear around the corner, and then taking Grace by the hand, walked through the school gates. She was early, so she decided that it would be nice to sit in the mild winter sunshine, on the retaining wall that bordered the memorial garden. Here were the plants that the children had dedicated to those who had lost their lives during the war. Edward had planted a rose in memory of his father, and Jess looked at it now, as new growth was beginning to sprout from its branches. So much had happened since then, and was still happening. Looking down at her hand, now scarred and swollen, she was reminded of the panic she had seen in Sid's eyes. Did she want retribution or did she just want him to disappear and never return?

"Mrs. DuBois?" Jess looked up to see Mr. Granger staring at her.

"Oh, Mr. Granger, I didn't hear you coming."

"I'm sorry if I startled you." He sat on the wall some distance away from Jess and Grace. "I have been meaning to get in touch with you regarding the position I had promised you here at the school." His pale face flushed slightly, and he ran his fingers through his thinning grey hair. "It was taken out of my hands, you see, and there wasn't much I could do about it."

"Don't apologise, Mr. Granger." Jess smiled reassuringly. "I understand."

"We have a young lady by the name of Beatrice White, I suppose Edward has told you, and she is doing a marvellous job. The reading levels have improved, I'm pleased to say."

"That's wonderful!" enthused Jess, as she tried to think whether Edward had told her about Miss White. "As things stand, at home, I may have had difficulty anyway."

Mr. Granger stood. "That's a relief to me." He coughed. "Are you waiting for your boys?"

"Yes, I am."

"Why don't you come into the staffroom and wait."

"No, it's quite nice out here in the sun."

He looked at his watch. "They won't be much longer. Good day to you, Mrs. DuBois."

*

"Are you sure you'll be alright, Jess?" It was the following morning, and Beau was ready for work.

"I've left the hospital number near the telephone if you need to contact me. Keep the doors locked, and please make sure you know who's on the other side, if anyone does come."

"Beau, stop fussing!" Jess was mildly exasperated. "I'll be alright." Beau was on the footpath with the bicycle, and Jess was on the verandah. She flapped her hands at him. "Go, or you'll be late!"

Beau gave her a searching look before straddling the bicycle and moving out on to the road. Jess watched him ride away, and sighed. She was not used to being under such careful scrutiny, and she looked forward to getting on with her work uninhibited. Grace also needed some normality. She had spent the previous night in their bed, and Jess knew that it was something that would have to stop. Beau was a very patient man, but she could see that patience wearing thin if Grace persisted with her tears. With the promise of a visit to the park, Jess was able to convince Grace that it was time to sleep in her own bed. There was nothing to fear now.

The day passed uneventfully, and Jess was able to complete most of the tasks she had set herself. Washing the bed-sheets was something she was unable to do, because of the heavy lifting, so she decided to leave those until Beau could help her.

Her mind shifted to Margaret several times during the day, but a walk around to see her was out of the question. She was debating on whether to telephone her, when it rang shrilly, making her jump. Jess picked up the receiver.

"Hello," she said into the mouthpiece.

"Mrs. DuBois?" a heavy male voice shouted in her ear.

"Yes."

"Senior Constable Whitley here, from the Bendigo Police Station."

Jess's heart gave a skip. "Yes." Her mouth was dry.

"You'll be pleased to know that we have Mr. Sidney O'Connor apprehended and here at the station." He paused. "Actually he was brought in by a Mr. William Maitland."

"Billy?"

"You know him?"

"Yes, I know him."

The constable laughed. "They both look as though they've been in a bit of a scuffle, so when we've had a chance to interview them, we'll let you know the results."

"Thank-you."

"My pleasure. You can enjoy the rest of your day now."

The receiver went down at the other end of the line, and Jess breathed a sigh of relief. Sid was no longer a threat, but Billy could find himself in a whole lot of bother. He had certainly tracked Sid down very quickly, and what had transpired between the two of them, Jess could only guess.

She picked up the paper with the hospital telephone number written on it, and put through a call. A receptionist answered. "Bendigo Hospital. How may I help you?"

"It's Jess DuBois speaking. Could I leave a message for Doctor DuBois, please?"

"The doctor is on his rounds, but I can track him down if you want to speak with him."

"Could you?"

"Certainly. Wait right there."

Jess waited, and was about to replace the receiver, when she heard Beau's voice.

"Jess!" He was out of breath.

"Beau, have you been running?"

"Yes. Are you alright?"

"Of course." Jess heard his sigh of relief. "I'm calling to tell you that Sid is at the Police Station. He was brought in by Billy Maitland."

"What did you say?"

"Billy took Sid to the station, and by all accounts, the two of them had been in a scuffle."

Beau laughed. "So Billy beat me to it, did he?"

"Beau, don't say things like that!" Jess was horrified.

"Well, Billy has saved me the trouble. I don't mind telling you, Jess, that had I been the one to find him, I would have…"

"Don't tell me, Beau! I don't want to know."

He drew a deep breath. "You're safe from him, that's the main thing, and I can concentrate on my work now. I'd like to know how Billy managed it."

"We'll hear soon enough."

Billy and Sid

Senior Constable Whitley replaced the telephone receiver, and looked across the top of his spectacles at the two battered and bloodied individuals standing before him.

"Well, Mr. Maitland, you've saved us the job of tracking this fellow down."

"My pleasure!" rasped Billy, through a mouthful of blood.

The constable turned his attention to Sid. "You've got some charges to answer for, Mr. O'Connor, and some explaining to do."

"I never meant to hurt 'er!" Sid spluttered, as Billy held fast to his sleeve.

"Then why did ya scarper?"

"I was scared."

"Scared?" Billy snorted scornfully. "You're a bloody coward, that's what you are, Sid O'Connor! It's time you got your comeuppance, an' I'm here t'see that you do."

"Alright, Mr. Maitland, we'll take care of things now," said the constable, removing Billy's hand from Sid's arm. "You're coming with me, Mr. O'Connor, and I'd like you to wait here, Mr. Maitland, if you don't mind. We will need to talk to you, too."

"I ain't goin' anywhere." Billy looked around for a chair, spotted one near the main door, and sat, crossing his arms in a gesture of satisfaction.

The Senior Constable raised his eyebrows, before steering Sid towards a door that led into a passageway.

"In here, Mr. O'Connor, if you please." He opened another door, on which was a gold-plated sign that read: Interview Room. Inside were a table and two chairs.

"Sit yourself down, Mr. O'Connor, and take off your cap, if you please." He called out into the passageway. "Constable Douglas, can you please come to the interview room?"

Sid sat on one of the straight-backed wooden chairs and removed his greasy cap, twisting it nervously in his hands. The Senior Constable sat opposite him, his beefy arms resting on the table between them. He stared at Sid for several moments, before a thickset constable entered the room, and stood with his arms akimbo behind his senior officer. Sid swallowed hard as Constable Whitley removed a notebook from his breast pocket.

"Now, Mr. O'Connor, I have had a complaint against you, from a Mrs. DuBois." He flicked open the pages of the notebook. "She says you followed her up the street, grabbed her wrist, and then flung her hand back against the brick wall of the Grey Goose Hotel, causing her injury." He looked at Sid over his spectacles. "Is that a correct account of the situation?"

"I never meant to hurt her, honest!"

"But nevertheless you did, it seems."

"I was angry."

"With Mrs. DuBois?"

Sid cleared his throat. "No, I was angry with that husband of hers. It was his fault that I… that I had me job taken away from me."

"And what job was that, Mr. O'Connor?"

Sid shifted uneasily on the seat. "Deliverin' their wood."

"That brings me to another issue, Mr. O'Connor."

"What's that?" Sid looked from one burly policeman to the other.

"We have found some outstanding complaints on you, pertaining to the theft of firewood."

Sid shook his head. "No proof o'that," he muttered belligerently.

"No, well anyway, I'm going to put you in the lockup for the night." The Senior Constable sat back on his chair, and grinned sardonically at Sid. "That way you can think about what you've done. You'll then be issued with a summons to appear before the Magistrate, and I can assure you, he won't be as easy on you as I have been. Keep out of trouble, Mr. O'Connor, and if you go anywhere near the plaintiff, Mrs. DuBois, you will find yourself incarcerated quicker than you can say Jack Robinson. Do I make myself clear?"

"Yes, sir," said Sid sullenly.

"Very well. Constable Douglas, take this man away, and send in Mr. Maitland, if you will."

*

Billy sat on the chair recently vacated by Sid, and folding his arms, looked squarely at the Senior Constable.

"So are ya goin' to lock 'im up?"

"Not so fast, Mr. Maitland." The Senior Constable considered Billy for a moment. "What's the problem with your voice?"

"Gassed durin' the war," rasped Billy.

"You were on the Front then?"

"Yeah. Survived against the odds. Some o' me mates weren't so lucky."

"And you have a history with Mr. O'Connor?"

"Ya could say that. Him an' me went to school together, but there was never any love lost between us." Billy shifted his position as the steely eyes surveyed him. "Then when I was doin' me trainin' at Williamstown, he stole me girl, an' I was nearly thrown out o' the army over that. Never did forgive 'im for makin' a fool o'me. Actually they both made a fool o'me." He shrugged. "Oh well, I was better off in the army, as it happens."

"What happened the other day, when Mr. O'Connor assaulted Mrs. DuBois? Were you there?"

"No, but I was in the pub, an' I saw her when she came in t'see Mrs. O'Malley. All upset she was, an' her hand all bloodied. I told 'er I'd find the little weasel, an' fix 'im proper."

"Which you did, obviously."

"Yeah." Billy wiped a hand across his mouth. "He wasn't hard t'find. I know all his hidin' places."

"He has several?"

"Yeah. Ev'ry time 'e's in trouble, 'e goes bush."

"He's in trouble a lot?"

Billy laughed. "He attracts trouble like flies to a carcass."

The Senior Constable studied Billy over his spectacles. He could sense that the lad was eager to exact revenge on the hapless Mr. O'Connor.

"You would like to see him behind bars?"

"Bloody oath I would," snarled Billy. "He's a menace to society. Lock 'im up an' throw away the key, I say."

"I should lock you both up, you know?"

"What for?" Billy sat forward. "What 'ave I done?"

"Breach of the peace. You were both involved in a brawl."

"I apprehended a felon," said Billy smugly, pleased with his explanation. "Saved you the job."

The Senior Constable laughed. "Yes, I suppose you did. Go on, get out of here, but don't go nicking off. We'll want to talk to you again."

The metal chair scraped on the floor as Billy stood. He touched his forehead in a mock salute.

"Yes sir!" he rasped, and stalked from the room. Constable Whitley shook his head, straightened the papers on the table, and muttered to himself.

"Both a pair of drongos, I reckon." He lifted his heavy body from the chair. "Time to give Mrs. DuBois a call, and give her the good news."

*

"What!" Beau thumped his hand on the kitchen table. "Jess, are you telling me that Sid O'Connor will be free to walk the streets again tomorrow?"

"Yes, Beau, I'm afraid he will."

"That's outrageous! What did the Senior Constable say exactly?"

"He said that Sid will be freed from the lockup tomorrow morning, and will then await the Magistrate's pleasure. He has been warned to stay away from us, and if he does come near, we are to contact the police immediately."

Beau looked keenly at Jess. "That is not good enough, Jess. He should have been remanded in custody until his hearing date."

"It's alright, Beau." Jess reached across the table and took his hands in hers. "He won't come near us, and I'm sure Billy will be keeping a close eye on him."

Beau ran his thumb across her scarred knuckles. "How did Billy find him?"

"I'm not sure, but he gave him a belting, by all accounts." Jess laughed softly.

"Hm. I need to be sure you and Gracie are safe here during the day, while I'm not here."

"I'll spend some time with Margaret, if that will make you happier."

Beau grinned. "Yes, it will."

"And," said Jess with a mischievous smile, "I've persuaded Grace to sleep in her own bed."

"So I get my wife back, do I?"

"I thought you'd be pleased." Jess sighed. "I'm afraid I had to use bribery."

"Oh?"

"Yes, I promised her a visit to the park."

"Make it the week-end, and we'll all go."

"A picnic?"

"Why not? It will make a nice change."

Deadly Consequences

Jess and Grace hurried around to Margaret's the following afternoon, to keep good the promise to Beau. Margaret was in bed, and her pale face brightened when she saw her granddaughter. Charles was relieved to see them, and confessed to Jess that he needed to check on his workmen. The new foreman was doing a sterling job, but they needed to see the boss once in a while.

Jess agreed, and told him to do what he had to do. She would remain with

Margaret until he returned. Charles smiled his gratitude and reached for his hat.

"I shouldn't be long, Jess," he said as he headed for the back door.

"Don't worry, Charles," she called after his retreating figure, "I'm sure Gracie will keep Margaret amused for the rest of the afternoon."

The door slammed and he was gone. How long was this going to continue, Jess wondered, as she walked slowly to the bedroom. She heard laughing as she reached the door, and Grace was showing her grandmother how she could turn somersaults on the floor. Jess stood and watched the antics for a few moments, before entering the bedroom.

"Show grandma how you can stand on your hands, Gracie."

Grace obliged, and Margaret clapped her hands. "Maybe you should join the circus, Gracie," she said, as Grace returned to her feet, and readjusted her pinafore.

"Don't tell her that, Margaret!" laughed Jess. "She might take you seriously." She straightened the covers on the bed.

"What happened there, Jess?" Margaret asked, pointing to Jess's hand.

"Oh, that was an accident." Jess looked quickly in Grace's direction, but the child was now preoccupied with a box of Margaret's gloves.

"Do you want to tell me about it?" Margaret was looking keenly at Jess. "It looks serious."

Jess sat on the side of the bed. "I had a run-in with Sid O'Connor."

"The woodman?" Margaret's eyes widened. "He did that?"

Jess frowned. "I don't think he meant to."

"Tell me about it."

Jess was reluctant to burden Margaret with the details of the altercation, but she insisted, so the story came out while Margaret leaned back on her pillows, her face a study of anxiety.

"Oh, Jess," she breathed. "That's awful!"

"Of course, Beau blames himself." Jess sighed. "He always does."

"No, he couldn't have predicted this." Margaret eased herself up from her pillows. "Sid has always been a problem. He grew up without his parents, you know. His grandfather was supposed to be responsible for him, but I don't think he cared for him, and he certainly didn't look after him. Whatever Sid has done, he's done it by himself."

"I was prepared to give him another chance," said Jess, "with certain conditions, but it didn't work out, so Beau asked Albie Blake to deliver our wood."

Margaret shook her head sadly. "Will he go to gaol?"

"I don't know, Margaret. That will depend on the Magistrate."

"Life can be very unkind to some people, Jess."

"Yes, it can." Jess noticed tears on Margaret's lashes. "I'll make us a cup of tea."

*

It was just after midnight when it happened. First there was a cracking, splintering sound, followed by a heavy thump. The curtains in the bedroom billowed and then cascaded to the floor beside the bed. Beau was awake instantly, and reached for the bedside lamp.

"What was that?" Jess struggled into a sitting position.

"I think it was something being thrown through our window." The lamp sprang into life, and Beau could see the shattered remains of the window, and splintered glass scattered across the floor.

He sat on the edge of the bed, staring out on to the dark street. "This is Sid's doing."

Jess clutched her nightdress to her as a cold draught of air hit her. She began to tremble as the fog of sleep lifted, and her brain told her that Beau was right. It had to be Sid.

Beau clambered over Jess, and headed for the door. In the passage she heard him fumbling for the light switch. When the passage flooded with light, she heard him lift the telephone receiver.

"Bendigo Police Station, please," she heard him say.

Beau kept his voice low, so Jess could only make out a little of the conversation, and within a couple of minutes she heard the receiver go down. Beau stepped back into the bedroom. Jess's heart constricted as she stared at him, standing there in only his pyjama pants and singlet. His face was grey in the guttering light from the bed-lamp.

"I am so sorry," he whispered.

Jess held out her arms. "Beau, come here." He moved slowly towards her and she placed her arms around him. "This is not your fault, so please don't keep saying you're sorry."

He sat on the bed beside her, and they held each other tight, while cold air from outside seeped in through the shattered window. Finally Beau stirred.

"I'd better get dressed. The police will be here shortly."

"In that case, I'll get my dressing gown on." Jess swung her legs over the side of the bed. "I hope all this hasn't woken the children." She reached for her gown. "I'll shut their doors."

*

Within half an hour, they heard the sound of heavy boots on the front verandah. Beau opened the door and hushed the young constable who stood there.

"The children are asleep," he whispered, "we'd like them to stay that way."

"Right you are, sir," said the fair-haired young man with a wide smile. "Lead me to the damage, if you please."

Jess was standing beside the bed as they entered, and the young policeman acknowledged her.

"Sorry to disturb you, ma'am," he said as he removed his helmet and tucked it beneath his arm.

"I've already been disturbed," murmured Jess, as she glanced towards the window.

"Yes, I see."

The policeman trod carefully across the shattered glass and fallen curtains, until he found the cause of the damage; a red house brick. He picked it up.

"Who would want to do this?" he muttered, turning the brick over in his hand. "It could have killed one of you."

"Yes, it could have!" said Beau angrily. "There's only one person who could have done this."

"You believe you know who did this?" the young constable looked keenly at Beau.

"Yes, I do. It was Sid O'Connor."

"I've heard that name recently. He was brought in for questioning on another charge, I believe?"

"He assaulted my wife!"

"Ah! The penny drops. You believe he has done this to get back at you?"

"Certainly he has," said Beau sharply. "Who else would do such a thing?"

The constable shrugged. "I don't know," he said slowly. "You tell me."

"Nobody!"

The constable looked around the room once more. "I suggest you remove the broken glass, and cover the window with something substantial. I'll take this brick with me." He smiled at the two watching him. "In the morning we'll bring Mr. O'Connor in for questioning, and in the meantime, I suggest you try to get some sleep."

"Sleep!" groaned Jess, after the young constable had gone. "I don't think that's going to happen."

"I think it is, Jess, but first, let's get this mess cleaned up and that hole blocked. Tomorrow I'll get on to a glazier."

*

Sid O'Connor sat facing Senior Constable Whitley, his arms crossed and his thin face set in a scowl. Whitley stared at him across the top of his spectacles.

"What did I tell you, Mr. O'Connor, about going near Mrs. DuBois?"

"Dunno what you mean." Sid glowered at the police officer.

"Where were you last night, at twelve o'clock?"

"In bed asleep."

"Anyone vouch for that?"

"Nope."

"Well, I'd like to suggest that you weren't in bed, that in fact you were in Oleander Street."

"What would I be doin' there at that time o'night?"

"You tell me." Whitley held his gaze, until Sid shifted uneasily on the chair, uncomfortable under the unwavering scrutiny. "I'll tell you why you were there, Mr. O'Connor. See this house brick?" He indicated the red brick sitting on the table between them.

"Yeah. What of it?"

"I believe you threw this brick through the window of a certain house in Oleander Street."

"Why would I do that?"

"Because you were still angry with the DuBois's."

Sid sat back on the chair, his bottom lip stuck out belligerently. "I never threw no brick!"

"No? Are you willing to swear that in court? Under oath?"

There was silence, as Sid contemplated his future. "They shouldn't've lost me my job," he muttered finally, staring at the floor.

Whitley drew a deep breath. "So you're now saying that you did throw this brick through the window of Mr. and Mrs DuBois's house?"

Sid nodded bleakly. "I s'pose I am."

"Do you realise that you could have killed somebody?" Whitley shook his head. "This means that you are going to have to be remanded in custody until appearing before the Magistrate. You should have heeded my warning, Mr. O'Connor. I did give you the chance to redeem yourself. Now you've only managed to make things much worse." He sighed. "We'd better get the paperwork done."

"Tell me somethin'. How'd you find me so quick?"

Whitley stared at the bruised, unshaven face before him. "We have our methods, Mr. O'Connor."

"It was Maitland, wasn't it?"

"I told you we have our methods."

Sid nodded his head. "Yeah, it was Maitland alright."

*

Jess replaced the receiver, and stood for a moment. They would not have to worry about Sid O'Connor for the foreseeable future. He had finally admitted to having thrown the brick, and would remain in custody until his hearing. She let out a deep sigh. It meant that she and Beau would have to attend the hearing, or send a written statement. She knew that Beau would be in favour of attending, whereas she felt somewhat diffident, knowing that a lot of past history could be dragged up. She didn't want that. She just wanted this last incident to be put to rest.

The sound of hammering broke into her thoughts. Beau had made contact with a local glazier, and he had come straight away. They had spent one cold, draughty night, and she didn't relish the thought of another. It seemed they wouldn't have to, after all.

A Picnic In The Park

The week passed without further incident. Beau was relieved that Sid was no longer a threat, and his mood lightened considerably. Jess noticed that he was spending more evening time with Edward, teaching him the finer skills of riding a bicycle. Edward was taking to it like a duck to water, and Jess would stand on the front verandah, in the twilight, watching them going back and forth along the road, until it was too dark to see.

Grace kept her to the promise of having a picnic, so when the following Sunday arrived, a hamper was prepared, and they all set off for the park. Jess had made the tentative suggestion to Charles that Margaret might like to come and sit with the family, and he had agreed, on condition the weather was favourable. He had borrowed a wheelchair from the hospital, and was able to stow it in the back of the car. Margaret was looking forward to being in the fresh air, and as the day dawned with the promise of sunshine and no wind, there was no reason why she couldn't join in the family fun. The past week had been harrowing, and they all needed a taste of normality.

Edward had been howled down when he had suggested that he ride the bicycle, and had to be content with taking the cricket set. Jess watched the two boys now as they walked ahead, Edward carrying the wickets and Ben carrying the bat and ball. She suddenly realised how much they had grown over the past few months, and was shocked to see that Edward was as tall as Ben, as they walked side by side, their heads close together.

Grace skipped ahead of the boys, and was happy to announce to anybody who cared to listen, that they were going on a picnic. Jess smiled to herself. Her baby was growing too fast, and at four, would soon be ready for school. Jess wondered fleetingly whether she would have any more babies. She glanced covertly at Beau, striding beside her and carrying the food hamper. He caught her glance, and smiled. It was in that moment that Jess could suddenly see Jack, and the memory of their final picnic. She turned away, her eyes prickling.

"What's wrong?" Beau sensed the change in her mood.

"Nothing." Her voice was husky.

"Jess? Out with it?"

"Memories, Beau. Precious memories." She turned to look at him.

"You're allowed to have your memories, Jess. They will always be there." He took her hand.

"They come when I least expect them."

"I know they do." Beau looked ahead to where the children were getting away from them. "Come on, my love, we'd better hurry. We don't want the children reaching Charing Cross before we do. The road could be busy."

*

They all made it safely to the park, and arrived just as Charles pulled up in the car. Beau handed the hamper to Jess, and went to assist Charles in unloading the wheelchair. Grace jumped up and down eagerly beside the car, waiting for Margaret to be helped into the wheelchair.

"Grandma!" she squealed excitedly. "Are you having a picnic with us?"

"Yes, dear," replied Margaret, as Beau lifted her carefully into the awaiting wheelchair.

Charles tucked a rug around her legs, and adjusted the shawl across her shoulders.

"Are you comfortable, dear?" he asked anxiously.

"Yes, Charles," Margaret sighed, flapping her hands. "I'm perfectly alright."

Jess and Beau looked at one another and smiled. This was a new role for Charles, and he was certainly going out of his way to make life as easy for Margaret as he possibly could. No man could be expected to do more.

With Margaret settled, Charles took the handles of the chair, and set it in motion. The children walked alongside, Grace chattering nonstop to her grandmother.

"Would you like to play hopscotch with me, grandma?" she asked eagerly.

"Not today, dear," said Margaret, as she looked up at Jess. "I'll watch you play."

"You're going to play cricket with us," said Edward matter-of-factly, "aren't you, granddad?"

Charles looked a little nonplussed, and glanced quickly at Beau. "If you want me to, Edward."

"Yes!" Edward nodded vigorously. "We don't have a side, do we, Ben?" Ben shook his head. "But that doesn't matter. Ma, are you going to play?"

Jess laughed. "No, Edward! I'll prepare the lunch." She caught Beau's amused glance.

"Go on!" he whispered. "If you can ride a bicycle, you must be able to play cricket."

"Behave yourself, Beau," Jess chided. "I do not play cricket."

So with the activities settled, all they had to do was find a suitable spot to lay their picnic rug. The park was dotted with people enjoying the late August sunshine, and the rose gardens were beginning to come into bloom.

They chose a spot beneath a large Elm, where the sunlight dappled through the foliage, giving them just enough protection without being too shaded. Jess spread a large checked rug on the ground, and the hamper was placed in the middle. Charles wheeled Margaret to one side of the rug, where she could see everything going on around them.

Grace found a stick and scratched hopscotch in the gravel path nearby. Immediately she had two little girls wanting to play. Jess watched as Grace eagerly allowed them to join in. Edward and Ben set up the wickets further away from the picnic spot, and Charles and Beau reluctantly removed their jackets and rolled up their shirtsleeves. Margaret smiled as she watched the two men cross the grass towards the boys.

"We'll give them half an hour before we call them for lunch," said Jess, as she began to empty the hamper. "I know who will have had enough by then."

"So do I," said Margaret, with a chuckle.

When the food was set out on the rug, Jess sat beside the wheelchair, and watched the activities in front of her. She was reminded of that final day with Jack, when the boys had insisted that he play cricket with them. Was it three years ago? Grace was only eleven months old at the time. Now she was nearly four, and very much in charge of her game of hopscotch.

"She is so like you, Jess." Margaret's quiet voice broke into her thoughts.

"She's bossy!" laughed Jess.

"Not at all," said Margaret. "She's taking charge; being a leader."

"Is that what she's doing?"

"Yes."

They were silent for a few minutes as they watched and listened to their family enjoying themselves. Even Charles was laughing, which made Margaret smile.

"He'll be alright when I'm gone," she whispered. "He has you and Beau and the children."

Jess sucked in her breath, as the words hit her like an icy blast. She turned to look at Margaret, whose expression was serene, as though accepting of her fate. Jess reached across and took her hand, squeezing it gently.

"We'll look after him, Margaret," was all she could say as her vision blurred.

"That's all I need to know." Margaret took a deep breath. "Now let's enjoy today."

*

They all agreed that the day had been very enjoyable, and as they said their goodbyes to Charles and Margaret, Jess couldn't help but wonder whether there would be any more days like this. She kissed Margaret's pale cheek, and then promised Charles that she would drop in during the week, to give him a chance to attend to his own work.

The family stood and watched as the car moved away, before continuing on their way home. Grace chattered excitedly about her new friends, and Jess listened distractedly, hoping she was giving all the right answers, until Beau nudged her, bringing her attention back into focus.

"Your daughter is talking to you, Jess," he said quietly. "You're miles away."

"I know, Beau. I can't help thinking of Margaret. She put the tough word on me today."

"Which was?"

"She wanted to be sure that Charles will have you and me and the children when she is gone."

"I see." Beau knew that it was going to be hard for all of them when the time came. "What did you say to that?"

"I told her we'd look after him."

"Which we will. There's no need to get maudlin yet."

"You're sure of that?"

"No, but I did notice that she's eating well enough, and her conversation hasn't deteriorated."

"They're good signs?"

"When she only wants to sleep, then we'll worry." Beau smiled at her frowning countenance. "Now talk to your daughter before she bursts."

Jess felt slightly more at ease, so turned her attention to Grace.

*

The children were in bed, the stories had been read, and Jess had prepared the porridge oats for breakfast. After banking the fire for the night, she made sure there was enough kindling for the following morning. Everything was in order. She locked the back door, turned down the light, and headed into the passage to find Beau. He wasn't in the lounge, so she guessed that he was probably having a last cigarette out on the front verandah. It seemed to be what men liked to do.

She found him leaning on the verandah railing. He turned as Jess approached, and after butting out his cigarette, lifted his arm. Jess moved into his embrace, leaning her head against his shoulder.

"It's a lovely evening, isn't it?" They watched the crescent moon slide behind a cloud.

"It's been a lovely day altogether." Beau squeezed her shoulder. "Where's your shawl?"

"I don't need it."

"The boys were delighted that Charles wanted to play cricket with them today. It's the first time he's done that."

"It is." Jess laughed. "I wouldn't say he wanted to; coerced more likely."

"Anyway, I do believe he enjoyed himself."

"That's good."

They were silent for a time, as they watched the moon reappear, throwing a faint glow over the dark street. The only sound was that of crickets connecting with each other in the damp earth. Beau turned Jess towards him, and wrapped both arms around her. They stood silently, locked together, as the pale moon played hide and seek with the clouds.

"I'm afraid sometimes," whispered Jess, "that I'm going to wake up one morning, and find that all this has been a dream."

"It's not a dream, Jess. It's all very real and…"

The shrill ringing of the telephone interrupted what Beau had been about to say.

"Who could that be at this time of night?" Jess pressed her hands to her face as they both turned towards the door.

Beau was the first to interrupt the sound before it woke the children. Jess turned up the passage light, and then stood behind him as he spoke into the mouthpiece.

"A call from Sydney? Yes, I'll hold the line." He looked at Jess. "Sydney," was all he said.

Jess's heart was hammering as they waited, and she feared the worst.

The seconds ticked by.

"Hello…yes…Clarence, is that you…No, it's not a good line. I can hardly hear you."

Silence again.

Jess watched Beau's face as he struggled to hear the message that Clarence was relaying. His face went deathly pale, and he leaned on the wall for support.

"I'll come right away," he said hoarsely, before returning the receiver slowly to its cradle.

"What's happened?" Jess grabbed his arm. "Is it Matthew?"

Beau nodded bleakly. "He's not expected to last much longer. Pneumonia has set in."

"Beau, I am so sorry." Jess wrapped her arms protectively about him, and felt his tears on her face. "You can't go until morning, so it will be two days before you reach Sydney."

"I know." Beau lifted his head. "It may be too late, but I have to go."

"Yes, of course you do."

"Raymond needs to know so that he can get a locum in for a few days." Beau brushed impatiently at his wet cheeks. "This couldn't have happened at a worse time, Jess."

"Don't think about it, Beau. You call Raymond, and I'll start packing your things."

Jess moved into the bedroom as Beau rang the exchange. No, it couldn't have come at a worse time, and Jess shook away the thoughts of what could happen while Beau was away. She pulled the Gladstone bag from the bottom of the wardrobe, and began flicking through Beau's clothing. How long would he be gone? He would need at least one change of clothing, plus his best suit. Matthew's death was imminent, so there would be a funeral to attend. Jess wished with all her heart that she could be with Beau, but that was impossible. She swallowed hard as she closed the bag and stood up. Beau appeared beside her.

"Raymond is going to hold the fort for the coming week," he said quietly. "I shouldn't be gone any longer than that."

Jess nodded mutely as they moved together in an embrace that held only anxiety and grief.

"I was going to say before the telephone interrupted me," said Beau against her ear, "that it's all very real and I'm not going anywhere. The reality is that nothing goes as expected, but I love you and that will never change."

Beau's Departure

The following morning, the boys were not impressed with the news that Beau was going to Sydney. They stared at him over their porridge bowls.

"Why?" asked Edward, his bottom lip stuck out belligerently.

"Because my best friend is very ill, and I need to see him," explained Beau carefully.

"How long will you be gone?" Ben was staring into his porridge.

"Not long, Ben. Possibly a week, but not longer." Beau looked at Jess standing beside him. "I need you both to take care of your ma while I'm away. Can you do that?"

"Yes," said Ben, picking up his spoon. "Dad said the same thing when he went away. He didn't come back." He stared up at Beau.

Jess gasped, and her hand flew to her mouth. "Ben! That was different. Your dad went to war."

"It's alright, Jess." Beau sat opposite Ben at the table. "You think I might not come back, Ben?"

Ben scowled. "Maybe."

"Ben, sometimes in life we have to do things that we feel are right, and not necessarily what we want to do. My best friend, Matthew, took care of me when I needed him most, and now I have to be there with him, when he needs me. Do you understand?" Ben nodded slowly. "I don't want to be that far away from your ma, and from you, but I must. You are my family, and I love you all. Please remember that, and I'll be back as quickly as I can be."

"Promise?"

"Yes, I promise."

Ben continued eating his breakfast, while Jess and Beau were both shaken by the moment and the revelation. Jess always knew that Jack's unexpected death had affected Ben deeply, but until this moment, she hadn't realised how deeply.

*

The mournful sound of the train whistle could be heard coming from further along the track. Beau placed his bag on the platform and turned to Jess, who was clutching Grace by the hand.

"Au revoir, my dears," he said softly. "I'll be back as soon as I can."

"Please take care, Beau, and give our love to everyone. I expect you will see Angela."

"I would think so." Beau put his arms around Jess, encompassing Grace as well. "I'm going to miss you," he whispered against Jess's ear.

"I'm going to miss you, too." She held him tight.

The train thundered into the station in a cloud of steam, enveloping all those on the platform. Beau picked up his bag, and with one final look at the two standing before him, made his way on to the train. Jess watched as he walked along the narrow corridor in search of a compartment. She held tightly to Grace, and tried to remain composed, although her heart was beating rapidly in her chest. This was a final goodbye for Beau and Matthew, and she wanted to be there to comfort him, when the time came. However it was not to be, and her mind kept leaping to the eventual goodbye with Margaret, hoping that it would not be while she was without Beau.

He appeared at a window, and leaned out to speak to her. At that same moment, the train lurched forward with a loud screech of wheels, and his voice was lost in the noise. She waved her hand as the train moved away, mouthing the words 'I love you' to the empty air. How many times had she been in this scenario? She wanted to scream 'take me with you!' but all she could do was watch as the train disappeared from her sight.

Grace was staring up at her with large eyes. "Has Beau gone, ma?"

"Yes, Gracie." Jess took a deep breath.

"So it's just us again?"

"For a little while, darling, and then he'll be back." As she spoke the words of reassurance to her daughter, Jess had an uneasy feeling in the pit of her stomach. She smiled down at Grace. "Come on, let's go home."

Her steps were heavy as she walked across the pedestrian bridge, and the uneasy feeling would not go away. The rhythmic rattle of the disappearing train kept saying to her, 'Beau has gone'.

Part Three

A Time To Love and a Time To Hate

Beau's Arrival

Beau stepped on to the platform, and the bustle of a city train station felt instantly familiar. He shouldered his way through the crowd, and hurried down the steps on to George Street. A tram rattled by, heading in the direction he wanted to go, so he ran alongside it, until it screeched to a halt. As passengers clambered out, others pushed their way on, and Beau joined them, managing to climb on board before the tram jerked into motion. He stood for the duration of the journey to Norlane Street, watching the familiar buildings as the tram rattled past them.

Finally the Clinic came into view, and Beau shouldered his way towards the doors. As the tram shuddered to a halt, he stepped out on to the road. Dodging a passing motorcar, he made his way to the footpath. The Clinic loomed above him, silent in the morning rush hour. He had arranged to meet Clarence here, and glancing along the street, saw Matthew's car parked some yards away.

The heavy doors of the building opened to his touch, and he stepped inside. The squeak of the linoleum beneath his feet was as if he had never left it. He walked slowly up the wooden staircase, breathing in the familiar smell of beeswax. At the top his footsteps faltered, as he gazed towards the door of Matthew's consulting-room, and then along the corridor to his own room. The sound of Clarence's voice came from the direction of the waiting room. Beau took a deep breath, and headed towards the sound.

He knocked on the door, and it was opened immediately. Clarence stood on the other side, his face haggard, and his appearance somewhat dishevelled. Beau saw Angela standing behind Celia's desk, and his face registered surprise.

"Ah, Beau!" Clarence sounded relieved. You're here at last."

"I hope I'm not too late."

"No, but we will have to get going immediately." Clarence looked at his pocket watch.

"Hello, Beau." Angela smiled at him.

"Hello Angela. I didn't expect to see you here."

"I'm helping out, while business is slow at the patisserie."

"I see."

Clarence turned to Angela. "You're in charge now, m'dear. The doctors should be here soon, and we'd better get going. It's a long drive to Willowbank."

Angela looked past Clarence to Beau. "I've packed you a hamper," she said, "in case you get hungry on the way."

"We're sure to," said Clarence as he moved to where Angela stood, and bent to kiss her cheek. "Thank-you, m'dear. We appreciate your concern for our welfare."

"Off you go." Angela handed Clarence a basket before giving him a gentle shove. Beau noticed that her cheeks had coloured slightly.

"Let's go, Beau." Clarence was already out the door. "Celia will be like a cat on hot bricks."

Beau smiled at Angela. "Jess sends her love," he said quickly, before following Clarence.

The door shut behind them, and Angela was left alone. She sighed. It was going to be a long day for them, and Beau looked exhausted after his train trip. Looking around the empty room, Angela prayed silently that they would get there in time. She reached for the files that were stacked on the desk. It was going to be a busy day.

*

It was late in the afternoon when the gates of Willowbank finally came into view. Clarence drove up the long steep drive until he reached a flat gravel area where he came to a halt. Beau had been sleeping for the greater part of the journey, and they had only stopped once, to refuel the car and to eat Angela's ham sandwiches and apricot tarts. These had been washed down with coffee from a flask that she had thoughtfully added to the basket.

"We're here, Beau," said Clarence, as he opened the door.

Beau rubbed his eyes and shook away the feeling of being woken suddenly. He had not had much sleep the night before, as he hadn't had time to organise a sleeping compartment, and so he had sat listening to the clatter of the wheels from Albury to Sydney.

As he stepped out of the vehicle, Beau saw a flash of black, and Celia came running down the steps, throwing herself into her father's arms with a cry of anguish.

"I'm so glad you're here!" she cried against Clarence's shoulder.

"Are we in time?" Clarence shot a look at Beau.

Celia nodded her head, and Beau sighed with relief.

"That's good." Clarence untangled himself from Celia's grasp.

She turned to Beau, and threw her arms around him, taking him off guard.

"Matthew has been waiting for you, Beau." She clung to him, her body shaking with sobs.

Beau took her shoulders and gently pressed her away from him. "He knows I'm coming?"

"Yes." Celia groped in her coat pocket for a handkerchief to wipe her tear-streaked face. "I told him he had to wait until you got here." She gulped.

Beau took her arm. "Then I'd better go and see him. Come on."

Clarence led the way up the stone steps and in through a wire door to a large vestibule with gleaming white linoleum and large urns of lush plants. They climbed a wide wooden staircase to the next floor, the layout reminding Beau of Serendipity. It was a grand building.

As they walked quietly along the corridor of the upper level, Beau pictured himself following Matthew as he strode the halls of Serendipity, looking for rooms to throw open to patients with influenza. It didn't seem so long ago that Matthew's energy was boundless. Beau's steps faltered now as they reached the room where Matthew lay. He didn't want to go in there.

Celia went in first, followed by Clarence, and lastly Beau, whose heart was pounding so loudly in his chest, that he feared they would hear it.

Celia sat beside the bed, and took Matthew's hand. "Beau's here, Matthew," she whispered.

Beau stood beside Celia and looked down on the figure lying on the bed, his face obscured by an oxygen mask. As his eyes locked with Matthew's, he saw only fear and helplessness.

"You sit here, Beau," said Celia, moving quickly to the window.

As Beau sat beside Matthew, he saw Clarence go to his daughter and place an arm protectively around her shoulders. Beau could hear the rattle of Matthew's chest as he struggled to breathe, and he knew that this was going to be a traumatic time for all of them.

He took his friend's hand and squeezed it gently. "Matthew," he said hoarsely, "I came as soon as I could." What could he say to his lifelong friend? "Please forgive me, Matthew," he whispered, tears of remorse and exhaustion sliding down his cheeks. "I let you down, and I am so sorry."

Matthew shook his head slowly, and with trembling fingers removed the mask from his face.

"Forgive me." It was so faint, Beau had to bend forward to hear him.

"For what, Matthew? You have done nothing wrong."

"Celia," was all he managed to say, before becoming distressed.

Beau replaced the oxygen mask, and sat back. Celia? What did he mean by that? He studied his friend's grey countenance on the white pillow, and pondered on what Matthew may have done that needed Beau's forgiveness. Did he blame himself for the breakdown of Beau's marriage with Celia? If so, that would have happened anyway, and Matthew needed to know that. Beau leaned forward.

"Matthew," he whispered, "you didn't take Celia away from me, if that's what is troubling you. We were over long before you stepped in." He placed his hand on Matthew's. "So there's no forgiveness necessary on your part, my dear friend."

Matthew closed his eyes, and his features suddenly relaxed.

"Matthew!" said Beau sharply, gaining the attention of Celia and Clarence.

They moved to the bedside, and Beau made way for Celia to sit beside her husband. The rattling in Matthew's chest slowed until there was hardly any movement at all. Celia stroked his face, as the tears streamed down her face. Beau choked back the tumult in his own breast, as he waited for Matthew's final moments.

They came quietly, peacefully, as the three looked on, and wondered what they would do now. When his final breath was taken, Celia laid her head against his breast and sobbed hysterically.

"No! Matthew, don't leave me!"

Clarence slipped out of the room, and went in search of a staff member, to let them know that Doctor Morley had gone, peacefully.

Beau stood weeping silently, with the knowledge that Matthew had waited for his arrival, to ask for his forgiveness before slipping quietly into the next world.

Celia raised her head, and looked at Beau through tear-filled eyes.

"What will I do now, Beau?" she whispered.

Beau took her arm, lifted her to her feet, and wrapped his arms around her.

"You'll carry on Matthew's work, Celia," he murmured into her hair.

"I don't have the heart for it."

"No, maybe not now, but you will, in time. You built that practice together, and you'll carry it forward, I have no doubt."

"You were there too, Beau."

"I know." Beau sighed, knowing that he had consciously walked away from it. "But it was yours and Matthew's, and his legacy is stamped on it."

"You can always come back, Beau." Celia lifted her head and stared intently at him.

"No I can't, Celia. I made my decision."

Celia moved out of his arms, and looked down on the now serene features of her husband. Bending over him, she kissed his grey cheek, and ran her fingers across his smooth brow.

"Good-bye, Matthew." Her voice choked. "Rest in peace, my darling."

Clarence returned at that moment with a doctor and two nurses, so Beau took Celia by the arm, and together they moved silently from the room. Clarence followed.

Returning to Sydney

Angela paced nervously around the waiting room, glancing every now and then out the window. The sky was overcast, and the view of the sea was grey and turbulent. She checked the street once more for a sign of Matthew's car.

They should be arriving soon. The Clinic had closed for the day, and the silence lay heavily around her.

At long last Angela spotted the car pulling in to the kerb. She walked quickly out into the corridor, and hurried down the stairs. Opening the heavy door to the street, she waited. Clarence was first, followed by Beau who was supporting Celia. They filed past Angela and headed up the stairs while Angela closed the door and followed. Nobody spoke.

Once in the waiting room, Clarence pulled off his thick coat and scarf, and sat heavily in the leather seat behind the desk. Beau made sure Celia was seated before he moved to the window and stared out across the bay.

"I have some sandwiches and hot coffee prepared for you," said Angela tentatively. "I thought you'd be hungry after your journey."

"Thank-you, m'dear." Clarence smiled up at her. "That would be lovely."

Beau moved to where Angela had set out cups and plates on a small table usually reserved for magazines. He put a couple of sandwiches on a plate, and poured a cup of coffee from the flask. Taking them across to Celia, who sat staring into space, he squatted down beside her.

"Celia, you need to eat something."

She turned to stare vacantly at him. "I'm not hungry," she murmured.

"Maybe not," insisted Beau, "but you have to keep your strength up."

"Why?" Her eyes stared dully into his.

"Because," said Clarence loudly, "we have a lot to do over the next few days, and you must have your wits about you."

Celia turned to stare at her father. "It will all have to wait," she said bitterly.

"It can't, I'm afraid." Clarence sighed heavily. "This Clinic needs to keep running."

Celia laughed harshly. "What if I don't want it to keep running?"

Clarence accepted a cup and plate from Angela. "You can't possibly mean that, Celia!" he said sharply. "Matthew put too much work into this place and Serendipity, for you to simply discard it!"

Celia dissolved into tears. "I'm sorry, Celia, but you need to hear this."

Beau stood and moved to the table where he poured himself a cup of coffee. His brain was fatigued, and he craved sleep after two sleepless nights. He needed to talk to Jess. She would be anxious to know what was happening. All of a sudden he felt so far away from the one person who could calm him with her gentle touch. He put his cup on the table.

"I need to make a call to Jess," he said, as he walked across the room to the telephone on the wall. The other three watched silently as he rang the exchange.

After several minutes he heard Jess's voice. "Beau, is that you?"

"Yes, my darling." He steeled himself against crying into the mouthpiece.

"What news do you have, Beau?" He was unable to speak for a moment, as he heard Celia weeping behind him. "Beau?"

"Matthew died just after I arrived, Jess."

There was silence on the other end of the line. "Oh, Beau, I am so sorry."

"I spoke to him briefly, and then…he was gone."

"And Celia? How is she?"

"It will take time, I'm afraid. We've just arrived from the Sanatorium, and are here at the Clinic, where Angela is plying us with food and hot coffee."

"That sounds like Angela." Jess paused. "So you'll be away for a while longer?"

"I'll have to wait until after the funeral, and that hasn't been arranged yet. I miss you, Jess."

"I miss you, too." Jess was close to tears. "Stay strong, my dearest, and give my love to Celia. I know how she must be feeling. It's the most devastating feeling on earth."

"I'll tell her you send your love." Beau heard the sound of the exchange about to interrupt. "I must go, Jess. I love you."

"I love you, too, Beau. Goodbye."

The line went dead. Beau slowly hung up the receiver.

"Jess sends her love," he said quietly.

*

Jess replaced the receiver and leaned against the wall. Suddenly all the uneasy feelings she had been experiencing since Beau's departure, evaporated, and she felt ashamed. He was devastated by the loss of his closest friend, and the grief was evident in his voice. How she wished she could be there to hold him, as he had been there for her during her time of grief.

"Ma, was that Beau?" Ben's voice broke through her thoughts.

"Yes, Ben."

"Is he coming home?"

Jess gave a watery smile. "Yes, he'll be home soon."

Ben seemed satisfied with that. "Can we have our bath now, Ma?"

Jess nodded. "Yes. I'll be there in a moment."

Matthew's Funeral

Celia stood before the cheval mirror in her bedroom, and surveyed the woman on the other side. Dressed in black from head to foot, she stared out at Celia through large tear-filled eyes. Her dark hair was pulled back severely and covered with a cloche hat and veil. The tailored suit hugged her slight body, and a fox fur draped itself around her shoulders. This was going to be a day like no other that she had experienced in her forty years. She ran a gloved hand across her pale cheek, and tried to pinch some colour there.

Matthew was gone, and she was now in full control of the Practice. The idea was daunting, and initially she had not been in favour of it, but Beau was right; she did have a duty to Matthew to continue his work. She knew she could do it, with her father's help.

A frown crossed her brow. Her father's association with Angela troubled her, but the woman was here to stay, that much was clear. Celia had to admit that her father was much more amenable since his relationship with Angela. She sighed heavily. If Beau would reconsider his position, then everything would fall into place, and her world would be as complete as it could be without Matthew. Did she have enough within her to convince him?

Celia straightened the front of her skirt, and pulled the black veil over her face.

A knock at the door made her turn.

"Are you ready, Celia?" It was Clarence.

"Yes, daddy, I'm coming." Celia walked resolutely to the door.

It had been Matthew's wish that he be buried on the grounds of Serendipity, so that was where they were all heading. The afternoon was mild, and sunshine squeezed through the clouds periodically, warming the air.

Celia walked slowly down the stairs to the living room. Clarence walked behind her, and at the bottom, Angela and Beau stood silently, both attired suitably in dark clothing. She managed a faint smile in their direction as she stopped at the foot of the stairs. Clarence moved to her side, and took her arm.

"Come, my dear," he said softly. "It's time to go."

Nobody spoke during the drive out to Serendipity. Celia sat in the passenger seat beside her father, while Beau and Angela squeezed into the back seat. The canopy was down, so they felt the sunshine while it was out and the faint breeze that stirred the trees alongside the road.

Beau thought back to his life here in the city, and while he didn't miss certain aspects of it, he missed the noise and constant bustle. People hurried along the streets, rather than dawdled, and that was something he still found hard to do. He smiled as he thought of Jess grabbing his arm and telling him to slow down. How he wished that she were seated beside him now, holding his arm and smiling up at him. He glanced at Angela. Her face was serene beneath the black netting that drifted down from her soft felt hat. She sensed his eyes on her and turned, smiling softly.

Clarence pulled into the gravel driveway, and drove slowly towards the Lodge. He heard Celia sigh softly, as they spotted people walking towards the rose garden. Near the large gumtree where Beau and Jess had been married, was a fresh gravesite, and beside it, Matthew's coffin. Celia whimpered as she saw it, and Clarence noticed how she clenched and unclenched her hands. He reached over and patted those hands gently.

"Be strong, my dear," he said softly.

As they all alighted from the vehicle, Beau saw Pastor Allenby hurrying towards them. As he glanced around the crowd gathering respectfully beside the grave, he saw Charlie Evans and his mother, Edwina. Charlie was waving at him, and smiling widely. He nodded his head in acknowledgement before moving to stand beside Celia. Clarence stood on the other side of his daughter, and Angela stood a little way behind them.

Pastor Allenby took Celia by the hand, and his ruddy face was sombre as he spoke to her.

"Mrs. Morley, my condolences on your loss. Doctor Morley will be greatly missed here at Serendipity, and as you can see, many patients have gathered to say their own goodbyes." Celia nodded stiffly. "When you are ready, we will begin the service. I have a seat for you if you wish to sit through the proceedings."

"Thank-you, but I will stand."

"As you wish." The Pastor shook Clarence by the hand, and moved across to Beau.

"Doctor DuBois, how nice to see you here. Everything is well with you, I trust?"

"Yes thank-you, Pastor, as well as can be expected."

"And Mrs. DuBois? She is well?"

"She is, thank-you."

The Pastor inclined his head to Angela, and moved swiftly to the front of the crowd. Raising his arms, he called for silence. "Let us begin." The crowd was hushed.

Clarence looked around for Angela, and beckoned her to his side. She moved silently, and he took her hand. His left arm he held protectively around his daughter. Beau stood with his hands clasped before him.

The Pastor began with the words: "The Lord giveth and the Lord taketh away."

As his words floated on the afternoon breeze, those gathered reflected on the influence Matthew Morley had had on their individual lives. Beau recalled the early days of boarding school, when he had suffered at the hands of bullies. Matthew had become his protector, and so life became bearable once again. Beau smiled as he recalled one particular incident, when the worst bully in the school had deliberately broken Beau's pencils and ruler, in front of a crowd of onlookers, and had flung the remnants into the air, shouting, "Catch them, DuBois, you miserable little Frenchie!"

He cringed now at the memory of what happened next. Matthew, a tall strapping lad, had charged at the perpetrator, grabbed him by the collar, and dragged him across the quadrangle to the Common Room. There he hung him up on a coat hook, and stood back, watching as the wretched boy wriggled and squirmed, and shouted abuse. Matthew, of course had received a caning from the Headmaster for his trouble, but was unremorseful.

"He won't bother you again, Beau!" he had laughed, slapping him on the back.

Beau blinked back the tears now as he stood listening to the final words of the service:

"Dust to dust, ashes to ashes; in sure and certain hope of the resurrection to eternal life, through our Lord Jesus Christ. Amen."

Beau could sense Celia trembling beside him as Pastor Allenby called for pallbearers to assist with the lowering of the coffin. He stepped forward, as did Clarence, Charlie and one of Matthew's security guards. Taking the ends of the two ropes, they slowly guided the coffin to the edge of the grave, and lowered it into the ground.

"I have rose petals from the garden here at Serendipity," said the Pastor, "for anyone who wants to scatter them on top of the coffin."

Two nurses walked through the crowd with cane baskets full of rose petals. Celia was the first to scatter a handful on to the coffin, and Clarence held her arm, fearing that she would fall into the hole. Thankfully she stepped back, and turning to her father, sobbed against his suit-coat.

Beau stood at the edge of the grave, and let a handful of petals fall on to the coffin.

"Good-bye, Matthew," he said silently. "I'm so sorry that things turned out this way."

"Doctor DuBois!" He heard a voice at his elbow. It was Charlie Evans.

"Hello, Charlie." He smiled thinly at the lad who not so long ago, had been traumatised by his experiences on the Western Front. "How are things with you?"

"Oh, I'm doin' real well, thanks. Workin' here in the garden has been the best thing for me."

"I'm so glad, Charlie."

Charlie danced from one foot to the other. "Now that Mr. Matthew has gone, I hope mum and I don't lose our jobs. I don't think I'd find another one as good as this one."

Beau frowned. "What makes you think you might lose your job, Charlie?"

Charlie was fidgeting. "We'll have another boss, and they mightn't want us."

"Mrs. Morley will be your new boss, Charlie."

"That's what I mean, Dr. DuBois. She mightn't want us."

"Nonsense, Charlie! I don't think you have any need to worry." Beau smiled. "Besides, Mr. Bonner-Smythe will have the final say when it comes to who works here."

"Are you sure?"

Beau patted the young man on the arm. "Of course I'm sure. I'll have a word in his ear if you think that would help?"

"Gee, thanks Dr. DuBois." Charlie nodded vigorously.

"I must say, Charlie, that the gardens look particularly beautiful at present."

Charlie's face suffused with colour. "You think so?"

"I do indeed. Keep up the good work, Charlie." Beau moved away, and headed towards Angela, who was trying to attract his attention.

"Beau, I need to go back to the Patisserie," she said hurriedly. "Clarence suggested that you drive me, I hope you don't mind." Angela smiled apologetically.

"I don't mind, Angela. What are we going back for?" asked Beau.

"Food." Angela shrugged. "There wasn't any room to carry the baskets, with us all in the car."

"Alright. I'm ready when you are."

"Thank-you, Beau." Angela breathed a sigh of relief. "We'll go now."

As they drove out through the gates of Serendipity, Angela expelled another sigh, as she relaxed into the leather seat. Beau glanced sideways at her.

"Are you alright, Angela?"

"Beau, cooking has always been my speciality, as you know, and I've been very comfortable with that. Now I find that my life is divided into two worlds, and I'm not quite sure whether I'm doing the right thing." She turned to Beau, her face anxious. "Do you know what I mean?"

"I know exactly what you mean, Angela. I'm experiencing a little of that myself."

"Tell me you're happy where you are now, Beau?"

"Oh, yes, I'm happy. Don't get me wrong, Angela, the move was necessary, but there are times when I miss all of this." He sighed. "And now that Matthew's gone, well..."

"It's not going to be easy for Celia to carry on where he left off. She has a different personality, and from what I've seen of her, tolerance is not one of her strong points."

Beau gave a short laugh. "You've noticed."

"Yes." Angela clasped her hands tightly in her lap. "She doesn't approve of her father's association with me, and makes it very clear."

"Try not to let it bother you. Clarence enjoys your company, that is obvious, so there's nothing Celia can do about that."

"She can make me feel very uncomfortable."

Beau was silent for several moments. "Don't let her intimidate you, Angela," he said finally.

"I'm not used to people like that, Beau, and I don't like feeling inferior."

"You're not inferior, Angela, far from it." Beau stopped for a moment. He didn't know how much Angela knew about his past association with Celia. "I was married to Celia for several years, before the war."

Angela turned startled eyes on him. "I didn't know that. Clarence hasn't mentioned it. Then you know exactly what I'm talking about."

"I do." Angela was silent, so Beau continued. "Celia always craved the high life. She loved parties and excitement. Matthew had a motorcar and was able to take her where she needed to go."

"You didn't mind?"

"No. I could see the writing on the wall before I went off to the war. When I returned I was incarcerated in an asylum, and Celia no longer saw me as her husband. I was this damaged, scarred, bitter individual who bore no resemblance whatsoever to the man she had married. She was unable to cope with the way I was, so I walked out of her life, and tramped the countryside, and that was when I met Jess."

"I didn't know any of that."

"There's a lot more to the story, Angela, but I won't bore you with it."

"You and Jess were made for each other, Beau." Angela looked searchingly at his profile. "Don't let anything spoil that relationship."

Beau turned briefly to make eye contact. "I don't intend to, Angela. Jess is my world now."

"Good." Angela grunted her approval. "I do believe we're here."

Beau pulled the car into the kerb and looked at the familiar buildings around him. He glanced upward to the room he had lived in, and Angela answered the question that was on his mind.

"A young man lives there now. Every week-end he gets drunk and sits on the balcony and serenades the passing population." She laughed. "He's quite entertaining. I think he's Scottish, because the songs he sings definitely have that flavour." She opened the door and stepped out on to the footpath. "This won't take long. Everything is packed and ready to go."

The shop door creaked as she opened it, and Beau watched her disappear inside. He sat and waited, while his thoughts went back to his time here, and the camaraderie he'd found in Angela's little shop. Reluctantly he knew he missed it.

The door swung open, and Angela appeared, followed by Sandra, her assistant. Beau climbed out of the car, and opened the rear door. Taking the baskets from their hands, he placed them on the back seat. Angela threw a rug over the top, before turning to Sandra.

"I don't think I'll be back before five, Sandra, so if you wouldn't mind locking up, I'll see you in the morning."

"I'll do that, Miss Rickard." She turned to Beau, smiling prettily. "Hello, Doctor DuBois."

"Hello, Sandra. Still working hard, I see?"

Sandra shot a glance at Angela. "Yes," she said quickly, before scurrying back into the shop.

Angela shook her head as she climbed back into the car. "She's a good girl;

very reliable."

Beau shut her door, and returned to his own seat. Releasing the brake, he negotiated the car back into the traffic. He needed to talk to Angela about her visit to the Convent, and now that they were alone, it seemed like the perfect opportunity. Charlotte was never very far away from his mind, and he knew that he would have to settle the mystery while he was here in Sydney.

They drove in silence through the central part of the city, and it wasn't until they were in the quieter suburban streets, that Beau voiced what he was thinking.

"Angela, where exactly was the Convent where you found my sister?"

"Oh!" Angela's brow creased. "Clarence would be the best one to ask. I think it was in the northern suburbs, somewhere near Manly."

"And they were the Sisters of Mercy?"

"Yes. Do you know the Convent?"

"I believe I do. It wasn't far from where I lived as a child."

Angela turned to look at Beau. "You mean your sister was close by, and you didn't know?"

"It seems like it."

They were both silent, as the significance of that information dawned on them. Beau felt his hands clench the steering wheel, as he tried to remember anything at all from that period of his life, but nothing would come. The only thing he could remember was that his mother had gone into a decline about that time, but as for conversations, he could only recall hearing the whispered discourse between his father and his grandmother. He thumped the steering wheel in frustration.

"I wish I could remember more!" he said angrily.

"Beau, you were only a little boy. How could you possibly remember something so traumatic?"

"That's just it! It was traumatic, and that's why I was shunted off to boarding school. They didn't want me to know whatever it was that was going on." Beau turned to Angela. "I have to see her, Angela. I won't rest now until I know what happened."

Angela smiled. "You do that, Beau. I think you should."

*

Celia opened the front door of her terrace house, and stepped inside. There she kicked off her shoes and removed her hat and veil, before rubbing her fingers through her hair.

"Ah!" she sighed. "It's good to be home."

Clarence and Beau had followed her into the living room, where she collapsed into one of the two plush couches. Clarence went straight to the sideboard and poured himself a drink.

"Wine, anyone?"

"Yes, please, daddy." Celia removed her coat and gloves.

Beau shook his head. "Not for me, thanks Clarence. I might go for a walk to the Clinic and put through a call to Jess."

"No need to walk, Beau; take the car." He delved in his coat pocket, producing a set of keys. "And you'll need these to let yourself into the building."

"Thank-you, Clarence." Beau took the keys. "But I'll walk."

"Before you go, Beau," said Celia, "I'd like a word with you."

"What about?"

"I need you back here. I can't run this place without you."

Celia's statement brought with it a shocked silence. Clarence frowned at his daughter, and Beau pressed his lips together as he stared at the keys in his hand.

"You know I can't do that, Celia," he said quietly, without looking at her.

"This is not a good time, Celia," admonished her father, as he handed her a glass of red wine.

"Of course it's a good time!" Celia took a sip of wine. "Strike while the iron is hot, as they say!"

Beau looked up into those intense brown eyes, and felt the earth slipping away from him, as it had done so often in recent times. He struggled to regain composure.

"I made my decision, Celia, and I won't change my mind."

"Even if we change the rules?" The eyes challenged him.

"Celia!" Clarence's tone had a note of warning.

"Daddy, we have to make Beau see reason!" Celia waved her arm in the air. "He is a part of this establishment, whether he likes it or not!" She placed her glass on a small side table. "Beau, I am prepared to put you solely in charge of both precincts…"

"Celia!" shouted Clarence. "That is enough!"

"I can do it, daddy! I have the power!"

"No, Celia." Clarence lowered his voice. "You don't have the power to make decisions like that. The committee has that power."

Beau was staring at the two of them as they bantered backwards and forwards. He wanted to get out of the room, away from the firing line.

"Well, I can influence the committee," Celia's voice was rising. "I can make them see that Beau is crucial to the success of this Practice. I can make them see that…"

"No, Celia!" Beau's voice cut across the heated atmosphere. "I cannot and will not return, and that is final. Please don't make this any harder for yourself."

"You owe it to Matthew!" It was the knife that turned in Beau's chest.

Clarence stood motionless, as Beau and Celia glared at one another across the room. She had gone too far this time, and he could sense Beau's dilemma. The silence was deafening.

"Celia, you are overwrought," said Clarence finally. "Stop this nonsense at once! You've had a harrowing time and need to go to bed." He turned to Beau. "Go and make your telephone call, Beau. When you return, we'll head on over to my place."

Celia glared balefully at Beau. "I thought I could persuade you to come back where you belong, but it seems I was wrong." She took a deep breath. "I hope you won't be sorry down the track, and wish that you'd taken me up on the offer."

"I'm happy where I am, Celia." Beau moved towards the door. "Now if you'll both excuse me, I must talk to Jess before it gets too late."

*

Beau stepped out on to the footpath, his legs trembling. Celia certainly knew how and where to strike her blows. Had she overheard his final words to Matthew, and was she playing on his feelings of guilt? Beau couldn't be sure, but he knew that he had to cut the ties once and for all. The Practice was something he had always longed for, but it came at a price he wasn't prepared to pay.

Beau gritted his teeth and stepped out along the footpath, heading in the direction of the Clinic. Within ten minutes he was unlocking the big wooden door, and letting himself into the building. Street lighting showed him the way upstairs, and he hurried towards the waiting room. It was locked, so he searched amongst the keys for the one that fit the lock.

Finally he was in, and groping in the semi-darkness for the light switch. Electricity had recently been installed, and the room flickered into a hazy light. Beau crossed the room to the telephone, and picking up the receiver, turned the handle. Within seconds a voice answered him, and after being connected to the Bendigo Exchange, it was only a matter of moments before he heard Jess's voice on the other end of the line.

"Beau?"

"Yes, darling girl, it's me." Beau swallowed the lump that was threatening to choke him. "I needed to hear your voice." The words tumbled out. "Matthew's funeral was today, out at Serendipity. He's buried where we had our wedding service."

"Oh! How is Celia?"

"Not coping very well at this stage, but she has her father, and now she has a medical Practice. She'll be alright."

"How are you? Where are you staying?"

Beau sighed. He didn't want to tell Jess what had transpired before his telephone call. "I'm alright, but I need to come home. I need to see you." He took a deep breath. "I've been staying with Clarence. What's happening there, Jess? How is Margaret?"

"Oh, she's gradually getting weaker, and spending more time in bed." Beau heard her voice crack. "I take Gracie around there every afternoon, to give Charles a chance to attend to his work."

"Have you heard anything from the Courts?"

"No, but I have written a statement and taken that to the Police Station. I'm hoping that's all I'll have to do. When are you coming home, Beau?"

"There's something I have to do tomorrow, and then I plan on being on the overnight train. I should be back in Bendigo the following afternoon."

"That's good. I..."

"Are you extending?" interrupted a bright female voice.

"No," said Beau quickly. "I'm at the Clinic, Jess, so I'd better hang up. I look forward to seeing you, my love, in a couple of days."

"Yes, Beau. I..."

The telephone went 'click'.

Beau replaced the receiver and stood for a few moments, savouring the silence. He had not told Jess that he planned on seeking out his sister the following day. He had a feeling that it was not going to be a joyous occasion, but it was something he had to do. Angela and Clarence had opened the way for him, so it was up to him to follow through.

Slowly he turned off the light, and locked the door behind him. Hopefully Celia would be tucked up in bed by now, and he wouldn't have to face her again tonight.

*

Jess replaced her receiver, and stood silently, listening to the chatter of her boys, as they waited for their bedtime story. Beau would be home in two days time, and then she could tell him what she knew he was waiting to hear. She smiled to herself as she headed for the boys' bedroom. Yes, all would be well when Beau came home.

Beau and Charlotte

Beau stood outside the massive iron gates, and looked towards the red brick building that towered ahead of him. It was the same vista that Angela and Clarence had studied as they waited for someone to appear. Beau pulled the rope attached to a large iron bell that hung beside the gate. The sound reverberated through his brain, and he shuddered. The Convent was just as Angela had described it - eerie.

Beau waited for what seemed like minutes before a black-clad figure came hurrying out of the building and across the compound. She stopped opposite Beau, and studied him closely through thick spectacles. When she spoke, it was with an Irish brogue.

"What can I do for you, sir?"

"I wish to speak with Sister Agnes."

"I'm sorry, sir. You'll have to speak first with the Reverend Mother."

"Very well."

The nun produced her large bunch of keys, and proceeded to unlock the gate. "May I ask what happened to y'face, sir?" she asked politely.

"I was hit with shrapnel during the war."

"You were in France?" Her voice had a musical lilt.

"Yes, I was."

"Terrible business." The nun tut-tutted as she swung open the heavy gate. "Mind how y'go across the grass. It is rather slippery."

Beau stepped inside the compound, and the heavy gate was immediately closed and padlocked. It was all as Angela had described. He followed the nun as she hurried back to the building, which seemed to loom out of the ground, blocking off all sunlight. Beau shivered. What was his sister doing in a place like this?

The empty corridor echoed to the sound of their footsteps as Beau followed his guide through to a heavy oak door. The nun smiled briefly at him as she knocked at the door.

"Who is it?" came a voice from within.

"Sister Miriam, Reverend Mother. I have a gentleman here to see you."

There was silence for a moment, and then they heard, "Send him in."

Beau stepped into the darkened room, and stood for a moment, as his eyes adjusted to the gloom. A disembodied voice came to him from behind a large desk.

"What can I do for you, sir?"

"I have come to see Sister Agnes." Beau stood rigidly to attention. It was reminiscent of his boarding-school days, except that the person behind the desk then had been the Headmaster.

"Social visits are usually organised by the Convent. Why do you want to see Sister Agnes?"

"I believe you had a visit recently from a Mr. Clarence Bonner-Smythe?"

"I did. He left a generous donation, I might add."

"He was enquiring about a young woman who had been sent to a Convent many years ago?"

"Yes." The disembodied voice suddenly seemed to have a face, as the Reverend Mother leaned forward to study her visitor. "And you are her brother, if I am not mistaken?" she whispered.

"I am. My name is Beauregarde DuBois."

The Reverend Mother sat back again, expelling a long breath. "I can see the resemblance. What happened to your face?"

"The war."

Her head moved in response, and then there was silence. Although the atmosphere in the room was chilly, Beau felt himself sweating beneath his suit coat.

"If you have come to convince Sister Agnes to leave the Order, then I fear you have wasted your time. Sister Agnes has no desire to join the outside world."

"I merely want to see her."

"After all these years?"

"A lot has happened during those years, as you can see," said Beau tightly.

"Very well." The Reverend Mother stood. "I will see if she wants to see you. Wait here, please."

She was small of stature, and seemed to glide across the floor, her rosary beads rattling at her side. Beau breathed a sigh as she wafted through the door, closing it with a bang behind her. Angela had described the room so perfectly, that Beau almost felt as though he'd been there before.

He waited for what seemed like a long time, with only the slow ticking of a clock to keep him company. Then the door opened slowly, and a figure appeared. She was taller than the Reverend Mother, and held herself erect as she advanced into the room. Beau felt his knees give way, and he gripped the edge of the desk for support. He would have known her anywhere, even though her face was framed in stiff white linen. They stood staring at each other across the room, while the clock ticked somewhere behind Beau.

"Charlotte." Beau finally found his voice

"What are you doing here, Beau?" Her voice was low, and reminiscent of another voice.

"I had to see you." He cleared the lump from his throat.

"Why, after all this time? Thirty-two years, isn't it?"

"Yes." His heart was thumping painfully. "I have to know why you did this, Charlotte."

She was silent as she took in all the physical attributes of the brother she had not seen since he was eight years old. His face was horribly scarred, and the black hair she remembered was grey, but the eyes were the same. It was like looking into a mirror.

"What happened to you, Beau?" There was sorrow in her voice now.

"I grew up, and went to war, and then got old." He shrugged. "Why a Convent, Charlotte?"

"I can't talk about it, Beau. I took a vow that I would never speak of it again."

"Speak about what? What happened to you, Charlotte?"

"Please, Beau, the past is… dead and buried." There were tears on her lashes.

Beau silently watched the changing contours of her face as she struggled to keep her composure.

"You had a child. I am certain of that," he said slowly and without emotion.

Her chest heaved. "Beau, you must go!" Her eyes darted from side to side.

"Tell me I'm wrong!" There was more he wanted to say. "Charlotte, did we live with a monster?"

"Beau, please!" she moaned. "I'm begging you, don't do this!"

"We did, didn't we?" Beau was beginning to understand. "Our father did this to you, didn't he?" There was no answer. "Didn't he?"

The door swung open and the Reverend Mother appeared beside Charlotte.

"Mr. DuBois, you must leave these premises at once! Sister Agnes will not be subjected to such shameful behaviour. You will not set foot in this Convent again, do you hear?"

Beau slumped. "It doesn't matter. I have the answer I was looking for." He looked at Charlotte. "I am so sorry for what you must have endured. I wish I had been older, and able to protect you."

"Beau, you must understand…"

"I know. You buried yourself here, half a mile away from our home. All those years I walked past this Convent, and didn't know you were here."

"I found peace, Beau."

"Yes."

"You shouldn't have tried to find me. What good has it done?"

"It's made me understand a lot of things. Good-bye, Charlotte." Beau moved to the door. "Don't worry, Reverend Mother, I won't be troubling you again." He stepped out into the corridor.

Cold air pressed against him as he headed for the front door, and his footsteps rang on the slate floor. His back was stiff as he marched resolutely across the wet grass towards the padlocked gates. There he stopped, and gripping the iron bars, shook them angrily.

A black-clad figure appeared beside him. It was the Irish nun. She slid a key into the heavy lock, and it opened.

"Some things need to stay buried," she said quietly, as she pulled open the gate.

Beau stared at her. "Some things should never have happened," he said hoarsely.

"But unfortunately they do." She smiled, and touched his arm gently. "Sister Agnes has found peace. I hope you can find yours. You can't change what happened to her."

Beau frowned at her. "How much do you know about my sister?"

"I've been here a long time."

"As long as Charlotte?"

"Longer." The Irish nun indicated that he should leave. "Good-bye, Mr. DuBois."

Beau stepped outside the gate, and it closed behind him. He turned.

"Then you'd know if she had a child."

The Irish nun closed the padlock and smiled at Beau.

"Leave well alone," she murmured, before hurrying back across the compound. Beau watched her disappear inside the building, before turning and retracing his footsteps along the uneven path that led towards the city.

His worst fears had been realised this day, and suddenly he wished he'd never agreed to find the sister who had disappeared so suddenly from the family home. Anger boiled up inside him as he walked, and his whole life crumbled beneath him. He had been the spawn of a monster, and there was nothing to say that he wouldn't become the same kind of monster. Beau blinked back the tears. What was he to do now? He couldn't go back to Jess with this awful knowledge. He had to find somewhere to think. His head hurt, and the old feelings of helplessness pressed around him.

He stumbled like a drunken man on the grass verge, with no idea where he was going. When he finally stopped, he knew exactly where his steps had led him. He was standing outside the house where he had spent his childhood. He blinked as the memories flooded back into his tired brain. It looked so different.

The two-storey, red brick house before him looked forlorn and neglected, its windows boarded up and the paintwork peeling. The rose garden was a jungle of briers and the once immaculately clipped hedge, trailed its branches across the footpath. The gravel driveway, once swept clean of leaf litter, was now strewn with litter of a different kind; bottles, newspapers, scrap iron and timber.

What was he doing here? It was another reminder of the life he had chosen to forget.

"It's a mess, isn't it?" The voice sounded beside him.

Beau turned to see an elderly man coming towards him. He was dressed warmly against the chill wind that blew, and a small terrier scampered at his side.

"It looks abandoned," said Beau slowly.

"Nobody's lived here for ten years." The old man peered at him. "You're not from around here?"

"No." Beau shook his head.

"It must have been a lovely home once."

It was, thought Beau. *It was a lovely house with secrets.*

The terrier was digging in the leaves under the hedge. "Come out of there, Maurice!" The dog obeyed, and stood wagging his tail in front of the old man. "Well, I must get on. I walk past here every day with Maurice." He smiled. "Loves his daily walk, he does." He doffed his brown tweed cap. "Good day to you, sir."

"Good day," returned Beau, and he watched the old man shuffle on along the street.

When he was out of sight, Beau stepped on to the littered gravel path. A large sign which read: KEEP OUT lay discarded against the side of the house. Beau walked the length of the building, and stood looking across the back yard. He remembered it as being a large manicured area, with fruit trees and vegetable plots. Now it was feet deep with grass, the fruit trees either dead or gone.

He glanced up at the verandah along the back of the house. The timber was rotted, and the deck in disrepair, with floorboards missing. Stepping gingerly on to the verandah, he saw that the back door was open, and hanging from its hinges. He knew that he was trespassing, but he had to see what was inside. The boards creaked as he stepped into what he remembered as the kitchen. Curtains hung in tatters at the two windows, and dust lay thick on the old iron stove. The room was empty, apart from an old table leaning precariously against the far wall.

Beau walked through to the passage, and along to the stairs that led to the bedrooms. Slowly he trudged up the stairs, and stood at the top. His mother's room was directly on the right, and his father's room on the left. His heart was thumping as he peered into his mother's room. It was empty, except for a faded rug on the floor. In his father's room was an iron bed frame, leaning against one wall, and a bureau with drawers askew.

The next room on the left was Charlotte's. Beau stepped into it, and he wanted to scream out loud for the horrors his sister must have endured in this room. Backing out, he crossed the passage to his own room. It was empty. There was no trace of anything familiar, but of course there wouldn't be. Another family had lived there after his father had died. Beau sank down against the outside wall, and tucked his arms around his knees. His head thumped and he cried silently into his arms. Jess's face swam before him, and he knew that he couldn't go back. Long-suppressed memories were now raging through his head like a tidal wave, and his fuddled brain had nowhere to escape. He was filled with sorrow.

Jess

Saturday

Jess stood on the platform, waiting for the afternoon train from Melbourne. She had heard nothing more from Beau since his telephone call, but that didn't bother her. He would have had a busy time, as he prepared to leave Sydney and all its association behind him.

The day was pleasant, and it seemed that the winter chill had finally gone. A whistle sounded in the distance. Jess smiled to herself as she pictured Beau's reaction when she told him her news. She had no doubt that he would be thrilled.

The locomotive appeared around the bend, issuing forth a cloud of steam, and within moments was thundering into the station. Jess scanned the windows as the train moved by. It stopped with a shudder, and people began pouring on to the platform. Eagerly she waited for a familiar figure to step off and sweep her into his arms, but he didn't appear.

Where was he? The last of the passengers were heading away from the platform, and Jess was alone. She felt sick inside, as she realised that Beau had not been on the train. She walked the length of the carriages one more time, in the hope that he was there, but she saw no sign of him.

Jess began to tremble. There had to be a rational explanation, she told herself, as she climbed the steps of the pedestrian bridge. He had missed the connection to Bendigo. Yes, that was it! She needed to hurry home and wait for a telephone call.

The call did not come. Jess became increasingly anxious as the evening wore on and there was no word from Beau. As she tucked Ben into bed, he looked up at her with those serious brown eyes.

"I thought Beau was coming home today, ma."

"Yes Ben, so did I." Jess brushed a hand across his tousled hair. "He must have missed the train." She smiled. "Don't worry. He'll be here tomorrow."

As she closed the bedroom door behind her, Jess sensed that Ben could see through her smile. She moved mechanically through her evening chores, hoping to hear the sound of the telephone, or Beau's footstep on the front verandah, but there was nothing. Finally, unable to bear the silence any longer, she decided to put a call through to Angela. Maybe she knew what was happening.

After going through the exchange to Sydney, Jess finally heard ringing at the other end of the line.

"Hello," a voice said. "Jess, is that you?"

"Yes, Angela." Jess felt the flood of relief. "Did Beau catch the train yesterday afternoon?"

There was a slight pause. "I expect so, Jess. That was his plan. Why? Is he not home yet?"

"No, Angela, he's not."

"Oh! Jess, there has to be a logical explanation. Perhaps he had to stop in Albury."

"He would have called me."

"Maybe he has no access to a telephone."

"Perhaps."

"Look, Jess, what if I call Clarence and see if he can shed any light on Beau's whereabouts. I must say I was a little puzzled that he didn't call and say good-bye to me, but I suspected that he must have run out of time. Stay put, Jess, and I'll call you back."

The line went dead. As Jess leaned against the wall, the door of the boys' bedroom opened, and Ben appeared.

"Who was that, ma?"

"Angela."

"Does she know where Beau is?"

"No, but she's going to find out." Jess smiled at her son. "Now you go back to bed. I'll let you know when I have some news."

The door closed behind Ben, and Jess slumped. There had to be a logical explanation. Perhaps he was stuck in Albury, unable to contact her. Her mind went back to her conversation with him after Matthew's funeral, and she suspected that Beau had taken it very hard. She should have been with him, to share his grief, but that had not been possible under the circumstances. Grief was becoming a regular part of their lives.

The telephone rang sharply behind her. Jess picked up the receiver, and a voice asked her if she wanted to accept a call from Sydney.

"Yes," said Jess quickly, and waited to hear Angela's voice.

"Jess?"

"Yes, Angela."

"Clarence was visiting his wife yesterday, so wasn't home when Beau left, but he said he's taken all his things, and left a scrawled note which said 'thank-you' and that was all."

"Alright. I suppose I have to wait until I hear from him, wherever he is."

"There's one other thing, Jess. Beau and I had a heart to heart discussion on the day of Matthew's funeral, and he did tell me that he should go and find his sister while he was in Sydney. Maybe that's what he did, and lost track of time in the process."

"He would have found a way to call me, Angela; I know he would!" Jess's voice was rising with her feelings of uncertainty.

"Yes, I know he would." Angela sighed, feeling her friend's pain. "See what happens tomorrow. He'll make contact soon, Jess, I feel sure. In the meantime, try to stop worrying, do you hear me?"

"Yes, I'll try. I'm sorry to be a bother."

"No bother, Jess. Beau will turn up, and you let me know as soon as he does, eh?"

"Yes, I will. Goodnight, Angela."

"Goodnight, Jess."

Jess replaced the receiver. How much did Angela know about Beau's past? Was she aware that he had disappeared once before, because he could no longer control the situation he was in? No! She mustn't even think about that! Beau loved her, and he had no reason to contemplate anything other than coming home to her. She pressed a hand to her stomach. She should have told him about her suspicions before he went away, instead of waiting until she was certain.

Jess spent a restless night, trying to rationalize the situation and see it as simply a case of Beau having no access to communication, but behind her rationalizing, there was that little niggle of fear. He had done it before; could he do it again? Sleep claimed her eventually, but her dreams found her thrashing about in the bush, and calling out his name, without making a sound.

Sunday

It was the shrill sound of the telephone that awakened her from her terrible nightmares, and she jerked herself awake, stumbling out of bed, and into the passage. The linoleum was cold beneath her bare feet. She picked up the receiver.

"Hello," she said breathlessly.

"Jess," came a strong masculine voice, "Raymond Simmons here. Sorry to trouble you on a Sunday morning, but I need to know whether Beau will be at the surgery tomorrow." He paused. "Jess?"

"Oh, Raymond, I thought you were Beau."

"He's not home yet?"

"No." Jess gulped. "He was supposed to be home yesterday, but he didn't arrive, and I've had no word from him." She was breathing erratically.

"He's probably stuck up at Albury. I don't know why they're still bothering to separate the States. The influenza is on the decrease. Um, could you let me know if he arrives home today? I need to sort out the roster."

"Yes, Raymond, I'll do that."

"Listen, Jess, don't worry if he can't get home yet."

"Thank-you, Raymond. I'll let you know as soon as I hear something."

The receiver went down at the other end. Jess stood in the cold passage, until she heard the pad of feet behind her. It was Ben.

"Who was that, ma?"

"Doctor Simmons."

"Did he want Beau?"

"Yes."

Ben slid his arms around his mother's waist, and leaned against her. "It'll be alright, ma."

"Of course it will." Jess took a deep breath. "Come on, let's get some breakfast."

*

The day continued, and still there was no word from Beau. Jess wanted to go and see Margaret, but she was reluctant to leave the house, in case he called in her absence. The silence was deafening, and the waiting unbearable. By mid afternoon Jess knew that she had to do something. With shaking hands, she picked up the telephone receiver and asked the exchange to put her through to the Albury train station. Eventually a masculine voice answered, asking what he could do for her. Jess took a deep breath.

"I'm trying to track down someone who should have been on the overnight train from Sydney on Friday night. Did any passengers remain in Albury under the quarantine rules?"

"No, ma'am. They all changed trains and went straight through to Melbourne. What is the name of this person you're looking for?"

"Doctor DuBois; Beau DuBois."

"Let me check for you. I won't be a moment."

Jess was left standing in the silence, while her heartbeat thumped in her ears.

Finally the voice returned. "I'm sorry, ma'am, I can't find any record of a doctor being on board on Friday night." He paused. "I hope you find him."

"Yes, so do I," said Jess weakly. "Thank-you for your trouble."

She replaced the receiver, her anxiety suddenly shifting to real fear. **Where are you, Beau?**

What should she do now? Beau was obviously still in Sydney, but where? Had he been to find his sister, and if so, what was the outcome that had caused this silence? She had to call Angela again, but decided to wait until the evening, in case Beau made contact. The knot in Jess's stomach tightened as she thought of the possible scenarios that could drive him to do something desperate, as he had done once before. No! She tried not to think about that, and concentrated for the rest of the day, on being ready for his return. Every time the train whistle blew, she waited to hear Beau's footsteps on the front verandah, but they didn't come.

The boys were silent, as they sensed their mother's anxiety, and on more than one occasion, Jess caught their covert glances in her direction. She smiled at them, reassuring them that Beau would be home soon. Whether they believed her or not, she couldn't tell. She hardly believed it herself.

When the evening came and there was still no word, Jess contacted Doctor Simmons and tried to explain that Beau had been delayed in Sydney, and he should probably organise the roster without him. Raymond was unperturbed. He had experienced delays in the train service himself, from time to time. Jess couldn't tell him that Beau had not actually caught the train.

When the children were in bed, Jess put another call through to Angela. What a blessing the telephone had been to her, and she sent a silent thank-you to Charles. Margaret would be wondering why she hadn't called during the afternoon, but what could she tell them? She couldn't tell them that Beau was missing. Missing – such a horrible word, with such connotations…

"Jess!" Angela's voice broke through her musings. "Any word yet?"

"No." Jess wanted to cry, and swallowed hard. "I've been in touch with the Albury train station, and Angela, he didn't board the train."

"Oh dear! That means he's still in Sydney. I've been wracking my brain, trying to think where he could be, and the only place I have come up with is the Convent where his sister resides." She shuddered. "I told you what an eerie place it is, didn't I?"

"Yes, you did."

"Look, Jess, I'll see if Clarence can take me back out there tomorrow, and we can at least find out whether Beau has been there."

"Thank-you, Angela. I don't know where to go from here."

"Jess, there is one other thing, and I'm not sure whether I should tell you."

"Tell me, please?"

"Clarence did tell me that Celia has been putting pressure on Beau to come back to the Practice. I just thought that, combined with Matthew's death, it could have all suddenly became too much for him. Maybe he needed some time to himself?"

"Without telling me?"

"I'm clutching at straws, Jess. I really don't know."

"Are you extending?" came a bright female voice.

"No," said Jess quickly.

"Leave it with me, Jess, and please try to stay strong. We'll find him."

The line went dead.

We'll find him! Missing! The words kept ringing in Jess's head, while the apprehension increased.

The Search for Beau

Monday

Angela shivered as she stood with Clarence at the gate of the Convent. This was déjà vu, and she wasn't shivering because of the cold. Clarence put his hand to the bell rope, and tugged it forcibly. It wasn't long before a black-clad figure came hurrying to see who was at the gate.

"What do they do in here?" muttered Angela. "And why keep the place locked like a fortress?"

Clarence turned to look at her. "You're not a Catholic?"

"I'm not anything," shrugged Angela. "I find that's the safest way."

"They actually work very hard, Angela," said Clarence, as he watched the nun coming towards them. "They grow produce, and sell to the markets."

"Then why lock the public out?"

"It's safer that way. Many of the nuns have chosen this life to escape the domination of men."

Angela turned to him, wide-eyed. "Is that why Charlotte is here?" she said slowly.

"Could very well be." Clarence removed his hat as the nun reached the gate. She was the same one who had let them in previously.

"Oh, it's you two again," she said, with her quaint Irish lilt. "What do you want this time?"

"We're here to see Sister Agnes," said Angela quickly.

The nun sighed. "Then you've wasted your time, I'm afraid. Sister Agnes has retreated to her cell to meditate and pray, so she's unable to speak to anyone."

Clarence scowled at the nun. "What has she done, Sister...er?"

"I'm Sister Miriam. I'm afraid I am not at liberty to say, sir."

"It wouldn't be because her brother came to see her, by any chance?"

The eyes behind the heavy spectacles widened in surprise. "I beg your pardon, sir?"

"Did Sister Agnes have a visit from her brother recently?" pressed Clarence.

"Why do you want to know, sir?"

"Because her brother has not returned to his home, and we are looking for him."

"Oh dear!" Sister Miriam pressed her hands to her face. "I shouldn't be telling you this, but yes, he was here on Friday, and spoke with Sister Agnes. When he left he was very distraught and angry. I told him that the past should have been left in the past. Nothing good ever comes from dredging up old wrongs. Sister Agnes is not the sister he remembers."

"Where did he go from here?"

"I don't know." Sister Miriam peered through the gate. "I think he went in that direction." She pointed to the left. "And you don't know where he is?"

"No," said Angela. "Are you sure we can't speak with Sister Agnes?"

"I'm afraid not."

"Thank-you anyway, Sister," said Clarence, taking Angela by the arm. "We won't trouble you further, but if you do remember anything, the Reverend Mother should know where I can be reached. I'm Clarence Bonner-Smythe."

"Yes sir, I know. I believe you left a substantial donation to the Order, on your last visit."

"I did. Come Angela, I don't think we can achieve anything else here. At least we know he was here on Friday. Good day to you, Sister."

"I hope you find him." Sister Miriam watched as they climbed into the motorcar parked on the roadway. "I'll pray that you do."

Clarence inclined his head as he started the engine.

Angela slumped against the seat, as the car pulled out on to the road. "Where could he have possibly gone from here?" She sighed heavily. "It's mostly bushland."

"That's what I'm afraid of," said Clarence, and Angela glanced sideways at his grim features.

"Why do you say that?"

"M'dear, there's probably a lot about Beau that you don't know."

"Then tell me, Clarence, please?"

Clarence was silent for a moment, as the car bumped along the dirt road. "Did you know that he was once married to my daughter?"

"Yes, he told me that recently."

"And did he tell you that he tried to take his life a couple of years back?"

Angela stared, open-mouthed at Clarence. "No, he has never told me that. No wonder Jess is so anxious. Do you want to tell me about it?"

"It was while he was in Bendigo. After he was sent home from the Front with what they called 'shellshock', he received treatment in an institution for several months. Celia could not come to terms with the man he had become, and so he walked out, leaving everything behind him. He finished up in Bendigo, and that's where he met Jess. Her husband at that time was training to go to the Front. To cut a long story short, Celia had second thoughts about his disappearance, and I employed a Private Detective to track him down, which he did, eventually. Beau was under a great deal of pressure from Celia, and with the way his brain was working, couldn't cope with what was happening to him. He went into the bush with alcohol and pills, and tried to end it there."

"Oh, poor Beau," whispered Angela. "No, he didn't tell me that."

"Jess found him, and that was where we stepped in and had him moved back to Sydney." Clarence shrugged. "There's a lot more to the story than that, which I won't go into now, except to say that he needs to be found quickly. If he has suffered more mental trauma, then goodness knows what he will be thinking." Clarence swerved to dodge a branch on the road. "And I'm afraid Celia has put more pressure on him, by insisting that he come back to the Practice." He smiled thinly at Angela, whose eyes were brimming. "Pressure is not something he needs right now."

"We have to find him."

"We do."

"The war left its mark on everyone, didn't it?" Angela wiped her eyes with a white handkerchief.

Clarence patted her hand. "It did, m'dear, it did."

"Where do we go from here? We're not going to get any more information out of the nuns."

"No, I'm afraid not." Clarence slowed the car, as the gravel road forked on to a bitumen surface, and houses appeared. He negotiated the turn carefully. "I would like to make contact with the newspapers, and get a photograph circulated."

"Do you have one?"

"I have several from his wedding day at Serendipity."

"Clarence?"

"Hm?"

"Beau left you a note, didn't he?"

"If you could call it that."

"Does that mean he came back into the city after his visit to the Convent?"

Clarence thought for a moment before answering. "I don't know. I didn't see him leave."

"So if he did come back, then that makes the search even wider," said Angela despondently. "Beau could be anywhere."

"Let's not get too down-in-the-mouth, m'dear. Before we do anything, a quick call to Jess to see if he's turned up, might just solve everything."

"And if it doesn't?"

"Then I'll get on to the newspapers."

"Should we contact the police?"

"Not yet. We'll do our own investigating first." Clarence smiled and Angela stifled a giggle.

"Maybe we should start our own Private Detective Agency."

"Yes, maybe we should."

They both laughed but it was a hollow sound; there was no mirth in it.

*

The call to Jess brought with it no good news, and as Angela explained their visit to the Convent, she heard the stifled sobs at the other end of the line. She wished she could throw her arms around her friend and tell her that everything was going to be fine, but it wasn't, as each passing hour brought with it only a deafening silence.

Jess Shares The News

Jess slowly replaced the receiver after talking to Angela. What did she do now? It was clear that Beau had left the Convent in a state of anxiety, and there were no obvious places to look for him.

His sister had withdrawn completely from the scene. How would they ever know what had transpired between brother and sister? Was it something so shocking that it had driven Beau to do…what? Could Angela and Clarence find him before it was too late?

All these thoughts were running around in her head, and Jess had to accept the fact that something had happened to Beau. She had no doubt that he would have contacted her if he had been able. Two days had passed, and they were no closer to an answer. Clarence had assured her that they would do everything in their power to find him, before the Police had to be informed. All of a sudden, Jess felt so far away and so helpless. She wanted to be part of the search, but that was impossible. All she could do was be close to the telephone, in case Beau called.

The children were unsettled, as they watched their mother struggling to remain calm and rational. Her mind was not on the everyday mechanics of the household, and Ben reminded her several times that he and Edward needed school lunches.

Doctor Simmons said he understood, as Jess tried to play down the seriousness of the situation, telling her not to worry too much. He could hold the fort for another week.

Tuesday

The time had come to inform Jean and Charles of what was happening, so on the Tuesday morning, when the boys had gone to school, Jess reluctantly left the house with Grace, and headed for the hotel. Jean met her at the side door.

"Jess, love, what brings you out so early in the morning?"

"I need to talk to you, Jean."

"Is something wrong, love?" Jean led the way to her sitting room.

"It's looking very much like it," said Jess, as she followed Jean into her private sanctuary.

"Come on then, out with it!" Jean sank into her favourite armchair.

"Beau is missing." It came out as a whisper, and Jean leaned forward, thinking she had misheard.

"What do you mean – missing?"

"He hasn't returned from Sydney, and he should have been back on Saturday." Jess slumped into the matching armchair. "Jean, I don't know where he is!"

Jean was silent for a moment. "You'd better tell me all about it."

Jess wiped her eyes, and related the series of events to Jean, who sat motionless, except for the occasional shake of her head. When Jess had finished, Jean sat back with a heavy sigh.

"I can't believe what I'm hearing, Jess. You don't think…"

"I don't know what to think, Jean. We were happy, and he was getting used to the changes in his life. The last thing he said to me was that he wanted to come home, and couldn't wait to see me."

"I wouldn't be waiting too much longer before contacting the police, if I were you, Jess."

"I know, but I keep willing him to appear on the doorstep. That's not going to happen, is it?"

"You have to stay positive."

"I want to be up there, looking for him, Jean. I feel so helpless sitting at home waiting for the telephone to ring."

"I could look after the children, if you think that would help, Jess."

"No Jean, I couldn't ask that of you," Jess whispered.

Jean thought for a moment. "What about Audrey Maitland? If you feel you should be in Sydney, I'm sure Audrey would jump at the chance to look after the children." She smiled at Grace, who had been standing quietly all this time, beside her mother's chair.

"Yes, she probably would. I'll wait until I hear from Angela before I make a decision."

"Don't wait too long, Jess." Jean's tone held a note of warning.

*

Jess knew that she must act soon, or it would be too late. She clutched Grace's hand as they walked towards the grandparents' house. What would Charles have to say? Her eyes pricked as she thought of Margaret and her situation. Why were all these things happening now?

Grace banged on the front door and they waited to hear Charles's tread on the passage inside. He opened the door eventually, and smiled at the visitors.

"Ah, Jess! Gracie! We've missed you the last two days."

"Yes, I'm sorry, Charles. I'm here to tell you why."

"You'd better come in. Margaret is feeling a little better today, so she's sitting in the lounge. We'll go in there. She's been anxious about your non-appearance."

Jess stepped into the lounge, and Grace darted past her, to stand close to her grandmother's chair. Margaret looked up, and a smile lit her pale features as she put her arms around Grace.

"I've missed you. Where have you been?" She looked questioningly at Jess.

"I've been waiting for Beau to come home from Sydney. I don't know where he is."

"What do you mean, you 'don't know where he is'?" Charles looked closely at Jess, his eyes narrowed. "He hasn't come home?"

"No. He was supposed to be home on Saturday, and I've heard nothing from him."

"Have you checked the railways?" Charles sat abruptly on his straight-backed chair.

"Yes. He didn't catch the train, and the last news I had of him was that he went to see his sister."

"I didn't know he had one."

"She's a nun," said Jess, without going into detail.

Margaret reached out and clasped Jess's hand. "I thought you two were happy," she whispered.

"We were – we are!" Jess shook her head. "I have no explanation for this."

"You'd better tell us precisely what you know, Jess," said Charles, his voice rising. "Maybe we can see things from a different perspective."

"Sit down, dear," said Margaret quietly. "There has to be a perfectly simple explanation."

"I thought so, too, Margaret, but I'm beginning to think that something has happened to him."

"Like what?" Charles's eyebrows rose dramatically.

"I wish I knew, Charles. I wish I knew."

*

There was only one more person to contact, and that was Izzy. Jess was reluctant to call her, because she knew what Izzy's reaction would be; that Jess had better get herself off to Sydney posthaste. The longer she delayed, the worse things could get! Jess already knew that. In her heart she felt sure that her love had not been enough to keep Beau safe from his past.

When the children were finally in bed, Jess resigned herself to calling Izzy. Charles had been emphatic that she contact the Sydney Police immediately, but she knew that would lead to authorities swarming all over the Convent, because Charlotte had been the last person to see Beau. Jess wanted to avoid that if she could.

"Hello!" Izzy's voice broke through her thoughts. "Jess?"

"Yes."

"What are you doing calling at this hour of the night? Nothing wrong, is there?" There was silence from Jess's end of the line. "Jess? Are you alright?"

"No, Izzy. I have some bad news."

"Is it Margaret?"

"No. Margaret seems to be fine at present. It's… Beau."

"What's happened?"

"I don't know where he is."

"What?"

"He's missing, Izzy, somewhere in Sydney, and nobody seems to know where he's gone."

"Just a minute, Jess. Back pedal, and tell me all. What's he doing in Sydney?"

Jess took a deep breath before launching into the story she'd told so many times before. Izzy listened as Jess stumbled over her words, amid the flow of tears. Finally Jess was quiet.

"Are you extending?" a voice filled the silence.

"Yes!" said Izzy sharply. "Jessie, you need to pack your bag and get straight up there to Sydney."

"I can't, Izzy. I have the children to think about."

"I'm coming down, little sister. I'll be on the early morning train, then you can go and find that man of yours. I think it's time you involved the police."

"I can't let you do that, Izzy. I'll…"

"Fiddlesticks! I'm coming and that's final. Harry and Nancy are quite capable of dealing with things here." She paused. "What do you think has happened, Jess?"

"I really don't know, but I'm very afraid for him. There's been such a lot going on lately, and if he's cracked under the pressure, then…"

"Don't even think about it, Jessie. Just get there as soon as you can, do you hear me?"

"Yes. I hear you, Izzy."

Wednesday

Jess spent another restless night, thinking about the journey ahead of her, and the possible outcomes. When daylight finally filtered through the curtains, she was exhausted, and not looking forward to spending the next night on a train.

She lay for some time, thinking about the future if something had happened to Beau. She thought about the child now forming inside her, and the possibility that he or she would never know their father. Tears formed at the corners of her eyes; bitter tears for the injustices that kept crashing around them.

Stop feeling sorry for yourself she told herself finally, as she threw back the covers and reached for her dressing gown. As she did so, she heard a loud knock on the front door. Her mouth was instantly dry, and her fingers trembled as she buttoned her dressing gown. Who could it be at this time of the morning?

Jess opened the front door slowly. It was the nice young Police Constable who had come to their aid the night Sid hurled the brick through the front window. Jess stared at him blankly, as she gripped the door for support.

"Sorry to trouble you, ma'am." He was smiling broadly. "I'm here to let you know that Mr. O'Connor's case comes up before the Magistrate today."

"Do I have to attend?" Jess asked faintly, while her brain screamed **I don't need any of this right now!**

"No, ma'am, not unless you want to." He peered closely at her. "Are you alright, ma'am?"

"Yes. Yes, I'm alright." Jess forced a smile. "What – what is the likely outcome?"

"Don't know, ma'am. It depends on the Magistrate." He shrugged. "Could be looking at three months with his track record."

"I see. Thank-you, Constable."

"My pleasure, ma'am." As he turned to leave, he added, "I see your window has been fixed."

Jess nodded, as the young Constable headed jauntily down the steps and out the front gate.

Closing the door, she leaned against it for several moments, her eyes closed and her head spinning. When she opened her eyes, she saw three children standing in the passage, looking sombrely at her. Jess opened her arms.

"Come here," she whispered. "I have to tell you what's happening today."

The three children moved silently into her embrace, as she prepared herself to tell them that Auntie Izzy would be looking after them for a few days, while she went in search of Beau.

They were happy with that.

Wednesday's Paper

Angela yawned as she opened the door on to the alleyway, and stepped out to retrieve the morning newspaper. The asphalt was wet and so was the newspaper. Picking it up carefully, she returned to the warmth of her kitchen, where she spread the wet pages out on the table. Clarence had placed an advertisement, and her eyes quickly scanned the print in front of her. There it was!

Angela leaned over the table, and there on page two she saw the headlines: HAVE YOU SEEN THIS MAN? Below the heading was a rather grainy picture of Beau, but she could tell who it was, and hoped others would, too. Under the picture was a brief paragraph, detailing where he was last seen, and a telephone number to call. It was Clarence's number.

Angela breathed deeply. Apart from the nuns at the Convent, who would have seen him, she wondered? The only thing that people might remember was the scar on his face, and that was all… The telephone rang shrilly. Angela went into the hallway to answer it. It was Jess. She was catching the midday train to Melbourne, she told Angela tearfully, and then the night train to Sydney.

Angela was pleased to hear that news. Whatever the outcome, Jess needed to be in Sydney, and part of the search, particularly if the Police had to be informed. If the picture in the paper brought no results, then there was no other alternative but to inform the Police. This troubled Angela, as she feared that the Convent might become a focal point for their search, and the sister who had remained hidden from society for over thirty years, might suddenly be thrown into the spotlight. Angela didn't want to see that happen. She picked up the receiver to call Clarence. He needed to know that Jess would soon be on her way. Clarence was also relieved to hear this news.

Angela opened the firebox of the black wood stove, and picking up the poker, raked the coals until she had a flat bed of glowing embers. They would be perfect for making toast, and she didn't have time to cook a proper breakfast this morning. This was her day at the Clinic, and she liked to spend more time dressing suitably, on these days.

As she sat before the fire, eating toast and musing on the way life was heading, she wondered what Celia thought about all the drama that was unfolding. Clarence had told her, of course, but he had said very little about her reaction to Beau's disappearance. The only thing she could glean from conversations with him, was that Celia was still smarting from the fact that she had not known about Beau's sister, and that she in no way felt responsible if he had cracked under the pressure. She would carry on the Practice with or without him. She knew where her duty lay, even if Beau didn't! That remark left Angela fuming, and she wondered how those two had ever got together in the first place. It must have been purely physical, she mused, because they had nothing else in common. Her thoughts turned to Jess, and how she must be feeling right now, as she prepared to make the journey to Sydney; an onerous trip at any time, but especially for a woman on her own.

Heaving herself off the chair, Angela threw several pieces of wood on the fire, closed the firebox, and headed for her bedroom. She had wasted enough time, and now she had to get ready for work.

*

Jess and Izzy had very little time together, between arrival and departure times, and as they stood on the platform, both felt overwhelmed by what was happening. Izzy wrapped comforting arms around her sister as the time drew closer, and felt her body tremble.

"What if we can't find him, Izzy?" Jess whispered.

"You mustn't think that, Jessie. You will find him, I'm sure."

The whistle sounded, and a voice called out: "All aboard!"

Jess picked up her bag. "I'll let you know when I get there, Izzy."

"Yes, and don't worry about the children, Jess. They'll be as good as gold."

"I know they will. Thank-you, Izzy."

With one last watery smile, Jess hurried for a carriage door. She didn't want Izzy to see her tears.

Izzy stood and watched as Jess made her way along the corridor to a vacant compartment. They waved to each other, before the train shuddered into motion. Izzy waited until it had disappeared around the bend, before she moved towards the pedestrian bridge.

Despite her words of reassurance to Jess, Izzy had a worrying feeling in her breast. It was almost like a premonition, and she hoped that she was wrong. Her little sister had proved her strength in the past, but how strong was she?

Izzy headed slowly for the Grey Goose, where Jean was looking after Gracie.

*

Angela was clearing away the last of the files for the day, and was looking forward to kicking off her high-heeled shoes. The last of the patients had left, and there were only the consulting-rooms to check and prepare for the following day. Then, when the two doctors left, she could lock up and walk the short distance home. She could hear their tread on the linoleum outside her door, and the soft undertone of their voices as they made their way to the stairs.

Finally the building was silent. She made her way to what used to be Matthew's room, and was about to open the door, when she heard footsteps behind her. Turning, she saw Celia coming towards her. Angela frowned. What did she want at this time of the day?

"Can I have a word with you, Angela?" Her voice rang through the silent halls.

"Certainly." Angela smiled tightly. There was no love lost between them.

"Have you seen today's paper?" Celia had a copy of the Sydney herald in her hand.

"Yes, I have."

"So Beau hasn't shown up yet?"

"No, he hasn't." Angela opened the door, and stepped into Matthew's consulting-room.

"Where do you think he could be?" Celia followed Angela into the room.

"If I knew that, Celia, I wouldn't be here." Angela picked up the files on the desk. "We're hoping that somebody has seen him, and that will give us a starting-point to look for him."

"By 'we' you mean daddy and yourself, I presume?"

Angela looked into the cool brown eyes. "Yes, I do."

"You've been seeing a lot of daddy in recent times, haven't you?" The brown eyes were unblinking as Celia stared at Angela.

"I have, yes." Angela gripped the patients' files tightly. Where was this leading?

Celia was silent for a moment. "My mother has been in an asylum for the past twelve years, and daddy has visited her once a week for all of those years, without fail."

"Yes, I know that."

"I haven't been to see her for maybe eight of those years." Celia's eyes were still on Angela. "There is no point, really. She doesn't know us, so why put yourself through that pain?"

"Your father remembers the good years, and so he thinks about that when he sits holding her hand." Angela felt her voice quiver as she spoke.

Celia's focus shifted, and her eyes narrowed. "He told you that?"

"Yes." Angela's voice softened. "I think he would like you to accompany him some time, and share the precious moments with your mother."

Celia's expression hardened. "I don't think I want to do that. There was never a time when she was in full control of her emotions."

Angela glanced up at the clock on the wall. It was five-thirty, and she needed to get home. "Celia, I'm sorry to end this conversation, but I must finish off here and get home. I have a room to prepare for Jess."

"Jess is coming to Sydney?" Celia's attention had shifted once again.

"She'll be on the early morning train."

"Very well. I'll get out of your way." Celia glanced around the room, and seeing it for the first time, her eyes filled with tears. "This was Matthew's room," she whispered forlornly, and then, as if shaking away the memory, said, "I only came to see if you'd read the paper."

"Thank-you, Celia." Angela smiled.

"I hope he's found soon." Celia wiped a hand across her eyes.

"So do I."

Angela remained where she was as Celia left the room, waiting until her footsteps descended the stairs before she moved. Then taking a deep breath she headed back to the waiting room. That was a strange conversation! As Angela locked the consulting-room door, she had a strong feeling that Celia might need to be watched closely. Her grieving for Matthew was still to be realised, and her ties to Beau had never been severed completely.

Angela picked up her coat and made her way down the stairs. It was time to get ready for her visitor.

Jess's Arrival

Thursday

Angela pulled her coat around her as she stood on the platform, waiting for the incoming train from Albury. There was a biting wind this morning, and the platform was an ideal place for it to move freely amongst the people gathered there.

It didn't seem that long since she and Clarence had journeyed to Bendigo to meet Jess's family and close friends, and to share with Beau and Jess, the beginning of their life together. They had been so happy, and Beau had publicly professed his undying love for Jess. Angela felt her eyes sting with tears at the memory. Had something gone so horribly wrong, that he felt the need to absent himself from their lives? No, she couldn't believe that. It had to be something else, and in her heart she feared that it had to do with his sister, Charlotte. What had he learned from her that had sent him into hiding, if that was what had happened? Of course, there was always the thought that it had nothing whatsoever to do with any of this. Had it been an accident that was preventing him from contacting his family? Was he lying somewhere, waiting for help to arrive?

Stop it! Angela told herself severely. You're letting your imagination run riot!

The sound of the train saved her from any more self-admonishing, and she concentrated on searching the crowd for Jess's slight figure. Angela held a handkerchief to her nose as steam spewed on to the platform. As the wheels ground to a halt, there was a sudden rush of human activity, and Angela stood on tiptoe as she scanned the hurrying crowd. Then she saw her, moving slowly as porters with trolleys of luggage dodged in and out of the crowd.

"Jess!" She saw Jess lift her head.

Angela pushed her way through the moving tide of humanity, until she stood in front of Jess. Opening her arms she gathered her into a warm hug. Jess was overcome by the moment, and had no control over the tears that poured down her cheeks.

"Oh, Angela!" she sobbed. "It's so good to see you. Is there any news?"

"I'm so glad to see you too, Jess." Angela released her hold, and stood back to inspect Jess closely. "I'm afraid I don't have any news." She was shocked to see how pale and drawn her friend looked. Taking her by the arm, she led her to a seat away from the noise and bustle. "Clarence had an advertisement in yesterday's paper, with Beau's picture, to see if there's anyone out there who has seen him." She smiled. "He's at home in case the telephone rings, otherwise he would have picked you up in the car." Angela rubbed Jess's fingers. "Would you like a cup of tea before we make our way to my place. We have to walk, I'm afraid, or try our luck with the trams."

"I'm alright to walk. The air might clear my head."

"Did you have breakfast on the train?"

Jess shook her head as she immediately thought of her previous trip to Sydney, and her fear when Beau was not there to meet her. Her heart did a little plummet, and she looked apologetically at Angela. "I couldn't eat breakfast." She couldn't tell her the real reason for that.

"Hm. Well, you might feel like something when we get to the shop. I'm leaving Sandra in charge today, so when you've rested, we'll catch a tram to Clarence's place. Does that sound alright?"

"Whatever you have planned is alright with me."

"You will tell me if you are too tired to do something, Jess? I do tend to get carried away, when I'm on a mission." She grinned suddenly. "This is a mission, Jess, and we will find an answer."

"Yes, of course we will." Jess tried valiantly to smile. She desperately wanted it to be true.

"Come on, then, let's get you home." Angela picked up Jess's valise. "Here, let me take that."

Jess offered no resistance. Angela linked her free arm though Jess's, and the two women headed out of the station.

As they walked, Jess thought back to her walk along the same route with Beau, only a few months ago. The streets were the same, and as they passed the Clinic, she looked up, half expecting to see Beau walk out through the big front doors. Nobody appeared. Angela, glancing in her direction, saw the shadow that passed across her face, and felt the quiver that ran through her body. They hurried past, and on up the hill towards Angela's Patisserie.

As they neared the little bakery, Jess's steps faltered. It was all so familiar, and she glanced up at the balcony where she had sat with Beau and watched the sunsets over the ocean. Angela heard the faint whimper that escaped her mouth, and squeezed her arm gently.

"What went wrong, Angela? Were we too hasty, and now Beau has regretted it?"

"No!" Angela's eyes widened with consternation. "This is something beyond your control. It has nothing to do with whether Beau loves you or not.

He does, and you have to hang on to that, Jess."

"Then where is he?" Jess's green eyes stared blankly at Angela.

"We don't know, Jess, but we're doing everything we can to find him." Angela opened the door to her shop and ushered Jess inside. "Come through to my lodgings, and we'll get you settled into your room before we depart. I'll have to wait until Sandra arrives, and that should be any tick of the clock now. I've already started some of the baking." She laughed. "I've been up since four."

"Since four?"

Angela shrugged. "That's the usual time to start baking."

They stepped into the room Jess had slept in prior to her wedding, and Angela placed the valise on the bed. At the same time, the sound of a door slamming made her look up.

"That will be Sandra. I'll leave you to arrange your things, Jess, and I'll go and issue some instructions." Angela smiled at Jess's downcast countenance. "Chin up, Jess, we're going to find Beau, and that's a promise." She touched her nose conspiratorially. "You have Bonner-Smythe and Rickard on the job, so what could possibly go wrong?"

Jess did smile then. "Can I hold you to that promise, Angela?"

"You most certainly can. Now, when you're ready, go into the kitchen, and we'll have some breakfast as soon as I've finished with Sandra."

With that, Angela was gone, and Jess stood listening to her footsteps hurrying along the passage. She turned slowly, and caught her image in the cheval mirror standing at the foot of the bed. She caught her breath, as she saw how pale and drawn she looked. The last time she had looked upon herself in this mirror, was when she was dressed in Angela's wedding dress, and had glowed with all the anticipation of a young bride. How quickly things could change. Jess ran a hand across her pale cheek, and pushed back the strands of golden hair that had escaped from the tortoiseshell combs.

Slowly she opened her bag, and began to take out the things she would need for her stay here, however long it may be. She placed her brush and comb on the table beside the bed, and tucked her nightdress under the pillow. Angela had thoughtfully left coat hangers on the bed, so Jess took her spare skirt, blouse and jacket, and hung them in the wardrobe. All her movements were without thought. Leaving her spare underwear in the bag, she placed it at the bottom of the wardrobe. That done, she went to the bathroom before venturing into Angela's cosy kitchen with its big range, where a black kettle was singing merrily. Jess knew that she would have to eat something, or Angela would become suspicious, and she didn't want that news to escape just yet.

As she was reaching for the tea caddy on the mantel above the stove, Angela appeared at the door, brushing flour from her hands.

"That's done!" she announced. "Now for some food. I fancy some bacon and eggs. What will you have, Jess?"

Jess felt her stomach churn at the mention of bacon and eggs. "I'll just have some toast, please."

Angela's brow lowered. "Your appetite hasn't improved, Jess," she said with a smile. "It's no wonder you're able to keep your figure." She groaned. "It's too late for me, I'm afraid."

So while Angela tucked into a plate of eggs and bacon, Jess sipped on tea and nibbled a piece of toast, while trying to suppress the nausea that threatened to rise from her stomach.

As Angela cleaned the last morsel from her plate, the telephone rang in the passage between the house and the shop. She pushed back her chair.

"That might be Clarence," she said as she hurried from the kitchen.

Jess took the opportunity to flee to the bathroom where she retched up her meagre breakfast into the toilet bowl. She sat for a moment, panting as beads of perspiration formed on her brow. Angela mustn't see her like this. Jess struggled to her feet, and filling a dipper with water at the sink, poured it into the toilet bowl. As she turned, she saw Angela watching her from the doorway.

"So that's the way it is, is it?"

Jess wiped a hand across her mouth. "Yes," she whispered. "At any other time I would be thrilled, but as things are…"

"No, Jess! Don't say it!" Angela was across the room in two strides. She gripped Jess by the arms.

"That was Clarence on the telephone. He's coming to fetch us straight away." Her eyes gleamed. "He's had a call from a chap who is certain he saw Beau last Friday."

"Last Friday?" said Jess weakly. "That's nearly a week ago."

"I know, but it's a start, Jess."

"Yes, I suppose it is."

"Do you feel well enough to go for a ride?"

"Yes, of course, as long as I don't have to smell bacon and eggs." Jess smiled wanly.

"Oh, I'm sorry, Jess." Angela groaned. "Please forgive me for being so thoughtless?"

"You didn't know, Angela, and besides, you were really enjoying it."

"That's the trouble," sighed Angela, "I always do." She clapped her hands together. "Clarence will be here in ten minutes, and we must be ready for him."

"Is it alright if I give Izzy a quick call to let her know that I've arrived safely?"

"Certainly, Jess! I'll just wash the breakfast things while you're doing that." Angela smiled. "Does Izzy know… about the baby?"

"Good heavens, no! I've only just realised it myself."

"So you haven't seen a doctor?"

"No." Jess smiled at the irony of the situation. "No, I haven't."

"Let's hope you'll see a very good one, soon."

Jess was reluctant to become too optimistic too soon. A sighting a week ago wasn't definitive proof that Beau was still in the area. He was very experienced at travelling on foot, as Jess knew. Still, as Angela had said, it was a starting point.

The Old House

Jess's telephone call to her sister was brief, and Izzy was relieved to know that she was safely in the care of Angela, whom she considered to be a strong and practical woman. Jess didn't have news to tell her, except that they were about to see a man who had seen Beau, or had seen someone fitting Beau's description. It was too early to become too optimistic. The police were not involved as yet, but Jess could see that if this sighting turned out to be a dead end, then they had no choice but to involve the police. That thought did not give her any joy.

Clarence arrived ten minutes later, and assisted the women into the car. Jess murmured that she was pleased to see him, as he squeezed her hand in greeting.

"I hope we've got something for you, Jess," he said as he climbed into the driver's seat. "The gentleman seemed very sure that he'd seen the man with the scarred face."

"Where did he see him?" asked Jess, from the rear seat.

Clarence pulled out into the traffic before he spoke. "Our witness, a Mr. Marshall, was out walking his dog, and by the way he described the location, it wasn't far from the Convent." He pressed the horn at a slow-moving pedestrian. "So we're meeting him there, if I can follow his directions."

Jess sat back against the soft leather seat and closed her eyes. She had not slept on the train, and the stress of the last few days was beginning to take its toll. Her head ached persistently, and Beau's face kept floating into her consciousness. She remembered vividly the time she had rescued him from the bush, and she prayed silently that she was not heading for the same scenario. No matter how she suppressed the thought, it wasn't far from her mind.

Nobody spoke as Clarence drove in the direction of the Convent, until he had to turn off the sealed road and on to a dirt road. The going was rough for a quarter of a mile, as they travelled through bushland, but then it opened out into a clearing. Several houses appeared on the horizon ahead of them, and the road was less corrugated. "I think we're nearly there," said Clarence, as he looked at a sheet of paper covered with jottings.

He slowed the car, and they all saw an elderly gentleman standing beside the road. He was dressed smartly, and reminded Jess of pictures she'd seen of the English landed gentry, with his tweed jacket and cap, and calf-length boots.

He smiled at them from beneath impressive whiskers.

"Mr. Marshall?" Clarence climbed out of the car, and shook the man by the hand.

"The name's Henry, and you must be Mr. Bonner-Smythe?"

"Call me Clarence." He looked at their surroundings. "So this is where you saw our missing friend?" All Clarence could see was a run-down house, partly hidden behind an overgrown hedge.

"Yes, I did," said Henry Marshall. "He was standing on this very spot, staring at the old house. I said 'hello' to him, and he answered me. I'd not seen him in the area before, and I walk here most days with my dog."

"And you're sure it was the same man you'd seen in the paper?"

"Absolutely certain, old chap!" He touched the side of his face. "The man I spoke to had a scar running down his face, just like the picture."

Jess scrambled out of the car, and stood staring at the old house. "What was he doing here?" she murmured, partly to herself.

"When I walked away, he was still standing here, transfixed almost."

Angela climbed out of the car, and stood beside Jess. "I have a theory," she announced, and they all stared blankly at her. "The Convent is not far away from here, am I right?"

"Yes, it's about half a mile from here."

"I thought so." Angela nodded her head sagely. "Beau was here because this is the house he grew up in." She turned to look at Henry Marshall. "How long has it been empty?"

"Dear me! Ten years at a guess." He scratched his whiskers. "I've been in the area for the past nine years, and it was empty when I came."

"Do you have any idea who owns it?" Angela persisted.

"No, I haven't." He gave a gruff laugh. "Whoever it is, I wish they'd clean it up."

"If you're right, Angela," Jess persisted, "and Beau did come here after he'd seen his sister, that in itself shouldn't have stopped him coming home. I don't understand it." Her eyes filled with tears.

The old man looked at Jess with concern. "Who is this man you're looking for?"

"He's my husband," whispered Jess.

"Oh, I am so sorry, my dear. I wish I could be of more help to you."

"You don't think he could still be here, in the house?" Angela was afraid to suggest what she had been thinking. "Should we have a look?"

Jess stared at her. "What are you thinking, Angela?"

"I'm thinking that he could have decided to have a look at the old place, for old times' sake, and perhaps fallen or had an accident or…"

Clarence laughed. "Angela, you have a vivid imagination!"

"I'm serious, Clarence. I think we should go and have a look."

"That would be trespassing," whispered Jess.

"Who's going to see us?" Angela looked meaningfully at the old gentleman. "You're not going to tell anyone, are you, Mr. Marshall?" She flashed him her most winning smile.

"No-one's been interested in the place for ten years, so who would I tell?" He smiled suddenly. "Actually, I wouldn't mind having a peek inside. It must have been a fine house in its day."

"Very well!" challenged Angela. "Who's coming with me? Jess? Clarence? Or is it just Mr. Marshall and me?"

"If you insist on this, Angela, then we'll all go," said Clarence, shaking his head. "Come on, Jess. We'd better humour the lady." He held out his arm to Jess. "The path looks a bit hazardous, with all that broken glass. I'd say this place has been used by a lot of vagrants over its ten years of being empty." He felt Jess shudder.

They picked their way through the strewn debris, until they reached the back corner of the house. The overgrown back yard encroached on the path that led to what had once been a closed-in verandah. Wire netting hung in shreds and birds had taken refuge on the ceiling beams. The three steps leading up on to the verandah were rotted, and hung precariously.

"We'll have to be very careful," said Clarence, as he tested the first step with his weight. "It will hold me, so it should hold the rest of you."

"I don't think this is a good idea." Jess stepped back, suddenly afraid of the neglected house.

"Why, Jess?" Angela wanted to know. "What are you afraid of?"

"I don't think he's here."

Angela took her hand. "Maybe he's not here now, but he might have been here. Come on! We've got this far."

Jess felt herself propelled up the steps to the creaky verandah, with its missing floorboards. The back door hung askew on one hinge, and as they all stepped cautiously into what looked like a kitchen, the smell of decay assailed their nostrils. They saw a black lead stove, now covered with dust, and a large table was pushed against the far wall, its legs unable to support it.

Beyond the kitchen was a passage, with a scullery now covered in cobwebs, and what looked like a bathroom, minus its fittings. Further along the passage they came across what had at one time been a dining room, but showed evidence of recent occupation. A filthy kapok mattress lay on the faded carpet square, surrounded by papers and beer bottles.

Jess began to shiver. "I can't do this! I need to get out!" She was perspiring freely, and her stomach wanted to heave.

Clarence, who was standing beside her, took her arm and led her from the room. He looked around for Angela. She was nowhere to be seen. Jess needed somewhere to sit. She was as pale as a ghost, and beads of perspiration had formed on her forehead.

"I'll find you a chair, Jess," he said, looking around as if a chair was about to materialize.

"Jess! Come up here!" They heard Angela's voice coming from the floor above. "I think I've found something."

Jess remained frozen to the spot. What had Angela found? Her legs refused to move. Clarence and Henry Marshall headed up the staircase, but she was afraid as her mind flashed back to searching for Beau in the bush. That discovery had been traumatic. Now she was doing it all again, only this time she had more to lose. Willing her feet forward, she began to climb the stairs.

At the top, a passage ran the length of the building, with rooms on either side, presumably bedrooms. Jess followed the sound of voices to a room on the right. Angela, Clarence and Henry Marshall were standing in the centre of the room, peering through the gloom at something Angela held in her hand. She looked up as Jess appeared in the doorway.

"I think I've found something of Beau's," she said quietly, holding out her hand.

Jess moved forward mechanically, and saw what Angela was holding. She sucked in her breath. It was a cuff link, and she recognised it immediately. The floor began to sway beneath her, and she felt strong arms holding her up.

"I remember Beau wearing these at Matthew's funeral," whispered Angela. "He was here, Jess, in this room."

Jess took the cuff link from Angela's hand. Yes, it was Beau's; she recognised the black onyx interlaced triangles framed in gold. Closing her fingers around it, she felt the clip biting into her flesh, and in her mind she was taken back to the day she had learned of Jack's death. She remembered squeezing his wedding ring until her hand hurt. Her eyes stung as she suppressed the cry that rose in her throat. Three pairs of eyes were watching her.

"Do you think he could still be here?" she heard herself saying.

"If he is," said Angela gently, "I don't know where he would be. I've been in all the rooms up here, and there's only dust and cobwebs, and a couple of iron bed frames."

"It might be a good idea to speak with the neighbours," offered Henry Marshall. "They might have noticed activity here over the past week."

"I didn't think there were any neighbours; not close ones anyway." Angela had moved to a grimy window that looked out over the west side of the house. "Look!" she exclaimed. "There's a house hidden behind those trees over there." She turned. "That's a very good idea, Mr. Marshall." Angela marched to the door, her footsteps echoing in the empty room. "Come on then!"

Jess held back, reluctant to leave the room where Beau had been. Clarence took her arm. "There's nothing else here, Jess," he said gently.

They clattered down the dusty staircase, along the passage and out through the kitchen. As Clarence helped Jess down the rickety back steps, she turned to look behind her. What if Beau was still in there somewhere? Had they covered every inch of the house? As if reading her thoughts, Clarence said, "He's not here, Jess."

She sighed. "Part of me wants him to be here, and part of me thinks that if he has gone, then he's still alive." She didn't see the shocked expression on Clarence's face.

They picked their way back along the driveway, and out on to the street, where Angela pointed to the right. "There's a house just along the street," she said, and with that, picked up her skirts and set off through the long grass.

The others followed until they reached the front fence of a garden that was well maintained in comparison to the one they had just left. Henry Marshall turned to Clarence as they all stood looking towards the red brick cottage, with its trimmed rose bushes.

"I might leave you good folk, if you don't mind. The wife worries if I take too long with my ramblings." He held out his hand to Clarence. "I'd appreciate it if you would let me know when you find the missing gentleman."

"I'll certainly do that," said Clarence, shaking him by the hand.

Henry Marshall then turned to Jess and doffed his cap. "I hope you find your husband, ma'am."

"So do I," said Jess, "and soon. Thank-you for your assistance."

"The pleasure was all mine." He doffed his cap at Angela, and smiling at the trio, strode off along the grassy footpath.

"Well," said Angela, "let's go and see what the neighbours have to say."

She opened the freshly painted wrought-iron gate, and led the way along the neat gravel path to the front door. It was open to let in the spring sunshine. Angela knocked on the open door.

"Anybody home?" she called out.

From the shadowy interior of the house emerged a small woman, in her sixties Angela estimated. She looked at the trio at her door, and wiped her hands nervously on her apron.

"Yes? What is it you want?"

Clarence removed his hat as he spoke to the woman. "Please excuse our intrusion, ma'am. We are seeking information on the house next door."

Her top lip immediately curled. "That place!" She said scornfully. "It should be demolished."

Clarence nodded in agreement. "We were wondering if you had noticed any activity around there, over the past week?"

The woman shook her head. "Not recently, but we do have trouble every now and then with people living there illegally."

"And nothing recently?"

"No." Her brow furrowed. "Come to think of it, I did hear what sounded like banging, about a week ago, but I thought it was just corrugated iron moving in the wind."

"I see. Who owns the place, do you know?"

"No idea. It used to be a lovely house, with a garden that was worth looking at. That was when the doctor owned it."

"The doctor?" The woman had their attention.

"Yes." She thought for a moment. "That's going back twenty years or so. He was French, if I remember correctly."

"Does the name DuBois mean anything to you?"

"Yes!" Her round face lit up. "That was it. Why do you want to know?"

Clarence, Jess and Angela looked at one another. It was Jess who now spoke. She told the woman briefly what the situation was concerning Beau's disappearance. Her eyes rounded with concern.

"My goodness! How awful for you." Jess saw tears on her homely face. "I wish I could be more helpful, but my hearing is not all that good, and I don't take a lot of notice when there are noises. As you can see, it's rather isolated out here; not a lot of houses around."

"So you haven't seen any strangers about here over the past week?" persisted Jess.

"No, I'm afraid not. I keep myself to myself." She smiled. "I will keep an eye out now, of course." She clasped Jess by the hand. "I do hope you find him, my dear." Looking off into the distance, she sighed. "My husband died many years ago, and I've been on my own here ever since."

"Well, thank-you, Mrs...?" Clarence interrupted.

"Mrs. Harding."

"Thank-you, Mrs. Harding. You have been very helpful." Clarence was anxious to be gone. He ushered Jess and Angela back along the path, as the woman watched them from her front door.

"We now know for certain that the house was where Beau grew up," said Clarence, as they made their way back to the car. "So where do we go from here?"

"We inform the police?" said Angela.

"No!" said Jess sharply. "Not yet. I want to visit Beau's sister at the Convent. I feel sure that whatever transpired between them, is the reason for Beau's disappearance."

"They won't let you see her," warned Angela.

"Nevertheless, I want to try." Jess stepped purposefully into the car.

Charlotte

The convent loomed ahead of them, silent and forbidding. Jess, Angela and Clarence stood outside the massive iron gates and pondered their next move. What was the likelihood of them being received cordially a third time?

Clarence pulled on the bell rope, and loud clanging penetrated the quietness. Jess winced, and placed her hands over her ears.

"Now we wait," said Angela matter-of-factly.

They waited for several minutes before a black-clad figure materialised from the building, and hurried in the direction of the gates.

"Thank goodness!" breathed Angela. "It's Sister Miriam." She was relieved to see the Irish nun coming towards them.

"Oh!" Sister Miriam frowned as she recognised two of the trio standing outside the gate. "If you've come to see Sister Agnes, she's still in seclusion, and unable to speak with anyone."

Clarence stepped forward and respectfully removed his hat. "Sister Miriam, this is Jess DuBois, wife of the man who is missing." He acknowledged Jess, and Sister Miriam smiled in her direction. "It is imperative that she speak with Sister Agnes, as it could be a matter of life and death. Since we were last here, we have discovered that Doctor DuBois was last seen at an empty premises near here, which we believe to be his childhood home, and also the home of his sister, Charlotte."

Sister Miriam looked genuinely grieved, and shook her head sadly. "I am so sorry, but I cannot allow you to enter."

"May we speak with the Reverend Mother?" asked Angela hopefully.

Again there was a shake of the head.

Jess stepped forward, and placed her hands tightly around two of the iron bars. "Please, you must help us!" she pleaded. "I feel sure that what has happened has been as a result of Beau's conversation with his sister. Is there anything YOU can tell us that could help us in finding him?"

Sister Miriam regarded them solemnly. "All I can say is that there are some family secrets that should remain hidden." She sighed. "Otherwise… the consequences are too great."

"They spoke of this?"

A shadow passed across Sister Miriam's face. "I've said too much already. You really must go."

Clarence was not going to be put off so easily. "Sister Miriam," he said as gently as he could, "I have to warn you that, in the event of us not being able to find Doctor DuBois, we shall be forced to involve the police. That would mean having uniformed men tramping all over your Convent, and I don't have to tell you how inconvenient that would be for you and your fellow Sisters."

Her brown eyes widened with alarm, but Sister Miriam lifted her chin resolutely. "I'm sorry, but we cannot allow Sister Agnes to be bullied into some sort of confession. She has suffered enough."

"What of me?" whispered Jess. "Don't you think I'm suffering, not knowing why my husband has chosen to walk away from me like this?"

Sister Miriam placed her hands over Jess's clenched knuckles. "Believe me, if I were at liberty to speak candidly with you, I would. I am so sorry." With that she turned and hurried back across the compound. The trio watched her disappear into the building.

Jess banged her forehead against the gate. "She knows something and won't tell us!"

"Can't tell us," said Angela drily. "Come on, we're not going to learn anything more today."

"We'll have to inform the police, Jess," said Clarence slowly. "The longer we leave it, the worse the situation could get." His voice trailed off, and the two women stared despondently at him.

"You mean he could be dead?" The question sat heavily on the silent air.

*

Sister Miriam glided swiftly along the dark corridor until she came to a closed door. After looking around her to make sure nobody else was in the vicinity, she knocked quietly before entering the room. The door closed silently behind her.

Sister Agnes was on her knees beside the single cot, her hands clasped in prayer. She didn't look up as Sister Miriam stood beside her.

"Sister Agnes," she began tentatively, "I will have to do penance for being here, but I have to speak with you. I have just left the main gate, where I spoke once again with the people who have been looking for you... and your brother." She took a deep breath. "This time they had his wife with them, and they told me that he is still missing." Sister Agnes raised her head. "They had come from your family home, now empty, where they believe your brother was last seen." She stopped. "His wife wished to speak with you, as she believes his disappearance is connected to his visit here to see you. They are extremely concerned for his welfare, and...are ready to call the police. I didn't tell them anything, but I thought you should know." She wrung her hands together. "Reverend Mother is going to be extremely angry if the police arrive on our doorstep."

The silence in the small room was palpable. Sister Agnes lowered her head to the cot, and a low moan escaped her throat. Then slowly she rose to her feet.

"It's time for me to break my silence," she murmured. "I must speak with the Reverend Mother."

"Are you sure?"

"Yes. Dear Sister Miriam, I have been hiding for the past thirty-two years, as you very well know. People are suffering because of what happened to me, and none of it is their fault. I must try to put it right. I must find my brother."

"Do you know where he is?"

"I have an idea where he might be." Sister Agnes smiled at her companion's startled expression. "If he was seen at the house, then he could still be there."

"Hiding, you mean?"

"Yes. When he was a child, we had this little game, and whenever f..." She stopped, and her expression hardened. "Never mind. It's time to uncover the truth."

Sister Agnes strode to the door, followed by the bemused Sister Miriam, and together they walked the length of the corridor to the Reverend Mother's office. The only sound was the swish of their habits on the worn linoleum. Sister Agnes knocked on the door.

"Come in," came a voice from within.

They entered the shadowy room where the Reverend Mother sat at her desk.

"Ah, Sister Agnes, what brings you out of your cell?"

"I must speak with you, Reverend Mother. It concerns my brother."

"Oh!" The Reverend Mother sent a glance in Sister Miriam's direction. "Sister, leave us, please."

"No!" said Sister Agnes quickly. "I would like her to stay."

"As you wish." The sharp gaze returned to Sister Agnes. "What news of your brother?"

"He is still missing, Reverend Mother, and I would like permission to leave the confines of the convent to go and look for him."

"Why? You do not know him."

"I believe I know where to find him."

The Reverend Mother sat back in her creaky leather chair. "Do you?" The blue eyes regarded Sister Agnes coolly.

"If I may interrupt, Reverend Mother," began Sister Miriam nervously. "That Mr. Bonner-Smythe and his female companion were here not so long ago. They had Mrs. DuBois with them – the wife of the missing man – and they had been at the DuBois family home, where he had been seen."

"Go on?"

"Mrs DuBois wanted to speak with Sister Agnes, but I sent them away." Sister Miriam looked down at the floor. "The poor woman is distraught."

The Reverend Mother turned her attention once more to Sister Agnes. "So you wish to end your time of meditation and prayer, and go out into the countryside to look for a brother who hasn't shown any interest for over thirty years? Am I correct?"

"Not only do I wish to end my seclusion, I wish to be relieved of the vow I made when I entered this Convent – the vow never to speak of my past."

The scratchy ticking of a clock broke the silence.

"You will have to speak with Father Thomas at St. Mary's about that." The Reverend Mother spoke harshly. "He is the only one who can absolve you." She paused. "You are not thinking of leaving the Order, are you Sister?"

"No." Sister Agnes laughed softly. "The outside world holds no place for me now. I am happy with my life here, but I have to set right a wrong made a long time ago."

The Reverend Mother studied the two Sisters for a moment. "I cannot allow you to go out alone, you understand. You must take someone with you."

"I would like to take Sister Miriam, if she is willing to go."

"Very well. Sister Miriam, are you prepared to accompany Sister Agnes on this wild goose chase?"

"Oh, yes, Reverend Mother," said Sister Miriam eagerly.

"Where do you think your brother may be hiding?"

"At Plaisir D'amour," murmured Sister Agnes, "our family home, ironically."

"The place is empty, presumably?"

"I believe so, Reverend Mother."

"Very well, you may go, but if he's not there, you will return immediately, do you understand?"

"Yes, Reverend Mother."

"And if you find him, what then?" The question hung in the air for several moments.

"I will have to consider that, when I find him."

"You mean 'if' you find him?"

Sister Agnes was at the door. "No, I mean 'when' I find him."

"Let this be the end of it, Sister. We cannot keep having these interruptions to our lives here." The Reverend Mother shook her head sadly as the door closed behind the two Sisters. "The world has a habit of leaching into our community like a dripping tap," she murmured to herself, as she reached for her pen and paper. Father Thomas would have to be informed of recent developments.

*

Two black-clad figures moved swiftly through the bush until they reached a gravel road. Sister Agnes turned to the right, and as though she had been in this direction recently, knew where her footsteps were taking her. They didn't speak as they walked, and the only sounds were the rustle of their habits and the soft jingle of their rosary beads.

They passed several houses before coming to a clearing. Sister Agnes stopped, looking ahead to where chimneys rose from a grey slate roof.

"Plaisir D'Amour," she whispered.

"That's where you lived?" Sister Miriam was breathing heavily.

"Yes."

Sister Agnes pressed on until they were standing on an overgrown footpath, and looking towards the sad remnants of a once stylish home. She gasped with dismay, unable to believe what her eyes were seeing.

"It looks a bit tumble-down and deserted, doesn't it?" Sister Miriam said slowly. "It must have been quite nice in its day."

"It was quite a mansion in its day." Sister Agnes stepped gingerly on to the littered driveway, and together the two women walked to the back of the house. As they stepped up on to the verandah, Sister Agnes was suddenly transported back thirty-two years, and her eyes were those of eighteen-year-old Charlotte. She gasped, and Sister Miriam grabbed her arm.

"What's wrong?" she whispered.

"I shouldn't be here!" Her voice had an unnatural squeak. "There are too many ghosts."

"You shouldn't believe in ghosts, Sister."

"I know, but they're here, nevertheless."

They were standing in the dust-filled kitchen, and Charlotte could hear the pounding of her own heart. She reached the door that led to the airless passageway, and looked beyond to the scullery, the bathroom and the staircase. It was then that she began to chant, quietly at first and then with more strength as she stepped into the passageway.

"Come out, come out wherever you are. I'm coming to get you! Ready or not, here I come."

Sister Miriam followed anxiously behind, as Charlotte headed for the staircase. There she stopped, and still chanting, reached a hand out to open the cupboard beneath the stairs. It swung wide, and Charlotte stepped towards the opening.

"It's safe to come out now, Beau." Her voice had a husky quality.

There was no movement from inside the cupboard, so Charlotte bent to peer into the gloom, while Sister Miriam stood with her hands pressed against her mouth. She didn't like what was happening. It was frightening and very ungodly. She crossed herself anxiously.

Charlotte leaned further into the opening, and her hand encountered something tangible. She knew immediately that it was Beau, and she thanked God as she felt a hand beneath her fingers. The flesh was warm but motionless.

"He's here," she whispered to Sister Miriam. "We must try to get him out." She turned back to the form in the dark space. "Beau! It's Charlotte! You can come out now. It's safe."

There was no response.

"How did you know he'd be here?" whispered Sister Miriam.

"I knew that if he was at the house, then this is where he would hide." Charlotte crawled on hands and knees into the tiny space. "I wish I had a light." She could just make out Beau's hunched form pressed against the back of the airless space, his arms wrapped around his knees and his head bent over his arms. "Beau! Can you hear me? It's Charlotte. I'm going to try and get you out of here." How she was going to achieve that, she had no idea, particularly if there was no response from Beau.

"How long do you think he's been here?" Sister Miriam watched on helplessly.

"I don't know. I need to get some water into him."

"I don't have a flask on me," said Sister Miriam miserably. "Should I go back to the Convent and get help and some water?"

"That would be a good idea, Sister. I don't think you and I are strong enough on our own to lift him. If you can find a litter, please bring that and two strong Sisters. Oh, and bring a lantern."

"Yes, right away. Is he going to be alright?"

"I hope so."

Charlotte heard Sister Miriam's running footsteps along the passage, and then there was silence. She pulled herself up beside the inert figure of the man who had once been her little brother. Wrapping her arms about him, she wept bitter tears into his jacket.

"I am so sorry, Beau, that life has had to come to this. I thought hiding myself away from the world all those years ago would heal the wounds, but I was wrong. Please forgive me if you can."

She felt a slight movement beside her, and Beau's hand raised enough to touch her face. Charlotte clutched it to her wet cheek. "We are going to get you out of here, and restore you back to health. Do you hear me, Beau?"

"Yes." It was just a faint murmur, but Charlotte was overjoyed to hear it.

Gently she rocked him in her arms, seeing once again the small boy hiding, terrified, until he no longer heard the sound of his father's tread on the stairs above him. She had tried to protect him by diverting her father's attention to her, but he was a Jeckyll and Hyde, and there had never been any guarantees of Beau's safety. Charlotte shuddered as the memories came flooding back - wicked, shameful memories.

"Help is coming, Beau," she whispered, as she continued to rock him in her arms. He shuddered against her. "Beau, I need to say something before Sister Miriam comes back. I made a vow never to speak of this, but I can tell you a story, because I know you now understand. A long time ago a couple had a daughter they loved very much. They lived in a big house and life was easy until the mother gave birth to a son; a beautiful boy with hair the colour of a raven's wing, and a winning smile. The mother doted on the boy, so much so that the father became jealous, and would cane him for no apparent reason. The daughter, who was many years older, noticed that things were not as they should be for her little brother, and spoke to her mother about the beatings. The mother was in shock and, unable to comprehend that her husband could do such a thing, retreated to her bed, where she would languish for days on end." Charlotte stopped here and had to control the anger that was flowing through her. "She knew what was happening to her son, but was powerless to protect him. So the daughter took it upon herself to protect her brother." She shuddered. "The only good thing was that the father was away from home for long stretches at a time, and during those times, the household seemed almost normal. But then he would return, and it would all start again. The young boy spent most of his time with tutors, most whom he did not like." She smiled now. "He could be a very obstinate little boy, and his father would cane him on his return from his Medical trips. So the daughter devised a plan to protect her little brother, and when the father was on the warpath, she would hide the boy in the cupboard under the stairs, and distract her father. However this started to go horribly wrong, when the father misread the daughter's intentions, and began to…" She steeled herself to say the words that were like gall in her mouth. "He began to pay attention to her in ways that a father should not. She was now almost seventeen - a woman in his eyes. Whether her mother knew what was happening, she couldn't tell, but the abuse continued. Then the mother died, possibly from a broken heart, and the young boy was immediately sent off to boarding school. The daughter thought he would be safe there, and began to plan her own escape. However it was too late, as she discovered that she was pregnant. That was when she was sent to a place where soiled girls had their babies, and never saw them again. The baby died at birth, and she held him for only a moment before he was whisked away. Thinking that her little brother was safely away from his father, the daughter decided to join the order of nuns who had looked after her, and that is where she remained. Each day she would pray for her little brother, and she still does, but she knows in her heart that she should have been there for him, through it all. She begs forgiveness from him." Her voice trailed off, as the man beside her began to cry.

The sound of hurrying footsteps in the passage, brought Charlotte to her knees, and she crawled to the opening, pushing wide the door. Sister Miriam appeared with a lantern.

"I've brought help," she panted as she handed Charlotte the lantern. "I have some water here."

Charlotte took the proffered flask, and kneeling beside her brother, held it to his lips. He drank thirstily before pushing it away. Two faces appeared in the opening, and Charlotte recognised Sister Roberta and Sister Bridget. She smiled at their startled expressions.

"I hope you are feeling strong, Sisters," she said without mirth.

"Where are we taking him?" asked Sister Roberta.

"To the Convent," answered Charlotte, taking the ends of a litter as they pushed it through the opening. "Beau, I am going to try sliding this beneath you. If you can straighten your legs, I'll lift them on, and we can move you."

Charlotte could see that his strength had gone, as he tried to move his legs, so with Sister Miriam's help, they gradually managed to pull him on to the litter. He was panting with the exertion.

"How long has he been here?" murmured Sister Bridget.

"Too long," answered Charlotte, as together with Sister Miriam, they managed to slide the litter across the doorway, where the other two Sisters pulled it into the passageway.

Charlotte swung the lantern around the small dark space, to make sure there was nothing else in there. She saw a leather bag with clothing folded neatly inside. Closing the bag, she crawled out of the opening, and got to her feet. Her legs were cramped and she had only been in there for an hour. Looking down on her brother, Charlotte could see that the effort of moving had exhausted him. His eyes were closed, and his unshaven face had that grey pallor of near death.

"Come on, ladies, let's put our backs to the litter, and get him out of here."

So the four nuns carried the semi-conscious Beau out of the house, along the littered driveway, and out on to the street. There was nobody in sight as they trudged along the roadway, and although extra help would have been greatly appreciated, Charlotte was thankful that they were able to make it back to the Convent without questions being asked.

The gates were open when they arrived, and Sister Miriam quickly locked them once they were inside the compound. Their footsteps swished on the wet grass as they walked towards the building, and Charlotte noticed curious faces at several of the windows. She could sense the whispering that was probably going on, particularly among the young novices.

The front door was opened for them, and they carried the litter along the gloomy corridor to where the Reverend Mother stood outside her office. There was concern etched on her face as the procession reached her.

"Where shall we put him?" panted Charlotte, her arms aching from the exertion.

"In the cell next to yours, Sister Agnes," said the Reverend Mother. "You will be responsible for him while he's here. I will make contact with Mr. Bonner-Smythe and let him know that Mr. DuBois is safe. In the meantime, make sure he does not disrupt the running of the Convent. Sister Agnes, as soon as you have your – er- brother settled, I want to see you in my office."

"Yes, Reverend Mother."

"And change your habit. You look as though you've been crawling about underground." With that the Reverend Mother went into her office, and the door closed behind her.

Charlotte smiled at the other Sisters. "Not far from the truth," she murmured.

When they reached the empty cell, Charlotte sent Sister Bridget to the kitchen for some warm broth, and Sister Roberta to the pantry for a bowl of warm water and a cloth. When they had gone, she stood with Sister Miriam, looking down upon the scarred features of her brother.

"He hasn't had it easy," she murmured.

"No, he hasn't, poor lad." Sister Miriam sighed. "His wife will be relieved that he's been found." She clucked her tongue. "Just imagine it! They must have walked up the stairs, right over where he was hiding, and didn't know he was there."

"This is all my fault, Sister." Charlotte knelt beside the cot, and took Beau's hand in hers. "I could have prevented this."

"Now, now! I won't hear you saying such things. You were the one who knew where he could be found, and you are the one who can restore him to good health."

Charlotte rose to her feet, and bending over the bag that had come with Beau, found men's pyjamas folded neatly at the bottom. She sighed with relief.

"While the younger Sisters have gone," she said to Sister Miriam, "we'll strip him of his soiled clothes, and put him in these pyjamas. Are you alright with that, Sister?"

"Of course!" snorted Sister Miriam. "A man's body holds no mystery to me, my dear Sister. I grew up in Ireland with five brothers." She raised her eyes heavenward.

"Very well." Charlotte smiled to herself.

As they stripped Beau of his clothing, they couldn't help but gasp at the scars on his body, and they looked at each other in horror. Charlotte immediately wondered whether her father had been responsible for them, but decided that they were more recent than that. She concluded that the war was the most likely cause. Thinking of the horrors her brother had had to endure in his life, she was moved to tears. Everything was so unfair.

When they had him comfortable on the cot, with clean sheets and blanket, the two younger Sisters appeared, and Charlotte began the task of washing the grime from his face. At one point, his eyelids flickered and she heard him murmur a name. She bent closer and his lips moved again.

"Jess." It was so faint she could hardly hear it.

"Is his wife's name Jess?" she said, turning to Sister Miriam.

"Yes, I think it is."

Charlotte leaned closer over the cot. "We'll let Jess know that you're safe, don't worry."

He said the name again, and this time his head moved from side to side. Charlotte frowned.

"You want us to inform your wife, don't you, Beau?" She saw tears form at the corners of his eyes, but he was too weak to respond further.

Taking the bowl of warm broth, Charlotte began to drip some into his mouth. As it stimulated his taste buds, he was able to take more, until the bowl was nearly empty.

"That's enough for now," said Charlotte. "I'll give him some more in an hour's time." She rose stiffly to her feet. "In the meantime, I have to speak with the Reverend Mother."

"I have no duties at present," said Sister Miriam quietly. "I'll sit with him while you're gone."

"Thank-you, Sister." Charlotte smiled.

"Don't forget to change your habit."

Charlotte turned at the door. "I wouldn't dream of forgetting."

*

"How did you know your brother would be there?"

"I didn't." Charlotte stood before the Reverend Mother's desk.

"So what prompted you to look there?"

"He had been seen at the house, so I knew that if he was in a state of agitation, he would hide where…"

"Go on, Sister," prompted the Reverend Mother.

"Forgive me, Reverend Mother, but I am not at liberty to say."

"Your vow of silence?"

"Yes, Reverend Mother."

"I see. Well I think it's about time you paid Father Thomas a visit, don't you?"

"Yes, Reverend Mother."

The Reverend Mother glanced up at the clock. "You may go over to St. Mary's now, and while you're there, give Father Thomas this letter." She handed Charlotte a sealed envelope. "And you'd better telephone that Mr. Bonner-Smythe and give him the good news."

"Yes, Reverend Mother."

"Make sure you're back in time for vespers."

"Yes, Reverend Mother."

*

Before heading along the road to St. Mary's, Charlotte went to speak with Sister Miriam, and left instructions that if she was not back within the hour, then Beau was to have more broth. Sister Miriam shooed her out of the room.

"I can attend to him, Sister Agnes. Go about your business!"

Charlotte hurried across the compound to the heavy gates, and unlocking them, made her way along the dirt road in the direction of the Church of St. Mary. The afternoon was drawing to a close, and she realised that she had not had a midday meal. Chastising herself that she had only missed one meal, while her brother had missed many, she quickened her pace. How long had he been in that confined space, she wondered? He had been missing for a week, so had he been there all that time? Charlotte was horrified by that thought. What had he endured during that time of solitude? Had he suddenly reclaimed memory of his childhood? He must have, if he had sought the safety of their secret place. *Oh Beau*, she whispered to herself, *I have to make it up to you. I owe you that much, little brother.* The perpetrator has gone, so his punishment is with God.

At the Church of St. Mary, Charlotte made her way to the Priest's office. Father Thomas's hearty laugh could be heard as she reached the door. He obviously had a visitor. Charlotte waited, her heart hammering. It was time to bring to a close the thirty-two years of suppressing what had happened to her and her brother, and inside she felt a sense of relief.

The door opened and a young couple emerged, their faces wreathed with smiles. They were heading for the altar, Charlotte guessed. She smiled at them as they passed, and wished them well. Father Thomas appeared behind them, his round, jovial face pink with the exertion of laughter.

"Sister Agnes!" His bushy eyebrows rose to his receding hairline. "This is a surprise. Come in! Come in!" As Charlotte entered his inner sanctum, he followed and shut the door. "What brings you here today? Has the Reverend Mother finally decided to have a telephone installed?"

"No, father, but I do need to use the telephone."

"I thought so."

Charlotte straightened her aching back. "I have come to see you on another matter."

Father Thomas sat his bulk on the chair behind his cluttered desk. "I'm listening." His blue eyes regarded Charlotte over the top of heavy-rimmed spectacles.

Charlotte handed him the sealed envelope from the Reverend Mother, and waited while he carefully slit it with a silver letter opener, and unfolded the paper within. His face registered a number of expressions as he silently read the contents of the letter.

"Well, well!" he said finally, placing the paper in front of him, and settling back on his chair. "You'd better tell me all, Sister Agnes."

Jess

Clarence replaced the receiver, and immediately put through a call to Angela. This was the call they had all been praying for, and which seemed destined never to happen. He waited, and finally Angela answered.

"Hello."

"Angela, m'dear! Beau has been found!" He heard a strangled squeal at the other end of the line.

"Clarence, is it true? Is he alright? Where is he?"

"Calm down, m'dear. Yes, it's true, and he is going to be alright."

"I'll put Jess on the line. She needs to hear this from you."

Clarence waited until he heard Jess's voice.

"Clarence?" Her voice was shaking. "What news do you have?"

"Beau has been found, Jess." He heard her quiet sob. "I've just this minute received a call from Sister Agnes. She found him, at the house where we were all searching. He was there all the time, apparently. He is now at the Convent, being looked after by the nuns."

"Am I able to see him?"

"Not immediately, Jess. He is in rather a sorry state, according to Sister Agnes, and it will take a lot of nursing care to bring him back from serious dehydration."

"Dehydration?"

"Yes, m'dear. Sister Agnes said that she would like to speak personally with you in a day or two, and explain how this whole episode unfolded." Clarence cleared his throat, as he began to feel the onset of emotion. "At least we know that he is safe and in good hands. Contact your family, Jess, and let them know that the search is over. That's all I can tell you at this point." His voice shook. "I'd better let Celia know. She has been like a cat on hot bricks waiting for news."

"Thank-you, Clarence. We are indebted to you."

"No, m'dear. I am pleased that Beau has been found, whatever the circumstances. I will take you out to the Convent on Saturday, to talk with his sister, and hopefully to see him."

Jess heard Clarence replace the receiver, so she replaced hers, and turned to Angela, who was standing behind her, hands clasped to her mouth.

"What did he say?" she squeaked.

"Beau was found by his sister, at the house where we had already been. He's suffering from dehydration, and is now at the Convent, where the nuns are looking after him."

"Oh, Jess! Come here. You need a hug."

Jess walked into Angela's open arms, and felt the tears gush as she was pressed against her comfortable shoulder.

"I thought I'd never see him again," she sobbed.

"There, there! Everything's going to be alright! You'd better telephone Izzy and let her know. She'll be anxious to hear good news."

*

Jess spent the next day anxiously killing time, and desperately wanting to be with Beau. She sensed that his sister did not want to rush things. There was so much she needed to know and understand. If he had been at the house when they searched it, why hadn't he called out and why hadn't they found him? She shuddered each time she thought of this. Had they unknowingly walked past him as they entered each room? She tried to think where he could possibly have lain, unnoticed. There was nowhere that came to mind.

Izzy had been relieved to hear the news, but wanted all the answers that Jess couldn't give her.

"You'll have to be content, as we are, knowing that he is safe," she had said, after receiving a grilling from Izzy. "I'll let you know when I've spoken to him."

Izzy had to be content with that.

The day dragged so slowly that Jess sought the activity of the patisserie, to keep herself occupied. Angela put her to work making scones, and watched covertly as Jess forced her mind away from Beau and into a working mode. There were moments when she perceived Jess staring into the distance, her hands idle and her brow furrowed. These were the moments when Angela wanted to reassure her that everything would soon be explained, but a nagging doubt lingered in her own mind. How was Beau going to come out of this episode? Angela could see it taking a while, and in the meantime, Jess had the added concern of being pregnant. Did Beau know about the baby? Angela was not sure that he did.

At one point, Jess looked up from kneading dough, to see Angela studying her. She looked away.

"I'm his wife," she murmured. "I should be with him."

"I know, Jess, but there's a lot about this situation that we don't understand. Charlotte will tell us at the right time."

"I know you're right, but I feel excluded." Jess bent over the dough, kneading it with vigour.

"You'll see him tomorrow." Angela could see the agitation in Jess's movements. "In the meantime, those scones are going to be like bricks if you keep punching them like that."

Jess stopped. "I'm sorry, Angela. I'm frustrated."

"I can see that." Angela watched, as Jess's movements slowed. "Jess?"

"Yes?"

"Does Beau know about the baby?"

"No. I had my suspicions before he left, but it was too early to be absolutely certain."

"And you're certain now?"

"Going by my other pregnancies, yes I'm certain."

"Think about telling Beau that wonderful news. It could make all the difference to his recovery."

Jess smiled. "I hope so."

The Truth

The bell clanged once more, and Jess, Angela and Clarence stood at the gates of the Convent, waiting to see a black-clad figure dart across the grass towards them. It didn't take long. It was not Sister Miriam, but a young novice with a fresh round face and an intense stare. Angela wondered how young women of her calibre could contemplate a life shut away from the normal happenings of society.

"Yes?" the novice looked them all over.

"We're here to see Reverend Mother about the matter of a patient here at present, a Doctor DuBois." Clarence respectfully removed his hat.

"Oh, yes!" she breathed, her eyes shining. "It isn't very often we have a man on the premises, except Father Thomas, of course." The novice began the task of unlocking the gate. "Reverend Mother and Sister Agnes are expecting you."

The gate swung open and the three entered the compound before it was shut with force behind them. Jess quivered involuntarily, and Angela clasped her hand.

"It won't be long now, Jess," she whispered.

"I'm nervous, Angela. What sort of reception am I going to get?"

"You stop that now!" Angela squeezed her hand. "It's going to be fine."

They followed the fast-moving novice along the passage to the Reverend Mother's office. She knocked quickly, and received the invitation to enter.

"The visitors have arrived, Reverend Mother." The novice inclined her head.

"Thank-you, Rachel. Show them in, please."

Angela and Clarence were ushered into the familiar surrounds of the Reverend Mother's office, and Jess, who had not been in there before, peered into the gloom, searching for a familiar face. As her eyes became accustomed to the half-light, she found herself looking into eyes that made her catch her breath. The face was surrounded by white linen, but she was looking at Beau.

"Charlotte?" She hardly dared say the name.

"I am Sister Agnes." The woman inclined her head.

Angela gripped Jess's arm to steady her as she stared at the sister who had disappeared from Beau's life so long ago.

"You must be the wife of our patient, am I right?" The voice came from behind a desk that took up most of the small space.

Jess tore her eyes away from the tall, graceful figure. "Y-es," she stammered slightly. "I'm Jess."

"Sister Agnes would like to speak with you. If you wish to be alone, that can be arranged."

"No," said Jess quickly. "My companions know what is going on, and I would like them to stay."

"Very well." The Reverend Mother lifted herself from her chair. "I will seek work elsewhere. You may use my office, Sister Agnes."

"Thank-you, Reverend Mother."

With a swish of black skirts, the Reverend Mother left the room, leaving an awkward silence behind her. Jess stared blankly at the tall figure before her, as she wondered why she hadn't been sent straight to Beau's side.

"Where is Beau?" she asked finally.

"He is resting," said Sister Agnes quietly. "I would like to talk with you before you see him. There are some things you need to know… about us."

"Very well." Jess leaned against the desk for support.

"When Beau came to see me a little over a week ago," began Sister Agnes, " he asked questions that I was not at liberty to answer. However, I think he already knew the answers; he just wanted to hear them from me." She took a deep breath before continuing. "When I knew he'd last been seen at the house where we grew up, and nobody had seen him since, I suspected that he would seek the one place where as a child, he had been safe."

"Safe from what?"

"Safe from our father."

"Oh." Jess felt faint, and Angela, watching her closely, pulled out a chair for her.

"Our childhood was not exactly a happy one, Jess, and as I am now able to talk about it, I would like to tell you what it was like for Beau, and for me. Maybe then you'll understand my hesitation in letting you see him."

"Where was this safe place?" asked Jess suddenly. "We searched the house, and he wasn't there."

"Yes, he was. Beneath the staircase is a cupboard, hardly visible to those who don't know the house, and this is where I found him."

Jess gave a little sob. "So we walked by him and above him?"

"Yes."

"Why didn't he call out?" Jess wiped the tears from her cheeks. "Did he know we were there?"

"I don't know. He hasn't spoken yet, except to say your name, Jess."

"You'd better tell us what we need to know," said Jess slowly, as she felt Angela's hands upon her shoulders.

"Very well, but you'd better prepare yourselves for some shocks." Sister Agnes glanced around the three faces, and clasping her hands tightly together, began the story she had related to Beau as they had sat huddled in the dark cupboard under the stairs. As Jess listened, her fear and anxiety mounted, but she gained a better understanding of some traits in Beau's character. Angela listened with undisguised horror, and Clarence, from a father's point of view, was disgusted beyond words.

When Sister Agnes had finished, there was silence for a full minute before Jess finally spoke.

"Beau has told me none of this," she whispered.

"No, he wouldn't have. I doubt whether he even remembered a lot of it." Sister Agnes smiled thinly. "It's amazing what the human brain can shut out for self protection." She looked squarely at Jess. "If he had not come searching for me, then none of this would have surfaced, until something triggered it, of course."

"Beau didn't want to come searching for you, at first, and I couldn't understand why he was reluctant. It's my fault that all this has come about. I should have left well alone."

"No, Jess, please don't blame yourself. The important thing now is to see that he recovers."

"When may I see him?"

"I'll take you to him now, but with a warning, Jess. He may not react the way you expect him to."

Jess nodded slowly, and rose to her feet.

Sister Agnes turned to Jess's companions. "It might be an idea to let Jess go in alone."

"Yes, certainly," said Clarence. "We'll wait here, Jess."

Angela grasped her by the arm. "Go to him, Jess."

Jess followed Sister Agnes from the room, and along another dark corridor, until they came to a closed door. Jess held her hand below her heart. It was beating so fast, she was sure that it could be heard. Sister Agnes opened the door, and gestured for Jess to enter. She stepped into the small cell containing a narrow cot and a small cupboard. Her eyes went straight to the cot where a figure was lying. Clasping her hand across her mouth to stop the cry that wanted to escape, Jess approached the cot. Beau was lying there. She could just make out his features in the poor light. Sister Agnes stood at the foot of the cot, while Jess stood beside his head. She dropped to her knees, and her trembling fingers found Beau's hand on the coverlet.

"Beau," she whispered, as she tried not to cry.

His eyes were closed, and for a moment there was no response. Jess squeezed his fingers. Opening his eyes, Beau turned to look at her. She could not read the expression in his eyes, but they held hers for a long moment, before he turned away with a rasping sigh.

"Jess," she heard him whisper.

"Yes, Beau, it's me." Jess was close to tears, and she wanted to stroke his cheek as she always did, but the very act of turning away from her, stilled her hand. "Beau, please don't turn away from me, my dearest." She gulped. "I have been desperately worried about you."

"Jess," he said again, and this time she could hear the anguish in his voice. "Go, Jess!"

"What?" Jess stifled the sob in her throat. "I'm not leaving you, Beau!"

"You must!" It was scarcely more than a whisper.

"No! You don't mean that, Beau!" Jess was sobbing now.

Sister Agnes moved swiftly to her side. "He is distressed, Jess. I must ask you to leave."

"No! I am not leaving here without him. Beau! I don't care what has happened to bring you to this, I love you and I'm not going anywhere without you!"

Sister Agnes pulled her gently to her feet. "Please, Jess. He is not ready for this. You must do as I say. We'll try again tomorrow, now that he knows you are here."

"I am not leaving here without him!" She was ushered towards the door. "I'm his wife and I have some say in what happens to him."

"I know, and you will, but at this moment he is still reconciling himself to his past."

"We both know that we can't change what has happened in the past, but Beau and I have a future, and I am not about to give that up."

They were back at the Reverend Mother's office, and Angela and Clarence turned expectantly as they entered. They could see by the smudges on Jess's cheeks that it had not gone well.

"What happened?" Angela asked tentatively.

Before Jess could speak, Sister Agnes stepped in. "Beau is not ready for reunions just yet."

"Jess?" Angela looked squarely at her.

Jess sighed. "Sister Agnes is right. I have to be patient. He will come around in his own time." She gave Angela a watery smile. "I'll come back tomorrow."

"I can't drive you tomorrow, Jess" said Clarence apologetically. "I have a Board meeting out at Serendipity."

"That's alright, Clarence. I'll catch the tram. Don't worry about me. I'll get here somehow." Jess wiped her puffy eyes and turned to Sister Agnes. "I must apologise for my outburst, Sister. I will try to keep a level head tomorrow. Thank-you for what you are doing. I do appreciate it. It can't be easy for you, knowing that you've exposed such a vile secret."

"In some ways it is a relief, but when I see what it has done to my brother, I have to believe that it has all been for a reason, and he will come to terms with it."

"I'll make sure he does."

As they left the confines of the Convent, Jess looked back at the imposing building with its fortress-like gates, and said a silent prayer for those inside. Angela, who was watching her, took her arm and squeezed it gently.

"Come on, Jess. Beau is in good hands, and only time is going to heal all the old wounds."

Clarence opened the car doors for them, and picking up their skirts, the two women stepped onto the running board. Jess sank gratefully against the leather upholstery of the rear seat, and Angela seated herself beside Clarence.

"Jess, I have been thinking," said Clarence as he started the engine. "I don't feel happy about you wandering the city alone tomorrow, so what if I bring you out here tomorrow morning, and then pick you up again later in the afternoon?"

Angela breathed a sigh of relief. "That is a wonderful idea, Clarence. I was also worried about Jess wandering about, looking for trams. I have to work at the Clinic tomorrow, so I'm not able to help. What do you think, Jess? Are you happy with that idea?"

Jess was sitting with her eyes closed. "Thank-you, Clarence, but I don't want to put you about."

"You won't be putting me about, Jess. As a matter of fact, it will give me an excuse to leave the meeting early." He laughed. "They do tend to drag on sometimes." He had another thought. "I will have Celia with me. That won't be a problem, I hope?"

"Not with me, Clarence." Jess still had her eyes closed, and felt herself slowly being enveloped in a warm cloud of sleep, as the car bumped along the gravel road.

Angela swivelled around to look at her, and could see that exhaustion had finally overtaken her. She turned to Clarence. "Jess is asleep, the poor love," she whispered. "I do hope she can handle all of this."

Beau's Return

As Jess stood at the Convent gates the following day, she wondered how things would be this time. Would Beau still want her to leave? She had to prepare herself for negative reactions. His world had come crashing down around him, and as much as she wanted to put her arms around him and comfort him, she knew in her heart that it might not happen.

Celia had been full of questions on the drive out to the Convent, and as Jess struggled to find answers, Clarence had tried to put a stop to the barrage.

"Celia, for goodness sake! Jess does not need this right now!" he said sharply.

Celia was unperturbed. "What is his sister like, Jess?"

"Celia!" growled her father. "That is enough."

"She looks just like Beau," said Jess calmly. "She's taller, but very straight and very elegant."

"Hm. She's certainly caused a lot of grief by remaining silent all these years."

Clarence turned to face his daughter. Her face was in profile, and he had a knee-jerk reaction when he looked at her. That passive expression was just like her mother's used to be, and the level of insensitivity was the same. He forced himself to look away.

"Celia! You don't know what she's had to deal with, so stop making assumptions." His voice shook, and his hands clenched on the steering wheel.

Jess put her thoughts of Celia aside as she watched Sister Miriam hurrying towards the gate, her black veil flying in the wind. She smiled at Jess as she unlocked the large padlock.

"This is becoming a habit, isn't it?" Her eyes twinkled as she spoke.

"I don't suppose you have a lot of visitors," said Jess, as she stepped inside the compound.

"No, we don't." Sister Miriam locked the gate.

"How is Doctor DuBois today?" Jess asked tentatively, as she hurried to keep up with her companion.

"He's managing a little food now, so that's a good start."

"Is he speaking at all?" asked Jess hopefully.

Sister Miriam looked at her keenly through the thick lenses of her spectacles. "Not a lot, but... he does say your name quite often."

Jess prayed silently that this was a good sign that he would be ready to talk to her.

As they passed along the corridor, Jess could hear voices coming from Beau's room. She recognised the voice of Sister Agnes; calm and even in tone as she said something to Beau. Jess couldn't make out the words, but she heard Beau's reply.

"I can't go back! I can't!"

"Oh dear," murmured Sister Miriam, "this doesn't sound very promising."

As they reached the door they heard Sister Agnes speak again. "Beau, your wife is not leaving here without you. You can't abandon her because of what your father did. You are not like father!"

Jess felt the hairs on the back of her neck crawl. This was not something that was going to go away easily. The hurt was too deep. She looked despairingly at Sister Miriam.

"What am I to do?" she whispered.

"Pray for a miracle, Jess," was all Sister Miriam said before knocking on the door.

The voices stopped as they stepped into the room. Sister Agnes, who had been bending over the cot, straightened up and smiled tightly at Jess. Beau turned his face to the wall. Jess felt sick inside. Sister Miriam touched her arm gently and propelled her towards the cot.

"Beau, your wife is here," said Sister Agnes. "I will leave you two together. Jess, I'll be in the next room if you need me." She walked silently from the room.

Sister Miriam smiled encouragingly, whispered, "I'll be praying for that miracle," and followed.

The door closed quietly behind the two nuns, and Jess was alone with Beau. He was her husband, but she felt like a stranger, standing awkwardly beside the cot, while he refused to look at her. She glanced around for a chair, saw one against the wall, and carried it quietly to the bedside, where she sat in the brooding silence.

Jess could hear her own heartbeat as she sat silently waiting for some response from Beau. She wanted to reach out and touch him, to feel his flesh against hers, but the fear of rejection was too great. The minutes ticked by.

Finally she found her voice and leaned forward.

"Beau, I feel your pain," she whispered.

The silence continued, while Jess felt her misery increasing with every second. Then he turned his head to face her, and Jess saw the undeniable pain in his eyes. She shrank from their intensity.

"You cannot even imagine my pain, Jess." There was anger in his tone.

"Then share it with me, Beau, please!"

He looked at her for a long moment and then sighed. "Jess, I've brought you enough grief. Walk away while you can. Find a life where you can be happy. You don't need this kind of ugliness."

Jess blinked at the unexpectedness of the remark. "Beau, you can't mean that! I thought you loved me! We can climb this mountain together. We've climbed other mountains. Beau!" Her voice rose to a sob. "Don't make me leave. I couldn't bear it." The tears were gushing now.

"Please Jess, don't make this harder than it already is."

"Are you saying that you don't love me?"

For a moment Jess saw a glimmer of the tenderness in the man she knew, but then it was gone. "No, I could never say that, Jess."

"You promised to love me until your dying breath." Anger was now taking the place of fear.

"And I will, but I have rotten blood in me, Jess, and I cannot let it mingle with yours."

Jess sat back on the chair, and pushed her fingers into her eyes. What was she to do now? Should she tell him about the child and accept the consequences, or could this be the miracle that Sister Miriam was praying for?

Beau was lying quietly, staring at the ceiling, his hands clutching the coverlet. Jess reached out and covered his hand with hers. She felt his fingers stiffen, and he turned once more to look at her.

"Beau, I need you beside me more than ever now."

He frowned as Jess lifted his hand and placed it against her stomach. She waited as the realization dawned on him.

"What are you trying to tell me, Jess?"

"I'm trying to tell you that our blood has already mingled, Beau." Jess saw tears forming at the corners of his eyes as he stared at her. "It's true, Beau."

The fingers beneath her hand turned and gripped hers tightly, while his other hand covered his eyes. He began to tremble, and Jess moved swiftly into the hug that she had been afraid to give him. His arms immediately wrapped around her, and they clung together, the pain temporarily forgotten as their tears mingled.

"I have no intention of leaving you, Beau," murmured Jess finally. "The past cannot be changed, no matter how hurtful it is, but we have a future, and we must look towards that."

"Oh my darling girl, it was the one thing I thought about most while I was in that very dark space, and I could see no other way out."

"Well our child has shown you that there is another way." Jess lifted her head, and gently brushed the wet hair from Beau's forehead. "Sister Miriam told me to pray for a miracle. Maybe this is it."

He smiled. "Maybe it is."

"We have to get you well before we can go home with our good news."

The door opened and Sister Miriam stood there, her eyes twinkling.

"So we have our miracle after all?" Her smile was mischievous.

Jess had the suspicion that she had been listening outside the door. It didn't matter. The important thing was that Beau had taken the first step out of the dark place he was in.

"Yes, Sister. We have our miracle." Jess smiled tremulously.

"God does move in mysterious ways, my dear."

Sister Agnes appeared at the door. "What is going on?" she asked, looking from one to the other. "Sister Miriam?"

"Ah, Sister, you could say we have a miracle happening right here in this room."

"Meaning?"

"Meaning there's to be a bairn," said Sister Miriam smugly.

Sister Agnes looked quickly at Beau and then at Jess. "A baby," she said quietly.

"This will make all the difference!" declared Sister Miriam, as she bustled across to the window and pulled up the blind. "Let's have some light in here! There's been enough darkness." She turned to Beau. "You'll be up and about in no time now, young man. That light at the end of the tunnel just got a whole lot brighter." She was smiling broadly.

"What will happen now?" asked Jess, looking at Sister Agnes.

She stared at Beau, and Jess could see a soft expression in her eyes that clearly indicated her feelings for her long-lost brother. Blood would always be thicker than water.

"I will have to speak with Reverend Mother of course, but I think Beau should stay here for a few more days, to make sure he has his strength back, and to allow us to talk openly about our past in order that we might put it to rest."

You don't want to let him go, thought Jess, watching the changing expressions on her face.

"I suppose we can wait another few days." Jess took Beau's hand and squeezed it gently. "Are you happy to be subjected to all this attention for a while longer, my dear?"

Beau looked across the room to his sister. "If it allows me time with Charlotte, then I'm happy."

"Good!" Sister Miriam headed for the door. "This calls for a celebratory drink. It will have to be a cup of tea, I'm afraid. There's nothing stronger in the pantry."

She laughed gaily, and without waiting for a response, was gone, her footsteps echoing along the empty corridor. Sister Agnes shook her head and sighed loudly.

"She is an angel," she said quietly, "but I do wonder why she chose the Order as her vocation."

"Perhaps she has ghosts somewhere in her past," murmured Beau.

Putting the Past to Rest

As Jess stood at the gates of the Convent, waiting for Clarence to arrive, her heart felt much lighter than it had done on her arrival. Beau was ready to accept that he was in no way responsible for the behaviour of his father all those years ago. Charlotte, who had been his protector, was now free to talk about the past wrongs, and reunite with the brother she had fretted over for years. Life with its ups and downs was going to continue, but Jess felt certain that the ghosts could finally be put to rest.

As she thought about the family back home, Jess wondered how Margaret was getting on, and a frown touched her brow. That would surely be the next hurdle for them all to negotiate, and it would not be easy. She would call Izzy as soon as they arrived at Clarence's house.

A car horn sounded, and Jess saw the black Ford bumping along the gravel road towards her. Celia was in the passenger seat, holding her hat against the breeze and looking decidedly peeved. Jess guessed that she had been forced to leave Serendipity sooner than she would have liked.

Clarence waved a hand as he slowed beside her.

"I hope you haven't been waiting too long, Jess." His smile behind the whiskers was wide.

"Only a few minutes, Clarence."

"Good!" He climbed out of the driver's seat, and opened the rear door.

"How was everything today, Jess?" he asked as he returned to his own seat.

"Beau has turned a corner, and he will go forward from here. Sister Agnes wants him to stay a few more days, to make sure."

Celia turned, her hand still on her straw hat, and frowned at Jess. "He should go to Serendipity to recuperate. It would make much more sense than being here with all those nuns."

"I'm not even going to suggest it, Celia," said Jess smoothly. "His sister wants to take care of him, and they have a lot of memories to share."

"Memories best forgotten."

"Not all of them are bad memories, Celia. There'll be some good memories there, too."

*

When Jess had gone, Sister Agnes paid a visit to the Reverend Mother, to ascertain whether it was permitted for Beau to remain at the Convent, under her care. The Reverend Mother took some time considering the request, and her fingers drummed on the desk as she looked at Sister Agnes over her spectacles.

"It is highly irregular," she said at last, "but under the circumstances I will grant your request, on the understanding that you will have full responsibility for him."

"Yes, Reverend Mother."

"I take it that his wife will be a regular visitor?"

"I would expect so."

"How long do you anticipate him being here?"

"It depends on his recovery, Reverend Mother, but I would say no longer than a week."

"A week?" Sister Agnes detected a note of alarm in the Reverend Mother's voice.

"Maybe less," she added hastily. "He has surprised us today with his progress."

"Very well, but I don't want this in any way to interrupt the work here. Is that understood?"

"Yes, Reverend Mother."

"If you need assistance, I expect Sister Miriam will make herself available."

Sister Agnes smiled. "Yes, I daresay she will."

"I will have to inform Father Thomas, of course. He may find the situation unmerited."

"Father Thomas is aware of all that has transpired. I expect him to be sympathetic."

The Reverend Mother shook her head. "Nevertheless, he needs to know what is happening."

*

Charlotte stood looking down on her brother as he slept. The colour was returning to his features, and the drawn look was gone, but he needed a shave. She had noticed a razor and brush amongst the items in his bag. Would he be receptive to her attempting to shave him, or should she leave it for Jess? While she was considering this, he opened his eyes and looked up at her. Charlotte smiled as she pulled up a chair and sat down.

"Hello, Beau." She received a brief smile in return. "I have been considering giving you a shave. Do you feel up to it?"

Beau ran a hand across the stubble on his chin. "I definitely need one."

"I saw a razor and brush in your bag, so if you'd like me to, I'll fetch some hot water and soap. Then when Jess comes back, you'll be more like yourself."

She laughed softly.

"She might not recognise me."

"Oh, I think she will." Charlotte rose and moved towards the door. "I'll be back in a moment."

Charlotte moved quickly to the kitchen, where she searched for a suitable bowl. Finding a small enamel dish, she filled it with water from the battered kettle that sat on the black lead stove. In the stores cupboard she found a bar of soap, and made a mental note that she would have to account for it on the stores list. Grabbing a towel, she hurried back to Beau.

When she opened the door, she was surprised to see him sitting on the edge of the cot, his bare feet on the cold linoleum.

"I thought it might be easier for you if I'm sitting up." His breathing was ragged.

Charlotte pulled a rug around his shoulders, and whisking a pillow from the cot, placed it beneath his feet.

"There! We can't have you catching a chill."

Beau smiled at her concern. "Thank-you. Should I call you Sister Agnes or Charlotte?"

Charlotte was delving into his bag. "You can call me Charlotte when we're alone," she said conspiratorially, "but Sister Agnes when anyone's about."

As Charlotte set to work, she began to talk, asking questions and trying to piece together the life of the brother she had cared about, but whom she had inadvertently abandoned all those years ago. Beau answered her questions, and touched on all the years leading up to meeting Jess. She felt remorse when she heard about the bullying at school, and Matthew stepping in to protect his friend. Her eyebrows were raised when he mentioned his first marriage to Celia, but she said nothing. The war years and the repercussions shocked her to the point of tears, and her hands became still when he talked about his life on the road with only a dog for company.

"That was when I met Jess." Beau ran a hand across his now smooth chin, and smiled up at his sister. "I don't suppose there are any mirrors here?"

"No! Definitely not!" she retorted, with mock horror. "You look perfectly fine from this angle."

"I'll take your word for it."

Charlotte put aside the bowl, soap and razor, and sat beside her brother.

"Tell me about Jess," she asked quietly. "She loves you very much."

Beau's expression softened. "She is my world, and to think that I was prepared to die rather than let her know about all this." He stopped. "I don't deserve her."

"That's not how she feels, Beau."

"It's not the first time… I've put her through such trauma." Beau spoke hesitantly, unsure whether he should be telling his sister the awful truths of his life.

Charlotte raised her eyebrows. "What are you saying, Beau? That you've done this before?"

"Worse." He hung his head, unable to meet the intense stare.

"Tell me about it. We need to expose all these demons and let them go."

Charlotte listened, horrified, as Beau went into the details of his attempted suicide and the repercussions of that on everybody, especially Jess.

"She must be a very special woman, if she can deal with all you've put her through, and yet she still loves you." Charlotte shook her head sadly.

"We only got married three months ago. It was here in Sydney, and Jess had just recovered from the influenza virus. I was working with patients here at the time."

"So she had the influenza? Is it slowing down? I've heard reports that it is."

"Yes, I believe it is. You haven't been affected by it here?"

"No." Charlotte chuckled. "We don't mix with the public very often, as you can see."

"What has your life been like, Charlotte?"

She shrugged. "Very structured and orderly. The only time we venture out of the grounds is to go to St. Mary's or to take our produce to the local market."

"You don't miss the contact with the outside world?"

"Not at all. In spite of this place looking like a prison, and what may seem to you as a lack of freedom, it's not like that at all." She smiled at his frowning face. "We share a common bond, and I am happy, Beau."

A bell sounded not far away. Charlotte stood.

"That's the bell for prayers before mealtime. I must go. Lunch will be brought to you shortly. Thank-you for telling me about yourself, Beau."

"There's a lot more to tell."

"Another time perhaps. Enjoy your lunch. It will only be soup and bread, I'm afraid."

Beau waved her away. "Don't be late for prayers."

Charlotte smiled and was gone.

*

When Jess returned to the Convent the following day, she found Beau sitting outside on a seat in the sunshine. He was wrapped in a blanket, and she smiled as she noticed that his feet were encased in thick black hand-knitted socks, probably belonging to one of the nuns. She sat beside him, and they smiled at each other.

"You've had a shave," was her first comment.

Beau ran a hand across his chin. "Sister Agnes thought I might look more appealing to you if the stubble was removed. Do I look appealing? There are no mirrors here."

"Yes, you look more like yourself now. You've even got colour back on your cheeks." Jess shivered. "You were a ghastly grey last time I saw you."

"I'm so sorry, Jess. I should never have put you through all of this." He touched her cheek.

"Tell me, Beau, what were you thinking when we went through the house? You must have known we were there."

"Yes, I knew you were there."

"Why didn't you call out?"

"I couldn't, Jess. I was shutting down, and my brain was past caring."

Jess felt the tears well in her eyes. "Is that what it was like all those years ago, when you hid from your father?"

"Not quite. I knew Charlotte would come and get me when the coast was clear." Beau took her hand. "We have had a long discussion about…everything. Charlotte knows a lot more about me than she did a few days ago. She said we all have to let go of the demons." He leaned over and kissed Jess's cheek. "Are we able to do that, Jess?"

"Yes, Beau, of course we can. We have something far more precious to think about."

Beau smiled. "This was the one thing that I was afraid of; continuing the bad blood."

"Don't think about it any more. Think about going home and picking up where we left off."

"I've disrupted your precious time with Margaret, and I'm sorry about that, too. How is she? Have you heard anything?" Beau turned to look at her, as though seeing her for the first time. "I haven't even asked who's looking after the children." He shrugged helplessly.

"Izzy is looking after them, and she says that Margaret is doing well." Jess laughed. "Izzy is making sure that she eats lots of green vegetables. That, she says, will keep her iron levels from dropping too far."

"Yes, it will. It's not a cure, but it will help in the short term."

Jess leaned her head on his shoulder. "It's so good to have you back, Beau," she whispered. "I thought I'd lost you forever."

"If Charlotte hadn't gone looking for me, then…"

"Sh!" Jess placed her fingers over his mouth. "I don't want to hear it."

A tall black-clad figure was approaching them across the grass. It was Charlotte. She stopped in front of them.

"This is a sight I am very pleased to see," she said brightly, smiling at each in turn.

"We have you to thank, Sister," replied Jess.

"My footsteps were guided, Jess. I didn't do it alone."

"Nevertheless, you knew where Beau could be found."

"Yes." She stared at Beau for a long moment. "Beau, the Reverend Mother is anxious to know how long you are likely to be here. I told her possibly a week."

Jess and Beau looked at one another, before Beau turned back to his sister.

"If Reverend Mother is uncomfortable with my intrusion into Convent life, then I'm happy to be discharged. What do you say, Jess?"

"If you think you're ready, Beau?"

He nodded. "I'm ready, Jess."

"I'll inform the Reverend Mother." Charlotte turned to go, but Beau stopped her.

"Charlotte!" She turned. "I may not get another chance to say this – I owe you my life, and I will never forget what you have had to do to make this come about. I – We want to keep in touch with you, if that is possible. You are still my sister, whatever name you choose to go by."

Charlotte was silent for a long moment.

"May we both live in peace now, Beau. The demons have left us." Charlotte smiled softly. "Write to me and let me know how you are both going and… when the baby arrives, I want to know about it. Is that clear?" There were tears on her lashes.

Jess and Beau watched her stride away across the grass, towards the main doors of the Convent.

"I don't think she wants to let you go," whispered Jess, slipping her arm through Beau's. As she turned to look at him, she noticed tears on his lashes. "We will keep in touch, Beau. Whatever mess has been made in all our lives, she will always be Charlotte, your sister."

"Take me home, Jess. It's time for me to start making amends to the people I love." Beau turned to face her, and Jess leaned forward to kiss him. "Should you be doing that?" he murmured, as he returned the kiss. "This place has eyes and ears everywhere."

"I don't care." Jess wrapped her arms firmly around him. "You are my husband, and I will kiss you whenever and wherever I like."

Beau laughed. "I seem to remember a time when you became all embarrassed when I tried to kiss you in public. Have you forgotten?"

"No. It was here in Sydney at the quayside."

"Hm. These are the memories we need to hold onto, Jess."

"Yes, and we have lots of those." Their eyes met and held.

Going Home

Jess turned around as the black Ford moved slowly along the bumpy road. She saw the black-clad figure standing at the gates, and she raised her hand in a farewell wave. The figure lifted her hand in response, before lowering it. Jess cast a furtive glance at Beau, seated beside her. He was looking straight ahead, and she could tell by the set of his jaw that he was reluctant to look behind him. She slipped her arm through his, and squeezed it gently.

"Charlotte is still at the gate, Beau," she said softly.

"I know."

Jess said no more. She could see that the parting was causing him great pain. He took her hand and held it tightly, while his eyes stared straight ahead. Clarence, seated in the driver's seat, could sense the poignancy of the moment, and concentrated on the road ahead. Angela, seated beside him, also knew that the moment did not call for conversation. Beau's harrowing experience had come to an end, and he had to say good-bye to the one person who had saved him from certain death. Angela blinked away the tears as she searched in her handbag for a handkerchief.

Clarence threw her a glance as she patted at her eyes, and he knew that Angela would soon have to say good-bye to two people who had become very dear to her. He had to admit that the past few days, although harrowing, had indeed brought everybody closer together. His thoughts turned to Celia, who was finally beginning to understand the situation. She had lost Matthew, and her attempts to regain Beau had failed, leaving her on her own and vulnerable in a man's world of business. Clarence knew that she would be strong enough, in time, and with his guidance, to take control, but there was a lot Celia would have to learn.

He smiled to himself as he recalled their last conversation. Celia had agreed, reluctantly, to accompany him to the asylum to see her mother. That was a giant step forward, and he had a feeling that it was Angela who had sowed the seed. Maybe these two would begin to get along. He hoped fervently that they would, as he was very fond of Angela.

Clarence pulled the car into the alleyway beside the patisserie.

"I believe this is the end of the road," he said, smiling at Angela.

"Thank-you, Clarence," said Jess. "You have made all this possible and we are very grateful."

"It has taken my mind off other things, Jess, so we all have a win." Clarence turned to smile at Jess. "Besides, it started out as a kind of adventure, didn't it, Angela?" She nodded. "Then, of course, when things became serious, we couldn't rest until this man was found."

Beau reached across the seat and grasped Clarence by the hand. "I'll never be able to repay the debt I owe to so many people," he said gravely.

"Nonsense!" Clarence shook his hand vigorously. "Your recovery is all the reward we need." His face became serious. "When are you planning on returning to Victoria?"

Jess glanced at Beau, to gauge his reaction to the question. He hesitated before answering.

"I'd like to leave here tomorrow," he said, looking in Jess's direction.

"Will you be strong enough to travel?" Jess asked anxiously.

"Yes, I think so."

"Tomorrow?" said Angela wistfully. "I thought we might have had you longer than that."

"We need to get home, Angela." Beau touched her shoulder as he spoke. "I'm sorry, but I must end this episode of my life as quickly as I can."

"Yes, I can understand that, Beau." Angela smiled at him. "It's just that I've never had a friend like Jess before, and…"

"We'll pop down occasionally to see them, my dear," interrupted Clarence, glancing indulgently at Angela. "Now that we know the way."

Angela smiled coyly. "Thank-you, Clarence. "I'd like that very much."

Clarence climbed out of the car. "Well, my dears, I hate to break this up, but I must get back to Celia. She's expecting me for tea," and as he opened Angela's door, he added conspiratorially, "and she's actually doing the cooking." He reached out a hand to Angela, who took it, and stepped gracefully out of the car.

Clarence then opened the rear door, and handed Jess out on to the narrow roadway. "Take care of yourselves, m'dear," he said quietly.

"We'll try, Clarence," Jess murmured, as she watched Beau alight from the car before retrieving his Gladstone bag from the floor.

"Well," said Clarence. "I'd better say good-bye now, if you good folk are leaving tomorrow." He turned to Angela. "Celia has agreed to accompany me to the asylum tomorrow, to see her mother."

"Oh, Clarence, that's wonderful!" Angela was genuinely pleased for him

"It's a start." Clarence shook Beau by the hand. "It's good to have you back, Beau, and I wish you both well." He turned to Jess. "We will come and see you, Jess, in the not too distant future. That is a promise." He kissed her.

"Thank-you once again Clarence, for all you did for us. We are extremely grateful." Jess felt her eyes fill up, and she wanted to give him a hug, but he had already turned to Angela.

"I won't see you tomorrow, m'dear, but we can go to Mario's on Sunday evening if you like."

Angela nodded eagerly. "Yes, Clarence, I would like that very much."

As Clarence stepped back into the car, Beau, who had been silent throughout the goodbyes, put a hand on the driver's door.

"Say good-bye to Celia for me, Clarence. I won't get to see her. Tell her I wish her well in the Practice. I know she will make a success of it, and between you, it will flourish."

"I'll tell her, Beau. She'll be sorry she missed saying good-bye, but I think it's best that way."

Beau stepped back as the black Ford eased on to the roadway. Clarence waved a hand, honked the horn, and moved off into the traffic.

When he had disappeared from sight, Angela linked arms with Jess and

Beau. "Time to get you two settled," she said brightly. "You can have my room. The bed is bigger." She giggled.

"No, Angela!" Jess was horrified. "We wouldn't dream of tossing you out of your bed."

"No arguments!" Angela was adamant as she marched them towards her front door.

Once inside, they were escorted reluctantly to Angela's room, where she quickly moved to the window and opened the curtains. The bed was larger and higher than the one Jess had slept in, but as she opened her mouth to protest once more, Angela placed her hands emphatically on her hips.

"Not another word, Jess! Now I'm going to leave you to freshen up, while I get some food organised." She laughed as she headed for the door. "I promise it won't be bacon and eggs."

With that she was gone.

Beau was frowning. "What did she mean by that?"

"I was sick the other morning when Angela was eating bacon and eggs. The smell turned my stomach." Jess smiled at the memory.

"Oh." Beau had a quizzical look on his face. "So it is true then? Morning sickness never lies."

"Yes, it's true." Jess moved into his arms. "Are you happy now, Beau?"

"I'm over the moon, my precious girl." His arms tightened. "I just pray that I'll be a good father."

"You will be." Jess choked on the words. "No more doubting, Beau."

*

The following afternoon, as the train quietly belched steam, Jess, Beau and Angela stood silently on the platform. It was time to say good-bye, and Angela was holding back tears as she hugged her friends. The whistle sounded and a voice called out: "All aboard!"

"This is it," she murmured. "I'm going to miss you both."

"We're as close as the telephone, Angela." Jess felt a sudden wave of emotion. "Be happy, Angela, and make sure Clarence keeps his promise."

"I will. Take care, Jess." Angela turned moist eyes on Beau. "You have something very precious to look forward to now, Beau." The whistle sounded once more. "Off you go, or you won't get a compartment." She watched as they boarded the train. "Write to me, Jess!" she called out. "Let me know what's happening in your little country town."

Jess followed Beau along the narrow corridor, as Angela hurried alongside the train. "Little country town indeed!" she murmured to herself. "Yes, Angela!"

The train jerked forward, and they waved handkerchiefs until they could see one another no longer. Beau had found an empty compartment and they closed the door firmly behind them.

Part Four

A Time to be Born and a Time to Die

Arrival

The house was quiet when Jess and Beau stepped through the back wire door. They stopped and listened for the sound of running footsteps along the passage. There were none.

"We're home!" called out Jess. "Where are you?"

Still there was no sound.

"Perhaps Izzy's taken the children to the park," offered Beau. "It's a pleasant enough day."

Jess's brow was furrowed. "She knew we were returning this afternoon."

"Maybe they're at Margaret's?"

Jess put down her suitcase. "You don't suppose something has happened to Margaret?" She looked beseechingly at Beau. "Izzy did say she was becoming weaker."

"It's possible, Jess." Beau placed his bag on the table. "That's where we'll look first."

"I could telephone to see if they're there."

"Very well. You do that, while I put our luggage in the bedroom."

"Oh!" Jess had a sudden thought. "Izzy has been using our room. I would say she's probably moved her things around to Margaret's, to let us have our room back."

"Maybe." Beau smiled wryly. "Make that call, Jess."

"Yes, Beau," said Jess meekly, and smiled as she headed into the passage to use the telephone.

It was Charles who answered the call, and in his booming voice, declared that they were all in the kitchen, Margaret included, preparing a homecoming feast for the weary travellers. Jess put down the receiver, and as Beau returned from the bedroom, stretched out an arm to stop him.

"They're all at Margaret's," she said as she wrapped both arms around him. "Izzy thought we'd be on the later train, that's why there was no-one to greet us. They're preparing a feast for us."

"Are they?"

Beau returned her embrace, and they stood silently for a few moments, contemplating the past couple of weeks and the enormous impact that it had

had on their lives. They were home now, but the questions would still have to be answered.

"What will they all think of me?" Beau murmured against Jess's hair.

She raised her head to stare at him. "What do you mean?"

"Will they think me a weak man who can't handle stressful situations?"

As Beau met her gaze, Jess could see the same sadness in his eyes that she had witnessed when he first arrived at her gate, and which she had caught glimpses of during their time together.

"They'll think no such thing!" she scolded, although her voice trembled. "You'll never be weak in my eyes, Beau. You have endured more than enough over the years, and now it's time to think about the future." She placed his hand on her stomach.

He smiled softly. "Are we going to tell them?"

"Of course we are." Jess took his hand. "Now come on, we'd better get around there and share in their celebration of your safe return."

"Jess?" Beau pulled her to a halt. "I never stopped loving you, even while I was in the darkest corner of my life. I want you to know that."

"I believe you, Beau."

*

They heard running footsteps as they waited at the door of the Stanley residence. Suddenly it was flung open, and three sets of arms competed for hugging rights, while three young voices all talked at once. Jess found herself struggling to stay upright, and finally she had to put an end to the commotion.

"Children, please!" she laughingly implored. "Let us inside and we'll answer your questions." She looked up to see Izzy smiling at her from the doorway. "What a welcoming committee!"

"They have been so anxious," said Izzy, as she ushered the children along the passage. "I had to put them off, because I thought you'd be on the later train, but here you are!" Izzy stretched out her arms to embrace them both. "It's so good to have you both home." She looked at Beau, and her eyes filled. "Welcome back, Beau."

"It's good to be back, Izzy."

"What an ordeal you've had, both of you." Izzy brushed the tears from her eyes as she led the way into the kitchen. "We've been busy making fairy cakes, and Grace has insisted that we need green icing to decorate them, so we've had to do a search for green food colouring."

Jess laughed. "Why green icing, Grace?"

"Because it's your favourite colour, ma," said Grace impishly.

"Yes, Gracie, it is." Jess looked around as she spoke.

Margaret was seated to her right, and Charles stood behind her chair. He smiled as her eyes sought his face.

"It's good to have you home," he said gruffly, his eyes blinking rapidly.

Jess reached for Beau's hand, as he stood beside her. "It's good to be home, Charles." She looked at Margaret, who was smiling serenely. "You look well, Margaret." Jess was surprised by the colour in Margaret's cheeks.

"I have my good days, and I have my bad days," said Margaret, as she reached out a hand towards Jess. "Today is a good day." She looked up at Beau. "I hope it's a good day for you, Beau."

"It is, Margaret." Beau cleared his throat. "It's a very good day."

The two boys were leaning against the table, and finally tiring of the dull adult conversation, Edward turned to Izzy. "When can we have our cakes, Auntie Izzy?" he asked solemnly.

Izzy laughed, as she rumpled his hair. "Not good at waiting, are you, Edward? We'll have them soon. Let your mother and Beau rest for a while. Go and play while you're waiting."

Edward shook his head. "No, we'll wait here."

Ben grabbed his arm. "Come on, Edward! Let's go up to the lounge and finish our game of snakes and ladders."

Edward sniffed. "Oh, alright."

"Wait for me!" Grace followed the boys as they left the kitchen.

Silence reigned, broken only by the singing of the kettle on the stove. Jess looked up at Beau. With the children out of earshot, it seemed like a good time to tell the family their news.

"Will we tell them now, Beau?"

He smiled at her. "If you like."

"Tell us what?" Izzy looked keenly at her sister.

"Beau and I are expecting a baby," said Jess quietly, and waited for the penny to drop.

Izzy clasped her hand to her mouth to muffle the squeal that erupted. "You are?"

"Yes."

"Jessie! Beau! That's wonderful news! Let me be the first to congratulate you." Izzy pounced on her sister, and enveloped her in an enthusiastic hug.

As Jess released herself from Izzy's grasp, she saw Ben standing in the doorway. He had heard the news, and his face was set in an accusing scowl as he looked at his mother.

"Ben, come here," said Jess quietly, as Izzy turned to envelop Beau in the same enthusiastic hug.

"No!" He ran through the kitchen and out the back door.

"Ben!" Jess made to follow him, but Beau pulled her back.

"Stay here, Jess. I'll go after him." He followed Ben out the back door.

"Sit down, Jess," said Izzy, pulling out a chair from the table.

As Jess sat heavily, concerned about her eldest son, Margaret touched her arm softly.

"We are very pleased for you, Jessie," she began. "Aren't we, Charles?"

"Yes, certainly," said Charles gruffly.

"When?" Izzy sat beside her sister.

"I don't know." Jess laughed. "It's very early days, and I haven't seen a doctor yet. I had my suspicions before Beau went away, but I didn't say anything, because I wasn't sure."

"And now you're sure?" Izzy insisted.

"Yes."

Izzy clapped her hands. "A baby! How wonderful!"

Charles sat beside Jess, his eyes full of concern. "How is Beau, really?" he asked.

Jess looked him squarely in the face. "He's not himself, Charles. He's very withdrawn, and I fear it will take some time for him to come to terms with what has happened to him." She smiled. "But he has come a long way, even now." She wanted to tell them all how afraid she had been, initially, but she refrained.

"And his sister?" asked Izzy, her eyes wide.

"She put herself out on a limb to find him. I believe she has always loved him, and wondered about him. She was very reluctant to let him go."

"It's very sad, isn't it?" Izzy wiped her eyes. "Some families just don't have that warmth and security that we have known." She sighed as she pulled herself to her feet. "Well, I'd better cream these cakes before we have Edward back again."

Jess looked across at Margaret. There were tears in her eyes as she reached for Jess's hand.

"You're the right person to see him through this, Jessie," she whispered. "And you will."

*

Beau followed Ben across the back yard, with its well-maintained vegetable plots, to where the boy had flung himself beneath the over-hanging branches of a gnarled old apple tree.

"Do you mind if I join you, Ben?" he asked, before awaiting the invitation to sit.

Ben looked up at him and shrugged his shoulders. "If you like," he muttered.

Beau sat and folded his arms around his knees. "I've never been out here before," he said as he looked about him. "Your grandfather keeps a very neat garden, doesn't he?"

Ben nodded. "I suppose so."

Beau was silent for a few moments.

"Ben," he said eventually, "sometimes we have to go through changes in our lives that don't necessarily fit in with the plans we have for ourselves."

Ben squinted up at him. "Like you marrying ma?"

Beau pulled at a blade of grass. The boy was not going to mince matters. "Yes, like me marrying your ma." Ben was silent. "And now we're going to have a baby sister or brother for you."

"I don't want another brother or sister. One of each is enough." Ben was becoming belligerent.

"What about your ma, Ben? Maybe she wants to give you a brother or sister."

"But…dad's not here." He scowled. "She can't!"

Beau scratched his head. This was going to be a little more difficult than he had at first thought.

"No, your dad's no longer here, Ben," he began slowly, "but I married your ma because I love her, and we want to have children." He swallowed hard as he thought about his recent ordeal. "I have tried hard to be a good replacement dad for you, but you will always keep your dad's name. Do you understand me, Ben?"

"Yes."

"The new baby will be my child, and will take my name."

Ben's brow wrinkled. "That's silly!"

"Never mind, Ben. The point is you will always be your father's son, no matter what happens in the future." Beau smiled at the bemused expression on Ben's face. "Anyway, the baby will not arrive for quite a few months, so you'll have plenty of time to get used to the idea." Beau stood up. "Come on. Let's go inside. We don't want to miss out on any of these cakes with the green icing."

Ben wrinkled his nose. "Who ever heard of green icing?"

"Gracie obviously has."

Ben got to his feet, and together they walked towards the house.

"Well," he said sagely, "if there has to be a baby, I hope it's a boy."

"Do you?" Beau smiled to himself.

Unwelcome News

The children were in bed, the house was quiet, and Jess sat beside Beau on the old brown couch, tucking up her knees. Leaning her head on his shoulder, she thought about the day. It had been a day of positives, except perhaps for Ben's reaction to the news about the baby. Margaret had been in good spirits, and that meant Charles was in a more jovial mood. Izzy, of course, was dying to know every little detail of the past two weeks, but Jess had hushed her, saying that it was not a subject for general discussion. Beau had been quiet throughout the afternoon tea, with its green cakes, and Jess had watched him covertly. He caught her eyes on him at one point, and before she looked away, she saw the faint glimmer of a smile.

She turned to him now, and tucked an arm through his. "What did you say to Ben, today? He seemed in a better frame of mind when you both returned from the garden."

Beau shrugged. "I didn't say much." He turned to look at her. "In some ways, Ben is very astute, but today I realised that he's just a little boy."

"Oh?"

"Yes. He said that you couldn't have a baby, because his dad was no longer here."

"He said that?"

"I thought he might have understood that our love could also produce a baby, but I don't know that he did." Beau ran a hand through her hair. "He did say that if there has to be a baby, then he hopes it's a boy." He laughed softly. "What do you think, Jess?"

"I don't care one way or the other," she laughed. "Although another girl would be nice."

"Hm." He kissed her forehead, and Jess felt some of the tenderness returning. "And do you have an inkling as to when this event will take place? You women seem to have inside knowledge about these things, that even the doctors don't have."

Jess thought for a moment. "I'm thinking that I'm about six weeks." Her brow furrowed. "That means we're probably due sometime in May, next year."

"Edward and I have birthdays in May."

Jess wrapped her arms around his neck. "Wouldn't it be nice if it was born on your birthday?"

"I couldn't wish for a better present." Beau bent his head to kiss her, igniting the familiar flame in both of them.

Jess sent up a silent prayer of thankfulness that her Beau was returning to her.

*

The following morning, after Beau had walked the boys to school, Izzy arrived at the back door, having spent the night at Margaret's. She called out: 'Hello! Anybody home?"

"I'm in the washhouse!" Jess called back, and immediately saw Izzy at the door.

"Should you be doing that?" accused Izzy, as she watched Jess dragging towels out of the copper with her washing stick.

"Why not?" shrugged Jess. "It's got to be done."

"Where's Beau? He could do it for you."

Jess brushed the damp tendrils of hair from her face. "He walked the boys to school, and then he's going to see Raymond Simmons." She turned back to her washing. "He wasn't looking forward to explaining to Raymond why he's been gone so long."

"Does he have to explain?" Izzy took the washing stick from Jess's hand and dunked the towels in the trough of cold water. "I kept him fairly well up to date with what was happening."

"Yes, but Beau feels it needs to come from him." She stopped. "He's hoping Raymond will be sympathetic and allow him a few more days away from the surgery."

"Oh, I'm sure he will. He knows how traumatic the whole thing has been for Beau, and for you, for that matter." Izzy grabbed the handle of the wringer. "Here, let me do that! You put them in the basket."

Jess shook her head in exasperation. "Izzy, I am not an invalid!" she retorted.

"I know," said Izzy smoothly, "but you can never be too careful, Jess."

Jess didn't answer, because she knew that Izzy was speaking from her own personal experience, having miscarried several times.

Together they managed to get the towels into the basket and outside to the clothesline. As Jess pulled down the hoists, Izzy reached for the peg bag, and in no time the line was up and the towels flapping in the late spring breeze.

As they stood watching the washing, they heard heavy footsteps coming along the path beside the house. Jean appeared, breathing heavily.

"Oh, there you are!" She put a hand to her chest. "Jessie! You're home!"

"Yes, Jean, we arrived home yesterday afternoon." Jess grabbed Jean by the arm and led her towards the verandah. "Sit down, Jean. You shouldn't have been hurrying." She pulled the old wooden chair towards her friend.

Jean sat with an audible sigh. "I know, but I wanted to tell Izzy what I've just heard from Billy Maitland." She wiped her perspiring brow on a handkerchief.

"What have you heard, Jean?" Jess leaned over her anxiously. "Is it about Sid?"

"Yes." She took a deep breath. "He's out of gaol, and on the warpath, according to Billy."

Izzy stepped onto the verandah. "What's going on, Jess?" Her brow was creased with concern.

Jess turned to her sister. "I'm sorry, Izzy, with all that's been happening, I neglected to tell you about Sid."

"Tell me what about Sid?"

"Didn't he get three months in gaol?" Jess had turned once more to Jean.

"No. The Magistrate gave him two weeks to ponder on his misdemeanours, and then he has to report to the police station three times a week for the rest of the three months."

"What?" Jess felt faint. "And you heard that from Billy?"

"Yes."

"Jess!" Izzy was becoming irritated. "What is going on?"

Jess sat heavily on the top step, suddenly unable to remain on her feet. "I'd almost forgotten about Sid," she mused to herself.

"Jess!"

She looked up at her sister. "It's my fault he went to gaol." Jess lowered her head to her knees.

Izzy sat beside her, and placed an arm about her shoulders. "Tell me about it, Jess."

Tearfully, Jess related the events that had led to Sid's arrest, and Izzy listened with horror, murmuring the occasional mild expletive.

"Oh, Jess," she said slowly, when the story had been told. "You have had a terrible time, haven't you? What do you think he'll do?"

"I don't know, Izzy. Maybe Billy has it wrong."

"No!" said Jean emphatically. "Billy hasn't got it wrong. Sid's out for blood, according to Billy."

"If he does anything, the police will be straight on to him, and then the Magistrate might not be so lenient." Izzy was fuming. "Do you think he'll be after Beau?"

"Yes," said Jean cautiously. "I would think so."

The three women stared glumly at one another, uncertain of what to do next. It was not news that Jess wanted to hear, after all that they had been through.

"If it's any consolation," said Jean finally. "Billy did say he'd keep a close eye on him."

"I don't want Billy getting into trouble." Jess knew that Billy wouldn't hesitate in dealing out his own punishment on Sid, for wrongs done to him in the past.

"Billy can take care of himself." Jean hoisted herself off the chair. "Anyway, I thought you should know how the land lies. I'd better get back to the pub." She smiled at Jess. "It's good to have you back, Jessie love. Izzy has kept me informed, and I am so sorry about what has happened to Beau."

"We'll get through it, Jean." Jess got shakily to her feet. "But we can do without Sid's revenge."

Izzy took her arm. "Come inside and sit down, Jessie. You look done in."

"I am feeling a little faint, I must admit." As Jess allowed Izzy to lead her to the back door, she turned. "Thank-you, Jean. We did need to know that. I'll catch up with you tomorrow."

"Righto, Jessie." Jean trudged down the steps. "We'll all keep our eyes and ears open."

*

Meanwhile, Beau had arrived at the Simmons' stately residence. He rapped on the brass knocker, and waited. The moments ticked by and nobody came. Finally, as he moved to step off the verandah, he heard the click of a latch, and turned to see Louise peering at him through the half-open door.

"Oh, it's you, Beau! If you're looking for Raymond, he's at the surgery." She opened the door fully. "He'll be very pleased to see you back, I can tell you!"

Louise was clad in a flimsy dressing gown of a silky soft pink fabric. She attempted to pull it around her, but not before Beau noticed her extended belly. He took a step back to the edge of the verandah.

"Thank-you, Louise. I'll find him there."

As he closed the gate behind him, Beau took a deep breath. If he was not mistaken, Louise Simmons was pregnant. He wondered how Raymond felt about that. As he walked, he thought about his own situation, and knew that if he had not discovered the devastating truth about his family, he would have been shouting the news of Jess's pregnancy to the world.

Inside he knew that he was excited, for it was what he had craved for a long time, but there was a reservation there now, and only time could remove that reservation. He smiled to himself as he realised that both he and Raymond would experience fatherhood together, and neither of them were young.

The surgery loomed ahead of him, and Beau had to divert his mind back to the reason for his visit. He opened the gate and stepped along the path to the front door. As he opened it, Norma met him, her eyes wide but her smile even wider.

"Doctor DuBois! You're back! How wonderful! Doctor Simmons is due to start surgery in half an hour, and I'm sure he'll be pleased to see you."

"Thank-you, Norma." He stepped past her into the passage, with its familiar smell of antiseptic.

"We were so sorry to hear about your friend," she said quietly, referring of course to Matthew.

Beau nodded, realising that Norma probably knew nothing about the drama that unfolded after Matthew's death. "He will be sorely missed, Norma. We had known each other since our early school days."

They had reached Raymond's door. Norma rapped loudly.

"Yes, Norma," came the voice from within.

Norma opened the door. "Doctor DuBois's here," she said brightly, and ushered Beau into the room, closing the door firmly behind him.

Beau stood silently as Raymond gazed at him over the rims of his spectacles. Slowly he placed the pen he had been using, on the desk, and sat back, folding his arms. Beau waited for the reprimand that would surely follow, but Raymond finally extended a hand across the desk.

"Welcome home, Beau," was all he said and Beau reached out and shook his hand.

"I owe you an explanation, Raymond."

He shrugged. "Not necessary, Beau. Your sister-in-law has kept me up to date with what happened."

Beau was relieved that Raymond's relationship with him had mellowed to the point where he was prepared to free Beau from any further explanation. However, Beau felt he owed it to Raymond to put him completely in the picture, even if it meant putting a strain on their working relationship.

"No, I'd like you to hear it all from me, and then you can judge whether or not I am fit to continue working here with you at the surgery."

Raymond raised his bushy eyebrows. "Very well," he said slowly. "But can I ask why you think there's a question over your working here?"

"My lack of emotional control, for one thing."

Raymond shook his head. "Beau, these were unmitigated circumstances. I don't know how I would react under the same duress. Besides, it's not up to me to say whether you are fit for this job. That's for the Board to decide, and they won't hear any complaint from me. You've proved yourself more than capable." He laughed. "I know what you're thinking. I wouldn't have said that a few months ago. Now...if you really want to plead your case, or otherwise, I have twenty minutes before people start walking through that door." There was an uncharacteristic twinkle in his eyes.

Beau didn't know where to go from here. Raymond's benevolence had left him speechless, and he could only guess that maybe the prospect of fatherhood had mellowed him to this point. He shrugged his shoulders.

"Well, in that case I won't take up any more of your time, Raymond." He hesitated for a moment. "When would you like me to start work again?"

"Oh, next week should be time enough. I have a young Intern helping me out, and it seems that the influenza cases are on the decrease. We've had no new cases since you left." As Beau turned to leave, Raymond added, "Beau, how about you and Jess coming for dinner next Saturday night? It might be a good time to discuss all manner of things."

Beau looked at him quizzically. "Thank-you, Raymond, we'd like that."

"Good. We'll see you then."

Beau closed the door behind him, and was smiling as he headed towards the front door. He hadn't expected such a response from Raymond, and could only put it down to his impending fatherhood. Norma stepped out of the waiting room as he passed.

"You look pleased with yourself, Doctor DuBois," she said as she opened the front door for him.

"Yes, Norma. Doctor Simmons is in a very agreeable mood."

"Ah!" said Norma in an undertone. "He has every reason to be, Doctor." She looked towards the waiting room door to make sure nobody was listening. "His wife is expecting their first child."

"Oh?" Beau feigned surprise. "That accounts for it, I would say."

"It's wonderful!" Norma giggled like a schoolgirl. "I'd given up on them, but..."

"Wonders never cease, Norma." Beau smiled at her excitement. "I'll be back at the surgery next Monday morning."

"Very good, Doctor. I'll look forward to that." She became conspiratorial again. "To tell the truth, that young Intern who has been here while you've been away, has been the bane of my life! 'Norma do this' or 'Norma do that'!" She raised her eyebrows. "I'm always running after him!" She grinned. "It will be good to have you back, is all I can say!"

"Thank-you, Norma."

Beau stepped out on to the verandah and down the steps. He had crossed another hurdle today, and felt quietly confident that he would be able to resume where he had left off. His steps quickened as he headed for home. He felt sure that Jess would be pleased.

As he turned into Oleander Street, he saw a familiar figure heading his way. He frowned. It was Sid O'Connor. Beau stopped and waited until he drew near.

"Doctor DuBois!" he yelled. "Just the man I wanna see!"

"What is it, Sid?" Beau asked tersely.

"I've been in gaol because o'you, and now I want me job back. I've done me time, an' I reckon you owe me." Sid glared at Beau, as they stood face to face.

"No, Sid! I owe you nothing." Beau was trying to curb his anger. "You attacked my wife and threw a brick at my home, and you expect me to give you your job back? I don't think so."

Sid stood with his feet apart and his arms akimbo. His expression was ugly. "You dunno how it is for the likes o'me, havin' no work an' no-one t'help me, do ya? You've probably had it easy all y'life; born with a silver spoon, as they say, but me, I have t'fight for everythin' I want."

Beau smiled thinly and shook his head. "No, Sid, I certainly wasn't born with a silver spoon, as you put it, and I can appreciate your position, but I cannot trust you to uphold your part of the bargain. My wife gave you a chance, and you let her down."

Sid's pale eyes stared into Beau's for several seconds. "I need the work," he said hoarsely. "Most o'me customers've heard what I did t'you, an' they've cut me off without even a 'by my leave'."

"I'm sorry, Sid, but it's out of my hands."

Beau spotted Jess and Izzy standing at the front gate, watching them, and he frowned. Jess had a hand to her mouth, and he saw Izzy place an arm around her shoulders. Beau turned back to Sid.

"What did the Magistrate advise you to do?"

"Him!" There was derision in Sid's tone. "I gotta front up at the police station three times a week. That's not gunna earn me any money!" Sid scuffed a shabby boot on the ground.

"Maybe Albie Blake can help you out."

"Yeah, doin' what?"

Beau shrugged. "He may have customers who don't know you."

"Hardly."

"I'm sorry, but I really can't help you, Sid."

Jess and Izzy had started walking towards them, and Beau didn't want Sid to see the two women. However, Sid heard the approaching footsteps, and turned. As they drew level, he snatched his dirty cap from his head.

"'Mornin', ladies," he muttered.

Ignoring him, Jess looked at Beau. "What's going on, Beau?"

"It's alright, Jess. Mr. O'Connor and I were having a civilized conversation."

Jess turned angrily to Sid. "You've got a cheek coming back here, Sid. Weren't you told to keep well away from us?"

Sid was looking at the ground, as three pairs of hostile eyes focused on him. "Yes," he mumbled.

"Well, we could report you for breaking the terms of your release." Jess was in no mood to be lenient with the errant Mr. O'Connor. She'd had enough of his troublemaking.

Sid placed his greasy cap back on his head. "Kick a man while he's down, would ya, Mrs. DuBois? You never struck me as bein' that sort o'lady."

Jess blinked as Sid's words struck a chord within her. "I'm not, Sid," she retorted sharply, "but you have given us more than our fair share of trouble in recent times."

Beau took her arm. "Come on, Jess, we're not getting anywhere here." He looked at Sid. "Be off with you, Sid, and in your best interest, keep away from this street."

Sid stared balefully at the three watching him, and with a curl of his lips, loped across the road, stopping on the opposite side of the street.

"What do I do now?" he yelled. "Answer me that!"

"I'll have a word with Albie!" returned Beau.

"Fat lotta good that'll do!" Sid spread his arms in a gesture of hopelessness, before loping away.

Jess took a long shaking breath, and gripped Beau's arm tightly. "I hope that's the end of it. I don't wish to set eyes on him again."

"He's a very unfortunate fellow, isn't he?" said Izzy, as they walked towards home. "I often wonder what happens to people like him, who find themselves without a friend in the world, and with no means of support." Suddenly she realised what she had said, and blushed crimson as she looked sideways at Beau. "I'm sorry, Beau. I do suffer from foot in mouth disease, as you are well aware. You would know very well how that feels."

"I certainly do, Izzy." Beau laughed softly. "Yes, I certainly do."

The Dinner Party

It was nearly time for Izzy to travel back to Swan Hill. Jess felt that she was ready to manage on her own, and Beau seemed to be recovering well. The fact that he was to be received back at the surgery with open arms, had indeed heartened him, and that, coupled with the unexpected invitation to dine with the good Doctor Simmons and his wife, had lifted his spirits considerably.

After making contact with Albie Blake, Beau was confident that the matter of Sid O'Connor could finally be put to rest. Albie had agreed to take him on, under certain strict conditions, which included his sobriety and his promise to keep away from Oleander Street. According to Albie, Sid had agreed to both conditions. Jess had been relieved when she heard that, and reported to Jean that Billy Maitland could relax his vigil over Sid. Jean had laughingly said that Billy was reluctant to do that. "Can't trust the mongrel," were his words to Jean.

Margaret seemed to be in a state of remission, and although her limbs were weak, her spirits were high, and this meant that Charles could safely leave her to attend to his own work.

On the morning that Izzy was to leave, Jess had a pang of guilt that she had not told Jean about the baby, so after waving Izzy off, and promising to telephone her regularly, Jess made her way up the hill towards the Grey Goose. Beau was at home, working in the garden, and Gracie was with Margaret, so it meant that Jess could spend some time with her friend.

As she approached the Grey Goose, she met Audrey Maitland arriving to take care of Jean's washing. Audrey smiled at her as she opened the side door.

"Lovely morning, Jess," she said brightly, ushering Jess in ahead of herself.

"It is, Audrey. Summer will soon be here."

"My old bones will appreciate that, I can tell you." Audrey laughed.

"Oh, go on with you! Your bones aren't that old, Audrey." Jess was in good spirits this day.

"Old enough," returned Audrey. "Oh, by the way, Jess, Billy tells me that you've been having some trouble with our friend, Sid O'Connor."

Jess shrugged. "It's all been sorted out now, Audrey."

"He's a public nuisance, that one, and according to my Billy, won't ever be out of trouble."

"Well we hope he is now, Audrey. Albie Blake has taken him under his wing."

"Albie Blake, eh?" Audrey pulled an apron from the bag she was carrying. "If anyone can fix Sid, it will be Albie. Does my Billy know that?"

"Yes, he does, Audrey."

"Good. Maybe he'll concentrate on his own business now, instead of wondering what Sid is up to." Audrey tied the apron around her ample middle, and hung her bag behind the Bar door.

"What's Sid up to now?" Jean appeared beside them, from somewhere along the passage.

"Nothing, Jean," laughed Jess.

"He's either heading into trouble or heading out of it." Shaking her head, Audrey marched off down the passage towards the washhouse.

Jean turned questioning eyes on Jess. "You're not here to talk about Sid, are you?"

"No, Jean." Jess took Jean by the arm. "Can we go to your sitting room?"

Mystified, Jean led the way, and once inside, she turned to Jess. "Well?"

"You might want to sit down, Jean, to hear what I have to say."

Jean raised a quizzical eyebrow and sat heavily on her favourite chair. "Well?" she repeated.

"Beau and I are expecting a baby."

Jean stared at her for a long moment before letting out a long slow breath. "That's wonderful news, Jess. I couldn't be happier for you both." She struggled out of her chair. "Here, let me give you a hug." Jean wrapped her ample arms around Jess. "You both deserve some good news. When is the happy event to be?"

"By my reckoning," said Jess, extricating herself from Jean's grasp, "it will be sometime next May, but it hasn't been confirmed yet."

"You need a good doctor," laughed Jean.

"I have one, Jean, although he may not want to be my paediatrician."

Jean snorted. "What's wrong with a midwife?" she declared airily.

"Nothing, Jean. I had my other three with the midwife. The doctor arrived when it was all over."

"That's what usually happens," declared Jean airily. "Did you have Mrs. Davidson?"

"Yes, I did."

"The best in the business is our Essie Davidson. She's been delivering babies around here for a very long time."

"Maybe too long…" began Jess.

"Don't say that, Jess! Essie will be around to deliver your baby, I can guarantee."

"We'll see. Now I must have a word with Audrey, before I forget. Beau and I have been invited to dine with Doctor Simmons and Louise on Saturday night, so we'll be needing her services to look after the children."

Jean smiled. "That sounds wonderful. You do that, Jessie. Things are beginning to smooth out for you now, aren't they?"

"Not quite, Jean." Jess was thinking of Margaret. "However, Margaret seems to be doing well at the moment, so that in itself is a blessing."

"It is; it certainly is."

*

It was Saturday night, and Audrey Maitland had arrived to look after the children. Charles had offered the use of the motorcar, as he said it was too far for Jess to walk. She had argued, but eventually had to give in, and now she could hear Charles pulling up on the front street.

Jess wore her red dress, as she felt that it was loose enough to be comfortable. Already she had noticed a slight thickening around her waist. Beau was unperturbed, and slid his arms around her.

"You look stunning, my love," he admitted. "I am looking forward to the changes this child is going to have on you." He kissed her lightly.

He hadn't told her about Louise. It would be best to come from them, although he knew that Jess would be cross with him for holding out on her.

The car horn sounded. Jess picked up her shawl from the bed, and took one last look in the cheval mirror. Her hair was loose, and she had pinned an artificial gardenia over her left ear. Beau smiled at her reflection with its worried frown.

"I've already told you that you look stunning," he whispered, as he dropped a kiss on the back of her neck. "We're not meeting with royalty, you know."

Jess sighed loudly. "Medical royalty, Beau, and I want to impress."

"You'll certainly do that. Now come on, before Charles toots that confounded horn again."

Together they stepped into the passage. As they passed the lounge, Jess poked her head around the door, and issued her final instruction to the children.

"Be good, children," she said firmly. "I don't want Mrs. Maitland saying that you misbehaved."

"They'll be fine, Jess." Audrey was seated on the floor, and they were all playing pick-up-sticks. "You go and enjoy yourselves." She waved Jess away.

As they closed the front door behind them, Charles climbed out from the driver's seat, and smiling widely, opened the passenger door for Jess.

"You look lovely tonight, my dear," he said quietly, as he handed her into the car.

"Thank-you, Charles." Jess glanced at Beau who grinned widely as he settled into the driver's seat.

"No need to bring the car back tonight, my boy." Charles closed the driver's door.

"How are you going to get home, Charles?" Jess called out as Beau eased the grey Chevrolet on to the road.

Charles waved them on. "I'll walk," he called back. "It's a lovely evening."

Jess settled back on the comfortable leather seat, and smiled serenely. "I remember a time when Charles would not have considered lending his pride and joy to anyone." She thought for a moment. "I think Izzy was the first outsider to drive this car, when…" She stopped, because it was when Jess was in the hospital, after Beau's suicide attempt.

"When?" Beau prompted.

"It doesn't matter." She smiled and waved a hand in the air. "It was some time ago."

They reached the Simmons' residence, and Beau handed Jess out of the car. He took her arm, and they walked along the path between the well-tended roses. Beau rapped on the brass knocker.

Footsteps were heard and Louise opened the door. She was wearing a satin gown of the most brilliant blue, which brought out the colour of her eyes, and her blonde hair was coiled at her neck, with a marcasite clip fastened above her left ear. She smiled broadly.

"Jess! Beau! Come in! It's been quite a while, Jess."

"Yes, it has, Louise."

They were ushered into the front lounge, where Raymond was pouring drinks at the sideboard.

"Ah! Welcome. Can I offer you a drink? Beau?"

"Thank-you, Raymond. I'll have a beer."

"Jess?"

Jess shook her head. "Nothing for me, thank-you, Raymond."

"Nothing? A lemonade perhaps?"

"No, thank-you." She still felt a little awkward in his presence.

Louise was hovering at her elbow, and Raymond handed her a glass of lemonade. Jess noticed that she wasn't drinking wine, and silently applauded her decision. Louise took her arm.

"Let's leave the men to their beer," she whispered. "I have something to tell you. Come into the kitchen while I check the vegetables."

As Jess caught Beau's eye, he shrugged, so she followed Louise to the kitchen.

"I've been dying to tell you my news, Jess!" Louise declared. "Raymond and I are having a baby!"

Jess stared at her blankly for a moment. "You are?" she squeaked. "Louise, that's wonderful!"

"We've waited so long, and now it's finally happening!"

"I am so thrilled for you. When is it due?" Jess sat on the nearest chair, suddenly feeling faint.

"I'm three months gone, so I'm due at the end of March." Louise's blue eyes quickly detected that Jess was feeling overcome. "Jess, are you alright?"

Jess laughed softly. "Yes, I'm alright, Louise, but I have something to tell you, too."

"You're not? Are you?" The blue eyes crinkled at the corners. "Are you telling me that you're also having a baby?" Louise laughed merrily. "Oh, Jess! That's wonderful! When?"

"Towards the end of May, according to my reckoning."

"You haven't seen a doctor?"

"No."

They were both laughing now, unable to contain themselves. Raymond and Beau appeared in the doorway, curious about the hilarity that was issuing from the kitchen.

"What ARE you doing? Louise?"

Louise wiped a hand across her streaming eyes. "Oh, Raymond, you'll never believe this! Jess is having a baby, too." She shook a finger at the two bemused men standing in the doorway. "What have you doctors been up to, eh?" She pulled a chair from beneath the table and sat down, the tears still rolling down her face.

Raymond looked at Beau, his expression without humour.

"If this is what pregnancy does to women, Beau, then I'm not altogether sure I can handle it."

Beau smiled. "I suppose we'll have to get used to it, Raymond."

Raymond frowned, the hilarity lost on him. "Louise," he muttered tersely, "I think it would be a good idea to get the meal started, don't you?"

"Yes, Raymond." Louise sighed, the mirth suddenly gone from her eyes.

Raymond turned and walked away, motioning Beau to follow. He did so, but not before he glanced back at Jess, who was staring in the direction of Raymond's retreating back. He felt a slight feeling of disappointment for Louise. Raymond had certainly succeeded in dousing her enthusiasm.

Louise and Jess looked at one another, as the men retreated, and Louise raised her eyebrows.

"I must apologise for my husband, Jess," she said, as she stood and picked up an oven mitt from beside the stove. "He is happy about the baby, really."

"He has a funny way of showing it, Louise."

"I know. I won't change him, but the baby might." She opened the oven door, and the sweet aroma of baked meat and vegetables filled the kitchen.

"That smells delicious," said Jess, "and I don't say that very often these days."

Louise turned to look at her. "The dreaded morning sickness, Jess?"

"Oh, yes."

"I'm over that now, thank goodness." Louise surveyed her roasting pan. "I'd better get an apron on, and we'll get this meal underway."

The meal progressed pleasantly enough, in the spacious candle-lit dining room, with its mahogany table and chairs, and gleaming silverware. Conversation moved easily between the success of the Red Cross home visiting program, and the gradual decrease in the number of influenza patients being treated at the hospital auxiliary wing.

Beau complimented Louise on the meal, to which she blushed prettily and thanked him. Jess, watching her in the flickering candlelight, knew that all Louise needed was to be told that she did something well. Raymond, she suspected, was not generous with his handout of compliments, whether to his wife or anyone else, for that matter. Beau, on the other hand, had always been more than generous with his compliments. She smiled at him across the top of the candles, and received that special look reserved just for her.

"So, Beau," Louise was saying, "what was it like to meet your sister for the first time after many years? Was she as you expected?"

Beau lowered his fork, and wiped his mouth on the linen napkin, a sign to Jess that he was considering his answer. She saw the narrowing of his eyes, and held her breath for a moment.

"I...I was reminded of my - our mother." He stumbled over the words. "When she spoke, I could hear my mother's voice, and when I looked at her, I saw ..."

"She looked like you, Beau." Jess held his gaze across the table.

"But why did she take the veil?" Louise had not finished. "That seems a strange thing for a young girl to do, particularly..."

"Louise!" Raymond snapped at his wife. "Beau did not come here to be interrogated." He looked from Beau to Jess, his brow furrowed. "We'll have dessert now, if you please."

"Yes, Raymond, right away. I was only..."

"You were sticking that inquisitive nose of yours where it wasn't wanted." Raymond laughed uneasily, trying to make light of a tense moment.

"It's alright, Raymond," said Beau, now in control of his thought process. "I will answer your question, Louise. My sister chose the veil to escape a cruel and dominating father, who made everyone's life a misery, including my mother's." He stared at Jess as he spoke.

Her eyes glistened and she forced a smile to her lips. It was the first time he had spoken of his father since returning home, and her heart skipped a beat. It was another tiny step forward.

Louise took a deep breath. "I'm sorry, Beau. That must have been awful."

"I hadn't remembered most of it," said Beau hoarsely, "until I set eyes on Charlotte."

"Charlotte? Is that her name?" Louise began removing plates from the table.

"It was her name. Now she is Sister Agnes."

Louise shook her head sadly. "I still don't understand it."

"Louise?" Raymond reminded her. "Could we have dessert, please?" Louise flashed him an apologetic smile, and hurried from the dining room. Raymond looked at Beau, and in hushed tones, said: "Louise doesn't need to know all the facts, Beau."

"Very well, Raymond."

"Why not?" asked Jess, her voice sharp with indignation. Did Raymond presume that Louise was not able to deal with cold hard facts?

Raymond shot her a look of surprise, as did Beau. Jess blushed, but she had no intention of backing down.

"Why not?" Raymond had taken an imperious tone. "My dear Mrs. DuBois, Louise is a very sensitive creature, and therefore I feel that certain subjects do not need to be discussed in her presence." Jess knew that he was humouring her.

"I think you underestimate Louise, Raymond." Jess stuck her chin out defiantly.

"Jess! Please!" Beau was staring at her, his expression pained.

"Let me finish, Beau!" Jess knew that she was on very dangerous ground, but she had spoken her mind, and needed to continue. "There are some things that cannot be hidden, and finding out about them openly is, in my opinion, the best option."

"It may be your opinion, Jess, but it is not the opinion of this household." Raymond's voice was tight as he struggled to keep control.

"Jess! Apologise to Raymond. We are guests in his house." Jess could see that Beau was mortified, but she was unrepentant in defence of her friend. Raymond could turn her out of his house for her opinion if he liked, but she was not going to apologise.

At that moment, Louise returned with a tray of desserts. She looked around the glowering faces, and halted, the smile dying on her lips.

"What have I missed?" she asked tentatively, as she placed the tray on the end of the table.

"Nothing, my dear." Raymond managed a tight smile. "We were simply airing our opinions."

"Oh!" Louise looked at Jess, whose face was flushed. "I see."

"We are ready to eat," said Raymond, picking up his spoon. "What do we have, my dear?"

"Poached pears and chocolate sauce." Louise placed the crystal dessert bowls in front of everyone, before taking her seat.

They ate their poached pears in silence, and Jess knew that there would be repercussions once they got home. She had spoken her mind, and the whole scenario had put her in mind of Charles and Margaret, when Charles had refused to let his wife have an opinion. She smiled to herself as she thought how Charles had mellowed. Maybe Raymond would, too.

The evening continued, and conversation was strained as they skirted all the controversial issues, and merely chatted about mundane, day-to-day happenings. Louise, blissfully unaware of what had transpired in her absence, tried several times to lighten the mood by relating stories from her Red Cross home visiting ladies, but the laughter was far from spontaneous.

Finally it was time to say goodnight, and as they stood on the front verandah, Louise clutched Jess by the arm, and whispered in her ear.

"Did you say something that upset Raymond?"

"I had an opinion which wasn't his, Louise." Jess spoke lightly. "It happens to me sometimes, when I tend to speak my mind."

Louise giggled. "Raymond doesn't like people disagreeing with him. He can be very arrogant, in case you hadn't noticed." She squeezed Jess's arm. "Anyway, I'm so glad we're having our babies more or less together. I'll have someone to talk babies with."

"Are you ready, Jess?" Beau came up behind them, and placed Jess's shawl across her shoulders.

She nodded, and Louise moved beside Raymond who stood rigidly in the spill of light from the front door. When the 'goodnights' had been said, Beau took Jess by the elbow and without a word, walked her along the path towards the gate. Raymond called out from the verandah.

"You will be at the surgery on Monday, Beau?" It was more a statement than a question.

"Yes, I'll be there, Raymond." Beau opened the gate, and helped Jess into the car.

"Good."

Jess knew that Beau was upset with her, and the drive home was made in stony silence. She would have be the one to break it somehow. When they pulled up outside their home, Beau cut the engine and they both sat staring straight ahead. Jess stole a glance at Beau. His jaw was set and his hands were gripped around the steering wheel.

"I'm sorry if I embarrassed you tonight, Beau," she said finally, looking down at her lap.

Beau didn't answer immediately, and when he did, his voice was unsteady. "Jess, we are different to most households. Wives don't always get to air their opinions." He turned to look at her. "I'm sure you knew that already."

"Yes." Jess met his gaze.

"Raymond is over-protective of Louise, I'll grant you that, but the discussion was about my personal life, and that's where I had the problem. If Raymond had chosen not to tell Louise all the raw details, then surely that was up to him."

Jess stared at him miserably. "But my issue was that he doesn't give Louise credit for having any understanding of real life issues, and that's his big mistake."

"You're probably right, Jess, but I would have preferred it if you had said nothing."

"I know. You have to work with the man, boorish as he is." Jess stifled a giggle.

"What's so funny?"

"Louise is very excited about us having our babies together, and Raymond will probably now think of me as a bad example."

"It is ironic, isn't it?" Beau smiled as he thought about that.

Jess slid across the seat and rested her head against his shoulder. "So am I forgiven?"

Beau sighed. "Yes, you're forgiven." He kissed the top of her head. "Don't do it again."

"Are we going to sit out here, or do you think Audrey will wonder what we're up to?"

"Hm, she might." Beau wrapped his arms around her, and his mouth found hers.

Jess sighed when he finally lifted his head. "I hate it when you're cross with me, Beau." She laughed as she had a sudden thought of her sister. "Aren't you glad I'm not Izzy?"

"Why's that?"

"Because Izzy doesn't care what she says and makes no apologies for it."

"Yes, I had noticed, and yes, I'm glad you're not Izzy. Now come on, let's get you inside, and then I think I'll put the car in the back yard. I'd hate anything to happen to it, parked out here on the street."

"Whatever you say, Beau." Jess traced a finger down his cheek.

"You little minx!" Beau pulled her tight against him. "I don't care how outspoken you are, just make sure it's not in front of Raymond Simmons." He kissed her again, and this time she felt the promise of what would come later.

Margaret

Life resumed with a vague sense of normality, although Jess knew that the time was coming once again for heartache. Her daily visits to see Margaret left her with the feeling that each visit would be the last. Charles was putting on a brave face, but Jess could see that he knew the time was coming.

As they sat beside Margaret's bed on a pleasantly warm afternoon in November, Jess looked across at Charles. His expression as he watched Margaret sleeping, was one of deep sadness, and her eyes misted, causing her to drop a stitch in the baby shawl that she was knitting.

"Damn!" she said under her breath.

Charles looked up. "Did you say something, Jess?"

"No, Charles. I dropped a stitch and I swore." She shrugged. "That's all."

"Oh." He resumed his observation of Margaret's pale face. "Margaret won't get to hold the new baby, will she Jess?" he said suddenly.

"No, Charles, she won't." Jess's fingers became still as this reality settled on her, too.

Margaret stirred. Her eyes opened and her voice was just a faint whisper as she spoke.

"If it's a girl, name her after me."

Jess and Charles looked at one another, and then down at Margaret, whose eyes were now closed.

"We can certainly do that, Margaret," said Jess quietly, as she laid a hand on Margaret's arm.

"I want to see the children," Margaret said softly.

"The boys are at school, Margaret," said Jess. "Gracie is here."

"Let me see her."

Jess put down her knitting, and went out into the passage. "Gracie!" she called.

Grace appeared at the lounge door. "I'm here, ma."

"Grandma wants to see you, sweetheart." There was a lump in Jess's throat as she spoke.

Grace skipped into the bedroom, and leaning against the bed, patted her grandmother's arm.

"I'm here, grandma," she whispered. "Did you want me for something?"

Margaret opened her eyes, and placed a hand over Grace's chubby fingers. "No, darling, I just wanted to see you, that's all."

Margaret smiled and Jess had difficulty hiding the tears that had sprung to her eyes. Charles looked across at her, his eyes wide with fear as he had to acknowledge what was now happening to his beloved Margaret.

"Do you want me to sing to you, grandma?"

"Yes, dear, that would be lovely. Grandma's tired, and a song might just send me off to sleep."

So as Grace sang 'Twinkle, twinkle little star' in a piping voice, Margaret slipped quietly out of this world into the next. Jess and Charles let the tears fall unrestrained.

When she had finished singing, Grace looked at her grandma, and said, in a soft whisper:

"Was that alright, grandma?"

"Grandma's asleep, Gracie," murmured Jess, through her tears, "and that was perfect." She took Grace by the hand. "Let grandma sleep now. You go back to your toys in the lounge."

As Grace skipped out of the room, Jess moved towards Charles and wrapped her arms around him. Together they looked down on the porcelain features of Margaret, and wept quietly.

"She looks peaceful," said Charles finally, as he groped in his trouser pocket for a handkerchief.

"Yes, she does." Jess wiped a hand across her eyes.

"I haven't always appreciated her," said Charles, his voice thick. "She was always there for me, and I took her for granted. I'm so sorry, Margaret."

Jess squeezed his arm. "Margaret knew that you loved her, Charles," she said tearfully. "Maybe we all took her for granted. She was the kind of person who was always there for everyone, and no matter what you had done, she still loved you."

Charles stood looking at Margaret for several minutes, as though taking in every detail of her face. Jess stood beside him, and thought of all Margaret had done for her in her times of need.

"We're all going to miss you very much, Margaret," she whispered.

Charles blew his nose. "I must call Doctor Simmons," he said eventually, heaving a great sigh.

"If he's not available, Charles, Beau is at home."

"Doctor Simmons was Margaret's doctor," said Charles stoically, "so he'd better be the one to sign the death certificate."

"Very well. Do you want me to stay until he comes?"

"No, Jess. You go home to Beau, and…let him know what's happened." Charles smiled weakly.

"Will you be alright?" Jess felt a twinge of guilt at leaving him.

"Yes. I'd like some time alone with Margaret."

"I understand." Jess patted his arm. "I'll collect Gracie and we'll go home." Jess gathered up her knitting. "Call me if you need us to be here."

Charles nodded. "Yes, alright."

As Jess moved into the passage, she heard his stifled sob, and it was as much as she could do to stop herself rushing back into the room. He wanted to be alone with his wife, and she had to respect that.

Grace was reluctant to leave her toys, and wanted to know why she couldn't stay. Jess merely said that grandma was sleeping, and grandddad didn't want to be disturbed. Grace was content with that.

Jess hurried home, her footsteps heavy and her heart breaking. She was reminded painfully of Jack's death, of which the anniversary was coming up in just over a week, and all the same emotions came flooding back. Life could never be the same as it was.

They reached home, and Jess opened the front door, expecting to be greeted by Beau, but he wasn't in the house. Rushing out the back door, she saw him in the vegetable patch, his sleeves rolled up, and a shovel in his hands. He turned at the sound of the back door opening, and plunged the shovel into the ground as he saw Jess running towards him, her hands clasped to her mouth.

"What's wrong, Jess?"

He had hardly got the words out, when Jess flung herself into his arms, her body shaking with sobs. Beau knew immediately what was wrong. He held her until her sobs had subsided.

"So Margaret's gone?"

Jess nodded against his chest. "Yes."

"I'm so sorry, Jess."

She lifted her head. "Charles said he'd call Raymond, and…he wanted to be alone with Margaret, so we left." Jess wiped a sleeve across her eyes. "Gracie sang 'Twinkle, twinkle little star' and…it was beautiful. Margaret just went to sleep."

Beau smiled. "It's not always dramatic, Jess. Where's Gracie now?"

"In the house. She doesn't know what happened."

"Let's leave it that way for the present. The boys will be home from school soon, and then I suppose we'll have to tell them all."

"Margaret did say that if we have a girl, we could name her after her."

"I don't have a problem with that." Beau smiled as he took Jess by the arm. "Come on, I've had enough gardening for one day. Let's go inside and I'll make you a cup of tea."

"Did I hear you right, Beau? You'll make me a cup of tea?"

"Yes, well I thought you might be busy calling your sister."

Jess shook her head. "I'll do that later. There are several telephone calls I'll have to make."

They walked slowly towards the house, their thoughts now on what would happen next.

*

That evening, after the children had been bathed, Jess sat them on the couch in the lounge, and knelt down before them. Beau stood behind her, his hand on her back.

"Children," began Jess cautiously, "we have something we need to tell you, and I'm afraid you're not going to like it." Three pairs of eyes were watching her closely. "Grandma…grandma went to be with your dad, today." She swallowed hard, and felt the pressure of Beau's hand on her back.

"What do you mean?" Ben's eyes narrowed. "Do you mean she died?"

"Yes, that's what I mean, Ben."

"Why?" Edward blinked back the tears. "Why did she have to die?"

"Your grandma was very sick, Edward." Beau knelt beside Jess.

"You're a doctor!" said Edward belligerently. "You could have fixed her!"

"No, I couldn't, Edward."

"But I sang grandma to sleep." Grace's voice was high-pitched and anxious.

Jess looked at Beau, and reading her plea for help, he took Grace by the hands.

"Yes, you did, Gracie, and your ma said it was beautiful, but your grandma has gone into a special kind of sleep; one that takes her far away to where we can't get to see her."

"I can't get to see her?" Grace's face crumpled and her green eyes filled with tears.

"But do you know what?"

"What."

"She'll always be with you, although you can't see her."

"How does that work?" Ben was sceptical.

Jess could see that Beau was struggling with what he had started, so she quickly placed a hand above Ben's heart.

"She'll be in here, Ben, along with your dad. You'll have memories of both of them, and they will be special, because nobody can take those memories away. Do you understand?"

Ben scowled, Edward nodded slowly and Grace dissolved into floods of tears.

"I want to see grandma!" she sobbed, while Jess moved to pacify her.

"Why does everybody have to die?" mumbled Ben, stoically refusing to give way to tears.

"It's part of living, Ben," said Beau matter-of-factly. "We're born, we live a certain length of time, and then we die. It's the natural order of things."

"We'll be very sad for a time," said Jess, her arms around Grace, "but after a while we'll remember all the good times we had, and we'll be so glad that she was our grandma; our special grandma." Tears filled her eyes as she looked at the three sober faces in front of her. "I remember when my grandma died, and my mother told me that she was on a journey to a much better place, and that I wasn't to be too sad." She smiled as she remembered that long ago time. "It will be the same for you, and one day you will understand."

"Can I sleep in your bed, ma?" Grace patted her mother's face.

Jess looked at Beau and saw the frown that furrowed his brow, but he nodded cautiously.

"Just for tonight, alright?" Jess didn't want a repeat of what had happened after Sid's attack.

"Alright, ma."

"Good, now it's bedtime. Off you go, and we'll be in to give you a kiss shortly."

The three children went reluctantly, and Jess pulled herself to her feet. The next few days were going to be difficult for everybody, but especially for Grace. She was Margaret's little girl – her little ray of sunshine. She sighed heavily. Beau slid his arms around her and held her close.

"We'll get through it, Jess," he murmured. "We've done it before."

*

Once the children were settled, Jess made the important telephone calls to Jean and Izzy. Jean was tearful, but knowing the situation with Margaret, was not surprised. She offered her premises, if there was to be refreshments after the service. Jess thanked her, and said she would tell Charles, when arrangements were being made.

Izzy was uncharacteristically silent when Jess broke the news to her.

"Izzy?" said Jess sharply. "Are you still there?"

"Yes, I'm here." Jess could sense that her sister was struggling with this information. Their own mother's death was still fresh in their memories. "How is Charles?"

"He's heartbroken, Izzy. In spite of all that we know about Charles, he loved Margaret dearly."

Izzy gave a short laugh. "I wouldn't have lasted long with a man like Charles."

"We all know that, Izzy. However, Margaret accepted things the way they were, and now…he's heartbroken. We'll have to watch him carefully."

"How are you holding up, Jess? You've had so much going on of late, you must be feeling the strain. Please take care of yourself. You have a little one to think about now."

"Yes." Jess smiled to herself. "If we have a girl, she will be named after Margaret."

"That's lovely, Jess." Izzy sighed. "Let us know when the funeral is to take place. We'll come down if we can."

"Izzy, it's the anniversary of Jack's death on the fourteenth of this month." Jess's voice quavered.

"Yes, of course it is. You take care little sister. We'll be thinking of you."

Jess hung up the receiver and stood for a moment. She would have to take care of herself. Her pregnancy was in its early days, and she didn't want to put it at risk, not after the events of the past weeks. It was a glimmer of hope on the horizon, after all the storms and emotional traumas.

Beau saw her standing pensively beside the telephone, and came up beside her.

"A penny for your thoughts, Jess?"

"Oh!" She turned, startled. "I didn't hear you coming, Beau." She smiled at him. "I was thinking about our baby, and how lovely it will be to look forward to something wonderful after everything that's happened."

"Yes, it will." Beau wrapped his arms around her. "How is Izzy?"

"Actually, she didn't sound her usual self. She was very quiet, for Izzy."

"The news has rocked her, too, I suppose."

Jess shook her head. "No, it shouldn't have been a surprise. It was more than that. She sounded very flat."

"I don't want you worrying your pretty head about Izzy. She's probably having an 'off' day."

"Yes, doctor." Jess smiled up at him. "I should be more concerned about Charles."

"Yes, you should."

Jess leaned her head against his chest. "I'd better telephone Angela and Mary, to let them know what's happened, not that I expect them to come, but they met Margaret and I'm sure they'd want to know."

"You do that, my love, and then I think it's time you went to bed. I don't want you over-doing things." He grimaced. "Besides, Gracie has been calling for you."

Jess sighed. "I'm sorry, Beau. I expect we'll both be kicked to death by Gracie tonight."

"You'd better believe it."

*

The following days were filled with sombre activity, as preparations were made for Margaret's funeral, and the date was set for the thirteenth of November. Jess was anxious about this decision, because it preceded the anniversary of Jack's death, but Charles was comforted by it. Mother and son would be together, he said.

Jess hovered on the sidelines, as Charles insisted on organising the day, giving advice where she felt it was necessary. Watching him closely, she was aware of his stoicism, even though at times he faltered, and insisted that he be left alone. These were the times when Jess became extra vigilant, and made sure that although his wishes were respected, she was close by.

Jean's offer to host the refreshments on the day was firmly, yet graciously turned down by Charles. The ladies from the Church had insisted that they organise the food, and mourners would mingle in the Sunday-School hall. Jean had to agree that it would be more convenient.

Jess called Angela and Mary, and they were both very sorry, but didn't think they could get to the service. Jess hadn't expected that they would come, and told them both that she understood. Angela had too far to come, and Mary had baby Jack to think about.

As she came off the telephone, Jess suddenly realised that Sally Mitchell would want to know about Margaret. After all, they had both attended the same Church since Sally was a child. Jess leafed through her list of contacts, and found a number. She had no idea whether it was Sally's current number, but she asked to be put through to it anyway.

After several moments, she heard a familiar voice.

"Hello. Sally Mitchell speaking."

"Sally, it's Jess – Jess Stanley." She gasped as she realised what she had said. "I mean Jess DuBois," she added hastily.

Sally laughed. "Hello, Jess. That's an easy enough mistake to make. How are you, anyway?"

"I'm very well, Sally, but I am the bearer of sad news, I'm afraid."

"What's happened?" The laughter had died from Sally's voice.

"It's Margaret." Jess swallowed hard. "She died two days ago."

"Oh, no! Jess, how awful! I am so sorry. Margaret was always so nice to me, even when I was an annoying child." Sally paused. "How is Mr. Stanley?"

"Charles? He's coping alright at present."

"When is the funeral?"

"On the thirteenth," whispered Jess. "The day before the anniversary of Jack's death."

"Oh, golly! You poor thing, Jess!"

"I don't expect you to be there, Sally, but I thought you should know."

"Oh, I'll be there, Jess. Simon is away at present. What time is the funeral?"

"Oh – er – two o'clock."

"I'll be on the morning train."

"Thank-you, Sally. It will be lovely to see you again."

"Ditto, Jess."

Jess slowly replaced the receiver. Looking up she saw Beau watching her, and she smiled at him.

"Sally's coming, but Angela and Mary couldn't promise to be here."

"They've probably both done enough travelling about the countryside."

"Yes, I suppose they have."

"You look tired, my love. Put your feet up for half an hour. There's nothing pressing that you have do now, is there? You've been on your feet all day, and I'm worried about you."

Jess smiled at his concern. "I'm alright, Beau, truly."

"I insist." Beau took her arm and led her to the lounge, where he pressed her gently on to the couch, and swung her legs up. "There!" He placed a cushion behind her head. "Stay put for half an hour. That is an order."

"But Beau…"

"No buts, Jess; Doctor's orders."

ess sighed. "The boys will be home from school soon."

Beau held up a hand. "I know. I'll attend to them." He bent and kissed her lightly on the cheek. "The next couple of days are going to be very harrowing," he said gently, "and my primary concern is for you."

"Yes, alright."

"Good girl."

As he left the room, Jess relaxed against the couch, suddenly aware that she was very tired, both emotionally and physically. She closed her eyes and was soon asleep.

Saying Goodbye

The little Church was full, and the only sound was the gentle wheeze of the pedal organ, as Mrs. Dutton played Margaret's favourite hymns. Jess sat between Charles and Beau, in the Stanley family's pew, and the two boys sat at either end. All were in their best clothes. Jess didn't have anything black, so she had chosen a dark grey skirt and fitted jacket, over a cream blouse with ruffles at the neck. On her head she wore a black straw hat over which she had added black netting.

Izzy and Harry, who had arrived on the midday train, sat directly behind them. Both were attired in black suits, Izzy's with a splash of pale pink lace at her throat.

Grace and Freya had gone to stay with Mrs. Maitland for the duration of the service, so Jess and Izzy could concentrate on the proceedings.

She glanced around to see who had come to pay their respects to Margaret, and was gratified to see so many representatives from the Church, the Red Cross and the Hospital Board. She saw Jean seated beside Louise Simmons who was discreetly wiping at her eyes. Raymond was not beside her. He was probably at the surgery. Sally Mitchell caught her eye, and they both smiled. She was dressed in a gown of deep maroon and Jess was slightly surprised to see the matching turban she had wrapped around her short hair.

Jess's gaze rested on Billy Maitland, who winked in her direction. That was so like Billy. She smiled as she turned her gaze along the other side of the nave, and her eyes immediately widened with shock, for there was Sid O'Connor seated on the aisle. Jess quickly shifted her gaze back to the front. What was he doing here? He looked sober enough, and his fine hair was slicked down with grease. She leaned in towards Beau.

"Sid O'Connor's here," she whispered.

Beau pursed his lips. "Showing some respect, I hope."

"He's with Albie Blake."

"Good."

"Billy's here, too."

Beau glanced around. "Charles asked him to be a pall-bearer." He frowned as he turned to the front. "I hope the two of them can behave themselves."

The organ wheezed to a halt as the doors of the Church swung open, and the Reverend Dawkins swept down the aisle, his robes rustling. All eyes moved to the pulpit. Beau squeezed Jess's hand.

Reverend Dawkins' gaze swept around the mourners and rested on the polished wooden coffin that stood before the altar. He took a deep breath.

"Friends," he began, "it is with great sadness that we are all gathered here today." Jess glanced swiftly at Charles, whose jaw was set. "As we say goodbye to Margaret Stanley, we reflect on the kind of person she was, and I am sure you have all been influenced in one way or another, by her kindness, her warmth, her generosity and her ability to make everyone she met feel important." Jess reached for a handkerchief. "We come to offer our condolences to Charles and the family, and to let them know that we will be here for them in the days that follow." He turned a page in his Bible. "One of Margaret's favourite Bible passages comes from Ecclesiastes, and of course you all know the one I mean. 'To everything there is a season; a time for every purpose under heaven.'" His droll voice continued. "A time to be born, a time to die;

a time to plant, a time to reap; a time to kill, a time to heal…"

When he reached the final verse, 'a time for war, a time for peace', he closed his Bible and looked across the congregation. "'Whatever God does is final – nothing can be added or taken from it.'" He raised his arms. "Let us pray." All heads bowed.

Jess glanced across at Edward. She could see his legs swinging backwards and forwards, so she reached across Beau and tapped him on the arm. "Sit still, Edward," she whispered.

"How long do we have to sit here?" Edward asked petulantly.

"Not long, now be quiet, please!"

The service continued with Margaret's favourite hymn, 'I come to the garden alone, when the dew is still on the roses,' and Jess took Charles by the arm as he swayed slightly.

At the conclusion, after the words 'the Lord giveth, and the Lord taketh away…' the pallbearers were called forward, and they included Charles, Beau, Harry, and Billy Maitland.

As they filed out of the Church, Jess took her boys by the hands, and smiling encouragingly at them, followed the coffin from the building. Izzy stepped up behind her, and Jess heard her whisper tearfully, "That was lovely, Jess."

Once outside, the coffin was placed in the back of the black hearse, ready for its journey to the cemetery. People milled around Charles, offering their condolences, and Jess noticed that he was gracious in his replies. Several members of the Hospital Board gathered around him, and solemnly shook his hand.

Jess let her gaze stray from Charles to the crowd, and she searched nervously for Sid O'Connor. There he was, talking to Jean, who was scowling ferociously at him. Jess made her way across to them. Ben and Edward had run off to join another group of children.

"Anything wrong, Jean?" she asked tentatively.

"No, Jess." Jean forced a smile. "I was just reminding Sid that this is a funeral, and he'd better not start anything."

"I won't, Mrs. O'Malley, honest! I wouldn't do that to Mrs. Stanley."

Jean squinted at him. "Don't you mean Mrs. DuBois?"

"No." Sid wiped a hand across his greased hair. "I mean Mrs. Stanley. She was a nice lady."

"Hmph! Well, don't you forget that, Sid O'Connor."

Sid turned to Jess, and she shrank from those pale eyes. "I'm real sorry, Mrs. DuBois."

"Thank-you, Sid."

"It might be a good idea if you push off now, Sid," muttered Jean. "You've paid your respects."

Sid stood stiffly, glaring at Jean. "I'll hang around, if ya don't mind. Albie an' me are off collectin' wood shortly. I'll wait for 'im."

"Hmph! There'll be a lot of eyes watching you, Sid."

"Yeah, I know." Sid's eyes strayed to where Billy and Beau were in conversation. They both looked in his direction. "Yeah, I know," he repeated before turning away.

"I don't trust him not to make a scene, Jess," said Jean tersely. "And Billy's just the one to provoke him."

"They won't, Jean."

Jess was watching Sid making his way through the crowd to where Albie Blake was talking to Charles, and she didn't see the young couple coming towards her. Jean touched her arm.

"Jess, isn't that Jack's young friend, Martin?"

Jess turned to where Jean was indicating, and her hands flew to her mouth. The handsome young man striding towards her was indeed Martin Weatherall, and beside him walked a slender young woman with long brown hair and a vivacious smile.

"Martin!" Jess found herself crushed in a hug that left her breathless. "I didn't know you were here!" she gasped as she tried to regain her composure.

"Mum said I should come." Martin turned to the young woman beside him. "Jess, this is Fleur Bovaird, my fiancé. We arrived in Australia last week, and we're getting married as soon as it can be arranged." He pushed the young woman forward.

Jess found herself looking into wide brown eyes. "I'm very pleased to meet you, Fleur."

"Bonjour, Jess. Martin tells me so much about you." Her English was fluent.

Martin grinned proudly down at her. "I've been teaching Fleur English, Jess."

Jess nodded. "Very good, Martin." She put a hand to her breast. "This is such a shock. I can't believe you're here."

"It was a last minute decision, Jess. Izzy and Harry don't know we're here, either."

Jess saw Beau walking towards them. "Beau!" she called excitedly. "Look who's here?"

Beau shook Martin by the hand. "Well, this is a surprise! How are you, Martin?"

"I'm very well, Beau. Meet my fiancé, Fleur." He grinned. "She's French, too."

"Bonjour, Fleur." Beau smiled at the young woman.

"Bonjour, Beau." She glanced swiftly up at Martin, before returning her gaze to Beau. "You fight in my country, also?"

"Oui! Yes, I did."

"I'm so sorry."

Beau shrugged. "We've moved on since then." He looked at Martin. "Tell me, how is the restoration going in France?"

"Slowly," said Martin, " but we will get there eventually."

By now Jess was feeling faint, and she grabbed Beau by the arm. "I have to sit down, Beau," she whispered, as she felt her knees buckle beneath her. Beau supported her, and assisted by Martin, led her back into the Church. As he sat her on the nearest pew, Izzy appeared beside them. She had just seen Martin for the first time.

"Jessie, are you alright?" she asked anxiously. "I'll get you some water."

"No, Izzy! I'm fine. I needed to sit down. Seeing Martin here was a shock."

"Nancy didn't say you'd be here, Martin?" said Izzy with mock annoyance. "We could have travelled down together. Hello Fleur."

"Bonjour, Mrs Dalton." Fleur smiled sweetly.

"We made a last minute decision," said Martin. "There wasn't time to make arrangements."

"Then we'll have to travel home together."

Harry appeared at the Church door. "Charles wants to head to the cemetery when you're all ready." He spotted Martin. "Martin, how did you get here?"

"The same way we did, Harry," snapped Izzy.

"But…"

"Never mind that now, Harry." She turned her attention to Jess. "Do you feel up to going to the cemetery, Jess?"

"Yes, certainly." Jess glanced swiftly at Beau as he placed a hand on her forehead.

"Do you think you should, Jess?"

"Yes, Beau. I'm perfectly alright now."

"You will ride in the car with Charles and the boys."

"It's not far," protested Jess. "I can walk."

"No, and that's final!"

Izzy raised her eyes as she marched out of the Church, and Jess heard her mutter, "Men!"

As Beau helped Jess to her feet, he whispered, "Trouble in paradise?"

"I'll have to find out," she whispered back.

Charles was waiting silently beside the hearse as they all filed out of the Church to join the crowd waiting to either walk or drive to the cemetery. Beau pressed Jess towards Charles's car, and helped her into the passenger seat. Jess watched as he spoke to Charles, who indicated that he was going to walk in front of the hearse. From the head nodding that followed, she gathered that Beau would drive her in Charles's car.

As she sat waiting, Jess saw Ben and Edward running towards their grandfather. They spoke to him, and he looked in Jess's direction. She saw Beau nod his head, before walking towards her.

"What are the boys doing?" she asked as he cranked the car into motion.

"They're going to walk with Charles." Beau sat beside her, and waited for the hearse to move.

"He'll like that," said Jess quietly.

Beau placed a hand on hers as they lay on her lap. "They're little men now, Jess, and this experience won't hurt them."

"No, I don't suppose it will." Jess felt her eyes prickle as she thought of Jack, and the sense that there had been no closure after his death.

Beau saw her face working, and squeezed her fingers. "Cry if you want to, Jess."

A voice beside her brought Jess back to the moment. It was Izzy.

"Can I ride in the car with you, Jess? These shoes are killing me!" Without waiting for an answer, she hitched her skirt and stepped up on to the running board. Jess heard her plop on to the back seat with a heavy sigh.

"Izzy, you never learn, do you?" said Jess drily, catching Beau's eye. "Your footwear is never suitable for the occasion."

"I know." Izzy covered her eyes with her hands. "Lecture me, if you like."

"No, I'm not going to lecture you, Izzy. You should know by now what I think."

Izzy groaned, and Jess half-turned to look at her. There was definitely something distracting her sister at present, and she would get to the bottom of it, but not now. This was Margaret's day, and she had to concentrate on that. Izzy could wait.

As Beau let the clutch out, Jess put a hand on his arm.

"Beau! Wait! Where's Jean? It's too far for her to walk to the cemetery."

"She's with the Doctor's wife," came Izzy's voice from the back seat.

"What's her name?"

"Louise."

"That's right. Jean is in Louise's car."

"That's good." Jess smiled at Beau. "Carry on, driver."

The car bumped away from the grass verge and on to the road. Ahead the hearse had slowly started moving, and people walked alongside. Charles and the two boys walked in front, and Jess felt her heart constrict. Beau was right; they were little men now. She wiped her eyes and concentrated on the road ahead.

It was about half a mile from the Church to the cemetery, and the weather was fragrantly warm, with a cloudless blue sky and a soft breeze. It was the kind of day Margaret would have enjoyed as she sat on the front verandah, looking out over her roses.

Jess scanned the crowd as they walked alongside, and she guessed that most of those who had been at the Church were now heading to say their final farewells to Margaret. She saw Sid walking with Albie, and she hoped that his respect for Margaret would keep him out of trouble this day.

"We will need two more men to lower the coffin." Beau's voice broke into her thoughts.

"Martin will probably do it," said Jess. "He's young and strong."

"You're right. I'll ask him."

Jess looked across the heads of the mourners. "There are plenty of men here, Beau."

The cortege entered the gates of the cemetery and drove slowly to the designated gravesite. Jess watched as Charles drew the two boys to his side. She saw him speak to them and they stood quietly while he went to speak with the reverend Dawkins, who had walked alongside the hearse.

Beau climbed out of the car, and turned to Izzy.

"Look after Jess, please Izzy. I need to organise two more pall-bearers."

"I'll do that, Beau." Izzy slid languidly from the back seat.

Jess was slightly irritated. "I don't need looking after, Beau!"

He gave her that look which said 'yes, you do', and hurried away towards Charles.

Jess clambered out of the car, and Izzy grabbed her arm. As she tried to pull away, Izzy clucked her tongue and grasped her firmly.

"We mustn't ruffle feathers, Jessie," she said as they walked towards the gravesite.

"Mustn't we?" Jess wasn't in the mood for Izzy's sarcasm. "Let go my arm, Izzy."

"No. The good doctor has spoken."

"For goodness sake, Izzy! What is wrong with you?" Jess immediately held up a hand. "No, don't tell me now. I will speak with you later."

Izzy let out a 'hmph!' and released Jess's arm. As she did so, Jess sensed someone walking a few steps behind her. She turned. It was Sally Mitchell.

"Sally!" she exclaimed. "I'm sorry I haven't had a chance to speak with you."

"That's alright, Jess. Hello Izzy."

Sally received a curt nod in response, and Jess frowned. This was so unlike Izzy.

"How have you been, Sally? Still enjoying the city lifestyle?"

Jess had already noticed that Sally's hemline was shorter than Izzy's, and her brown hair beneath its maroon turban was cropped short across the nape of her neck.

"Oh, yes. Simon and I are now living in a sort of commune with a lot of artists." Her face flushed slightly. "Simon is very artistic, and I've taken up pottery."

"Pottery?" Jess showed surprise. "What about the teaching?"

Sally shook her bobbed head. "No. This is much more rewarding."

"Financially?" Izzy asked drily.

Sally hesitated. "Not really," she admitted.

"So how do you keep yourselves?" Izzy, being artistic herself, could not hide her curiosity.

"Oh, we pool our resources. It works well enough."

"I see." Jess could see that Izzy was sceptical.

"Jess!" Sally grabbed her arm. "I have to catch the six o'clock train back to Melbourne, so I'm afraid I won't be able to stay long at the refreshments."

"That's alright, Sally." Jess patted her hand. "It's lovely to see you."

"Mrs. Stanley was always so kind to me."

"She was kind to everyone, Sally, even the likes of…" She broke off as she caught sight of Sid removing his grubby suit coat, handing it to Albie, and stepping up beside Billy alongside the coffin. She sucked in her breath as the Reverend Dawkins raised his hands for silence.

"We have come to the final moments of the service," his voice rang out, "but not the final moments for Margaret. She has moved on to better things. Before we commit her body to the earth, we will hear the words of the twenty-third Psalm." He cleared his throat.

"The Lord is my shepherd; I shall not want…"

All heads were bowed as his voice rang across the cemetery. Jess stole a glance across to where the six men were standing silently beside the coffin, waiting to lower it into the earth - Charles, Martin and Harry on one side, and Beau, Sid and Billy on the other side.

The service finished with The Lord's Prayer, and slowly the men tightened their hold on the ropes, bracing themselves as they lowered Margaret's body to its final resting place. Charles was crying unashamedly as the rope gradually slipped through his hands. Jess could see Beau watching him from across the grave, and tears filled her own eyes. Izzy and Sally moved as one to slip their arms through hers, and she was silently grateful for their presence.

When it was over, the gravediggers waited patiently for the crowd to disperse, before beginning their task of filling the grave. It was over.

Jess released her arms, and walked across to Charles, who was watching the grave being filled.

"Margaret is at peace, Charles," she whispered, "and she's not here."

"I know, Jess." Charles wiped his eyes. "It doesn't make it any easier, though, does it?"

"No, but at least you will have a place to come and remember her."

Charles looked closely at Jess. "You don't have that, Jess."

"No." Jess smiled through her tears. "Come on, there's nothing more we can do here, and all the food will be eaten if we don't get back to the hall." Jess saw Beau waiting beside the car, the boys and Izzy with him. "You'd better have a ride in your car, Charles." She took his arm. "It looks as though you already have passengers."

Her gaze strayed across the dispersing crowd, stopping when she saw Billy and Sid. They were standing awkwardly, a few feet apart, and as she watched, Jess saw Sid extend a hand towards Billy.   He looked at it for a moment before extending his hand. Jess looked away, not believing what she was seeing, but when she looked back, she saw that they were in conversation.

"Peace at last," she whispered.

"What did you say, Jess?"

"Charles, look at Billy and Sid over there. I do believe there's been a truce."

"Thank-you, Margaret," she heard Charles whisper.

Izzy's Admission

The afternoon wore on as people gathered in groups in the Sunday-School Hall, drinking tea and sharing stories about Margaret. The buzz of conversations and quiet laughter indicated the love they all had for the quiet, unassuming lady with the big heart. Jess kept a close watch on Charles, and for a time he handled the conversations well. The Church ladies kept him plied with cups of tea and sumptuous cakes, until Jess saw him hold up his hands and shake his head. Eventually she saw him head for the door, so she put down her cup and followed.

Stepping out on to the asphalted yard, she looked for him. He was standing beside his car, his head bent. Jess walked up to him.

"I'm sure nobody will mind if you make your excuses, Charles," she said quietly.

He turned. "I need to go home, Jess."

"Of course you do, Charles." Jess smiled. "I'd like to go home, too." She took a deep breath. "However, I can stay a while longer, and I will extend your apologies if you need to go."

"Thank-you, Jess. " Charles pulled a white handkerchief from his breast pocket, and wiped his eyes. "I need to be alone."

Jess touched his arm. "I understand. I'll come around and see you tomorrow."

She stood back as he cranked the car into motion, and then climbed into the driver's seat. Watching him pull away, Jess sighed deeply, and turned to go back into the hall. Beau was watching her from the doorway, and as he headed down the steps towards her, Jess smiled to herself. While she had been watching Charles, Beau had been watching her. She took his hand as he reached her, and planted a kiss on his cheek.

"Charles has had enough," she said quietly. "He needs to be alone."

"He got through the whole service very well."

"Yes. Now it's time to face reality, and that's the hard part."

*

Jess was glad to see the end of the day, and as she settled onto the old brown couch, her feet on a stool, she closed her eyes and reflected on the events. It had been a positive day in many respects, the most astounding being the reconciliation between Billy and Sid. That had left her speechless. She had seen her boys grow in character as they walked beside their grandfather, and her eyes misted even now as she thought of how proud Jack would have been of them.

The one thing that puzzled her most was her sister's changed attitude. She had never heard her speak to Harry the way she did this day. It was totally out of character. As if in answer to her thoughts, Izzy appeared beside her.

"You'll be pleased to know, Jess, that Grace and Freya are quite excited about sleeping together in the same bed." She flopped on to the couch beside Jess. "You're sure it's alright to leave Freya here for the night?"

"Yes, of course." Jess opened her eyes. "You can enjoy a child-free night at the hotel." She turned her head to look at her sister.

Izzy was pulling her blonde hair from its restraining combs, and didn't see Jess's studied gaze.

"Ah! That's better." She shook her curls loose.

"Izzy?"

"What." Izzy looked at Jess, frowned and then sighed. "Ah! THE conversation."

"Yes. Where are Beau and Harry?"

Izzy yawned. "Out on the back verandah." She leaned towards her sister. "Out of earshot!"

"Good! Now, tell me what is going on with you, Izzy? You have been as prickly as an echidna all day. In fact you have not been yourself for a while, so tell me what gives, big sister!"

Izzy remained silent for some moments as she considered her answer, and Jess waited.

"We have been trying for some time to have another child, Jess."

"And?"

"And it's not happening." Izzy folded her arms, and pushed Jess's feet along, so that she could share the footstool.

"You might have to give it some time, Izzy,"

"I have…The thing is, my doctor now tells me that I am entering that next phase of my life, and the likelihood of me falling pregnant now is very slim."

"Oh, I see."

"I'm not like you, Jess. You seem to be able to fall pregnant just like that!" She snapped her fingers. "I couldn't understand why I had not been blessed."

"But you're taking it all out on Harry, Izzy, and that's not fair. It's not his fault."

"I know, and I shouldn't, but when you said you were pregnant, that was the last straw! I'm sorry, Jess. You deserve every happiness, and I'm thrilled for you, I really am."

"But you wish it was you?"

Izzy nodded. "Pathetic, isn't it?"

"No, it's natural."

"The other thing that's got me all het-up is the fact that Nancy's leaving us. She's going to France with Martin and Fleur, Jess. Can you believe that?"

"She told me."

Izzy was silent. "There's something else."

Jess groaned. "What is it?"

"Do you remember Harry saying during one of our visits that he would like to get back to being a publican?"

"I do," said Jess cautiously.

"Now that Nancy's leaving, he's thinking seriously about it. Jess, I don't want to move around the countryside again."

Jess patted her hand. "It might just blow over, Izzy. I wouldn't worry too much about it."

"You don't know Harry. If he gets a bee in his bonnet, so to speak, he's not happy until he's shifted it."

"Look at it this way, Izzy." Jess laughed. "He might decide to come to Bendigo."

"Yes, well that would be different. I could go along with that."

*

Beau and Harry were sitting on the top step of the back verandah, beer glasses in their hands, watching the sun turn the sky pink behind the tall ghost gum that grew by the back fence. The air was warm, the silence broken by the chirping sound of crickets in the back lawn.

"You've got the place looking nice, Beau." Harry drained his glass.

"Thanks Harry. It was too much for Jess to upkeep, but you know Jess, she did try."

Harry gave a short laugh. "They're not that much different, Jess and Isobel. They're both stubborn and hate to give in."

"That's true." Beau took the empty glass from Harry, and getting to his feet, headed for the kitchen door. "The same again, Harry?"

Harry waved his hand. "No, I've had enough."

When Beau returned, Harry was standing beyond the verandah, on the gravel path that led to the lavatory. He had lit a cigarette, and was inhaling deeply. Beau went to stand beside him.

"Cigarette, Beau?"

"No thanks, Harry. I'll pass on that." He chuckled. "Jess doesn't like me coming to bed with the smell of cigarette smoke on my breath."

Harry laughed. "I don't very often smoke, to tell the truth, but sometimes the need is there."

"And the need is there now, Harry?"

"You could say that." Harry took a final puff on the cigarette, and butted it beneath his shoe. "Can I share something with you, Beau?"

"Certainly, Harry."

"Isobel knows nothing about this, so I would appreciate it if you don't say anything."

"What is it, Harry?"

"Well, as you may or may not know, Nancy is leaving us shortly, to go and live in France with Martin and Fleur."

"Yes, I think Jess said something about that."

"I'm thinking of selling the business, Beau, and going back to what I enjoy; being a Publican." Beau was silent, not knowing how to react. "Isobel knows that I have been thinking about it, but what she doesn't know is that I have my heart set on the Grey Goose."

"I see. Have you spoken to Jean?"

"Not yet. My plan tomorrow is to talk with Jean and see how she feels about the idea of me becoming a partner. As we all know, Jean is not getting any younger, and well…" He shrugged, "she might warm to the idea."

Beau thought for a moment. "In that case, Harry, you should tell Izzy your plans before you speak to Jean."

"You think so?"

"I know so. Jess has noticed how tetchy Izzy has been of late, and maybe she senses that you're not telling her everything."

"No, Isobel is tetchy for other reasons, Beau; women's reasons." He stopped. "She would dearly love another baby, but it looks like we've been very lucky to have had Freya."

"And Jess being pregnant hasn't helped the situation, am I right?"

"Yes, exactly."

"Well anyway, I'd be sharing my plans with Izzy, if I were you, Harry."

"Yes, maybe you're right."

Beau slapped Harry across the back. "I'm going inside. The girls will be singing out for a cup of tea very soon, and that has become my lot in married life."

Harry grinned in the gathering darkness. "Love, honour and obey comes in many forms, Beau."

A Time For Change

The following morning, when Beau had cycled off to the surgery, and the boys had gone to school, Jess decided that it was time to take Grace to see her grandfather. Izzy had asked if she could keep Freya for the morning, because she and Harry needed to speak with Jean. It all sounded a little mysterious, but Jess was happy to oblige. It would help her in dealing with Grace when she arrived at granddad's house to find grandma not there.

Jess set off with the two little girls, and smiled as she watched them running hand-in-hand along the footpath, their excited squeals echoing around the street. The morning was warm, and Jess had chosen to wear a paisley pinafore that she had worn during her pregnancy with Grace. It was cool and loose, and she had tied a matching scarf around her hair. Beau had earlier made the comment that she looked radiant, and she smiled now as she thought about that moment.

When they reached the Stanley residence, Grace banged on the brass knocker. Charles took several moments to answer, but finally the door opened. He looked haggard, and Jess suspected that he probably had not slept. Smiling down on the two children, he opened the wire door and ushered them inside.

"Come in, come in," he said. "I've done nothing this morning, so you'll have to take me as you find me."

"That's alright, Charles," said Jess. "Is there anything I can do for you?"

Charles shook his head. "No, Jess. You have enough to do."

Gracie ran through the house, and for once, Charles did not chastise her. He knew that she was looking for Margaret, and he waited until she stopped in front of him, her hands outstretched.

"Where's grandma?" Her brow was creased in a frown.

"Grandma's not here, Gracie," said Charles slowly.

Then, as if a tap had been turned on, Gracie began to cry. Jess moved to comfort her, pressing her against her thighs. Freya stood back, her face screwed up in bewilderment. Should she cry, too?

"Gracie," said Jess gently, "do you remember what we talked about the other night? That grandma has gone on a journey and we won't see her?" Grace nodded against her mother's pinafore. "Well, we all have to get used to that idea, and even granddad won't get to see her for a long, long time." She glanced up at Charles, whose eyes were brimming. "Now give granddad a big hug and tell him you love him."

Grace wiped her sleeve across her eyes, before reaching up to Charles. He buried his face in her neck, and Jess could see his shoulders heaving.

"I'm sorry, granddad," hiccoughed Grace. "I love you just as much as I love grandma."

Freya was crying at this stage, so Jess wrapped her in a hug, and they all stood together, weeping.

Finally Jess moved, pressing Freya away from her.

"I think it's time, girls," she said, "for you to go to the lounge and play with the toys there, while I make granddad a cup of tea."

Charles let Grace slide to the floor, and then reached for a handkerchief.

Grace grabbed Freya by the hand and led her to the lounge.

"Come on, we need that cup of tea." Jess took Charles by the arm.

Charles went willingly, and once in the kitchen, Jess moved towards the stove. The kettle was already singing, so she reached for the tea caddy on the mantel above, and spooned tealeaves into the enamel teapot. Seeing the sink stacked with dirty dishes, she was about to tackle them, when Charles stopped her.

"Leave those, Jess!" It was a command, albeit a quiet one. "I can do those later."

"It's no trouble, Charles."

"No, Jess! I have to do these things for myself."

Jess knew when to stop arguing with Charles, and continued making the tea. Charles sat quietly at the table, and Jess slid a cup in front of him.

"It's going to take some time to get used to the loneliness, Jess." He sounded so forlorn.

"Yes, I know, Charles. You won't get used to it, you'll learn how to live with it."

They drank their tea in silence, as the sound of the two girls playing in the lounge, reached their ears. They had recovered from their initial shock, and bounced back, as only children can do.

Jess smiled. "They're happy enough now," she said quietly. After a short pause, she added: "Charles, today is the anniversary of Jack's death, and I'm going to the school to place some flowers on the memorial garden there. Do you want to come?"

"No. Thanks all the same, Jess. I must get up to the hospital. Some of the Board are meeting there to discuss the possibility of closing the auxiliary wards at the Asylum. The influenza seems to have passed."

"Very well… I was wondering, can I pick some of Margaret's roses to take to the school?"

"Certainly. Help yourself. I won't pick them."

Jess reached across the table and covered his hand with hers. "We're here for you, Charles. Promise me you won't forget that?"

Charles placed his other hand on Jess's. "I promise."

*

Sometime later, as Jess walked towards the school with the two girls, and a bunch of Margaret's red roses wrapped in newspaper, she saw Charles drive by, on his way to the hospital. *Thank goodness he has something to keep his mind occupied. It will help fill in the empty days.*

It was morning playtime when Jess reached the school, and as she walked towards the memorial garden, she saw Edward running across the quadrangle towards her. Grace squealed with delight at seeing her brother, and headed in his direction. Freya followed, her stocky little legs unable to keep up with

Grace.

Jess watched the reunion with a smile. It was as if they hadn't seen each other for a long time. Children were such a blessing, and especially in times of trauma and heartbreak as they had all been experiencing of late. Jess was preoccupied with her thoughts, and didn't see Mr. Granger ambling towards her. As he reached her, he removed his hat.

"Mrs. DuBois! What brings you to the school today?"

"Oh!" Jess was surprised to see him smiling so warmly. "I've come to place roses on the memorial garden. It's twelve months since Jack died."

"Yes, of course. Please accept my condolences on the loss of Mrs. Stanley."

"Thank-you, Mr. Granger."

"The children have tended the garden over the past year, and they've done an exceptional job. The plants are thriving well."

"I'm so pleased."

"I'll – I'll get you a jar of water for those roses." He ambled away towards the school building.

Jess watched him go, before turning her attention to the two little girls. They were happily playing with the older children, so she walked across to the memorial garden, and stood for a few moments contemplating the significance of the roses, the rosemary and the border of forget-me-nots. They must never forget what these plants represented - the loved ones who had died for their King and their country, but most of all for the safety of their families.

"Will this do?" Mr. Granger's voice sounded at her elbow.

"That will be perfect." Jess took the jar, and unwrapping the roses, placed them in the water.

"Put them in the front there." Mr. Granger pointed to a space between two rosemary bushes.

Jess knelt and placed the jar, remaining on her knees as she bowed her head. Above her she heard Mr. Granger murmur the oath: "**They shall grow not old, as we who are left grow old. Age shall not weary them, nor the years condemn. At the going down of the sun and in the morning, we will remember them.**"

"We will remember them," repeated Jess, her eyes swimming.

*

The sound of the school bell meant the end of playtime, and as all the children headed for their respective class rooms, Grace and Freya found their way back to Jess. They were crestfallen that they were now alone, and wanted to know why they couldn't stay with Edward.

"You are both too young for school," Jess reminded them. "Besides, I need to get Freya back to her parents, and if you are both good, you can have a drink of lemonade. How does that sound?"

That was enough bribery, so they held hands and skipped ahead of Jess as she headed for the Grey Goose. The sound of laughter reached them, as Jess opened the side door of the hotel and ushered the girls into the passage. It was coming from the Ladies Lounge. She headed towards the sound. From the doorway she could see Jean, Izzy and Harry seated at one of the tables, their heads bent over a pile of paperwork. Izzy looked up as they entered, her face beaming.

"Oh, Jessie!" she cried. "You'll never guess what's been happening here?"

Harry tried to hush her. "It's not cut and dried yet, Isobel."

Freya ran to her mother, and clambered onto her knee, while Jess looked around the faces, trying to ascertain what was happening.

"What is going on?" she asked finally.

"Harry is going into partnership with Jean!" Izzy burst out, unable to contain herself.

"Isobel, there is a lot to be sorted out before we can say that for certain."

"I don't care, Harry!" Izzy hugged Freya to her. "It's near enough for me."

Jess looked at Jean. Her round face was beaming as she mopped it with a handkerchief. "It's true, Jess! This is a wonderful day for me. I've been praying for an answer to my problems here, and without having to give up my beloved hotel, I think we've found a way."

Jess let the idea sink in. Harry and Izzy were going to come and help Jean run the hotel. It was an idea that had crossed her mind several times over the past couple of years, but she had dismissed it as being impracticable.

"Where will you live?" she asked breathlessly, as she sought safety on the nearest chair.

"Here!" said Izzy, as if there was any doubt.

There was another question on Jess's lips. "What about Rodney?"

There was silence for a moment, before Jean snorted loudly. "There's nothing he can do about it," she said scornfully. "I'd already cut him out of any control."

"Well!" Jess was nonplussed. "This is exciting news. So when is this ball going to start rolling?"

"Just as soon as I can sell or lease the business in Swan Hill," said Harry jubilantly. "I have an interested party standing by." His eyes were twinkling.

"What about the family home, Izzy?" Jess asked slowly. "Are we going to sell that, too?"

Izzy sighed. "We'll have to, Jess. We were planning on moving into it, when Nancy sold her farm, but those plans have all changed now. The house will fall into disrepair if we don't sell it soon."

"I suppose the time had to come," said Jess reluctantly. "We can't hang on to things forever."

"No, we can't." Izzy looked across at Jess. "It will mean money in your pocket as well, Jessie."

"Yes." She smiled suddenly. "With the baby coming, we'll have to do some alterations to our home, or we'll be bursting at the seams."

"Exactly!"

"This calls for a celebration!" Jean struggled to her feet. "I'll get us some drinks."

"I'd already promised the girls a drink," laughed Jess. "It was the only way I could drag them away from the school."

"Just think, Jess," sighed Izzy. "Grace and Freya will go to the same school."

Life was about to change again.

The Letters

Jess breathed a sigh of relief as she watched the train pull away from the station, taking Izzy, Harry and Freya back to Swan Hill. Their plans to go into partnership with Jean had taken a step forward over the past few days, and a contract had been drawn up. Izzy had been unable to contain her excitement, while Harry had tried to keep a level head, saying that 'it's not a done deal yet, Isobel'. Jess smiled as she walked towards the pedestrian bridge with Grace. At least it had taken Izzy's mind off her disappointment at not being able to fall pregnant.

As they climbed the steps it was Grace who now voiced her disappointment. Tugging at her mother's skirt, she whimpered plaintively, "Where's Freya gone, ma?"

Jess turned her attention to her daughter. "Freya's gone home, Grace."

"But I wanted her to stay here."

"We'll see her again very soon. Now let's get rid of that sad face, and we'll go and see Mrs. O'Malley, and then granddad. How does that sound?"

"We won't see grandma, though, will we, Ma?" Grace reminded Jess, as they clattered down the steps to platform two.

"No, Grace, we won't."

They were both silent as they headed up the hill towards the hotel. Not seeing Margaret was one of the hardest things they both had to endure. Jess took Grace's hand, squeezing it as she smiled down on her.

As they arrived at the side door of the Grey Goose, Audrey Maitland was arriving too, swathed in a red floral pinafore, a matching scarf wrapped around her head, and a basket over her arm.

"Good morning, Jess," she said brightly. "Good morning, little Gracie."

"Good morning, Audrey," said Jess, while Grace stared solemnly at her. "Say 'good morning' to Mrs. Maitland, Grace!" Jess added sharply.

"Good morning, Mrs. Maitland," said Grace reluctantly.

"We've just seen her cousin off at the station," said Jess, as a way of explanation. "Grace didn't want her to go. Hence the glum face."

"That's alright, Jess." Audrey opened the heavy door. "I'm glad I've seen you, anyway. You'll never guess what has happened." Audrey stopped talking as they all stepped into the cool passage.

"What's happened, Audrey?"

Placing her basket on the small table in the passage, Audrey said, "It's my Billy, Jess!"

"What about Billy?" Audrey was not in a hurry to reveal her story.

"Well," she began, as she took a cloth and a tin of furniture polish from the basket. "Apparently Billy and Sid are back on speaking terms. Mind you," Audrey opened the tin of polish, "I don't see it lasting. That Sid's a bit of a mongrel, I think you'll agree." Audrey cocked an eyebrow at Jess.

"Let's hope he's had a change of heart, Audrey."

"Pigs might fly, Jess," Audrey snorted, "but Billy's old enough now to deal with Mr. O'Connor."

"What about Mr. O'Connor?" Jean had appeared at the bar door, wiping her hands on her apron.

"Him and my Billy are back on speaking terms," said Audrey with a sniff of disapproval.

"Oh well," muttered Jean. "It's time Sid O'Connor became a regular human being."

"He'd better not start anything, that's all I can say."

Jean smiled and changed the subject. "You can start the dusting in the Ladies Lounge, Audrey."

"Certainly, Jean." Audrey marched off towards the Ladies Lounge.

Jean turned to Jess, her eyes shining now. "Isn't it exciting, Jess?" she whispered, not wanting Audrey to hear. "Just think! Your sister will be living right down the street from you."

"Are you sure it's what YOU want, Jean? I mean, Izzy can be very overbearing, as we all know."

"It's an answer to my prayers, Jess. Don't worry about Izzy. I can deal with her." Jean's eyes were twinkling. "Harry will be a godsend."

"Yes, I'm sure he will." Jess paused. "Just a word of warning – don't let Izzy loose with a paintbrush, or you'll have the pub looking like a giant mural." Jess waved her hands in the air.

"That doesn't sound so bad." Jean was in the mood to agree with anything.

Jess shook her head. "Don't say I didn't warn you."

"Mrs O'Malley!" Norman's voice came from the direction of the bar.

"Coming, Norman!" Jean turned quickly to Jess. "Was there anything in particular you wanted to see me about, Jess?"

"No. We've been to the station to say goodbye to the family, and we just popped in to say 'hello'. We're off to see Charles, now."

"Hm. He's not doing so well, is he, Jess?"

"It will take some time, I'm afraid." Jess breathed deeply. "It's something we have to go through, that nobody can do for us."

"Yes, that's true." Jean nodded sagely. "I'd better see what Norman wants. Lovely to see you, Jess, and you too, Miss Gracie."

Jean disappeared into the bar, and Jess took Grace by the hand. "It's time to see granddad."

*

Grace knocked on the front door. There was no answer. Jess could see the car parked in the driveway, so Charles had to be somewhere nearby. Grace knocked again. There was still no answer.

"We'll go around to the back, Gracie. Maybe granddad's in the garden."

There was no sign of Charles in the garden, and the back door was unlocked. Jess pushed it open.

"Charles!" she called. "Are you there?" There was no response. Jess shivered. It reminded her of the empty house in Sydney, and her heartbeat quickened. She had to check the rooms, in case Charles had suffered a heart attack or…

Jess shook away the thoughts as she took Grace by the hand and walked through the kitchen. The dining room was empty, as was the bathroom, the spare bedroom and the lounge. The door to Margaret's bedroom was partially open, so Jess pushed it, slowly. The bed was neatly made, and at first glance there was nobody there. Jess was about to retrace her steps when she saw Charles. He was seated on the floor, his head resting on his knees, and an open photograph album beside him. Without wanting to frighten him by appearing suddenly beside him, Jess cleared her throat.

Charles looked up quickly. His eyes were red-rimmed and he had not shaved around his whiskers as he normally did. He looked unkempt and very unhappy. When he saw Jess and Grace, he broke down, sobbing uncontrollably. Jess moved swiftly to his side, and kneeling beside him, wrapped her arms around his heaving shoulders. Grace stood silently watching, her eyes large and unblinking.

"Oh, Jess," he sobbed. "What have I got to live for now?"

Jess quivered. She had uttered those words when Jack died, and as Beau had answered her then, she gave the same answer to Charles.

"You have us, Charles," she whispered.

He looked up at her, and wiped a sleeve across his face. "Yes, I do, don't I?"

Grace squatted in front of him, and patted his whiskered cheek. "Don't cry, granddad," she said in a soft husky voice. "I don't like it when you cry."

Charles took her chubby little hand in his, and sighed. "Alright, Grace – just for you."

Jess picked up the photograph album, and closing it, got shakily to her feet. "Let's take this out to the kitchen, where we can all look at it," she said, forcing a smile. "Besides, I need a cup of tea." Holding out a hand, she helped

Charles to his feet, and they all headed for the kitchen.

*

Two hours later, after sharing lunch with Charles, and reminiscing over old photographs, Jess felt reasonably happy leaving him alone. He said there was a plumbing job he needed to check on, so Jess and Grace took their leave.

They arrived home in time to see George, the postman, delivering the afternoon post.

"Good afternoon, Mrs. DuBois," he drawled. "I have two letters for you. One's from Swan Hill, and the other is from Sydney."

Jess hid a smile as she took possession of the letters. George didn't miss a trick. He knew everybody's business. "Thank-you, George."

"Good afternoon, little Gracie." George bent his angular frame to shake Grace by the hand. "Nearly ready for school then?"

"No!" said Jess quickly. "She has another year before she goes to school."

George nodded gravely. "I see." He looked up at Jess. "Sorry to hear about all your troubles, Mrs. DuBois. Mr. Stanley will surely miss his wife."

"He does, George."

"Hm." George lifted his hat to scratch his head. "Well, I'd better be on my way. Can't hold up the King's mail, can we?"

Jess watched him saunter to the next house, thinking wryly that George was never in a hurry to deliver the King's mail. She looked at the two letters in her hand. Turning them over, she saw that one was from Nancy, and the other was addressed to Beau. It was from his sister.

Stepping on to the verandah, Jess opened the letter from Nancy. It was an invitation to a wedding ceremony for Martin and Fleur. The paper was fine grained with gold lettering, and Jess could see that a very skilled hand had crafted the calligraphy. She ran a finger over it, admiring the accuracy of the letters.

The date was the last Saturday in November, and the venue was All Weather farm - Nancy's place. It was to be an informal garden wedding, attended by a few close friends. Jess wondered briefly whether Nancy had sold her farm, because the invitation also stated that the three of them would be leaving for France three day after the ceremony.

Jess placed the invitation back in the envelope, and cast her eye over the one from Charlotte. It was addressed to Beau, in a heavy black scrawl, so she felt it was not her place to open it. She was probably writing to see how Beau was coping with life after his ordeal. Jess had the feeling that Charlotte was now a part of Beau's life, and that was a good thing. She was, after all, his family.

"Ma!" Grace's voice broke into her thoughts. "Are we going inside?"

Jess unlocked the front door, and smiled apologetically down on her daughter. "I'm sorry, Grace. Ma was preoccupied."

Grace darted in front of her, running along the passage to her room. Jess followed, placing Beau's letter on the small telephone table beside their bedroom door. He would be home from the hospital soon, and would be surprised to hear from Charlotte so soon.

Jess grabbed an apron from behind the bedroom door, and tying it around her, made straight for the kitchen. She had spent more time than she intended with Charles, and although she didn't begrudge him that time, she now had to cook tea for the family. To make matters worse, the fire was out, and the boys were not home to bring in the kindling.

Sighing, she made her way out onto the verandah. There was enough kindling in the wood box to light the fire, but it meant that more would have to be chopped. Gathering the kindling in her apron, Jess straightened her back as she looked out across the yard. Beau had certainly made improvements to the garden, and even the chook pen had received a coat of paint, with Ben's help. Life was slowly gaining some normality, but there were times when she caught Beau staring out into space, as though trying to see what lay ahead. He was still reserved where the children were concerned, and Jess knew that it would take time for that bond to return to the way it was.

She had noticed that he was reticent about bathing the children, particularly Grace, so didn't force the issue. She knew that he was a good man, and that there was no reason to think otherwise. He, on the other hand, seemed unable to trust himself completely. She would have to convince him that she had no such qualms.

She sighed once more. It was time to get the fire going. Jess walked back into the kitchen as Beau appeared from the passage. He immediately removed the kindling from her apron.

"Let the fire go out, did you, Jess?" he quizzed, smiling at her.

Jess brushed herself down. "I was with Charles longer than I had planned, so yes, the fire is out."

Beau opened the firebox, and began to lay the kindling, as Jess reached for a pile of newspapers, and began scrunching up the pages.

"How was Charles?" asked Beau.

"It's starting to hit home that Margaret is not there." Jess handed him a matchbox. "He said the same thing that I said after Jack died; that he has nothing to live for."

Beau looked up quickly. "What did you tell him?"

"That he has us." Jess's voice began to tremble.

Beau watched as the small flame took hold in the firebox. "And so he has." He reached for some small pieces of wood and laid them carefully across the kindling. When he was satisfied that they were taking hold, he closed the firebox door and straightened his back. "Healing always takes time, Jess." He had his back to her, so she couldn't see the expression in his eyes.

"I know." Jess laid an arm across his shoulders. "Beau?"
"Yes?" He turned slowly.
"There's a letter on the table in the passage. It's from your sister."
"What does she have to say?"
"I haven't read it. I left it for you."
Beau frowned. "Jess, you can read my mail."
"I know, but this is from Charlotte, and you need to read it first."
"We'll read it together." Beau moved towards the kitchen door.
"We also received an invitation to Martin's wedding."
"Oh? When's that?" Beau stopped in the doorway.
"The last weekend in November, so about three weeks away."
"We'll go, of course?" It was a question rather than a statement.
"Yes, of course."
"Good." Beau disappeared from sight.

Jess picked over a bowl of potatoes that stood beside the sink, and chose four large ones. As she searched in the drawer for a vegetable knife, Beau returned, and sat at the table. He tore the envelope, and pulled out a sheet of heavy, homemade paper. Jess watched his face as he scanned the page. Looking up at Jess, he motioned her to sit.

"You need to hear this, Jess," he said quietly.
"What does she say?"
Beau began to read the black scrawl:

> *Dear Beau and Jess,*
>
> *I am writing to you, primarily to find out how you are coping with life far away from the Convent and secondly to say that I miss your presence here. My heart is divided now, so I must spend time in quiet prayer and contemplation, to rid myself of the desire to venture out into the world.*
>
> *The reverend Mother is advising me to leave this compound and perhaps seek God's work elsewhere. Her suggestion is the Congo, where she says the need for Sisters and medical personnel is great. I hope I can find the answer for my disquiet.*
>
> *I am so pleased that we had the chance to find each other, Beau, even in such trying circumstances, and my wish is that we make contact as often as we can.*
>
> *You are so fortunate to have a wife like Jess. She is a warm, compassionate person, and I feel you are destined now to have a happy life together. It is my fervent prayer that you do.*
>
> *Think of me, Beau, as I wrestle with my own disquiet, and if you are a devout person, please pray that I will find an answer.*

I remain
Your loving sister Charlotte
(Sister Agnes)
P.S. Write back soon

Beau looked across at Jess, his eyes moist. Slowly he folded the paper and tucked it inside the envelope. Placing it on the table, he sat back with a sigh.

"Poor Charlotte," he said quietly. "She has had her peace shattered by all of this."

"Beau," Jess reached across the table and took his hands. "Charlotte's peace was brought about simply by her choosing to forget. I don't want you feeling guilty about what's happened. If anyone should feel guilty, it's me."

"Why you?" Beau was frowning at her.

"Because if I hadn't persuaded you to find her in the first place, none of this would have come about." Jess shrugged. "It has happened, and now we must all deal with it, each in our own way. If it means that Charlotte goes to the Congo, then I believe that this is her destiny." She smiled.

"And our destiny?" The grey eyes were studying her intently.

"Our destiny is to have a happy life together." They stared at one another for a long moment.

"Now," her voice was husky, "I should start preparing tea. We can't fulfil our destiny on empty stomachs."

"Thank-you, Jess."

"For what?"

"For being you."

Martin's Wedding

The weeks slipped by, and soon it was time to prepare for a train trip to Swan Hill for Martin's wedding. The children were excited about the prospect, and asked on more than one occasion, 'how many sleeps until we go, ma?'

Charles was gradually accepting the fact that Margaret was no longer there, and spent more of his time at the hospital or overseeing his workers. Jess was relieved that he was finding ways to occupy his time, but in spending less time at home, the housework was being neglected. Charles had never been a man to share the workload with Margaret, until her sickness prevented her from fulfilling her duties.

On more than one occasion Jess found dirty dishes in the sink and the bed unmade. Margaret would have been horrified. Whenever she suggested that she do them, his eyebrows would lift imperiously, and the old Charles would emerge. "I will deal with it," was always his reply.

Jess wondered what she could do about it, without upsetting him, and suggested quietly one day, that he employ Audrey Maitland to do what he didn't have time to do. He warmed to that idea, much to Jess's relief, and she immediately arranged for Audrey to be his housekeeper.

With that problem hopefully solved, Jess was able to concentrate on preparing for the trip to Swan Hill. This time there would be five of them travelling, and because they were going to a wedding, good clothes needed to be laundered, pressed and hung up, ready to be packed.

As the time drew near, and everything was in place, Jess pulled two suitcases down from the top of the wardrobe in her bedroom. Upon opening them, she found a pile of Jack's clothes that she had forgotten about, and a small book of his poetry. She sat back on her heels and opened the book, which was musty from being shut away from the air. Her fingers traced across the open page, and she found herself reading aloud:

> *Today I picked forget-me-nots*
> *And pressed them in a book for you.*
> *A keepsake to remind you*
> *that my love is always true.*
> *Think of me when I'm far away*
> *On a distant, war-torn shore,*
> *And remember, just like the forget-me-not*
> *That it's you I'll be fighting for.*

Jess quickly closed the page, as tears welled in her eyes, and as she did so, dried forget-me-nots fell from the book to her lap. She picked them up carefully, fearful that they might disintegrate, and thoughts of Jack filled her mind.

"Oh Jack," she whispered. "You keep reminding me never to forget you." She smiled as she placed the flowers back in the book and closed it.

As she got to her feet, she saw Ben standing in the doorway, watching her. How long had he been there, she wondered?

"Was that one of dad's poems, ma?" Jess had her answer.

"Yes, Ben."

"Can I read them?"

"Of course." Jess smiled as she handed him the book. "Take it to your room. I think your father would want you to have this." As Ben walked away, she added: "Don't lose the flowers."

"What are they for?"

"They're a reminder that we mustn't forget your dad, even though life has changed for us."

"Hm." Ben opened his mouth to say more, but changed his mind, and smiling at his mother, retreated to his bedroom.

Jess watched him go, before sighing and returning to the suitcases. Would two be enough for all of them? Beau could only carry two, and she knew that he wouldn't allow her to carry one. The decision was made. Now it was time to pack them.

*

Finally the day arrived, and the family walked sedately to the station to catch the Melbourne to Swan Hill train. Jean was hovering in the doorway of the hotel as they passed, and stepped out on to the footpath to greet them.

"Tell Harry and Izzy that plans are proceeding well," were her first words to Jess, "and they should be hearing from my Solicitor very soon."

"They will be very pleased to hear that, Jean." Jess enveloped her friend in a hug.

"I am so excited, Jess. It's something I've been praying for."

"Izzy is excited too, believe me!"

"Jess!" Beau's voice sounded beside her. "We have a train to catch, in case you've forgotten." He smiled at Jean. "We really must get on."

"Yes, yes!" Jean flapped her arms at them. "Off you go." She turned to Ben. "I'll take care of your chooks while you're gone, Ben."

"Thank-you, Mrs. O'Malley."

"We'll only be gone for three days," laughed Jess.

"Have a good time!" Jean called after them as Beau led the way towards the station.

Jess turned and waved. "We will!" she called back.

Jess hurried after Beau, and the children ran ahead. As she caught up with him, he turned, his expression apologetic.

"I'm sorry, Jess, but once you and Jean get together, there's no knowing how long you are going to be, and we can't afford to miss this train."

"I know, but Jean is so excited."

"I'm sure she is." He added wryly: "We'll hear all about it when we get to Swan Hill."

*

They did hear all about it. Izzy was so excited, she could hardly contain herself, and when Jess passed on Jean's news, she giggled like a schoolgirl and did a little jig right there on the station platform.

"Oh, Jess!" she exclaimed. "It is going to be so wonderful, living near you."

"Yes, of course it is." Jess grabbed Izzy by the arm, as Beau struggled with the cases. "Now can we please go to the car before Beau collapses under the weight of the luggage?"

Izzy laughed out loud. "It's usually me with all the luggage. Here, give me one of those, Beau." She grabbed a suitcase from his hand. "What have you got in here, Jess?"

"We are going to a wedding, Izzy, so our best clothes are in there," said Jess sharply.

"Alright, Jess! I get your message. Follow me, everyone."

They all followed Izzy out to where the car was parked. Izzy pulled open the luggage compartment at the back, and hoisted the case in. Beau followed suit, marvelling at the strength of his sister-in-law.

"Right! Everybody in?" Izzy declared loudly.

As Jess ushered the three children into the back seat, she couldn't help but smile at the way Izzy was dressed. Over her bright pink dress she wore a dustcoat, like the one Charles always wore when he was driving the car. Her blonde hair was pushed under a peaked cap, and a pair of goggles hung loosely around her neck. Soft leather gloves covered her hands, and she clapped them together now as she moved to the front of the car to crank the engine. Shaking her head, Jess followed the children into the back seat. Izzy had always been the capable one; the one who had chased the cows into the milking-shed, regardless of the conditions underfoot.

Beau, who had been looking on with amusement, climbed into the front passenger seat, as Izzy settled into the driver's seat.

"Freya is so excited!" Izzy shouted above the noise of the engine, as she negotiated the large vehicle on to the road. "She has really missed Gracie."

"Gracie has missed Freya, too." Jess had to speak loudly to be heard over the engine.

The drive to Dalton's was a bumpy one, and Jess felt quite queasy by the time Izzy pulled up outside the shop. Harry appeared at the door, and bounded down the steps to meet them. Freya jumped excitedly at his feet.

"Welcome!" he called out, as he hurried forward to open the car door.

Freya and Grace immediately fell into each other's arms, chattering in high-pitched voices. Beau opened the luggage compartment, and handed Harry one of the cases.

"Good God, man!" exclaimed Harry. "Did Isobel pack this?"

"It feels like it, doesn't it?" Beau pulled the second case out and slammed the door shut.

"I heard that, Harry!" Izzy's voice floated back to them, and the two men looked at one another and grinned. "I'm the only one who can say things like that."

Harry opened his mouth to retort, but Izzy was no longer within earshot. She had gathered the children together, and was already crossing the verandah. Harry shrugged.

Jess, who had remained behind, laughed at the expressions on the two men.

"Just imagine what it's going to be like, Harry, when you get to Bendigo."

Harry groaned. "Don't think I haven't thought of that, Jess. I'll have to make sure I keep her so busy she won't have time to be wandering off to your place."

"Good luck with that, Harry," said Beau, as the three headed into the shop.

As they walked through the door into the house, they were in time to hear

Edward say:

"Where are we sleeping, Auntie Izzy?"

"You boys will sleep in the lounge," replied Izzy. "Grace will sleep with Freya, and your mum and Beau will have the spare room. Does that sound alright?"

"The lounge?" Edward screwed up his nose. "Can't we sleep in the spare room?"

"No, you can't!" Jess and Beau both spoke at once.

"Don't be silly, Edward!" said Ben crossly. "We don't sleep with the adults."

Edward pouted, sending Izzy and Harry into helpless laughter.

"I thought you might have suggested that we stay at the family home, Izzy," said Jess, as the men took the cases into the spare room.

"I thought about it, Jess, but that would mean you would be over there, and I would be here, and…" She shrugged theatrically. "I want you here. Besides, I have started going through things at the house, in case we sell it."

"I need to help you with that, Izzy," said Jess, as she shrugged herself out of her jacket, and laid it on the bed.

"Yes, I know, but there's plenty of time for that." The sound of childish laughter reached their ears. Izzy smiled. "It sounds as though the girls are happy enough. Come on through to the kitchen and we'll have a cuppa. You must be dying for one."

*

That evening, when the children were settled in their respective rooms, Jess, Beau, Izzy and Harry sat out on the back verandah, and watched the sunset. The sky was awash with random swirls of pink, red and orange, and magpies warbled their evensong in the branches of the eucalypts that grew along the street. Harry sat back on his chair and sighed.

"I am going to miss all this?" he said, as his arm did a wide sweep of the long back yard.

Izzy looked keenly at him. "We'll have the same sunsets in Bendigo, Harry," she said, frowning. "It's not like we're going to the other ends of the earth."

"I know," said Harry, his head nodding slowly, "but there's something very special about a Mallee sunset. Just look at those colours; aren't they brilliant?"

Izzy sighed. "Yes, Harry, they are, but they'll be gone in a few minutes, and we'll be in the dark."

"Thank-you, Isobel! I was just about to wax lyrical and…"

"Another time, Harry. I want to hear what Jean had to say." Izzy turned to Jess who was seated on a kitchen chair beside her.

"She didn't say much, Izzy. We were in a hurry to catch the train." Jess glanced down at Beau who was seated on the top step, at her feet. He looked up at her. "Weren't we, Beau?"

"We would have missed the train if you'd stopped and talked to Jean."

"Yes, I know." Jess turned her attention to Izzy. "Jean said that you'd be hearing from her Solicitor shortly, and that this was something that she'd been praying for." Jess shrugged. "That was as far as the conversation went, Izzy."

"I'm a bit concerned about Rodney," said Beau, in the quickly fading sunset. "He's caused trouble before; he could do so again."

"No!" Harry was adamant. "We've got him covered. He can't do a thing about it. His mother has taken him out of her Will."

"If anything happens to Jean, and we all know that her health is shaky, he could contest the Will, couldn't he?" Beau's statement hung in the air.

"If anything happens to Jean, yes, he could," said Harry slowly.

They were all silent, while the connotations of this statement penetrated their brains. It was Izzy who broke the silence. "Well, we're not going to worry about that now." She stood up, scraping her chair on the verandah. "I think it's time to take these chairs and head inside. The mosquitoes will be heading our way soon, and the darkness is now upon us."

"Ooh, Isobel!" Harry chuckled. "Very poetic, I must say."

*

Some time later, Jess lay in the darkened bedroom, waiting for Beau to return from his ablutions. The curtains at the window were open and she watched the moon playing hide-and-seek with the scudding clouds, plunging the world into blackness every now and then. The rainbow hues of two hours ago were gone, replaced by impenetrable grey cumulus. They reminded Jess of the days when she and Izzy had lain in the paddock, surrounded by their father's dairy herd, and seeing all manner of shapes in the clouds. She smiled at the memory.

Jess felt the bed move as Beau climbed in beside her, and instinctively she turned into his arms. They lay in silence for several minutes, content just to have that close proximity with each other. It was Beau who broke the silence eventually.

"It's time you went to sleep, my love," he murmured drowsily. "It's been a big day, and we have another one coming up tomorrow." He yawned.

"Hm." Jess didn't move. "Beau?"

"What is it?"

"There's something I want to do tomorrow, and I need to know whether you think it's foolish."

Jess felt him laugh softly. "You're never foolish, Jess." He kissed her brow.

"This might be."

"Then tell me, my love."

"When I was packing for our trip, I came across some of Jack's pressed forget-me-nots in one of the cases. I must have put them there for safekeeping. They were in a book of his poems." She paused. "I want to ask Martin if he could put the flowers and a copy of the poem, on Jack's grave for me. Is that a foolish idea, Beau?"

"No, it's not foolish, Jess, and yes, I'm sure Martin will do that for you."

"Good." Jess pressed her head into his chest. "Then that settles it."

Beau tightened his grip on her, and was suddenly glad that she couldn't see the expression on his face. She was his, of that there was no doubt, but her love for Jack would always be there beneath the surface. He had known it all along, but it was moments like this that reminded him of whose footprints he was following.

"I love you, too, Jess," he whispered to himself. "Don't ever forget that."

Jess was already asleep.

*

The road to All Weather farm was deeply rutted, and Harry drove the car with extreme caution for the last quarter of a mile. Dust plumed behind them in a dense cloud, and Jess and Izzy hung on grimly to their straw hats, as the vehicle shuddered and bumped for a bone-shaking ten minutes before arriving at the gate. The little girls shrieked with laughter as they were tossed about like corks on the back seat, while Ben and Edward, who were squeezed into the open luggage compartment, covered their mouths against the dust that followed them.

"Sorry about that," apologised Harry as he stopped at the gate.

It was Beau who jumped out to open the gate, and then waited as Harry drove through, before closing it. He jumped on to the running board and gripped the door as the car bumped its way across the home paddock towards the typical Mallee farmhouse with its wide verandahs protecting it from the hot summer sun. The weatherboards were sadly in need of a coat of paint, and a bed of bedraggled hydrangeas struggled to survive against the sheltered south wall.

Chairs had been set out on a small patch of watered grass, and several people were standing in small groups, chatting and laughing as they drank from long-stemmed glasses. Izzy leaned forward in her seat and tapped Harry on the shoulder.

"Do we know any of these people, Harry?" she asked anxiously as her eyes skimmed the guests.

Harry pulled up beneath the spindly shade of a gnarled old apple tree, and his eyes narrowed as he looked across the yard. "I don't think so, Isobel," he replied.

Ben and Edward tumbled out of the luggage compartment, their faces and clothes streaked with dust. Jess, who was feeling slightly nauseas after the jolting of the final quarter of a mile, looked at them with dismay. Shaking her head, she climbed unsteadily out of the car, and after straightening her pale grey suit, took the two boys by the arms.

"Straight to the washhouse, you two," she said briskly.

"Where's the washhouse?" asked Ben, slapping the dust from his pants.

"Ask Nancy," said Jess, shading her eyes as she watched a familiar figure in a pale blue linen suit hurrying in their direction. "Here she comes now."

Nancy opened her arms wide as she reached Jess, and enveloped her in a warm hug. "I am so pleased to see you all here," she said, as she glanced around the group. "Martin is anxious to catch up with you." She looked down at Ben and Edward. "My goodness! I didn't realise how dusty our road was!" She pointed in the direction of the house. "You'll find a washhouse on the verandah, boys, near the back door."

"Thank-you, Nancy," laughed Jess. "I had just finished telling them to go and find somewhere to clean themselves." She watched as the boys ran in the direction of the house. "I suppose I'd better go and supervise."

"No, Jess." Beau had stepped up beside her. "I'll go. Hello, Nancy. It's lovely to see you again, and on such a memorable occasion."

"Yes, it is. How are you, Beau?"

"Oh, I'm well thank-you." He smiled at Jess. "Excuse me while I check on these boys." He hurried across the yard, and Nancy turned back to Jess.

"I must say, Jess, that you are looking very…" She stopped short of saying the obvious and Izzy, who had been standing beside the car, suppressed a giggle. Jess and Harry frowned in her direction.

"I'm pregnant, Nancy," said Jess quietly. Nancy's fair complexion flushed.

"I – I thought that might be the case," she said, "but I didn't know whether I should say so."

Jess smiled. "We are very happy about it, Nancy; very happy."

"That's wonderful, Jess." Nancy took a deep breath as they made their way towards the grassed area where couples were gathered. "We're waiting on the Pastor, and then we can begin. Martin is somewhere about." She cast a glance around. "Yes, there he is. Martin!" she called out.

Jess saw Martin's tall frame emerge from the group, and the smile that lit his face as he saw them. He spoke to the man he had been talking to, and then headed in their direction.

Jess held out her arms and was immediately swung off the ground. Martin spun her around, before releasing her and standing back to look at her.

"Hello, Jess!" He beamed. "I am so pleased you could make it." He looked around at the rest of the family. "Hello Izzy. Hello Harry." He looked down at the two little girls staring up at him. "My goodness! Is this Gracie?"

Jess nodded. "And of course you will have met Freya."

"Yes. Hello Freya." Martin leaned forward and held out a hand to Grace. "Hello, Grace. You were only a tiny child when I saw you last. How old are you now?"

"I'm four," said Grace in a husky voice, her eyes never leaving Martin's face.

"Four, eh? You're nearly a big girl." Martin straightened up. "Where are the boys?"

"Beau had to take them to the washhouse to clean the dust off them," said Jess.

Martin threw back his head and laughed loudly. "Our wonderful road!" he exclaimed.

Jess saw the boys heading towards them, their hair damp and their faces clean. Beau followed, and Martin bounded forward to clasp him by the hand.

"Beau! How are you, mate?"

"I'm very well, Martin, thank-you, and I must say, you look every bit the bridegroom."

Martin flushed as he tweaked at his collar and tie. "A bit dressy for me, mate, but we have to abide by the rules on these occasions."

"I hate to break up this reunion," said Nancy quickly, "but I think the Pastor might be on his way, Martin. You'd better rally the troops."

Martin shaded his eyes as he looked out towards the road. Sure enough, a black vehicle was bumping and jolting its way towards them.

"Right!" Martin faced the visitors. "I hope somebody has a camera."

"I do," said Harry.

"Then let's do this!"

Nancy flapped her hands at him. "Go, Martin!" They all watched as he sprinted across the yard, coat tails flapping. "Fleur is in the house. I'd better make sure she's ready." Nancy smiled at her guests. "Find yourselves a seat over there, preferably in the shade, and we'll be under way shortly." With that she hurried towards the house.

"Come on then!" said Harry. "You heard the lady. The show's about to begin."

"Harry!" exclaimed Izzy crossly. "A little decorum would not go astray."

"No dear."

*

Jess sat beside Beau, on one of the wooden kitchen chairs that had been set out for the guests. The two boys sat on the ground at their feet, and Grace sat on Jess's knee. It was an unusual setting for a wedding, with the dairy cows mooing quietly in the background, and the hum of insects in the air. Jess brushed at an annoying fly and turned to watch as Fleur came down the steps of the back verandah, walking slowly towards Martin and the Pastor.

As she reached Martin, Fleur slipped her hand into his, and gazed adoringly up into his face. Jess was able to study the two of them as they stood side by side. Fleur was as petite as Martin was tall and rangy. Her gown of smooth cream satin clung softly to her youthful figure. Dark brown hair hung in a long braid down her back, and was threaded with white daisies.

Jess let the voice of the Pastor drift over her as she reflected on the past, and all that had happened since meeting Martin three years ago, when Jack brought him home for Christmas. The insecure young boy had gone, and in his place was a self-assured, confident young man who was embarking on the next phase of his life with a woman who adored him. Jess felt her eyes mist over, and reached for a handkerchief.

"What's wrong?" whispered Beau.

"Nothing's wrong," replied Jess as she dabbed at her eyes. "I was remembering Martin as he was when I met him three years ago."

"Life has changed him, Jess."

"He's a son Nancy can be very proud of."

"I'm sure she is."

Finally they heard the words 'I now pronounce you man and wife', and before the Pastor had given his final blessing, Martin scooped his bride up in his arms and kissed her thoroughly. The small crowd erupted into enthusiastic cheering and clapping, and Martin's mates leapt to their feet. Wolf whistles rent the air, sending cattle skittering away from the unfamiliar sound.

"You may kiss your bride." The Pastor was smiling as he finished the service over the noise. "That's if you haven't already," he added.

Everybody flocked around the happy couple, congratulating them, and admiring the ring. Jess hung back, waiting for an opportunity to speak with Martin alone. Nancy had headed into the house, where the refreshments were to be served. Izzy had gone with her, leaving Harry in charge of Freya, who wanted to look at the cows.

Beau knew that Jess was anxious to speak with Martin, so he took Grace by the hand, and followed Harry and Freya across the yard to the home paddock where curious Friesians stood by the fence, chewing their cud and watching proceedings through doe-like eyes.

Jess waited until Nancy had called from the verandah, to say that refreshments were ready, before approaching Martin. He was heading towards the house, Fleur close beside him.

"Martin!" He turned. "Can I speak with you, please?"

"Certainly, Jess. What about?"

"I'd like to ask a favour of you." Jess fell into step beside them.

"Ask away."

"Do you ever visit Jack's grave?"

"Yes, I've been there once. Why?"

"I have something that I want you to leave on his grave, if you can."

Martin stopped walking, and Jess opened the grey linen reticule that she had hanging from her wrist. She pulled out a small tin and lifted the lid. Martin peered inside it.

"Dried flowers?" He studied Jess's face.

"Yes." Jess cleared her throat. "Forget-me-nots. They hold significance for

Jack and me. There's also a copy of one of his poems."

Martin nodded his head slowly as Jess closed the tin and handed it to him.

"I can do that for you, Jess," he said quietly.

"M'oublie pas," Fleur murmured. "Forget-me-not."

"Yes, Fleur." Jess had tears in her eyes.

Fleur held out her right wrist, on which was entwined a sprig of rosemary. "I wear this for remembering," she said, her fingers twisting the rosemary.

"Who do you wish to remember, Fleur?"

"My papa."

"Fleur's father didn't return from the war," said Martin, placing his arm around her waist.

"I'm sorry, Fleur." Jess touched the younger woman on the arm. "It seems that most people suffered loss, one way or another."

"Oui."

Martin hooked his free arm through Jess's. "Come on!" he said brightly. "We'd better get to the food before it's all eaten."

*

The light was beginning to fade when Jess and the family stood beside the car to say their goodbyes to Martin, Fleur and Nancy. The rest of the party had gone, tooting horns loudly as they all departed into the night.

The group stood silently as they all contemplated this goodbye, knowing that they probably wouldn't see each other again. The Weatheralls were departing on the Tuesday, bound for Melbourne, and then the next ship that was sailing to England. Nancy had not sold the farm, but it had been leased to a neighbouring farmer, who needed the extra land to run his cows. The farmhouse would remain empty, until the marriage of his son, who would then move into it.

Nancy seemed happy with this arrangement, as it meant that if she did have to return to Australia, she would have somewhere to live. Martin had pooh-poohed the idea of his mother returning, to which Nancy had merely smiled and tilted her head as if to say 'we'll see.'

Now they had to say good-bye, and faces were glum as they all looked at each other in the gathering darkness.

Martin broke the silence. "I know we're all feeling the same at the moment, because we know this is final, but I want you to know that I will never forget what you have all done for mum and me. This wouldn't be happening if it weren't for Jack and Jess, and then you, Harry and Izzy." He blinked rapidly. "We won't forget you." He turned to Jess. "I will make it my business, Jess, while we're still in England, to visit Jack's grave." He patted his breast pocket. "Your message will be safe with me."

"Thank-you, Martin." Jess was close to tears, and felt Beau's arm around her.

"If it's alright, I'll tell him that you are happy, and that the children are doing well."

Jess nodded. "I'm sure he'll be listening somewhere."

Nancy stepped forward and clasped Harry and Izzy by the hands.

"I'll write to you when I'm settled in France, and let you know how things are going. I wish you well with your own venture, and hope that it is a move for the good, as I hope mine is."

"The whole world is changing, Nancy," said Harry solemnly, "and we have to change with it." He leaned forward and kissed her cheek. "Good luck and Godspeed. We'll miss you."

The hugs and kisses began, and cheeks were awash with tears. The children watched on, with wide eyes, until they were also encompassed in wet hugs. Finally everybody stood still.

"Let's not drag this out," said Harry sadly, as he opened the passenger door of the car. "Come on, Isobel. You be the first to break this up."

Izzy climbed into the car, followed by Jess, the little girls and finally Beau. Ben and Edward clambered into the luggage compartment, bringing a laugh from Fleur.

"Très bon!" she exclaimed.

Harry cranked the engine and lit the gas lamps before climbing into the driver's seat.

"Good-bye everyone!" He tipped his hat.

"I'll open the gate for you, Harry," said Martin, as the car moved slowly across the grass.

"Good-bye!"

"Au revoir!"

"Good luck!"

The voices echoed across the paddocks, as the car bumped away from All Weather Farm, and headed towards Swan Hill. Another chapter had closed, and Jess felt the awful finality of it weighing down her heart. She reached for Beau's hand and gripped it tightly.

A Christmas Invitation

Christmas was looking like being a very bleak affair, until Louise paid Jess a visit one day early in December, and requested their presence at the Simmons' residence for Christmas dinner, and that included Charles.

"You're inviting us all to Christmas dinner?" Jess blinked at Louise as she sat awkwardly on the brown couch, smiling up at her.

"That's what I said, Jess."

"But…"

"But nothing!" Louise waved her hands in the air. "I couldn't stand another Christmas dinner with just Raymond and me." She sighed as she rubbed her back. "This child is really making its presence felt. I'll be glad when it's out." Louise appraised Jess. "Look at you! Hardly a bump, and I'm like a ship in full sail." She groaned theatrically. "How do you do it, Jess? You look so neat."

"Louise!" laughed Jess. "You're due in March, and I'm not due until May. Perhaps that has something to do with it."

"Perhaps... Where were we? Even my head's out of order."

"Christmas dinner?" prompted Jess.

"Yes. You will come, won't you?"

Jess laughed, remembering their last meal with Louise and Raymond. "Hm! I'll have to watch my p's and q's then, won't I?"

Louise snorted. "Don't worry about that."

"We'll come on certain conditions."

"And they are?"

"That we provide some of the food. I know Charles will probably want to be in charge of the turkey. That's been his job every year." She stopped. "Margaret always made the pudding."

They were both silent for a moment.

"Would you like to do the pudding, Jess?"

Jess nodded slowly. "Of course. I'll find Margaret's recipe, although I know she used to make it at least two months prior to Christmas."

"That's settled then. I can do the rest, if the turkey and pudding are accounted for." Louise struggled out of the couch. "Thank-you, Jess. You have no idea how happy this makes me."

"Thank-YOU, Louise. I was wondering how we were going to deal with Christmas this year."

They were at the front door when Louise remembered something else.

"No presents," she said emphatically. "I have something else in mind." She smiled mischievously before treading heavily down the steps to where the car was parked on the side of the road. "If I think of anything else, I'll let you know."

"I'm pleased to see that you're not walking!" called Jess from the verandah.

Louise grimaced as she wedged herself into the car. "It is a bit of a tight squeeze."

"Be careful, Louise! You don't want anything to happen to the baby."

Louise waved her arms. "See you on Christmas Day, Jess."

The car jerked into motion, and Jess was left wondering about the invitation. It certainly wouldn't have come from Raymond, and she hoped that he had been consulted. Perhaps Beau could find out. There was nothing she could do, if he hadn't. What she had to do now was find Margaret's recipe for Christmas pudding, and see how Charles felt about the whole idea.

Charles reluctantly agreed to provide and cook the turkey, and helped Jess search through Margaret's cookbooks for her pudding recipe. They found it eventually, along with a collection of threepenny bits to place in the mixture. Jess also found bags of dried fruits and flour that Margaret had obviously bought in preparation for the Christmas pudding bake. So with permission from Charles, she collected the ingredients together and placed them in one of Margaret's cane baskets.

"It will make it feel as though Margaret had a hand in this," she said to Charles. "She must have been planning Christmas, in spite of her illness."

"You knew Margaret, Jess," said Charles, his eyes misting. "She liked to be organised. Perhaps she did this to help you."

"Perhaps she did." Jess looked at the basket full of fruit and flour. "I only need the eggs and the butter, and perhaps a little brandy, and we'll have ourselves a Christmas pudding. Thank-you, Margaret." She smiled at Charles. "Thank-you, Charles. We'll have Christmas after all."

The following day, Jess meticulously followed Margaret's recipe, and soon had the pudding steaming away in its calico casing. She sighed with relief as she peeked into the saucepan where the water was simmering gently. Soon the kitchen was filled with the pungent aroma of boiling fruit.

Jess decided that as she was now in a Christmas frame of mind, she had better write to Sally, Mary and Angela, and wish them all a merry Christmas, so she sat at the kitchen table and pondered over her writing paper.

Sally would want to know about Martin, and of course she could give her the news about the baby, now that her three months was past. She had no doubt Sally would be delighted. Mary hadn't been in contact for a while, and Jess wondered whether their current situation had changed. Maybe George had been transferred elsewhere? She would have to find out. Angela would be pleased to know that Charlotte had been in touch with Beau, and could possibly be heading to the African Missions, on advice from the Reverend Mother. They would all be thrilled with the news that Harry and Izzy were in negotiations with Jean, and would soon be living close by.

Jess sighed as she contemplated all the changes that had occurred recently, and she stared at a blank sheet of paper for some time, before actually writing anything. She was so pre-occupied she was only vaguely aware of the boys arriving home from school.

This was where Beau found her some time later, when he came in from putting the bicycle away in the shed. Jess didn't look up as he entered the kitchen, and he moved quietly behind her to plant a kiss on the back of her neck.

"Beau!" Jess spun around on the chair. "You frightened the life out of me! Don't do that!"

"You were totally absorbed in whatever it is you are doing, my dear." He peered over her shoulder. "What ARE you doing?"

"I'm letting Sally, Mary and Angela know what has been going on here, and wishing them all a merry Christmas."

"I see." Beau looked around. "Are the boys home from school?"

"I think so." Jess looked up at the clock. It was five o'clock. Her hands flew to her mouth. "Is that the time? I haven't started tea yet." She rose from the chair.

Beau sniffed the air. "But you have something nice cooking away there."

"It's the Christmas pudding."

"Oh! Margaret's recipe?"

"Yes." Jess folded away the letters until later. It was time to think about tea.

Ben and Edward, having heard Beau arrive home, appeared at the kitchen door. They had been home for an hour, and seeing their mother absorbed in her letter writing, had decided not to disturb her. Grace also appeared from the other end of the house, and immediately demanded eggs on toast for tea.

"Well, Gracie," said Jess, who was now feeling guilty about her lack of supervision, "that's probably what we will have." She glanced up at Beau, who was standing behind the children, his expression unreadable. "Go and collect the eggs, boys."

"We already have, ma!" they chorused.

Jess shrugged. "Good! How do you want them cooked?"

Again there was a chorus, until Jess held up her hands. "Enough! We'll have them poached." Catching Beau's eye, she saw him smile as he shook his head. "It serves me right," she said as she reached for a pan.

*

Later that night, as Jess lay in the crook of Beau's arm, listening to the rhythm of his breathing, she contemplated the day. Life was changing so quickly and it made her sad. There was an unmistakeable shifting of friendships that she had considered dear, and their absence would leave an enormous gap in her life. Margaret, Martin, Nancy, Sally and Mary were all connections with Jack, and all that had happened in the past. She knew that she had to let go of what had been, and concentrate on what was happening now and into the future. Looking at Beau, sleeping peacefully, she was reminded that he was her future, and no matter what it held, she loved him dearly. They had faced many challenges together, and no doubt would face many more. Life was not always going to be easy. Jess placed her hands on her stomach, feeling the 'bump' as Louise had referred to it, and she smiled in the darkness. There was plenty to look forward to, and she needed to embrace it all.

She kissed Beau lightly on the cheek. He stirred but didn't wake.

"Goodnight, my love," she whispered. "Sweet dreams."

Finale

New Beginnings

Christmas Day 1919

It was Christmas morning.

Jess and Beau were awakened by the sound of running footsteps along the passage, and suddenly the door burst open and three bodies hurled themselves on to the bed, all talking at once.

"Ma! Look what I got for Christmas!"

"Ma! Wake up!"

"Beau! Father Christmas has been! He left me this note, and I have to go and look outside!"

Jess struggled into a sitting position, and pushed the hair away from her face. Three children were sitting on the end of the bed, all holding something tangible. Grace had a porcelain baby doll, dressed in a pink crocheted outfit, with a matching beret and booties. Ben had a model airplane kit, and a bundle of books. Edward had a note saying that he should look in the back yard for his present. What could it be? He tugged at Beau's hand, in an attempt to get him out of bed.

Beau feigned reluctance as he reached for a dressing gown, but after winking at Jess, followed Edward from the bedroom. Jess also shrugged herself into her dressing gown, and rubbing the sleep from her eyes, tried to concentrate on the two children seated beside her.

Grace was showing her the doll, and Jess said a silent thank-you to Margaret, who had been the one busy with a crochet hook, leading up to her sickness. Ben was anxious to get started on his model airplane, but Jess reminded him that they were all going to Doctor Simmons' for Christmas dinner, and he would have to wait until Beau could help him.

A frown crossed Ben's face when told he had to wait, but he said nothing, instead unwrapping his books. The frown quickly turned into a smile as he found Mark Twain's The Adventures of Tom Sawyer and Huckleberry Finn.

"Ma!" he cried triumphantly. "I've been waiting for these books for so long!"

"Well now you have them, Ben." Jess rumpled his hair. "Come on, let's go outside and see what Edward has, shall we?"

They followed the sound of Edward's high-pitched voice, and there he was in the back yard with Beau. They were both bent over a bicycle - a smaller version of Jack's old bicycle.

"We'll take it out on the road," Beau was saying, "when we're dressed, and see how you manage this one." He turned as Jess came down the back steps with Ben and Grace.

"Look ma!" Edward squealed. "I got a bicycle!"

"Aren't you a lucky boy? It seems that everybody got what they wanted."

Beau stood back as the children gathered around the bicycle. Jess stood beside him, and tucked her arm in his.

"You did well for the boys, Beau," she whispered. "They couldn't be happier."

"Thanks to Charles for the books, and the local thrift shop for the bicycle. I gave it a coat of paint, and it looks as good as new. Edward should have no trouble with this one."

"I don't have a present for you."

"Yes you have," said Beau quietly, as he ran a hand across her middle. "I'll have to wait for it." He smiled. "Merry Christmas, my love."

*

At midday, Charles was honking the car horn, and activity within the household increased. Jess pulled the Christmas pudding off the stove, wrapped it in a towel and placed it in a basket. Beau called the children from their presents, and within no more than two minutes after hearing the car horn, they were all on the front verandah, and Jess was locking the door.

Charles was out of the driver's seat, and opening the passenger doors for everyone to climb on board. Beau steered Jess to the front passenger seat.

"You sit in here, Jess," he said, as he helped her up on to the seat. "We can't have you squashed in the back."

With everyone finally on board, Charles grated the gears and the big car moved forward. He turned to smile at the children in the back.

"Did father Christmas come last night?" he asked, and there was an immediate response.

"Yes, granddad!" came the chorus, followed by them all talking at once.

"Hang on!" laughed Charles. "One at a time, if you please!"

The three looked at Beau, who indicated that Ben go first, and so order returned, and they all told their grandfather that they had got exactly what they wanted. He nodded approval.

"That's good. You're very lucky children."

Jess had to agree, as she silently recalled the last-minute dash to make sure Father Christmas arrived on time. It had been touch-and-go with the new paint on the bicycle, which Beau had hidden around at Charles' place, in case the boys decided to snoop.

"How's the turkey, Charles?" Beau's voice cut through her thoughts.

"I think it's up to scratch, Beau," answered Charles, as the Simmons' residence came into view. "It's in the luggage compartment, wrapped up in towels to keep it warm. I'm surprised you can't smell it from where you are."

"I can!" shouted Edward.

"You would!" said Jess, shaking her head.

The big car pulled up outside the red brick terrace house, and Louise immediately appeared, dressed in a flowing red dress, her blonde hair tied up with a matching ribbon. Jess marvelled at how robust she looked, and as they hugged each other at the gate, she said so.

"You look wonderful, Louise!" she laughed. "Pregnancy certainly suits you."

"Do you think so, Jess?" Louise placed her hands across her back. "I'm like a ship in full sail."

They both saw Beau grin at this remark. "Go on, Doctor Smartie!" continued Louise. "Make a joke of it. Raymond does."

"I wouldn't dream of it, Louise," said Beau smoothly, as he lifted Grace down on to the footpath.

Charles was at the back of the car, retrieving the turkey in all its wrappings. Louise bent to smell the aroma that filtered through the towels.

"Ooh, Charles!" she murmured. "That smells delicious."

"Well it won't stay delicious if we don't get inside and carve it up," said Charles, trying to sound flippant, but receiving a tiny frown from Louise.

"Everything's ready, Charles." Louise looked at Jess, who merely raised her eyes skywards.

"Good!" said Charles. "Lead the way, McDuff!"

As they stepped into the cool interior of the house, Louise took Jess by the arm.

"I'm not sure how to take Charles today, Jess. Is he serious or what?"

"I think he's trying hard to act as though everything is normal. We need to cut him some slack. He really misses Margaret, although he won't say so."

"As long as I know. I don't want to say the wrong thing, which I can do very easily."

Raymond had appeared at the kitchen door. "Christmas greetings, everyone!"

Jess was surprised by the wide smile that welcomed them, and she responded in the same manner. It was going to be a joyous time after all.

*

The meal progressed with gaiety and laughter, and Louise's special surprise came in the form of handcrafted bonbons. As each person pulled open their bonbon, there was a present inside, and Louise sat smiling as gasps and cheers accompanied each opening. The children all received a lollypop and a bag of boiled sweets, making their eyes pop wide with excitement. Jess received a pair of hand-crocheted baby booties as well as a small bottle of perfume. For Beau there was a miniature bottle of whisky and an initialled handkerchief.

Charles received two cigars, also wrapped in an initialled handkerchief, as did Raymond.

"Louise, you shouldn't have!" exclaimed Jess, feeling embarrassed because she had nothing to give in return. "What's in your bonbon?" Louise was the last to open hers.

"I'll see, shall I?" Louise shared the pull with Raymond, and on to the table fell a gold chain bracelet. Louise sucked in her breath as she looked around the table. "I am not responsible for this one," she said quietly, and her eyes turned to Raymond.

"Merry Christmas, my dear," he said slowly, as a smile spread across his serious features.

Louise grabbed his head between her hands and pulled him into a kiss, which made the children giggle and the adults cheer.

"My stuffy husband had a hand in this, wouldn't you say?" Louise's eyes were shining as she looked around at her guests. "Merry Christmas, everybody."

"Merry Christmas!" was the group reply.

Conversation continued as the meal progressed, and everybody agreed that the turkey was the most delicious they'd ever tasted, and Jess had excelled herself with the pudding.

"Margaret would have been proud of you, Jess," said Charles, his eyes misting.

"It's your job every year now," said Louise loudly. "I think we should make this a regular thing, don't you agree, Raymond?"

He smiled. "It looks like it."

The telephone rang shrilly in the hallway. Raymond wiped his fingers on the linen napkin beside his plate, and rose to answer it. Louise sighed.

"I'll be there as soon as I can," they all heard him say and the receiver was replaced.

Raymond returned to the dining room, his face serious.

"I have to go," he said solemnly. "Mrs. Downing is in the last stages of labour, and the midwife thinks there could be a problem with the umbilical cord."

"Do you want me to go, too?" asked Beau.

"No, thanks all the same, Beau." Raymond smiled briefly. "Enjoy the rest of the day."

They heard the front door slam behind him. Louise slumped in her chair.

"Oh, the joys of being a doctor's wife," she said as she looked in Jess's direction. "Something for you to look forward to, Jess." She sighed as she straightened her back again. "Keep eating, everybody. We haven't finished this meal yet."

"A Christmas baby," said Jess softly. "I hope all goes well for mother and child."

New Year

Jess was relieved to find out, several days after Christmas, that Mrs. Downing and baby Joshua had both survived the difficult birth, and were doing well.

The postman, George, delivered letters from Sally and Mary on consecutive days. They both enthused over the news of the baby and wished her and Beau all the best for Christmas and the New Year. Sally was pleased to hear that Martin had found his future in France, and she indicated that both she and Simon would be travelling the countryside soon, selling their artwork, and if that didn't work out, then they would return to the artists' community.

Mary and George would soon be moving to Western Australia, where George, recently retired from the Armed Forces, had plans to buy a small plot of land to potter around on. His family were from over there, and had encouraged him to move his family to where they would be closer. Jess got the feeling from the letter that Mary was not happy with this idea, because it would take her away from all her friends. She promised to keep in touch with Jess, as she felt a special bond with her and Beau.

The next day a letter arrived from Angela, and the postman scratched his head as he pulled it from his satchel.

"You're a popular lady, Mrs. DuBois," he muttered, turning over the letter before handing it to Jess. "This one's from Sydney."

Jess smiled as she took the letter. "It is Christmas, George," she said. "Everyone should get mail at Christmas."

"Not everyone, Mrs. DuBois." He shook his head. "You know Mr. Fleming down the road a bit?" Jess nodded. "He don't get any letters, at any time of the year."

"Oh?" said Jess, wanting to beat a hasty retreat to the verandah, where she could read Angela's letter in peace. "Perhaps he doesn't have any family out of town."

George leaned on the fence. "Oh, he's got family alright. Do you know...?"

Jess didn't want to be rude, but she sensed a story coming. "I'm sorry, George, but I do have to go. Tell me another time, eh?"

"Oh. Sure thing, Mrs. DuBois. I'd better not hold up the King's mail."

"No. Thank-you, George."

Jess watched as he sauntered along the street, then climbing the steps to the verandah, she sat on the old stool and opened Angela's letter.

It read:

> *Dear Jess, Beau and children,*
> *It was so lovely to hear from you. I am thrilled that your sister is coming to live near you, Jess. That will be wonderful for all of you.*
> *I was sorry that I couldn't get down for Margaret's funeral. How is Charles? He reminds me so much of Clarence – pig-headed when*

it comes to seeking help or a little care from outsiders.

I am pleased to say that Celia and I are at last on speaking terms, and we have both travelled with Clarence to the Asylum to see his wife. Her name is Julia, and she must have been a beautiful but very temperamental woman in her early years. Celia carries some of the same traits as her mother, but Clarence hopes that now her mind is completely absorbed by her work, she will not lose her reason. One can only hope, when the genetic thread is so strong.

I am still working at the Clinic, but with the influenza now past, I will return full-time to my little patisserie. It's what I love. Clarence says I should spend a little money on the place, to bring it up to modern standards, and he is prepared to help me with that. He is a dear man, and I can't imagine life without him now.

I have not heard anything more about your sister, Beau, but the old house has been demolished. Clarence and I drove past there recently and saw a 'for sale' notice out the front.

Anyway, that's all the news for the present. I look forward to hearing when your baby arrives, and hope you are keeping well, Jess. Seasons greetings to you from all of us here in Sydney, and pass them on to the folk we met.
Your friend
Angela

Jess folded the paper and sat staring into the distance for a few moments. So the old house was gone? Jess shivered as memories of being there invaded her consciousness. There could be no more ghosts there, surely? They would have returned to dust. Thoughts of Beau's ordeal there, crept into her mind, followed by a moment of panic when she considered the consequences had he not been found. Her spine tingled and she found her hands clenched around Angela's letter. She had tried not to think of any of it since returning home, but it was moments like this one she was experiencing now, that made her shudder and thank God for Charlotte's intervention.

As if on cue, Beau appeared before her, pulling his bicycle through the gate.

"What's wrong, Jess?" he smiled up at her. "You look as though you've seen a ghost."

Jess retrieved her train of thought. "I've had a letter from Angela."

"What does she say?" Beau leaned the bicycle against the fence and joined Jess on the seat.

"Here, read it for yourself." Jess handed him the letter.

Beau read it and then turned to Jess. "I see where the ghosts are." He took her hand. "We have to believe they are all gone, Jess. They've been turned into dust."

"I know, and I try not to think of them, but sometimes…" Her voice caught in her throat. "What if you hadn't been found?" Jess turned tear-filled eyes in his direction.

Beau placed his arms around her and held her close, sensing the quiver in her slight frame. "I was found, Jess, and that's all that matters now. We can never comprehend the past, so we must let it go and concentrate on the future. Who knows what wonderful things are waiting for us? Now dry your eyes, and if you're a good girl, we can watch the fireworks tonight, because it's New Year's Eve, and even the children will be aware of that, I'm sure."

"Can we watch the fireworks?" It was Edward's voice that came from behind the front wire door.

Beau groaned. "I swear those children have ears everywhere, Jess." He turned to Edward who now stood beside them. "Yes, Edward, on one condition."

"What's that?"

"That we don't have any arguments when it come to chores tonight."

Edward nodded vigorously. "There won't be! Can I tell Ben?"

"Yes. Go on!"

Jess and Beau looked at each other as the front wire door slammed behind Edward, and they heard him shouting, "Ben! Ben! We're allowed to watch the fireworks tonight!"

*

It was almost midnight, and Jess, Beau and the three children stood waiting patiently on the front verandah for the air to explode with a kaleidoscope of flashing colours – stars and comets and cascading fountains of every hue.

"Why can't we go to the showgrounds to watch them?" asked Edward, pulling his mother's skirt.

"Because we can see them from here," answered Jess patiently.

"How much longer?" Grace was rubbing her eyes.

"Not long now." Beau checked his watch in the light from the doorway. "It looks as though half the neighbourhood is on the street tonight." He lifted Grace and swung her across his shoulders. "You should be able to see now, Gracie. Are you ready for this?"

"Yes!" came the chorus.

Then it happened – an explosion of colour that lit the night sky, and set the neighbourhood dogs in a frenzy of barking. One after the other the fireworks crackled and hissed high above their heads, raining down in a fiery trail until they disappeared behind the trees.

Beau felt an instant of panic as the deafening sound reminded him of gunfire, and he closed his eyes to shut out pictures that he hoped he would never see again. Jess turned at that moment, and caught the look of panic on his face. She tucked her arm in his and squeezed it tightly. Thoughts of war had been far from their minds until this moment, but it seemed they never really went away.

"Are you alright, Beau?" she whispered, as the boys shouted and cheered beside them.

Beau opened his eyes and stared at her. "For a moment I thought I was in France," he said hoarsely.

As the fireworks slowly evaporated into the air, the town clock began to strike midnight. The boys counted in the new year – one, two, three, four, five, six, seven, eight, nine, ten, eleven, twelve.

The street erupted with loud cheering. "HAPPY NEW YEAR!"

Beau bent to kiss Jess as he whispered, "Happy New year, my love."

"Happy New Year, Beau," she whispered back.

New Life

It was a new year – a new decade, and life at the DuBois household resumed a normal thread. Summer brought with it some searing days and nights, but by the end of February the worst of the heat had gone, giving way to the cooler breezes of an early autumn. Izzy reported that the move to Bendigo was about to happen. The shop had been sold, the family home was on the market, and a carrier van had been requisitioned to deliver their furniture to the Grey Goose during the last week of March. Her excitement was infectious, and Jess found herself counting the days to their arrival.

In the meantime, Louise was getting close to her delivery date, and she spent a lot of time visiting with Jess, where she sought advice from Jess's experience with having children. She was becoming increasingly apprehensive, and it took a lot of reassurance from Jess before she could acknowledge that everything would be fine. With two doctors between them, so what could possibly go wrong?

However, by the middle of March, with only days to go, Louise sought Jess's advice once more. Should she be experiencing what could only be described as contractions just yet? Jess sat her on the couch, and sitting beside her, took her hands, which were trembling.

"Louise, what you are experiencing is perfectly natural. It's the baby letting you know that it's almost ready for the outside world."

"Are you sure, Jess?"

"Yes." She smiled at Louise's troubled expression.

"Beau has assured me that everything is going well."

"Well then, stop worrying, Louise! You're in good hands, as I expect I will be when my time comes."

Louise smiled. "Funny, isn't it? Raymond is your doctor, and Beau is mine."

"It makes sense, Louise. No emotional ties to deal with."

"You're right, of course." Louise sighed. "I just wish it were all over. Do you know much about the midwife?"

"Mrs. Davidson?"

"Yes."

"I know she's been around for a long time, and she helped deliver my three."

"That's reassuring, Jess."

"Stop worrying, Louise. Very soon you will hold a beautiful bundle in your arms, and life will never be the same again." They laughed together. "Now let me get you a cup of tea."

*

It was after midnight when Beau got the call that Louise was in labour, and had been moved to the hospital at Raymond's request. He dressed hurriedly, and gave Jess a quick kiss before heading out into the night. Raymond was picking him up in the car, and Jess saw the headlights through the bedroom window as he pulled up on the street. A door banged and the car moved off.

Jess lay back on the pillow and contemplated what was about to happen. It would be a long night for Louise as she experienced something she had not experienced before, but which would be the most fulfilling, rewarding experience of her life. Jess had found it so, although she had heard tales from women who found the whole thing so appalling, they were never going back to do it again.

Jess smiled in the darkness, because invariably the ones who protested the loudest, were the ones who did go back again.

The sound of the front door woke her some hours later, as dawn was spreading its rosy hue across the sky. Beau stood in the doorway, his smile wide.

"What did she have?" Jess struggled to sit up, as her own 'bump' was now very visible.

"She had a boy." Beau sat on the edge of the bed. "Raymond is over the moon, Jess. I've never seen him so excited."

"I knew she'd have a boy," said Jess with a sigh of satisfaction.

"Did you, Miss Smartie? And what are we having?"

"A girl, of course." Jess smiled.

"Of course."

"Does baby Simmons have a name yet?"

Beau's brow furrowed. "Yes." He paused. "William Raymond, I think."

Jess said the name several times. "I like the sound of that," she said. "It's shows strength."

Beau laughed. "He had strength alright! He weighed in at nine pound and three ounces."

"Oh my goodness! Poor Louise!" Jess clapped her hands over her mouth.

Beau yawned as he began untying his shoelaces. "Now, my sweet wife, I need to get a couple of hours sleep before I begin the day shift."

He collapsed beside her, and was soon asleep.

*

Jess waited a couple of days before going to see Louise and baby William. Beau had allowed mother and child to go home, knowing that Raymond had hired a maid to take care of the household duties for the immediate future.

Not wishing to walk up the hill to Louise's place, Jess caught the tram near the fountain, and managed to find a seat for herself and Grace. The tram clanged its way up View Street, and turned into Barnard Street, heading towards the hospital. Jess pulled on the cord as they reached the hospital, and she and Grace alighted. It was only a short walk from there to Louise's place. It was also only a short walk to the surgery where Beau was working.

They stepped it out, and soon arrived at the red brick terrace house. Jess rang the doorbell. A fresh-faced young girl opened the door. Her head was swathed in a floral scarf, and she carried a feather duster in one hand.

"Can I help you?" she asked politely.

"I'm Jess DuBois, and I'm here to see Louise – Mrs. Simmons."

"Just one moment please." The girl disappeared, returning a few moments later to open the door. "Mrs. Simmons will see you," she said as she stepped aside to let Jess and Grace enter the house. "She's in the lounge room."

"Thank-you," said Jess. "I know the way."

Louise was on the red velvet couch, propped up with cushions, her feet covered with a rug. In her arms she held a carefully wrapped bundle.

"Jess! Gracie! How wonderful to see you!"

Jess peered over Louise's shoulder. All she could see was a little pink face with a mop of soft fair hair. Baby William was snuffling and mouthing the air, as he struggled to escape the confines of the swaddling blanket. Grace stood watching, a frown etched into her brow.

"He's very fair," said Jess, as Louise pulled the blanket from his face.

"I was always fair, Jess, and Raymond tells me that he was fair as a child. His hair went dark as he got older." She chuckled. "Isn't he simply adorable?"

"He's beautiful, Louise. What do you think, Gracie?"

"He's too small to play with." Grace lost interest and turned away.

"He'll grow, Gracie," laughed Louise.

"You look wonderful, Louise." Jess sat on an armchair opposite Louise. "How did you do it? Beau said that William was nine pounds and three ounces. He's a big boy."

"Yes, he is, and believe me it wasn't easy. Beau was wonderful, Jess. He talked me through it, and his voice was almost hypnotic. I've never heard him speak like that before. His tone was calm and even, and he didn't raise his voice once, even when I was flailing about in agony. Do you know what I mean?"

Jess blinked. "Yes, I do, Louise. When I was ill with the influenza, I could hear him speaking quietly to me, but it wasn't until I recovered that I realised his voice had probably kept me alive. Every now and then I remember things that he must have told me then because he hasn't spoken of them at any other time. So yes, I do know what you mean."

The two women were quiet as they thought of the man who had held their lives in his hands.

Finally Louise stirred and shook a brass bell that stood on the small table beside her.

"I'll ask Mabel to make us a pot of tea." She smiled warmly at Jess.

"That sounds like a wonderful idea."

Izzy and Harry

The telephone rang shrilly in the passageway. Jess hurried to answer it, and Izzy's voice came over the line, loud and clear.

"We're on our way, Jess!"

"You are?"

"Yes! It will take us a couple of days to reach Bendigo, as we have to follow the removalist van." Izzy laughed. "It's like a circus, Jess, truly! We have so much stuff, and yet we're leaving a lot of it behind."

"What about the family home? I was intending to help you clear that."

"Oh, a lot of that is coming too. I've kept the family heirlooms, and left the rest for the people taking it over."

"I should have been consulted, Izzy." Jess felt her voice getting tight.

"I'm truly sorry, Jess. I must have forgotten to tell you, in the chaos that we've been living under." Izzy noticed Jess's silence. "Anyway, you can have what you want of mother's things."

"That's not the point, Izzy!"

Jess was cross that she hadn't been consulted in the final negotiations, but living so far away, there was little she could have done anyway.

"Let's not argue about it, Jess. We can sort it all out when I get there."

"Are you extending?"

"No!" said Izzy quickly. "'Bye Jess! We'll see you in a couple of days. Have the kettle on for me."

The line went dead

"Yes, Izzy," said Jess to herself, as she replaced the receiver.

Beau appeared at the kitchen doorway, ready for work. "Izzy?"

"Yes." Jess sighed. "They are leaving Swan Hill now, and we'll see them in a couple of days."

"So why the long face?"

"Having Izzy around permanently may not always be a good thing."

Beau smiled as he dropped a kiss on her cheek. "I could have told you that, my love. Anyway, I'm off to work. I'll see you tonight."

*

The honking of a car horn made them all head for the front door en masse. Grace was the first to leap down from the verandah, into the arms of her cousin. Jess followed, smiling at the reunion between the two little girls. It was certainly going to be good for them, she mused, even if her own feelings were slightly askew. Beau and the boys were last out of the door, and stood on the verandah as Izzy climbed out of the car from beneath a pile of household paraphernalia. Stretching her back, she made her way on to the footpath.

"I won't grumble about the train trip ever again," she muttered, as Jess pulled her into a hug. "We're covered in dust, and insects and goodness knows what! The first thing I need is a bath."

"No!" laughed Jess. "The first thing you need is a cup of tea. Remember?"

Izzy grimaced. "Yes, I remember. Well, the second thing I need is a bath."

"That can be arranged." Jess looked around. "Where's Harry?"

"Oh, he's with the carrier. They've gone straight to the pub." Izzy turned to Beau. "Guess who our carrier is, Beau?"

"How should I know, Izzy?" Beau shrugged his shoulders.

"Remember Alf Peterson?"

"From Albury? How could I forget that bone-shaking ride from Albury to Swan Hill, for your mother's funeral? So Alf is on the job, is he?"

"He had to do a delivery run to Swan Hill, and then when we're unloaded, he has furniture to pick up and take back to Albury."

"I see." Beau turned to Ben and Edward. "Come on, lads, I think we might be required at the pub to help unload Auntie Izzy's things." He smiled at the two women. "You can have your cup of tea in peace, girls. It's good to have you here, Izzy." He slanted a glance at Jess, before heading off along the street, the two boys in tow.

Izzy tucked her arm in Jess's. "Lead the way to the cup of tea, sister dear." She laughed. "I see our daughters are delighted to see each other."

"Grace has been counting the hours," said Jess as they climbed the steps. "Maybe she'll leave me alone now."

"Oh, Jess, I can't wait to get settled in here." Izzy squeezed Jess's arm. "It's going to be such fun, don't you agree?"

Jess crossed her fingers behind her back. "Of course it is, Izzy."

The New Arrival

Izzy and Harry settled into pub life like ducks to a pond. Jess's fears that Izzy would overwhelm her were unfounded, as Izzy had plenty to occupy her. Jean was finally able to relax a little, and leave the heavy work to Harry.

As Jess had suspected, Freya's room was soon adorned with a mural of dragonflies and fairies. Jean was thrilled with it, and requested that Izzy paint a mural on one wall of the Ladies Lounge, preferably not fairies. Izzy pondered over the theme, and eventually came up with a poppet head and gold-panning miners. The patrons were so thrilled with it, that they brought their friends and relatives to see it. It increased liquor sales, and the Ladies Lounge became quite a tourist haven.

Harry knew that his wife's flair would not stop there, and fully expected that the bar would be next, but Izzy was a little reluctant to go into such a male dominated area.

"No," she told Harry firmly. "I won't be venturing in there, but I might try something in the outdoor garden area, if Jean agrees."

Jean told her to go ahead, and watched on eagerly as a picture of the Cascades emerged on the brick wall surrounding the garden.

"I've always loved the cascades in Rosalind Park," enthused Izzy. "This is my version of them."

They added a colourful extra dimension to the quiet garden, used during the summer by those who wanted to drink in relative peace and quiet.

"This is lovely, Izzy," said Jean as she surveyed the finished work. "You are so talented."

"I'm not very good at a lot of things, Jean, (as you will no doubt find out), but I do pride myself with being able to visualise scenes and replicate them on a flat surface."

"You can indeed."

*

In the meantime, Jess was getting closer to her due date, and not venturing very far while Beau was at work. With the cooler weather now upon them, and autumn on the wane, she had to relinquish her favourite spot on the front verandah, for the warmth of the lounge fire. There she would read or knit, and unless intercepted by Izzy, fall asleep on the couch. Her body felt heavy, and she tired easily, something she had not experienced with the other three children.

Louise came to visit on several occasions, bringing William for a walk in the fresh air. On one of these occasions, she encountered the postman, who duly told her that Mrs. DuBois had received mail from overseas - England, in fact. Not many people could boast that, he declared loudly.

Louise took the letter from him, and negotiating the big pram through the gate, bade the postman 'good day!' Shaking her head, she lifted William from the pram, and made her way up the steps to the front door.

"Jess!" she called out. "It's Louise! Are you there?"

She heard Jess answer from the lounge, and pushed the door open.

"How are you?" Louise crossed the lounge, and sat opposite Jess, reclining on the couch.

"Hello, Louise. You know how it is? I feel so cumbersome, I can hardly move."

Louise laughed. "I know exactly how you feel." She handed the letter across to Jess. "Your postman just delivered this." Her brow furrowed. "He's a very unusual man, isn't he? Does he know what's inside the letters, or simply wishes he does?"

"George?" Jess laughed. "I don't know, Louise, but he does know where every letter comes from." Jess tore open the envelope. "It's from Nancy." Her eyes quickly scanned the contents. "They arrived safely in England, and visited Jack's grave." She stopped, her jaw wobbling uncontrollably, while Louise looked at her curiously. "I asked Martin to place some dried forget-me-nots on Jack's grave," she said as a way of explanation. "He has done that, and Nancy says that the cemetery is very well tended, and she will send me a photograph when they get the film developed." She sighed, and read further. "They are now in the French village of Petite Colline, where Fleur's family live. She says the rebuilding has begun, and it is a very pretty little village. Nancy is learning the French language, and is settling in well. She awaits news of my baby." Jess folded the letter and placed it back in the envelope. "I'm so pleased for her," she whispered.

"I had a letter from Mary Walker recently," said Louise, as she rocked her sleeping child. "They have moved to Perth, so we probably won't see them again. They are such a nice couple. I was intending inviting them to stay with us again." She shrugged. "Oh well, that's the way it goes. I will write to her."

"I must, too. She wants to know when my baby arrives."

Louise giggled softly. "She got a surprise when I told her that William had arrived."

"I'm sure she did." Jess paused, her expression reflective. "Louise, had you noticed that everybody's moving?"

"Yes, I had, but don't worry, Jess, we're not going anywhere." Louise beamed at her.

"That's good."

The previously unlikely association between these two women had evolved into a friendship in which they now both felt at ease, and that bond had increased as they moved through their pregnancies together.

"Jess?"

She shifted her focus back to the present. "Yes, Louise."

"Did you ever think that we could become such good friends?"

Louise must have been reading her mind. "No, I didn't."

"It's strange how these things happen, isn't it?"

"It is, and I am so pleased that it did."

Jess felt the baby move, and let out a small gasp. "I think somebody else is pleased too, Louise."

*

The month of May was coming to a close, and Edward and Beau's birthdays were looming. Jess awoke on the morning of the twenty-fifth of May, with a familiar feeling of restlessness. It was usually her precursor to the onset of labour. She mentioned it to Beau as he got ready for work, and before she struggled out of bed, he ran his hands over her belly, prodding and feeling where the baby lay.

"The head is down, Jess, so it would be a good idea to get everything ready. I will inform Raymond, and the minute the contractions start, I want you to call me. Is that understood?"

"Yes, Beau." Jess smiled at his obvious concern.

"No waiting around for the two minute contractions. I'll borrow Charles' car, and that way I can be on the spot." He stopped and gazed at her. "It won't be long now, my dearest."

"Go to work, Beau, and stop fussing." Jess pulled herself up on the bed. "I have done this before, you know?"

"I know, Jess, but I haven't." He kissed her lightly. "Now be a good girl and do as you're told."

"Yes, doctor." Jess sighed as she reached for her dressing gown. "I'll call the midwife."

"Do that and make sure she gets here promptly."

Jess nodded. "You'll be late if you don't go, Beau."

"I'm going." He stopped at the door. "I love you, Jess," was his parting remark.

When he had gone, Jess moved slowly to the kitchen to prepare the porridge for the children. It had already been prepared and stood on the hob, keeping warm. He was a dear man.

"Breakfast!" she called out, and immediately running footsteps could be heard in the passage. Her back ached, and she was glad to sit down with the children while they all ate their porridge. It was not enjoyable, but she knew it would sustain her if she went into labour.

The boys were soon off to school, and Izzy was coming to collect Grace for the day. When she arrived, Jess tried hard to act as though nothing was happening, but seeing the look Izzy fixed her with, she knew that her sister hadn't been fooled.

"Are you alright, Jess?" she asked anxiously.

"Of course I am." Jess knew that she had spoken too quickly.

"I'll come back later to check on you, alright?"

"If you like." Jess shooed them out of the door.

After they had left, Jess moved slowly through the motions as she covered the bed with a large sheet, and collected towels, a bowl and disinfectant. Then she called Mrs. Davidson, who said she'd be there as soon as she could. Jess told her not to hurry, as the contractions hadn't started. However, Mrs.

Davidson had attended Jess three times, and was aware of how quickly she delivered.

Once the dishes were done and the beds made, Jess decided that it would probably be a waste of time getting dressed, so she wandered aimlessly from room to room, waiting for that trigger point which would surely come. At noon she made herself a sandwich and stepped out into the back yard to eat it. The chooks were running the fence line, and Jess realised that Ben must have forgotten to feed them. She headed for the shed to fetch some grain, and that's when the pain slammed her body. She fell to her knees and gasped, as she clutched at her stomach. Grabbing the shed door for support, she pulled herself to her feet, and taking quick breaths, headed for the house. Jess felt the telltale flow of liquid between her legs, and knew that her waters had broken.

Stumbling through the house, she reached for the telephone to call Beau, but the receiver slipped through her fingers and she collapsed on to the floor. Panting, she dragged herself into the bedroom, as the pain slammed her again. Was she going to have to do this by herself? Jess pulled herself up into a sitting position beside the bed, and waited for the next contraction. **Please God, don't make me do this alone**, she sobbed, as the pressure on her abdomen increased.

Another contraction and she took shallow breaths, trying not to push. Suddenly a face appeared beside her, and as the contraction subsided, she saw Mrs. Davidson. Jess sobbed with relief.

"Call Beau!" she gasped.

"Let me get you on to the bed first." Mrs. Davidson was a strong, heavily built woman, and in no time she had Jess on the bed, on her side. "Right! No pushing until I say so. How far apart are the contractions?"

"I don't know...very close."

The midwife vanished into the passage, and Jess heard her talking to Beau.

"Yes, Doctor... I found her on the floor in the bedroom...Her waters have broken and I'd say the contractions are about two minutes apart..." She laughed. "Usually the case with Jess...Alright, but Doctor Simmons needs to get here quickly." She heard a cry coming from the bedroom.

Slamming down the receiver, she rushed in to find Jess doubled up, her breath coming in ragged gasps.

"Hold on, Jess!" she said calmly. "Roll on to your back and I'll see what's going on down there."

"Is the doctor on his way?" panted Jess, as she heaved herself on to her back.

"Yes." The midwife lifted Jess's soaked nightdress, and looked carefully for signs of dilation. "You're not ready yet, Jess, so try not to push on the next contraction."

Jess listened for the sound of Charles' car, and prayed that they wouldn't be too long.

Another two contractions passed before she heard the slam of a car door, and running footsteps on the verandah. Doctor Simmons burst into the room, and immediately took control.

"How far apart are the contractions?"

"About a minute, doctor."

Jess felt his hands on her abdomen, and then he listened for the heartbeat through the stethoscope that swung around his neck.

"Alright, Jess," she heard him say gently. "We're nearly there, but don't push until I say so." He turned to the midwife. "Warm water please, Mrs Davidson."

Jess saw her scurry from the room, and then she heard Beau's voice as he said something to her. Gritting her teeth, she prepared for the next onslaught.

There were two more heavy contractions before Jess heard the word 'push!'

She pushed.

"And again!"

"One more should do it, Jess!"

"Good girl! That's it!"

Jess let the sob slide out of her, as she felt the baby emerge.

"Well done, Jess…You have given birth to a daughter."

"I knew it," she croaked. "Can I see her?"

"When I've tested her lungs and tied the umbilical cord."

With that she heard the sound of slapping on flesh, and a strong cry emerged from the infant.

"Good lungs," said Doctor Simmons.

Several moments passed before Jess heard him say, "There! Now clean them both up, Mrs Davidson, and I'll let her husband in on my way out."

Jess sensed the smile in his voice.

"Thank-you, Raymond," she managed to say weakly, before the door opened and he was gone.

She heard Mrs. Davidson's calm voice talking softly to the infant as she sponged her down, and then Beau appeared beside her.

"I haven't cleaned your wife up yet, Doctor!" she scolded.

"I don't care." Beau took Jess's hands and his eyes were swimming as he leaned over to kiss her. "So we have a daughter, Jess?" he whispered.

"Yes, Beau, we have a daughter."

"Here she is." Mrs. Davidson handed the tightly swaddled infant to her mother, and stood back to survey the introduction. How many times had she done this over the years? There were too many to count. She wiped her hands before busying herself with removing the water and blood-soaked linen.

Jess pulled the towel away from the child's face, and stared into deep grey eyes. Dark hair framed the tiny face, and it puckered as she let out a quivering cry.

Jess looked up at Beau as he sat beside her. His expression was rapt, and he placed a finger on the tiny rosebud mouth.

"She is so beautiful, Jess." His voice shook with emotion. "Thank-you, my darling."

"I'd like to name her Charlotte Margaret."

"I think that's a wonderful idea." He said the name softly. "Charlotte Margaret DuBois."

They sat gazing at the tiny bundle they had created, until Mrs. Davidson flapped a towel at Beau.

"There's still work to be done in this room, doctor," she said, smiling widely, "so if you wouldn't mind leaving me to my business, I would appreciate it. You can continue this mutual admiration thing after I've gone."

"Yes, Mrs Davidson." Beau kissed her plump cheek as he left the room.

"The cheek of the man!" She winked at Jess.

"He's happy, Mrs. Davidson." Jess sank back on the pillow, suddenly feeling exhausted.

"I can see that." Mrs. Davidson took the child from Jess's arms. "Come on, little Miss Charlotte, I need to weigh you, and then I can attend to your mother."

Jess heard the sound of a car, and then Izzy's voice, as Beau said something to her.

"What! She's had it already? Beau, I was talking to her only a few hours ago." There was a pause. "So you have a daughter? Let me be the first to congratulate you, Beau. That's wonderful news." Another pause. "I can't believe she had her so quickly."

Jess then heard Beau say something, and the car door slammed before she heard the engine roar into life. Where was he going?

Izzy appeared at the bedroom door, her face all smiles. "Jess, you clever girl! I can't believe how quick it has been. Let me have a look at the little darling."

"Who are you?" asked the midwife quickly.

"I'm Jess's sister, Izzy."

"That's alright then."

Mrs. Davidson unwrapped the tiny bundle, and Izzy studied the pink, screwed up features.

"Hm!" she said. "She'll be like her father, I think."

"Definitely," said Jess, brushing strands of wet hair from her face. "Where has Beau gone?"

"Oh, he's taken Doctor Simmons back to the surgery, and then he'll be home again. I don't think he can wait to hold his daughter." Izzy looked at Jess. "So you're calling her Charlotte Margaret? That's very pretty. I presume the Charlotte is after Beau's sister?"

"Yes."

"Can I interrupt?" Mrs Davidson was looking keenly at Izzy. "I need to get Jess cleaned up, so if you could make her a cup of tea, that would be helpful."

Izzy made a face at Jess. "I think I'm being told to get out." She smiled graciously at the midwife, before leaving the room.

Jess called after her. "Izzy, could you telephone Charles and tell him?"

Izzy's face appeared momentarily at the door. "I certainly will. This should cheer him up no end."

"I hope so."

"Out!" exclaimed Mrs Davidson in exasperation, and Izzy withdrew immediately. "I'm sorry, Jess, but I do need to have you looking respectable before that man of yours returns."

"I don't think he'd care," said Jess weakly.

"Maybe not, but I would, so off with that nightdress!"

Jess gave a long sigh and complied. She had given Beau a daughter and she couldn't be happier.

A Time To Embrace New Things

"Are you quite sure this is what you want, Sister Agnes?"

Reverend Mother sat behind her huge desk, surveying the figure standing erect before her.

"Yes, Reverend Mother." Sister Agnes stood with her hands folded at her waist, her chin high.

"You have thought of all the consequences should it not work out for you?"

"I have."

"Hm." There was a long pause. "I should stop you, you know?"

"I know."

The Reverend Mother expelled a long sigh. "The Congo would have been an ideal place for you, Sister Agnes, but I suspected that you had other ideas, when you refused to talk about it." She toyed with a pen as she held it poised over a sheet of paper. "We'll miss you."

"Thank-you, Reverend Mother. I'll miss you, too."

"You know what this means, of course?"

"Yes, I do."

"You'll have to say your goodbyes now, because when those gates are opened for you to leave, there will be no-one here to share your journey."

"I know."

A heavy silence ensued, filled only with the labouring tick of the clock above the fireplace.

"Why, Sister, after all these years, do you want to leave the one place that has given you solace?"

"I have a family out there, and I would like to get to know them." She paused. "My brother has written me that his wife, Jess, has recently given birth to a daughter, and…they have called her Charlotte, after me." Her eyes were glistening.

"Hm." There was another long pause. "Transferring to a Convent down south, isn't an option that you'd want to consider?"

"No, Reverend Mother."

"Very well, if I can't change your mind, I will inform Father Thomas, and we will begin proceedings at once."

"Thank-you, Reverend Mother."

"For what it's worth, Sister, your time here has been of great value to the Order, and you will be sorely missed by everyone here."

Sister Agnes smiled, but remained silent.

"That will be all." The Reverend Mother waved a hand as a sign of dismissal. "You'd better find Sister Miriam and explain yourself to her."

"I have, Reverend Mother, and she wishes me well."

*

Charlotte stood silently beside the cot that had been her bed for the past thirty-two years. Her eyes skimmed the sparse room, and stopped on the small suitcase that lay on the cot. Her worldly possessions were in there, and amongst the clothes she saw the tiny knitted baby's jacket that some kind soul had given her when she entered the gates of the Convent. It was yellow with age, and Charlotte slowly picked it up, handling the soft wool as though it were fragile.

She breathed deeply as she began to disrobe, laying each article of her habit on the cot. In the case she found street clothing that had been acquired for her from a local charity shop, and slowly she began to dress. There was no mirror to see how she looked, but it was of little consequence when her friends would not be there to see her go. Charlotte ran her fingers through her short grey hair, and feeling the need to cover her head, found a blue felt hat amongst the contents of the case. The clothes she had entered the Convent in were long gone; perhaps to some novice who had changed her mind at the last minute.

When she was ready she closed the case, and stepping out into the dimly lit corridor, began her solitary walk through the building. She paused outside Sister Miriam's door, and thought she heard the faint sound of weeping.

"Good-bye, Sister Miriam," she whispered before continuing on her way.

As she crossed the grass to the gates, she was aware that somebody was watching her progress, but she dared not look back. It would be Sister Miriam, and her heart ached for the kindly soul she was leaving behind.

Outside the open gate she saw a black car. Clarence Bonner-Smyth was her only local contact with the outside world, and he had agreed to take her to his friend, Angela, and from there she would make her plans.

Clarence stepped out of the car as he saw her approach, and quickly opened the passenger door for her.

"Hello, Charlotte." He raised his hat.

"Hello Mr. Bonner-Smyth," she replied as she handed him her case and then stepped up into the passenger seat.

"Please call me Clarence."

Charlotte smiled, but said nothing more.

Clarence climbed into the driver's seat, and pulling off the brake, eased the big car forward.

Charlotte was aware of the big gates clanging shut as they drove away, and tears prickled behind her eyes. Clarence saw the tears and handed her a clean handkerchief.

"This is a bold move, Charlotte," he said gently. "You are very courageous."

"Time will tell," said Charlotte, wiping her eyes.

"Angela is looking forward to seeing you again, and we hope we can help you out here." He glanced at her profile. "Is Beau aware of this move?"

"No."

Clarence let out a whistle. "So you're going to surprise him?"

"I'm not sure yet."

They continued the journey in silence, as Charlotte gazed around her at a city she had not seen for a lifetime. Traffic increased as they reached the inner city limits, and the competition for road space was fierce. Clarence watched as she flinched each time a vehicle came too close, or a horse shied in their direction. He smiled.

"The city has changed, Charlotte. A lot has happened during your time away from it."

"I can see that. I have a lot to get used to."

"You do." Clarence pulled into the alleyway beside the patisserie. "This is where Angela lives," he said, as he turned off the engine. "She has a pastry shop, and is a very good cook." He laughed. "You can see that I enjoy Angela's cooking." Patting his ample stomach, he alighted from the car.

Angela appeared at the doorway to her residence, and held out her arms to Charlotte.

"Welcome to my home!" She held the stranger for a moment, before standing back to look at her. "You look a little different to the last time I saw you, but I must say that you are so much like your brother, it is uncanny."

Angela ushered her guest into the house, while Clarence grabbed the case from the back seat and followed.

Charlotte looked around her at the things that make up a home, and which she had not seen for many years; things like plump cushions, ornaments, lace curtains and pictures on the walls. Angela opened a door, and gestured her to enter the room where Jess had previously slept. The bed was high and large, and covered with a brightly coloured counterpane. A mirror stood in the corner, and Charlotte surveyed the woman standing there. Was it her? She touched her pale cheek. Angela saw her dilemma, and squeezed her arm.

"There are a lot of things that will be overwhelming for a time, Charlotte," she said, "but you'll soon get used to it all."

"I hope so."

"I have tea cooking for us, and after we've eaten, we can decide what to do." Angela looked at Clarence, standing in the doorway. "You are staying for tea I presume, Clarence?"

"What a silly question."

*

After a delicious meal of thick lamb stew with lots of vegetables and soft fluffy dumplings, Charlotte sat back, fearful that she might burst. While the meals at the Convent were substantial, they were not considered over plentiful. She held back a burp with her hand.

"I'm sorry, Angela!" She laughed softly. "I'm not used to food in such quantities."

"You'll have to get used to it, if you stay here," laughed Clarence, wiping his mouth on a napkin.

"Which brings us to the subject," said Angela quietly, "of what your plan is, Charlotte?"

Charlotte looked at the two faces watching her. "I want to be with Beau," she said finally.

"Of course you do." Angela put down her fork. "Does he know of your…?"

"Renouncing of my vows?" Charlotte shook her head. "No."

"Well!" Angela stood up. "The first thing you must do is let him know." She went to a drawer in the massive dresser that filled the kitchen, and produced a piece of paper. "I have his telephone number here. Call him." She handed Charlotte the paper. "Call him now."

"What if he…?"

"The telephone is in the hallway. You do know how to use a telephone, I presume?" Angela glanced quickly at Clarence.

"Yes, of course." She frowned. "He may not want to see me under these circumstances."

"Charlotte!" Angela placed her hands on her hips. "Your brother will be delighted to see you, especially now that they have baby Charlotte. Go this instant and tell him you're on your way."

"Are you sure?"

"Of course I'm sure! You've come this far. You can't back away now."

"Thank-you, Angela. I can see why you are such a good friend to Beau."

"Because I'm a bully?" Angela laughed and Clarence shook his head.

"Exactly, Charlotte. She is a bully, but a very nice one aren't you, my dear?"

*

Beau replaced the receiver and leaned against the wall. "Jess!" he called.

Jess appeared from the kitchen, baby Charlotte in her arms. "What is it, Beau?" She looked at his tear-stained face. "What's happened?"

"It's my sister Charlotte." He choked on the words.

"What's wrong with her?" Jess touched his arm.

"Nothing's wrong, Jess." He wiped his eyes with his sleeve. "She's coming here to be with us."

"What?"

"She's left the Convent, Jess; renounced her vows, and wants to be with her family. She wants to be with us, Jess. Isn't that wonderful?"

"Yes, Beau." Jess had tears in her eyes. "I knew she didn't want to let you go."

Author's Acknowledgements:

I have reached the end of the journey. My little craft has finally come to shore, and I want to say thank-you to those who have shared the journey with me. Your encouragement and your enthusiasm along the way have kept me afloat, when I was tempted to throw down the anchor. You have shared every moment with people who lived through war and then pandemic. You have gotten to know them as I have, and shared their joys and their sorrows.

Saying good-bye to characters I have lived with for the past five years has made me very sad, but I feel it is time to let them continue their lives in peace now.

Thank-you Valerie and Fran, for always being available to read what I have written, and having such faith in me. I am humbled by your opinions.

Thank-you Joanne, for your expertise in putting the final drafts together for publication, and steering me in the right direction when it came to cover design.

I have learnt so much over the past five years, and no doubt I will continue to learn and grow as I hone my craft.

I don't know what lies ahead for me after this, but I look forward to stepping out into the unknown, and finding more characters willing to allow me into their lives. I have enjoyed the experience, as I am certain you have.

In Jack's own words: "I'll see you on the other side, Jess!"

Unfortunately he didn't, but life went on, and he was never forgotten.

Ne m'oublie pas – Forget me not.

Valmai R. Harris

Extracts from comments made by readers:

Forget Me Not

&

Forget Me Not – The Journey Continues

"Thank-you for taking us on this journey. It will live on in the hearts of many readers in the years to come." Kaye Nankervis

"Congratulations on writing such a wonderful story. Looking forward to No. 3." Jeanette McCracken

"Absolutely loved your first book 'Forget Me Not'. One of those books I couldn't put down but was sad because I had finished it. I had very quickly grown to love the characters, felt for their anguish and wanted some happiness for Jess and her family. Then came the sequel, some happiness finally but still a few loose ends and that feeling of wanting more. I will certainly be waiting for the more. Carolyn Priddle

"Don't be sad, the story will live on in many readers' hearts."
Amber Breewal

"The author, Valmai Ruth Harris has shared a privilege with readers, the close relationship with herself and family. A compelling read."
Fran Wright

"I am excited for me and sad for you, Valmai. We will be kind to your baby. Thanks for trusting us." Sue Kidd

"This has been a part of your life for so long, but now we can all enjoy your special words. I am very excited to read the third and last book of the series." Lorraine McSween

Valmai Harris

Growing up in country Victoria, Valmai spent much of her time writing stories, purely for her own amusement. This was curtailed when music became her priority, and piano practise took up much of her time.

Later, when her own family emerged, writing became a thing of the past. It wasn't until later years, when the children were off her hands, that Valmai began writing music. She found this to be both therapeutic and rewarding, and was involved in the writing of several musicals, which were performed locally. (By this time she was living in Bendigo.)

It wasn't until 2017, after having written a song about her grandfather not returning from the First World War, that she decided to use his experiences and write a novel, something she had always wanted to do. The first novel was called **Forget Me Not**.

Following its popularity, locally, and having the characters firmly fixed in her mind, Valmai wrote **Forget Me Not – The Journey Continues**.

Now she has completed of the trilogy, with **Forget Me Not – Journey's End**.

Thoughts of retiring with nothing to do are far from Valmai's mind, as she plans to continue writing.

www.ingramcontent.com/pod-product-compliance
Lightning Source LLC
Chambersburg PA
CBHW022032290426
44109CB00014B/839